THE
COLONIAL CLIPPERS

BY

BASIL LUBBOCK

*Author of "The China Clippers"; "Round the Horn Before
the Mast"; "Jack Derringer, a tale of Deep Water";
and "Deep Sea Warriors"*

WITH ILLUSTRATIONS AND PLANS

SECOND EDITION

GLASGOW
JAMES BROWN & SON (GLASGOW) LTD., PUBLISHERS
52 TO 58 DARNLEY STREET
1921

Kent.   Lightning.   White Star.   Malabar.

EMIGRANT FLEET IN HOBSON'S BAY.

From a painting by Captain D. O. Robertson, late commander of ship "Lightning."

[*Frontispiece.*

Dedication

Dedicated to all those who learnt the art of the sea so thoroughly and practised it so skilfully aboard the Colonial Clippers.

PREFACE

In this book I have attempted to give some account of the beautiful sailing ships which played so great a part in the development of the great British Dominions under the Southern Cross.

It is written specially for the officers and seamen of our Mercantile Marine, and I have endeavoured to avoid such a criticism as the following :—"Heaps about other ships, but my old barkey was one of the fastest and best known of them all and he dismisses her with a line or two."

I have made rather a point of giving passage records, as they are an everlasting theme of interest when seamen get together and yarn about old ships. The memory is notoriously unreliable where sailing records are concerned, so I have been most careful to check these from logbooks and Captains' reports. Even Lloyd's I have found to be out by a day or two on occasions.

A great deal of my material has been gathered bit by bit through the past 25 or 30 years. Alas! many of the old timers, who so kindly lent me abstract logs and wrote me interesting letters, have now passed away.

The illustrations, I hope, will be appreciated, for these,

whether they are old lithographs or more modern photographs, are more and more difficult to unearth, and a time will soon come when they will be unprocurable.

Indeed, if there is any value in this book it is because it records and illustrates a period in our sea history, the memory of which is already fast fading into the misty realms of the past. To preserve this memory, before it becomes impossible, is one of the main objects, if not the main object, of my work.

Note.—As in my *China Clippers*, when using the word " mile " I always mean the sea mile of 6080 feet, not the land mile of 5280 feet.

CONTENTS

PART I.—THE EMIGRANT SHIPS

ix

CONTENTS

CONTENTS

PART III.—THE IRON CLIPPERS

xii   CONTENTS

CONTENTS

ILLUSTRATIONS

ILLUSTRATIONS

THE COLONIAL CLIPPERS.

PART I.

THE EMIGRANT SHIPS.

Those splendid ships, each with her grace, her glory,
Her memory of old song or comrade's story,
Still in my mind the image of life's need,
Beauty in hardest action, beauty indeed.
" They built great ships and sailed them " sounds most brave,
Whatever arts we have or fail to have ;
I touch my country's mind, I come to grips
With half her purpose thinking of these ships.

That art untouched by softness, all that line
Drawn ringing hard to stand the test of brine ;
That nobleness and grandeur, all that beauty
Born of a manly life and bitter duty ;
That splendour of fine bows which yet could stand
The shock of rollers never checked by land.
That art of masts, sail-crowded, fit to break,
Yet stayed to strength, and back-stayed into rake,
The life demanded by that art, the keen
Eye-puckered, hard-case seamen, silent, lean,
They are grander things than all the art of towns,
Their tests are tempests, and the sea that drowns.
They are my country's line, her great art done
By strong brains labouring on the thought unwon,
They mark our passage as a race of men
Earth will not see such ships as those again.

—JOHN MASEFIELD.

The Power of Gold.

FROM time immemorial the progress of the world, in colonization, in the Sciences (shipbuilding especially), and in the Arts owes its advance to the adventurous spirit of the pioneer. Particularly is this the case in the opening up of new countries and in the improvements in ship transport to those countries.

1

Kipling has sung the song of the pioneer and has laid stress on the pioneer spirit, but he has not touched on that great magnet which has ever drawn the pioneer on and dragged civilisation in his wake—the magnet of gold. Gold and its glamour has been the cause, one can almost ,say, of all the tragedy and all the evil in this world, but also of nearly all its good and all its progress.

It was the discovery of gold which opened up the fair States of Western America and brought about the building of the wonderful American clipper. In the same way the great Dominions of Australia and New Zealand owe their present state of progress and prosperity to that shining yellow metal; and without its driving power there would have been no history of the great Liverpool emigrant ships to record.

Emigrant Ships to Australia in the Forties.

Before the discovery of gold in Australia, the trade of that Colony was at a low ebb, suffering from want of enterprise and financial depression; whilst the emigrant ships running from Liverpool and other British ports, owing to the want of healthy competition, were of a very poor description. The horrors of the long five-months passage for the miserable landsmen cooped-up in low, ill-ventilated and over-crowded 'tween decks, were fit to be compared with those of the convict ship. The few vessels with humane owners and kindly captains were in a class by themselves. These, indeed, thought of the health and comfort of the wretched emigrants and did not content themselves with merely keeping within the letter of the Government regulations, which might more fitly have been framed for traffic in Hell.

For first class passengers the splendid Blackwall frigates of Green, Money Wigram and Duncan Dunbar, and the beautiful little clippers of the Aberdeen White Star Line, provided excellent accommodation and a comfortable and safe, if not a particularly fast, passage. But the ordinary steerage passenger had to content himself as a rule with a ship that was little better than a hermetically sealed box: one as deep as it was long, with clumsy square bows and stern, with ill-cut ill-set sails—its standing rigging of hemp a mass of long splices; and with a promenade deck no longer than the traditional two steps and overboard.

These Colonial wagons were navigated by rum-soaked, illiterate, bear-like officers, who could not work out the ordinary meridian observation with any degree of accuracy, and either trusted to dead reckoning or a blackboard held up by a passing ship for their longitude; whilst they were worked by the typically slow-footed, ever-grousing Merchant Jack of the past two centuries.

Report on Steerage Conditions in 1844.

Nearly everyone has read of the horror of the convict ships, but the following report of steerage conditions in 1844 plainly shows that in many respects the emigrant's lot was every bit as hard and revolting: " It was scarcely possible to induce the passengers to sweep the decks after their meals or to be decent in respect to the common wants of nature; in many cases, in bad weather, they would not go on deck, their health suffered so much that their strength was gone, and they had not the power to help themselves. Hence the between decks were like a loathsome dungeon. When hatchways were opened, under which the people were stowed, the steam rose and the stench was like that from a pen of pigs. The few beds they had were in a dreadful state, for the straw, once wet with sea water, soon rotted, besides which they used the between decks for all sorts of filthy purposes. Whenever vessels put back from distress, all these miseries and sufferings were exhibited in the most aggravated form. In one case it appeared that, the vessel having experienced rough weather, the people were unable to go on deck and cook their provisions: the strongest maintained the upper hand over the weakest, and it was even said that there were women who died of starvation. At that time the passengers were expected to cook for themselves and from their being unable to do this the greatest suffering arose. It was naturally at the commencement of the voyage that this system produced its worst effects, for the first days were those in which the people suffered most from sea-sickness and under the prostration of body thereby induced were wholly incapacitated from cooking. Thus though provisions might be abundant enough, the passengers would be half-starved."

This terrible report was given before a Parliamentary Committee.

A Shipping Notice of 1845.

It does not even mention the overcrowding which took place, owing to the smallness of the ships, which can well be realised by the following shipping notice taken from a Liverpool newspaper of January, 1845.

NEW SOUTH WALES.

Will be despatched immediately :—

For PORT PHILLIP and SYDNEY, New South Wales.

The splendid first-class English-built ship

" ROSSENDALE,"

EDWARD DAVIDS GOULDING, Commander.

A 1 at Lloyd's, 296 tons per register, coppered and copper fastened, and well known as a remarkably fast sailer. This vessel has spacious and elegant accommodation for passengers, replete with every convenience and presents a first rate opportunity.

For terms of freight and passage apply to

MESSRS. FAIRFIELD, SHALLCROSS & Co.

The Discovery of Gold in Australia.

However, on the discovery of gold in 1851, the Colonial trade leapt out of its stagnation and squalor and at one bound became one of the most important in all the world's Mercantile Marine. And when the gold fever drew a stream of ignorant English, Scotch and Irish peasants to Australia, men, women and children, most of whom had never seen a ship before they embarked and who were as helpless and shiftless as babes aboard, it was seen that something must be done to improve the conditions on the emigrant ships. Government regulations were made more strict and inspectors appointed; but the time had passed when they were needed—competition now automatically improved the emigrant ships from stern to stem.

The discovery of alluvial gold in Australia was mainly brought about by the great Californian strike of 1849. That strike upset the theories of geologists and set every man on the world's frontiers searching for the elusive metal. The first authentic discovery in the Colonies was made near Clunes, in March, 1850, but it was not until September, 1851, that gold began to be found in such astounding quantities that large fortunes were rocked out in a few weeks.

The first licenses for diggers were issued in September, 1851; and the effect on the ports of Melbourne and Geelong was immediate—wages began to rise to fabulous heights, as did the common necessaries of life, even to wood and water. Shearers, harvesters and bushmen were soon almost unobtainable, and the very squatters themselves left their herds and flocks and rushed to the goldfields. The police and custom-house officials followed them, and in their turn were followed by the professional men of the towns—the doctors, lawyers and even clergymen. And as has ever been the case, sailors, running from their ships, were ever in the forefront of the stampede.

By the end of September there were 567 men at Ballarat; they, by means of the primitive Australian gold rocker, had rocked out 4010 ounces or £12,080 worth of gold, taking it at its then commercial value of £8 per ounce. There were only 143 rockers, yet this amount had been won in 712 days' work, representing a day and a quarter's work per man. At the beginning of November it was estimated that there were 67,000 ounces of gold in banks and private hands at Melbourne and Geelong. From this date new fields, to which wild stampedes took place, were discovered almost daily. Forrest Creek, Bendigo, Ararat, Dunolly and the Ovens all showed colour in turn.

Melbourne and its Shipping 1851-2.

It was some months before the news of the great Australian gold strike spread round the world, and one can well imagine the excitement on board the

incoming emigrant ships, when they were boarded
almost before their anchors were down and told the
great news. Often successful miners would come
off and prove their words by scattering gold on the
deck, to be scrambled for, or by removing their hats
and displaying rolls of bank notes inside them.
Settlers, bereft of their servants, sometimes even
came off with the pilot in their anxiety to engage men.
Indeed it was commonly reported in the winter of
1851 that the Governor was compelled to groom his
own horse.

With such stories flying about, and every native
apparently in a state of semi-hysteria, it is not surprising that often whole ships' crews, from the captain
down, caught the gold fever and left their vessels
deserted. Not even the lordly Blackwall liners
with their almost naval discipline could keep their
crews. The six-shooter and belaying pin were used
in vain. Shipmasters were at their wits' end where
to get crews for the homeward run. £40 and even
£50 was not found to be sufficient inducement to
tempt sailors away from this marvellous land of gold.
Even the gaol was scoured and prisoners paid £30
on the capstan and £3 a month for the passage.

By June, 1852, fifty ships were lying in Hobson's
Bay deserted by the crews. Nor were other Australian
ports much better. The mail steamer *Australian*
had to be helped away from Sydney by a detachment
of volunteers from H.M. brig *Fantome*; and at
Melbourne and Adelaide, where she called for mails,
police had to be stationed at her gangways to prevent
desertion, whilst at Albany she was delayed seven
days for want of coal, because the crew of the receiving
ship, who were to put the coal aboard, were all

in prison to keep them from running off to the diggings.

Some description of Melbourne at this wonderful period of its history may perhaps be of interest.

From the anchorage, St. Kilda showed through the telescope as a small cluster of cottages, whilst across the bay a few match-boarding huts on the beach stood opposite some wooden jetties. Williamstown, indeed, possessed some stone buildings and a stone pierhead, but in order to get ashore the unhappy emigrant had to hire a boat. Then when he at last succeeded in getting his baggage on the quay, he had to guard it himself, or it would mysteriously disappear. Rather than do this, many a newly arrived emigrant put his outfit up to auction— acting as his own auctioneer on the pierhead itself. And as an outfit purchased in England for the Colonies is usually more remarkable for its weight than its suitability, those who did this generally profited by their astuteness. Melbourne itself could either be reached by a river steamboat up the Yarra Yarra, which at that time was not more than 25 feet wide in places; or by ferry boat across the bay and a two-mile walk from the beach by a rough trail through sand, scrub and marsh. When emigrants began to arrive in such numbers as to overflow Melbourne, the beach became covered with tents and shacks and was known as " canvas town."

There were only 23,000 inhabitants in Melbourne at the time of the gold discovery. Its houses were mostly of wood and but one story high. With the exception of Collins, Bourke and Elizabeth Streets, which were paved, the streets were merely narrow muddy lanes, and there were no foot pavements.

In the wet weather these lanes became torrents of water and many a carter reaped a harvest taking people across the road at sixpence a time.

Lucky diggers, down on the spree, easily distinguishable by their plaid or chequered jumpers, cabbage tree hats, moleskin trousers, and bearded, swarthy faces were to be seen everywhere. Many of them spent their time driving about in gaily decorated carriages accompanied by flashily dressed women covered with cheap jewellery. Amongst these charioteers, the uproarious British tar could always be picked out. He disliked driving at a slower pace than a gallop, and as often as not, instead of handling the ribbons, he would insist on riding postillion— and he was also unhappy unless his craft flew a huge Union Jack.

As usual with gold so easily come by, the lucky digger made every effort to get rid of his dust. Just as the buccaneer in the days of the Spanish Main, when back from a successful cruise, would pour his arrack and rum into the streets of Port Royal and invite all and sundry to drink at his expense, so in Melbourne the Australian digger stood champagne to every passer-by. It was being done across the Pacific in California. It was done on the Rand. It was done in the Klondyke. And some day it will be done again.

The shops, as usual, made more money than the diggers; and tradesmen, made casual by prosperity, adopted the "take it or leave it" tone and gave no change below a sixpence. The police were a nondescript force, mostly recruited from the emigrant ships, and the only emblem of their office was the regulation helmet. Indeed, dressed as they were, in the clothes in which they had arrived out, their appearance was not very uniform. However it was beyond the power of any force to preserve strict law and order at such a time, and the most that was expected of them was to keep the side walk and gutters clear of drunken miners and to pacify the pugnacious.

The " new chum " had hardly landed before he was regaled with hair-raising stories of bushrangers— apparently these gentry had an awkward habit of holding one up in the Black Forest on the way to the diggings. Thus firearms of every description were soon at a premium, many of them being more dangerous to the man who fired than to the man fired at.

Before leaving Melbourne for the sea, I must not omit to mention a well-known character of those days, namely George Francis Train. He combined the businesses of packer to the diggings and agent to the White Star Line. He was a real Yankee with an unceasing flow of flowery talk; and, after amassing a fortune in Melbourne, he returned to his native State and became a candidate for the American Presidency; and he informed everybody, that if he was elected, he intended reforming the world. Alas! they turned him down—he went broke and sank into obscurity. Appearances at the present day, however, seem to show that old Train managed to plant some of his seed in the White House.

First Gold Cargoes Home.

The first ship to land Australian gold in the British Isles was admitted by most people to be the smart little Aberdeen White Star liner *Phoenician*, commanded by Captain Sproat, a great passage maker. She arrived off Plymouth on 3rd February,

1852, after a passage of 83 days from Sydney. This was considered a record for the run home. She brought 74 packages of gold dust, valued at £81,000.

The first ship to arrive in Liverpool with a gold cargo was the Eagle Line packet, *Albatross*, Captain Gieves. She arrived on 31st August, 1852, with £50,000 of gold dust; but, what was far more remarkable, was that she arrived with the same crew to a man with which she had left England.

This was a very different experience to that of her sister ship, the *Eagle*, which left Port Phillip on the 2nd September, after waiting six months for a crew, and then paying between £50 and £60 per man for the run home. Apparently though, the *Eagle's* expensive crew were worth their money, for she made the quickest passage ever known up to that date, arriving in the Downs on the 78th day out. She also had a record gold shipment of 150,000 ounces.

The Great Rush to the Gold Regions in 1852.

With the arrival in England of larger and larger consignments of gold, there was such a rush to take shipping to the Antipodes that both the Emigration Commissioners and the shipowners found themselves unable to put sufficient tonnage on the berth to carry the clamouring hosts of adventurers. In London the magnificent frigate-built Blackwallers of Green, Money Wigram and Smith were diverted from the Indian trade in a vain attempt to stem the rush; whilst Liverpool shipowners began hiring or buying American Transatlantic packets and clippers, besides sending a shoal of orders across to the Boston and Nova Scotian shipbuilders. As fast as driving could make them, ships came crowding into Hobson's Bay, just as they were still doing in San Francisco Bay on the other side of the Pacific; and it soon became no uncommon sight to see a dozen ships waiting inside the Heads for want of pilots to bring them up to the anchorage.

In the year 1852 102,000 people arrived in the Colony of Victoria, and in the 18 months following the discovery of Ballarat the population of Melbourne sprang from 23,000 to 70,000, and that of Geelong from 8000 to 20,000.

In the five years 1852-7, during which the rush to the diggings was at its height, 100,000 Englishmen, 60,000 Irish, 50,000 Scots, 4000 Welsh, 8000 Germans, 1500 French, 3000 Americans, and no less than 25,000 Chinese—not to speak of the other nationalities of the world, all of whom were represented—landed on the shores of Port Phillip.

The Need for Fast Ships.

Though undoubtedly the chief reason of orders to builders across the Western Ocean was cheapness, yet at the same time it was recognised that no ships that sailed the seas could approach the sailing records made by the "Down East" clippers of Maine and Nova Scotia. And everyone was in a violent hurry to get to the new Eldorado, so naturally took passage on the ship which had the greatest reputation for speed. Thus the Australian gold boom filled the shipyards of America with orders for large passenger carrying clippers. Indeed the only British firm which could in any way compete with the builders of the Yankee soft-wood ships—that of Hall, of Aberdeen—had not yet built a ship of over 1000 tons.

Maury's Improvements on the Old Route to the Colonies.

In more ways than one we owed America thanks for shortening the passage to Australia— and not least to the sailing directions advocated by her great wind expert Maury. In the days before the gold discovery vessels followed the route laid down by the Admiralty; they kept as much to the eastward as possible on their way south in order to avoid the dreaded Cape San Roque and. its leeward currents; they rounded the Cape of Good Hope close to, indeed often touched there, then kept well to the north of the forties running their easting down. Then a 120-day passage was considered very good going, and when Captain Godfrey, of the *Constance* and *Statesman*, went out in 77 days by sailing on a Great Circle track, his performance created a huge sensation in shipping circles.

Maury did not actually advocate running the easting down on a Great Circle; but what he did was first to dispel the bugbear of Cape San Roque, which, however much it may have worried the leewardly craft of the old days, could have but little effect upon the fast weatherly ships of the fifties. He next showed the advantages of sailing on a Great Circle from San Roque so as to get into the high latitudes as soon as possible. He was dead against bracing sharp up against the S.E. trades.

"Australian-bound vessels are advised," he writes, " after crossing the equator near the meridian of 80° W., say between 25° and 32°, as the case may be, to run down through the S.E. trades, with topmast studding sails set, if they have sea room, aiming to cross 25°

or 30° S., as the winds will allow, which will be generally somewhere about 28° or 30° W., and soon, shaping their course, after they get the winds steadily from the westward, more and more to the eastward, until they cross the meridian of 20° E., in about lat. 45°, reaching 55° S., *if at all*, in about 40° E. Thence the best course—if ice, etc., will allow— is onward still to the southward of east, not caring to get to the northward again of your greatest southern latitude, before reaching 90° E. The highest latitude should be reached between the meridians of 50° and 80° E. The course then is north of east, gradually hauling up more and more to the north as you approach Van Dieman's Land. The highest degree of south latitude, which it may be prudent to touch, depending mainly on the season of the year and the winds, the state of the ship, and the well-being of the passengers and crew.''

This last sentence was a very important qualification of the Great Circle route, and it is evident that Maury quite realised that only very powerful, well found ships could adventure far into the fifties without being made to pay severely for their temerity.

Early Fast Passages Outward.

Constance, Captain Godfrey, left Plymouth, 17th July, 1850, arrived Port Adelaide, 1st October, 1850—76 days.

Runnymede, Captain Brown, left Liverpool, 21st February, 1852; arrived Port Adelaide, 4th May, 1852—72 days.

Anna, Captain Downward, left Liverpool, 6th April, 1852; arrived Port Adelaide, 21st June, 1852—76 days.

Constance was owned by James Beazley, *Runnymede* was a ship hired by the Emigration Commissioners, and *Anna* was a Fox Line packet. They were all under 1000 tons. Other passages which I have been unable to verify were—*Bride*, 75 days to Adelaide; *Raleigh*, 81 days to Perth; *Cambridge*, 81 days to Melbourne; and *Progress*, 82 days to Melbourne.

The keen competition set about by the gold find not only produced larger, faster ships, but much improved victualling and accommodation.

Rules and Customs aboard the "Eagle" in 1853.

The improvement is well shown by this account of life aboard an Australian emigrant ship just nine years after that horrible 1844 report had been submitted.

The *Eagle* is a first-class ship, 187 feet in length, has three decks, viz., a spar or upper deck, main deck and 'tween deck. On the spar deck are placed the small boats, entrance to the cabin and main deck. Cabin and saloon passengers have the exclusive right to the poop; but, through the kindness of the captain, ladies from the 'tween decks are allowed to walk on it. On the main deck are situated the cabin and saloon, entrance to the 'tween decks, the galleys and the ropes to work the vessel with. The 'tween deck passengers have the right to walk on the spar deck from the poop to the bow.

The captain generally appears on deck about 6 a.m. After breakfast he mingles with the passengers, ready to hear and redress grievances.

At 10 a.m. Dr. Dunlevy attends at the hospital to give advice and medicine free of charge.

The passengers are divided into four leading divisions viz.:—Cabin passengers, saloon or house on deck passengers, second cabin passengers, 'tween deck and intermediate or third class passengers, who are again sub-divided into enclosed and open berths.

The accommodation in the berths is first rate. In the cabin the berths are 8 feet 2 by 5 feet 6 for two persons. There are a few double berths for families.

In the second cabin on deck, the sleeping berths are 6 feet by 4 feet 6 for two persons and there are a few double berths. The second cabin 'tween decks sleeping berths are divided into closed and open. The open berths are exclusively occupied by single men. The enclosed are occupied by families and single ladies.

Young ladies' sleeping berths are in compartments of 4 or 6 beds and placed on one side of the ship— young men on the opposite side of the ship; families occupy berths on either side.

The same system is followed in the enclosed and open intermediate with the exception that some of the compartments for single people contain 8 beds.

After being at sea for two or three days, Mr. Nolein, the purser, came round and arranged the 'tween deck passengers into messes, giving to each mess a card with the names of the parties forming it and also its number. On the other side of the card is a printed list of the provisions for each adult per week.

In the second cabin 'tween decks each mess consists of 24 adults; in the enclosed intermediate 12; and in the open 10.

The first cabin is provided with three stewards and a stewardess, who attend on the passengers exclusively; and they are supplied with fresh provisions daily.

The second cabin on deck has two stewards. In both cabins passengers have nothing to provide but bed, bedding and napery.

In the second cabin 'tween decks each mess is provided with a steward. Passengers in this part of the ship only provide bed, bedding, napery and a small cask or tin bottle to hold their daily supply of fresh water.

In the intermediate no attendance is provided.

Messmen.—Each mess elects two of its number to act as messmen for one week. The messmen go to the purser to receive the provisions allowed it for the week. The day appointed on the *Eagle* for this purpose was Friday. They have also to go every day and receive the water; and divide it out to each individual if required. They have also to make puddings for the mess three times a week, as well as oatmeal cakes, loaf bread, etc.

In the intermediate each mess has to provide bags or dishes wherein to keep the provisions for the week; and also a dish to bring their tea, coffee, beef, soup, etc., from the cook, as the company provide no utensils for this part of the ship.

Water.—Fresh water is served out by the third mate to every messman once a day. Each adult is allowed three pints per day and the same allowance is given to the cook for the tea, coffee, soup, etc., for each person on board.

Hours.—The hour appointed for passengers going to bed is 10 p.m. When the bell strikes the purser comes round and sees that all lights are put out except those allowed to burn all night. Parties not going to bed at that hour must either go on deck or remain below in darkness, and they are not allowed to make any noise that would disturb those in bed.

Each passenger is expected to turn out of bed at 6 a.m. The doctor generally comes round in the morning to see that all are up, more especially in the hot weather.

Provisions.—Provisions are served out to each mess by the purser in rotation. He commences with the messes in the second cabin. He first serves out tea, coffee and sugar to mess No. 4, and goes over the whole messes by rotation with the same articles. The flour, oatmeal and rice are then served out in the same order and so on with the other articles until he has given out all the provisions. He then serves the intermediate, following the same order as the second cabin.

Cooking.—The ship has two galleys, two cooks and four assistants. The provisions used in the first cabin, house on deck and second cabin 'tween decks are cooked in the starboard galley; and those used by the third cabin or intermediate passengers and crew in the larboard galley. They also cook anything extra as ham for breakfast.

Loaves, oatmeal cakes, puddings, etc., must be taken up to the galley before a certain hour in the forenoon. Between meal times hot water is sometimes exchanged for cold water to old and delicate passengers.

Breakfast, Dinner, Supper.—The hour for breakfast is 8 o'clock, dinner at 1 and tea at 6. As all the messes cannot dine at once, they take it week about in rotation: for example, if messes 1, 3 and 5 mess first this week, they will be last in the week following.

The stewards in the cabins grind the coffee for their respective messes. The messmen in the intermediate grind their own coffee in the mill in the galley and carry water from the cook to infuse the coffee for their own mess. The stewards and intermediate messmen bring the dinners from the galley to their respective messes.

Tea is brought in the same way as coffee. Coffee is generally used for breakfast and tea for supper.

The floor of the intermediate saloon is scraped daily by the messes in rotation.

Washing Days.—Two days are set apart in each week for washing clothes. If those washing have not saved up fresh or collected rain water, they must wash them in salt water. Whether fresh or salt, it is always cold and the clothes are dried by tying them in the rigging.

Cleaning the Berths.—The stewards, besides scraping the floor, collect the slops of the mess every day.

Ventilation.—As regards this most important point, the *Eagle* must be classed A1.

The ventilation of the ship is on the same plan as that of the Cunard steamers. The first cabin saloon has two ventilators on deck, covered with glass panes at top and opening in the sides. The sleeping berths in the cabin are ventilated by windows in the sides and openings above each door.

The second cabin on deck sleeping berths have the windows in the sides, which slide so as to admit plenty of fresh air and also openings above each door. The saloon into which the sleeping berths open is ventilated by a large skylight on deck.

The second cabin 'tween decks has two ventilators, one on each side of the main deck. They are made of iron with openings all round, and are glazed on the top to prevent the water from coming down. The berths in the after part of it, right astern, are ventilated by windows in the stern and in the sides.

In addition to all this, there are three hatchways, and a ventilator on the upper deck, glazed on the top; and four windows on each side of the main deck, which slide up to admit fresh air. A space is left at the top of each berth for the same purpose.

The vessel is lighted by these windows and also by dead lights in the deck during the day; and at night by lanterns in each compartment and also by lanterns belonging to private individuals. The lights must be put out by 10 p.m., but one is allowed to burn all night in each division.

Liquors.—Ale and porter are sold to the 'tween deck passengers from 10 to 12 a.m. Passengers must obtain an order from the captain to obtain wine or spirits. Provisions or groceries can be purchased at any hour of the day.

Luggage.—Two small boxes, say 30 inches by 19 by 16, are much better than a large one. The one marked "not wanted on the voyage" is placed in the hold and brought to deck, if requisite, every three weeks.

The other is for use on the voyage and is placed under the owners' sleeping berth. A carpet or canvas bag with pockets in the inside will be found a most useful article.

Clothing.—Each passenger must have two suits of clothing: one for cold, the other for warm weather. Any old clothing, provided it is whole, is good enough for use on the voyage. Coarse blue cloth trousers or fustian ones, with a short coat or jacket and vest of the same material, stand the voyage well; and light trousers such as canvas or shepherd tartan ones, that wash well, with an alpaca coat, are good for warm weather.

Articles for Daily Use.—A knife, fork, table and tea spoon, a pen knife, a hook pot, a baking can, a tin pot, capable of holding 2 or 3 gallons of water, a lantern, brushes, combs, a mirror and tooth and hair brushes with washing basin and a slop pail for each mess.

The Weekly Dietary Scale.

Second Cabin.

Day of Week.	Breakfast.	Dinner.	Tea or Supper.
Sunday.	Coffee, biscuits and butter.	Preserved potatoes, preserved meat, plum duff.	Tea, biscuits and butter.
Monday.	do.	Pea soup, & pork, biscuits, mustard and pepper.	do.
Tuesday.	Coffee, biscuits, butter, cheese.	Salt beef, preserved potatoes and plum duff.	do. do.
Wednesday.	Coffee, biscuits and butter.	Same as Monday.	do.
Thursday.	do.	Same as Sunday.	do.
Friday.	do.	Pork & pea soup or salt fish with rice and butter.	do.
Saturday.	Porridge with butter, molasses or sugar.	Salt beef and rice with molasses & biscuits.	do.

Intermediate Cabin.

Day of Week.	Breakfast.	Dinner.	Tea or Supper.
Sunday.	Coffee, biscuits and butter.	Preserved meat & plum duff.	Tea, biscuits and butter.
Monday.	do.	Pork, pea soup & biscuits.	do. do.
Tuesday.	do.	Salt beef, plum duff & biscuits.	do.
Wednesday.	do.	Pork, pea soup, & biscuits.	do.
Thursday.	do.	Preserved meat, plum duff and biscuits.	do.
Friday.	do.	Pork, pea soup & biscuits.	do.
Saturday.	do.	Salt beef, rice, molasses and biscuits.	do.

Each mess may have oatmeal cakes and loaf bread fired three or four times a week.

The *Eagle*, which was commanded by Captain Francis Boyle and owned by Gibbs & Bright, of Liverpool, may be taken as a good example of a well-run ship in the Australian emigrant trade during the fifties.

The above account was published in a newspaper printed on board, and gives a very thorough account of the routine. This, of course, varied in different ships and under different captains, but in the main points the methods of the best lines were the same.

On the passage during which the foregoing account was written, the *Eagle* went out from Liverpool to Hobson's Bay in 80 days, her best 24 hours' run being 315 miles.

Liverpool Shipowners in the Australian Trade.

Thanks to the activity and enterprise of Liverpool shipowners in ordering new ships, Liverpool became the starting point of the rush to the gold regions—the chief emigration port in the British Isles, not even excepting London. And such a name did Liverpool ships gain for their speedy passages that "Liverpool on her stern and bound to go" became a regular saying amongst seamen in the fifties.

Though many of the ships sent away from Liverpool to the Colonies were hired by the Government Emigration Department, these were only a small fraction of the vast fleet sailing out of the Mersey between 1852 and 1857. The most prominent firms in the great emigration trade from Liverpool to Australia were:—James Baines & Co., of the Black Ball Line; Pilkington & Wilson, of the White Star Line; James Beazley; Henry Fox, of the Fox Line; Miller & Thompson, of the Golden Line; and Fernie Bros., of the Red Cross Line.

MR. JAMES BAINES.

To face page 23.

Many of these firms, including the Black Ball and White Star, were brokers as well as owners, and very often the ships advertised in their sailing lists were privately owned.

James Baines, of the Black Ball Line.

The Black Ball Line, the most celebrated line of passenger ships, perhaps, in its day, owned its existence to a little self-made man named James Baines. And the Black Ball Line would never have become the great concern that it was in its palmy days if it had not been for this man's foresight and enterprise. He, it was, who realised the genius of the great American shipbuilder, Donald Mackay, and gave him an order for four ships, the like of which the world had never seen before—ships which knowing men in the business pronounced to be too big and likely to prove mere white elephants once the first rush of gold seekers was over. However, James Baines, although he was but a young man of barely thirty, had the courage of his convictions, and he proved to be in the right, for it was these big Mackay clippers which really made the reputation of the Black Ball Line.

James Baines was a very lively, little man, fair with reddish hair. His vitality was abnormal and he had an enthusiastic flow of talk. Of an eager, generous disposition, his hand was ever in his pocket for those in trouble; and he was far from being the cool, hard-headed type of business man. He was as open as the day and hail-fellow-well-met with everybody, nevertheless his far-sightedness and his eager driving power carried him to the top in so phenomenally short a time that his career has become a sort of romantic legend in Liverpool.

He was born in Upper Duke Street, Liverpool, where his mother kept a cake and sweet shop, in which many a present-day Liverpool shipowner can remember stuffing himself as a boy. Indeed, Mrs. Baines had such a reputation that she is said to have made one of the wedding cakes for the marriage of Queen Victoria.

The following is the most generally-accepted story of James Baines' first venture in ship-owning. In 1851 a dirty-looking ship with stumpy masts and apple-cheeked bows lay in the Queen's Dock, Liverpool, with a broom at her masthead, thus indicating that she was for sale. This ship, which seafaring men contemptuously compared to a barrel of pork, had been cheaply built at Miramichi, and was evidently going for a song. James Baines scraped together what little money he had and bought her, sent her out to the Colonies and made a good profit on her; and this was the humble beginning of the great Black Ball Line, which in 1860 possessed 86 ships and employed 300 officers and 3000 seamen.

How James Baines came to take the house-flag and name of the well-known line of American packet ships, which had been running between New York and Liverpool since 1816, I have been unable to find out. One cannot but think, however, that this must often have occasioned confusion in Liverpool business circles.

James Baines' success was, as I have said, meteoric, and to the end of the fifties he flourished exceedingly. He lived in a beautiful house, where he dispensed princely hospitality, drove a four-in-hand, and thought nothing of buying five ships in one day at Kellock's Auction Rooms. But in the year 1860 his star began to set. Like many another, he was tempted by the steam-kettle, with the result that he amalgamated with Gibbs, Bright & Co., who had already deserted sail for that doubtful investment, auxiliary steam, and had started a service with the ill-fated *Royal Charter* and the equally well-known *Great Britain*.

The packets and steamers of the combine provided a service to Australia from Liverpool twice a month, but it is doubtful if the experiment proved a success financially. The chief cause, however, of James Baines' downfall was the failure of Barnard's Bank. At the same time it must be remembered that his soft-wood ships, many of which were old Yankee clippers already past their prime when he bought them, were becoming more and more strained and water-soaked, with the result that his repair bill was ever on the increase, and this just when other firms were building iron ships on purpose to compete with his wooden ones. The two last ships, in which he had any interest, were the *Great Eastern* and the *Three Brothers*, once upon a time Vanderbilt's yacht and famous for its unsuccessful chase of the *Alabama*, now a hulk at Gibraltar.

Misfortunes, once they begin, have a habit of crowding upon one, and poor old James Baines, for some years before his death, had to depend for his subsistence on the charity of his friends. Indeed he was absolutely penniless when he died of dropsy on 8th March, 1889, in a common Liverpool lodging house. He was only 66 years of age at his death. Yet it will be a very long time before he and his celebrated ships are forgotten in Liverpool.

In the Black Ball Line I served my time.
Hurrah ! for the Black Ball Line.

The White Star Line.

The White Star Line, the great rival of the Black Ball, was started by two young Liverpool shipbrokers, John Pilkington and Henry Threlfall Wilson. The actual ships owned by them were never very numerous, though they included the famous *Red Jacket* and *White Star*.

In 1867 Pilkington & Wilson wisely sold their soft-wood ships, which by this time were thoroughly strained and water-soaked, to various purchasers; and parted with their well-known house-flag to the late Mr. T. H. Ismay for £1000. Mr. Ismay was joined in partnership by Mr. Imrie, and these two men started the present White Star Line with iron sailing ships for the Australian trade, whilst Messrs. Pilkington & Wilson retired on their laurels.

The Mail Contract.

I do not think anything shows the enterprise of the Black Ball and White Star Lines more clearly than the contracts which they signed in 1855 with Earl Canning, the Postmaster-General, for the carriage of the mails to Australia. Messrs. Pilkington & Wilson undertook to carry the mails in the following ships, *Ben Nevis, Shalimar, Red Jacket, Emma, Fitzjames, Mermaid* and *White Star*; and to land them in Australia in 68 days, or pay a penalty of £100 a day for every day over that time. James Baines was even more daring, for he accepted a contract to land the mails in 65 days with the same penalty attached.

The "Marco Polo."

The first ship to shorten the voyage between England and Australia was the famous *Marco Polo*,

"MARCO POLO."

To face page 27.

generally spoken of as the pioneer ship of the Black Ball Line.

The *Marco Polo* was built by Smith, of St. John's, N.B., and is described by those who remember her as a common six-year Quebec timber ship, "as square as a brick fore and aft, with a bow like a savage bulldog," a big thick lump of a black ship with tremendous beam, a vessel you could carry on to glory in, even to sporting lower and topmast stunsails in a strong gale.

The story goes that on her maiden voyage she arrived in Liverpool from Mobile with a cargo of cotton. Old Paddy McGee, the rag man and marine store dealer, bought her cheap and resold her at a great profit to James Baines, who refitted her from stem to stern for the emigrant trade.

It is hard to say whether there was really a touch of genius in the designing of *Marco Polo*, or whether she owned most of her reputation for speed to the wonderful driving power of her famous skipper. I am inclined to give James Baines credit for possessing a good eye for a ship, and this opinion is strengthened by the following description taken from the *Illustrated London News* of 1852.

The distinguishing feature of the *Marco Polo* is the peculiarity of her hull. Her lines fore and aft are beautifully fine, her bearings are brought well down to the bilge ; thus, whilst she makes amidships a displacement that will prevent unnecessary "careening," she has an entrance as sharp as a steamboat and a run as clean as can be conceived. Below the draught line her bows are hollow ; but above she swells out handsomely, which gives ample space on the topgallant foc's'le—in fact, with a bottom like a yacht, she has above water all the appearance of a frigate.

The *Marco Polo* is a three-decker, and having been built expressly for the passenger trade is nothing short in capacity or equipment. Her height between decks is 8 feet, and no pains have been spared in her construction to secure thorough ventilation. In strength she could not well be excelled. Her timbering is enormous. Her deck beams are huge balks of pitch-pine.   Her timbers are well formed and ponderous.   The stem and stern frame are of the choicest material.   The hanging and lodging knees are all natural crooks and are fitted to the greatest nicety.   The exterior planking and ceiling is narrow and while there has been no lack of timber there has been no profusion of labour.

The length of the *Marco Polo* from stem to stern (inside measurement) is 185 feet ; her beam is 38 feet ; her depth of hold from the coamings 30 feet.   Her registered tonnage is 1625, but her burthen will considerably exceed 2000 tons.

On deck forward of the poop, which is used as a ladies' cabin, is a " home on deck " to be used as a dining saloon.   It is ceiled with maple and the pilasters are panelled with richly ornamented and silvered glass—coins of various countries being a novel feature of the decorations.   Between each pilaster is a circular aperture about 6 feet in circumference for light and ventilation ; over it is placed a sheet of plate glass with a cleverly painted picturesque view in the centre with a frame work of foliage and scroll in opaque colours and gold.   The whole panels are brought out slightly by the rim of perforated zinc, so that not only does light from the ventilator diffuse itself over the whole but air is freely admitted.

The saloon doors are panelled in stained glass bearing figures of commerce and industry from the designs of Mr. Frank Howard.   In the centre of the saloon is a table or dumb-waiter made of thick plate glass, which has the advantage of giving light to the dormitories below.   The upholstery is in embossed crimson velvet.

The berths in separate staterooms are ranged in the 'tween decks and are rendered cheerful by circular glass hatch-lights of novel and effective construction.

This mid-Victorian account of a passenger ship and her internal decorations is interesting in more senses than one, but I fear that in these days when everyone seems to be an expert in the artistic merits of old furniture and house decoration, many of my readers will shudder at the *Marco Polo's* crimson velvet cabin cushions, stained glass panels and richly ornamented pilasters.   However, at the time all these fittings and arrangements for passengers were considered a great advance on anything previously attempted.

Captain James Nicol Forbes.

Marco Polo's first commander was the notorious Captain James Nicol Forbes, who had previously commanded with great success the Black Ball ships *Maria* and *Cleopatra* in the Australian trade.

Bully Forbes is one of the best known characters in the history of the British Mercantile Marine. His career was as meteoric as his owner's and had as sad an end. By two wonderful voyages in the *Marco Polo* and a still more wonderful one in the *Lightning*, he rushed to the head of his profession. Then came his eclipse in the wreck of the *Schomberg*. A life of Captain Forbes was printed in Liverpool at the time of his triumphs, but it is very scarce and practically unobtainable, and thus the history of this remarkable man has become shrouded in legend and fairy tale, and at this length of time it is difficult to separate the fact from the fiction.

He was born in 1821, a native of Aberdeen. In 1839 he left Glasgow for Liverpool without a shilling in his pocket; but he was a man who could not be kept down and he soon gained command of a ship; and at once began to astonish everybody by the way in which he forced indifferent ships to make unusually good passages. One of his first commands appears to have been an old brig, in which he made two splendid passages to the Argentine. His success with the Black Ball ships *Maria* and *Cleopatra*, which were neither of them clippers, gave him the command of *Marco Polo* and his chance to break all records.

In character Captain Forbes was a most resolute man, absolutely fearless, of quick decisions, but of a mercurial temperament. It goes without saying that he was a prime seaman—his wonderful passages in *Marco Polo* and *Lightning* are proof enough of this. And with regard to the *Schomberg*, I have little doubt in my own mind that Forbes was disgusted with her sluggishness and by no means sorry when she tailed on to the sandspit.   But he evidently failed to foresee the bad effect her loss would have on his own reputation.   In Liverpool, at the many banquets in his honour, he had been rather too ready to give wine-tinted promises as to what he would do with the *Schomberg*, and the chagrin of this, his first failure, was the real cause of his downfall.

After the wrecking of the *Schomberg*, he sank into obscurity, for though he was acquitted of all blame by the Court of Inquiry, he could not weather the disgrace. For some time he remained in Australia, a " very sad and silent man," the very opposite of his usual self. However, in 1857 he obtained command of the *Hastings*, but lost her in December, 1859.   All this time his star was setting, and for a while he was regularly "on the beach" in Calcutta.   Then in 1862 we find him home again and acting as agent for the owners of a Glasgow ship called the *Earl of Derby*, which was in distress on the Donegal Coast.   Soon after this in 1864, in the time of the cotton famine, he bobbed up in Hongkong in command of a ship called the *General Wyndham*, one of Gibbs, Bright & Co.'s, and there loaded cotton for Liverpool.   He is described then as being a seedy, broken-down looking skipper, with the forced joviality of a broken-hearted man.   He discussed the passage down the China Seas (it was S.W. monsoon time) with some of the tea clipper captains, and displayed all his old bravado, declaring that he would "force a passage." However in spite of his big talk, he took 50 days to Anjer.

I have come across one characteristic story of his visit to Hongkong. He was insulted by two Americans on the Water Front; in a moment he had his coat off and did not let up until he had given them a good thrashing.

He commanded the *General Wyndham* till 1866, and that was the end of his sea service. He died at the early age of 52, on 4th June, 1874, in Westbourne Street, Liverpool. His tombstone is in Smithdown Road Cemetery, and on it is carved his claim to fame, the fact that he was "Master of the famous *Marco Polo*."

As long as square-rig flourished, Forbes was the sailor's hero, and of no man are there so many yarns still current in nautical circles.

He is the original of the story, "Hell or Melbourne," though it has been told of Bully Martin and other skippers. The yarn goes that on one of his outward passages, his passengers, scared by the way in which he was carrying on, sent a deputation to him, begging him to shorten sail, and to his curt refusal, he added that it was a case of "Hell or Melbourne." His reputation for carrying sail rivalled that of the American Bully Waterman, and the same methods are attributed to him, such as padlocking his sheets, overawing his terrified crew from the break of the poop with a pair of levelled revolvers, etc.

Captain Forbes was a very lithe, active man, and one day, as the result of a challenge, he crawled hand over hand from the spanker boom end to the shark's fin on the jibboom, not such a difficult feat, though not a usual one for the master of a ship. Whilst on the *Lightning*, it was his custom to go out on the swinging

boom when the lower stunsail was set, and to calmly
survey his ship from the boom end, when she was tearing
along before the westerlies. The danger of this proceeding can only be realised by an old sailor. If a
man at the wheel had brought the ship a point or two
nearer the wind, the probability is that Forbes would
have been flung into the sea as the boom lifted or
perhaps the boom itself would have carried away, as
that was the usual way in which lower stunsail booms
were smashed up.

Every man is supposed to have a lucky day, and
Bully Forbes' lucky day was a Sunday. On his
record voyage in *Marco Polo*, he left Liverpool on a
Sunday, sighted the Cape on a Sunday, crossed the
line on a Sunday, recrossed the line homeward bound
on a Sunday, and arrived back on Liverpool on a
Sunday. After this you may be sure that he took care
to start his second voyage on a Sunday.

"Marco Polo's" First Voyage to Australia.

On her first voyage to Australia *Marco Polo*
was chartered by the Government Emigration Commissioners. She took out no less than 930 emigrants,
these were selected with care and reported to be nearly
all young and active Britishers. The married couples
were berthed amidships, single women aft, and single
men forward. There was a special hospital or sick
bay and she also carried two doctors. In ventilation
and comfort she was far ahead of any previous emigrant
ship; on deck there were even provided large tubs,
lined with lead, which the women could use for washing
clothes. And the proof of her great superiority in
arrangements for emigrants was at once proved on her
passage out when she only had two deaths of adults

THE BLACK BALL LINE
JAMES BAINES & Cº

THE EAGLE LINE
GIBBS, BRIGHT & Cº

GIBBS, BRIGHT & Cº

THE WHITE STAR LINE
PILKINGTON & WILSON

JAMES BEAZLEY.

ABERDEEN CLIPPER LINE
GEO. THOMPSON & Cº

J. DUTHIE SONS & Cº

THE ELDER LINE
A.L. ELDER & Cº

"TORRENS"
FLAGSHIP ELDER LINE.

DEVITT & MOORE.

THE ORIENT LINE
ANDERSON, ANDERSON & Cº

JOHN WILLIS & SON.

on board, both from natural causes, and only a few of children from measles, this at a time when ships carrying half the number of emigrants arrived in Hobson's Bay with from 50 to 100 deaths aboard.

Her officers were chosen from the best ships sailing out of Liverpool, Forbes' chief mate being McDonald, who succeeded Forbes in command of *Marco Polo* and afterwards made a great name for himself in command of *James Baines*.

The regular crew of the *Marco Polo* numbered 80 men, but 30 other seamen worked their passage, so Forbes could afford to carry on till the last moment, especially as in emigrant ships the passengers were always ready for "pully-hauly," in order to get exercise, and invariably tailed on to halliard or brace when there was occasion. *Marco Polo*, of course, had her full outfit of flying kites, and set three skysails on sliding gunter masts, man-of-war fashion, but she did not send aloft a moonsail at the main like her great successors *Lightning*, *James Baines* and *Champion of the Seas*. She had Cunningham's patent topsails, and on one occasion reduced sail from royals to double reefs in 20 minutes.

Marco Polo's departure was not allowed to take place without the usual banquet aboard previous to sailing, which was such a custom in the fifties. The *dejeuner*, as the reporters called it, was served on the ship's poop under an awning. Mr. James Baines presided, and his partner Mackay and Captain Forbes were vice-chairmen. After the usual round on round of toasts, there was the usual speechifying.

James Baines opened the ball by the customary optimistic speech. Mr. Munn, of the Cunard Company, followed with the hope that as the *Marco Polo* was the

c

largest ship ever despatched to Australia, so she
would be the most prosperous. Mr. Mackay said
that he never felt so much responsibility, as he did that
day, when he found nearly 1000 souls on board the
Marco Polo; and Captain Forbes finished up by the
characteristic remark that "he judged from the
appearance of her sticks and timbers that she would
be obliged to go; and that they must not be surprised
if they found the *Marco Polo* in the River Mersey that
day six months."

This prophecy the people of Liverpool duly saw
fulfilled. The *Marco Polo* was advertised to sail on
the 21st June, but she did not actually sail until
Sunday, 4th July.

The following is the first shipping notice of this
wonderful ship :—

SPECIAL NOTICE,

And under engagement to sail on the 21st June.

The Splendid New Frigate-built Ship—

" MARCO POLO."

A1 at Lloyd's.   2500 tons burthen; coppered and copper fastened;
now only on her second voyage* ; is the largest vessel ever despatched
from Liverpool to Australia ; and expected to sail as fast as any ship
afloat ; has splendid accommodations and carries two surgeons—

Apply to JAMES BAINES & Co.

After sailing on 4th July, the *Marco Polo* arrived
inside Port Phillip Heads at 11 a.m. on 18th September,
1852, after a record passage of 68 days, having beaten
the steamer *Australia* by a clear week. Running her
easting down her best day's work was 364 miles, and in
four successive days she covered 1344 miles, an average
of 336 a day.

On his arrival in Hobson's Bay, Captain Forbes
found some 40 or 50 ships waiting to sail, held up for

---

*Her first voyage was the one to Mobile.

want of crews; whereupon he promptly had his own crew clapped into prison on a charge of insubordination, with the result that they were ready to hand when he wanted them and thus he was able to set sail again for Liverpool on 11th October, 1852.

Leaving at 5 a.m. on the 11th, the *Marco Polo* passed Banks Straits on the 12th and sighted the Auckland Islands on the 17th. On her passage to the Horn she made three successive runs of 316, 318 and 306 miles, and on 3rd November when she made the Horn she logged 353 knots in the 24 hours, the weather being recorded as fine. On the 5th November she passed Staten Island; and on 19th December saw a barque apparently abandoned, and an empty long-boat painted stone colour. Forbes showed blue lights and fired rockets, but, receiving no reply and being naturally in a great hurry, proceeded on his way; and finally arrived off Holyhead at 3 p.m. on Christmas Day and anchored in the Mersey on Sunday, 26th December, 1852, 76 days out from Melbourne and only five months and 21 days out on the whole voyage.

This was so much a record that many shipping people when they recognised her lying in the Mersey though that she must have put back disabled in some way.

And the story goes that a waterman, meeting James Baines in the street, said:—"Sir, the *Marco Polo* is coming up the river." "Nonsense, man," returned Mr. Baines, "the *Marco Polo* has not arrived out yet." Less than an hour after this assertion, James Baines found himself face to face with Captain Forbes.

When the ship hauled into the Salthouse Dock, the quays were crowded with people. Between her fore and main masts a huge strip of canvas was suspended with the following painted on it in huge black letters:—THE FASTEST SHIP IN THE WORLD.

On this passage she again beat the *Australia* by more than a week, many bets having been made in Melbourne as to which ship would arrive first. After such a voyage *Marco Polo* was at once considered to be the wonder of the age and people flocked from all parts of England to see her.

Her officers declared that she made 17 knots an hour for hours together; and Doctor North, the chief Government surgeon on board, who had been in the ship *Statesman* when she made her celebrated passage of 76 days from Plymouth to Australia, declared that the *Marco Polo* was by a long way the fastest vessel he had ever sailed in and vastly superior to the *Statesman*.

The *Marco Polo* brought home £100,000 in gold dust, and her officers related that on her arrival out she was surrounded by boats, the occupants of which threw small nuggets amongst her passengers. She also brought home a nugget of 340 ounces, purchased by the Government of Victoria as a present for the Queen.

" Marco Polo's " Second Voyage to Australia.

After such a record voyage, I find the following notice advertising her second departure for Australia.

BLACK BALL LINE OF AUSTRALIAN PACKETS.

For passengers, parcels and specie, having bullion safes, will be despatched early in February for Melbourne.

THE CELEBRATED CLIPPER SHIP "MARCO POLO."

1625 tons register; 2500 tons burthen; has proved herself the fastest ship in the world, having just made the voyage to Melbourne and back, including detention there, in 5 months and 21 days, beating every other vessel, steamers included.

As a passenger ship she stands unrivalled and her commander's ability and kindness to his passengers are well known.

As she goes out in ballast and is expected to make a very rapid passage, she offers a most favourable opportunity to shippers of specie—

Apply to JAMES BAINES & Co., Cook Street.

Before the *Marco Polo* was hauled out of the Salt-house Dock for her second voyage, another large *dejeuner* was given on board, at which testimonials were presented to Captain Forbes and Charles McDonald, his first officer. The usual flowery speeches were made, but the remarks of Bully Forbes were especially characteristic. He said that "as regards his recent voyage, he had done his best and he could not say he would do the same again, but if he did it, he would do it in a shorter time. (Laughter.) He was going a different way this time, a way that perhaps not many knew of, and the *Antelope* must keep her steam up or he would thrash her (referring to the challenge of a race round the world sent him by Captain Thompson, of the steamer *Antelope*). Captain Thompson only wanted to get outside Cape Clear and he could make a fair wind into a foul one. (Laughter.) That he (Forbes) would do his best for the interests of his employers and while the Black Ball Line had a flag flying or a coat to button, he would be there to button it."

The *Marco Polo* sailed on her captain's favourite day and also on the 13th of the month, namely, on Sunday, 13th March, 1853. She had on board 648 passengers and £90,000 of specie. The emigrants were composed chiefly of men of the artisan class, and there were very few women amongst them. This seemed to be a matter of great regret, and as the ubiquitous newspaper reporter had it:—"One young gentleman, whose incipient moustache and budding imperial showed that he was shaping his course for the diggings, was heard to express his sorrow that there were not more ladies, as 'they exercised such a humanising tendency on mankind, don't you know.' " The reporter goes on to describe how one of the passengers was arrested for burglary just before sailing and his luggage found to be full of jewellery and watches; and how a first class passenger (who had left a good legal practice for the land of nuggets), dressed in huge sea boots, a blue shirt and marine cap, lent a ready hand in hoisting the anchor and setting the sails and joined in "the boisterous refrains of the sailors with evident pleasure." The anchor was weighed soon after 10 o'clock and the *Marco Polo* was towed to sea by the *Independence*. The day was beautifully fine, and James Baines and his partner Miller proceeded in the ship to beyond the N.W. Lightship, returning in the tug.

Bully Forbes was in a very confident mood, and, as soon as the ship was under weigh, had his passengers called together and addressed them as follows:— "Ladies and gentlemen, last trip I astonished the world with the sailing of this ship. This trip I intend to astonish God Almighty!" Then turning to his ebony cook, who went by the name of Doctor Johnson, he said:—"Search well below, doctor, and if you find any stowaways, put them overboard slick."

"Ugh, ugh!" chuckled the sable doctor as he shuffled below. In a short time he reappeared with an Irishman whom he had found concealed in the quarters of a married couple.

"Secure him and keep a watch over the lubber, and deposit him on the first iceberg we find in 60° S.," growled Forbes, with mock fierceness. The stowaway, however, was returned in the tug with the ship's owners.

The *Marco Polo's* best runs on the outward passage were the following:—

May 1	..	314 miles.	May 5	..	285 miles.
„ 2	..	300 „	„ 6	..	288 „
„ 3	..	310 „	„ 12	..	299 „
.. 4	..	304 „			

These were nothing extraordinary; however she again made a very good passage and arrived at Melbourne on 29th May, 75 days out. She left Melbourne again at 5 p.m. on 10th June, with 40 cabin passengers and £280,000 of gold dust.

Her best runs this passage were, of course, made on the way to the Horn, being:—

June 15	..	314 miles.	June 19	..	324 miles.
„ 16	..	322 „	„ 20	..	316 „
„ 16	..	322 „	„ 20	..	316 „
„ 17	..	294 „	„ 21	..	322 „
„ 18	..	260 „			

Total for week 2152 miles.

But on the 23rd in 60° S. her progress was severely stopped by large quantities of small ice, which tore all the copper off her bow.

On the 26th June, when in 141° W., a large ship was sighted astern which proved to be Money Wigram's famous Blackwaller *Kent*, which had sailed 5 days ahead of *Marco Polo*.

From 27th June to 1st July only small runs could be made, the ship being surrounded by ice, but with strong northerly winds to help her, she cleared the ice on the 1st and at once started to make up time, running 303 miles on 2nd July, 332 on the 3rd, 364 on the 4th and 345 on the 5th. And on 18th July in 49° 30′ S., with strong S.W. wind, she made her last run of over 300.

However, in spite of these fine runs to the southward, the passage was a good deal longer than Forbes anticipated, as *Marco Polo* was 95 days out when, on 13th September she arrived in the Mersey.

Nevertheless she had made the round voyage in the very good time of exactly 6 months, and when Captain Forbes appeared "on Change" about 1 o'clock on the

13th "the cheering was long and loud and he received a hearty welcome from all the merchants assembled."

After-Life of "Marco Polo."

At the end of her second voyage Bully Forbes left the *Marco Polo* to take over the *Lightning*, and was succeeded by his chief mate Charles McDonald.

Leaving Liverpool in November, 1853, with 666 passengers, McDonald took her out in 72 days 12 hours or 69 days land to land, and brought her home in 78 days. Then he left her to take over the *James Baines* and a Captain W. Wild had her. By this time it is probable that she was getting pretty badly strained, being a soft-wood ship, and whether Captain Wild and his successor Captain Clarke were not sail carriers or did not like to press her too much, I do not know, but her fourth and fifth voyages were not specially good, her times being :—

4th voyage, 1854-5, outward 95 days, under Captain Wild.
          homeward 85   „   „   „
5th voyage, 1855, outward 81 days under Captain Clarke
          homeward 86   „   „   „

She was still, however, a favourite ship, taking 520 passengers out and bringing home 125,000 ounces of gold under Captain Clarke.

On her sixth voyage she for the first time got into trouble as she parted her tow rope when leaving the Mersey and got aground off the Huskisson Dock, after first colliding with a barque at anchor in the river. However she came off on the flood without damage and sailed for Melbourne on 7th December, 1855, arriving out on 26th February, an 83-day passage. In 1856 she went out in 89 days, leaving Liverpool 5th September.

Her most serious mishap was on her passage home in 1861, when she collided with an iceberg on 4th March. Her bowsprit was carried away, bow stove in and foremast sprung; in fact, so seriously was she damaged that she was very near being abandoned. Eventually, however, she managed to struggle into Valparaiso after a month of incessant pumping. Here she was repaired and, continuing her voyage, at length arrived at Liverpool on 21st August, 183 days out from Melbourne.

Though Messrs. James Baines sold her to another Liverpool firm in the early sixties, she still continued regularly in the Melbourne trade, and as late as 1867 I find another fine passage to her account, which is thus described by Captain Coates in his *Good Old Days of Shipping* :—" Captain Labbet, of Brisbane, once told me that in January, 1867, he took passage home in the steamship *Great Britain*. The *Marco Polo* left at the same time and was soon lost sight of. A week later the look-out man of the *Great Britain* reported a sail right ahead, and shortly afterwards expressed his belief that it was the *Marco Polo*, in which ship he had previously sailed. His opinion, however, was scoffed at ; on the ship being neared he proved to have been right. She was again distanced and the *Great Britain* made what was esteemed a good passage. On taking the pilot off Cork, the first question asked was :—" Have you seen the *Marco Polo* ? " The reply came :—" Yes, she passed up 8 days ago." She had made the passage in 76 days.

Most Notable Clippers of 1853.

The *Marco Polo* was followed across the Atlantic by numerous other Nova Scotian built ships from the yards of W. & R. Wright and Smith.

The most notable of these were the *Ben Nevis*, which arrived during the summer of 1852, and the *Star of the East*, *Miles Barton*, *Guiding Star* and *Indian Queen*, which arrived at Liverpool in 1853. All these ships were intended to lower the colours of *Marco Polo*, but not one of them succeeded in doing so, though they made some very good passages.

"Ben Nevis."

The *Ben Nevis* was the first ship owned by Pilkington & Wilson. She was, however, too short and deep for her tonnage, her measurements being:—

Length over all	181 feet.
Beam	38 feet 6 inches.
Depth of hold	28 feet.
Registered tonnage	1420.

Commanded by Captain Heron, she sailed for Melbourne on 27th September, 1852, with 600 passengers, a cabin passage in her costing £25, and she took 96 days going out.

The "Star of the East."

A far more worthy ship to compete with the *Marco Polo* was the *Star of the East*, which arrived in Liverpool on 5th March, 1853, 20 days out from St. John's against strong N.E. winds. She was built by W. &. R. Wright, her dimensions being:—

Length of keel	206 feet
Length over all	237 ,,
Beam	40 feet 10 in.
Depth of hold	22 feet
Registered tonnage	1219 tons.

The following are some of her spar measurements:—

Mainmast—extreme length 84 feet; diameter 41 inches.
Main topmast—extreme length 53 feet; diameter 19 inches.
Main topgallant mast—extreme length 75 feet; diameter 14 inches.

Bowsprit and jibboom—outboard	55 feet.
Mainyard	89 ,,
Main topsail yard	70 ,,
Main topgallant yard	52 ,,
Main royal yard	36 ,,
Main skysail yard	27 ,

Sail area (studding sails excepted) 5500 yards.

At the time of her launch she was considered the finest ship ever built at St. John's. On her arrival in Liverpool she was at once bought by Mr. James Beazley, having cost him when ready for sea £22,683. She loaded for Australia in the Golden Line, and went out to Melbourne in 76 days under Captain Christian, late of Beazley's *Constance*. From Melbourne she went to Sydney and loaded across to Shanghai; then sailing from Shanghai in the favourable monsoon, arrived home in 104 days, 4 of which were spent anchored off Gutztaff Island in a typhoon. The whole voyage only occupied 9 months 27 days, and she cleared £8018 clear profit. Her second voyage on the same route she did still better, clearing £8920.

The "Miles Barton."

The *Miles Barton* measured:—

Length	175 feet.
Beam	35 ,,
Depth	22 ,,
Registered tonnage	963 tons.

She also was bought by James Beazley and loaded in the Golden Line. On her maiden voyage she went out to Melbourne in 82 days, and followed up this performance with two trips of 76 days each.

The "Guiding Star."

Arrived in Liverpool in October, 1852, and was at once chartered by the Golden Line for £12,000, considered a huge sum in those days. Her life, however, was not a long one, as she was lost with all hands between January and April, 1854, and it was generally supposed that she became embayed and back-strapped by a huge ice island in about 44° S., 25° W.

Tragic encounters with ice were by no means unusual in the fifties when every passage maker was trying to follow out Maury's instructions by running far down into southern latitudes in search of strong fair winds.

The "Indian Queen."

The *Indian Queen*, 1041 tons, the most notable Black Baller launched in 1853, and advertised as *Marco Polo's* sister ship, was a very fast vessel, her first voyage to Australia being made in 6 months 11 days, and in 1855 she came home from Hobart in 78 days. In 1859 she narrowly escaped the fate of *Guiding Star*. On 13th March, 1859, she sailed from Melbourne for Liverpool under Captain Brewer, with 40 passengers and the usual cargo of wool and gold dust. All went well until she was half way to the Horn, when on the 27th March the weather became thick with a strong N.W. wind and heavy westerly swell.

On the 31st March she was in 58° S., 151° W. by account; the day was wet, foggy and very cold and the ship logged a steady 12 knots with the wind strong at N.W. At 2 a.m. on the following morning those below were aroused by a violent shock, the crash of falling spars and a grinding sound along the port side, and the first of the frightened passengers to arrive on the poop found the ship lying broadside to broadside with an immense iceberg. All her spars and sails above the lower masts were hanging over the starboard side, the foremast was broken off close to the deck and was held at an angle by its rigging, the mainyard was in half, the bowsprit was washing about under the bows, and though the mizen topmast was still standing the topsail yard was in two, broken in the slings.

The night was dark and rainy and at first the watch below and passengers thought that all was lost. They found no one at the wheel, the port life-boat gone, and not a soul on the poop, but they were somewhat reassured by the appearance of the carpenter who had been sounding the pumps and pronounced the ship to be making no water. Then the second mate appeared aft and announced that the captain, mate and most of the crew had gone off in the port life-boat. Apparently there had been a disgraceful panic which involved even the captain, who actually left his own son, an apprentice, behind on the ship.

However those who had been so shamefully deserted began to buckle to with a will, headed by the second mate, Mr. Leyvret, and the cool-headed carpenter, a man named Thomas Howard. Passengers, cooks, stewards and those of the crew left on board were promptly divided into watches, the captain's son was sent to the wheel, and whilst some set about clearing up the raffle of gear and getting things ship-shape as far as possible, others shovelled the ice, which lay in masses on the decks, overboard.

With some difficulty the crossjack was backed and the head of the spanker hauled in. At the same time the boat was perceived tossing in the swell on the port beam and apparently endeavouring to regain the ship, and faint cries for help could be heard against the wind. She seemed to be without oars and with sea after sea washing over, she was soon swept past the ship by the back wash off the ice and lost sight of in the fog never to be seen again. The ship, though, with the backed crossjack, began to drift along the side of the berg and presently dropped clear of it into smoother water to leeward.

Day now began to break and all hands set about cutting away the wreck, but the mainyard and the rest of the raffle hanging from the stump of the main-mast was hardly clear before the terrible cry of "Ice to leeward!" arose and a huge berg appeared looming out of the mist. The crossjack was at once braced up, the spanker set and the foresail trimmed in some fashion or other, then in a tense silence the survivors watched the ship slowly forge ahead and, dragging the wreck of masts and spars and torn sails along with her, weather the new danger by a bare 100 yards. And scarcely had she done so when the foremast fell crashing on to the long-boat, the other boats having been already stove in by falling spars. The next business was to get the wreck of the foremast over the side and clear of the ship. Here the carpenter displayed the greatest coolness and skill, being ably backed up by the second mate and the 4 seamen left on board. With the last of the wreck overside, time was found to muster the survivors, when it was discovered that the captain, chief mate and 15 men had been lost in the port life-boat, leaving behind the second mate, car-penter, bosun, 4 A.B.'s, 1 O.S. and 2 boys, besides the cooks, stewards, doctor, purser, and passengers who numbered 30 men, 3 women and 7 children.

A course was now steered for Valparaiso, some 3800 miles away. It was not until the 7th April that the ship got finally clear of the scattered ice, but on the 3rd the wind came out of the south and with a lower stunsail and main staysail set on the main, the ship began to make 3 or 4 knots through the water.

One iceberg of huge size and square like a mountainous box was only just cleared before it broke in two, the smaller portion bursting into the sea like an avalanche, and sweeping a huge wave in front of it, did not bring up until it was 2 to 3 miles away from the rest of the berg. The last ice was seen in 54° S., it being reckoned that the accident had happened in 60° S.

As soon as 49° S. was reached, a direct course was shaped for Valparaiso. Sheers were now rigged and a topmast secured to the stump of the foremast, then topsail yards were crossed on the jury foremast and mainmast, which improved the ship's progress another knot. In this condition the *Indian Queen* slowly wandered north, weathering out gale after gale. On the 7th May a welcome sail was sighted. This proved to be the New Bedford whaler *La Fayette*, whose captain boarded them, offered them every assistance and corrected their longitude, which was 3° out. On the following day the French man-of-war *Constantine* appeared and promised to convoy them in. On the 9th May land was made some 20 miles south of Valparaiso, and on the morning of the 10th, as the crippled *Indian Queen* approached the Bay, the boats of H.M.S. *Ganges*, 84 guns, came out to her aid and towed her in to the Roads, where she anchored safely, just 40 days after her collision with the iceberg.

The Famous "Sovereign of the Seas."

My notes on the emigrant ships sailing from Liverpool in 1853 would not be complete without some mention of the celebrated American clipper *Sovereign of the Seas*. This ship was built by Donald Mackay for the American Swallowtail Line and at the time of her launch, June, 1852, was hailed as the largest merchant ship in the world, her measurements being:—

Length of keel .. .. .. ,. ..	245 feet
Length between perpendiculars	258 ,,
Length over all	265 ,,
Beam	44 ,,
Depth	23 ,,

Tonnage (American Register) 2421 tons.

Her lower masts from deck to cap were:—

Foremast 89 feet; mainmast 93 feet; mizen 82 feet.

Her lower yards measured in length:—

Foreyard 80 feet; mainyard 90 feet; crossjack yard 70 feet.

And her topsail yards:—

Fore topsail yard 63 feet; main 70 feet; mizen 56 feet.

She spread 12,000 yards of canvas in her working suit.

On her maiden voyage she carried a crew of 105 men and boys, including 2 bosuns, 2 carpenters, 2 sailmakers, 3 stewards, 2 cooks, 80 A.B.'s and 10 boys before the mast. She was commanded by Donald Mackay's younger brother, Captain Lauchlan Mackay, one of the best known skippers in the United States.

Loading 2950 tons of cargo and receiving 84,000 dollars freight, she sailed from New York for San Francisco on 4th August, 1852; and considering the season of the year, she made a wonderful run south, crossing the equator in 25 days and reaching 50° S. in 48 days.

[*To face page* 48.

" SOVEREIGN OF THE SEAS."

She was nine days making the passage of the Horn from 50° S. to 50° S.; but shortly after rounding the Horn she carried away her fore and main topmasts and sprang her foreyard. Captain Mackay, however, kept the seas and refitted his ship in 14 days, during the whole of which time he is said to have remained on deck, snatching what little sleep he allowed himself in a deck chair. The *Sovereign of the Seas* in spite of this mishap arrived in San Francisco only 103 days out, and this was considered the best passage ever made at such an unfavourable season of the year.

From San Francisco she went across to Honolulu in ballast and there loaded a cargo of sperm oil; it being the custom of American whalers to call in there and leave their oil for transhipment so as to clear their holds for a fresh catch.

The *Sovereign of the Seas* left Honolulu on 18th February, 1853, for New York, and once again made a most remarkable passage in spite of a sprung fore topmast, jury fore topgallant mast and a weak crew—no doubt a large number of her original crew deserted in San Francisco in the hope of reaching the gold diggings, but more probably only to be shanghaied on some homeward bounder.

Like all Mackay's wonderful creations, the *Sovereign of the Seas* was at her best in the roaring forties, and on the run to the Horn she made 3144 miles in 10 days, her best 24-hour runs being:—

March 11	..	..	..	332 miles.
,, 12	..	..	..	312 ,,
,, 16	..	..	..	396 ,,
,, 17	..	..	..	311 ,,
,, 18	..	..	..	411 ,,
,, 19	..	..	..	360 ,,

During this time she had strong quartering winds

and a heavy following sea, which drove her at times as much as 19 knots through the water.

After rounding the Horn, she had the usual weather up through the tropics, and arrived at New York on 6th May, 1853, having made the record passage of 82 days from Honolulu.

As she was considered to be too big for either the San Francisco or China trades, she was at once loaded for Liverpool, there to take part in the booming Australian emigrant trade.

And crossing the Western Ocean she once more made an extraordinary passage, as the following epitome shows:—

> June 18—Sailed from New York, passed Sandy Hook at 6.30 p.m.
> ,, 24—Sighted Cape Race at 6 a.m.
> ,, 26—Becalmed on the Banks.
> ,, 28—Distance run 344 miles—ship close-hauled under single ,reefed topsails.
> ,, 30—Distance run 340 miles, under all sail to skysails and royal stunsails off Cape Clear at 6 a.m.
> July 2—Anchored in the Mersey at 10.30 p.m.
> Passage New York to Liverpool, from dock to anchorage, 13 days 22 hours 50 minutes, and 5 days 17 hours from the Banks of Newfoundland.

Donald Mackay crossed the Atlantic on the ship and spent his whole time watching her every movement, and it was probably the experience gained on this passage which had much to do with the wonderful success of his later vessels.

On her arrival in Liverpool the *Sovereign of the Seas* was at once chartered by the Black Ball Line. Captain Lauchlan Mackay, however, did not remain in her, but returned to New York, his place being taken by Captain Warner, who had been in the ship since she was launched.

Captain Warner sailed from Liverpool on 7th

September, 1853, with 25 first cabin, 40 second cabin passengers and a cargo valued at £200,000, and wrote the following account of his passage to the *Liverpool Mercury* :—

I arrived here after a long and tedious passage of 77 days, having experienced only light and contrary winds the greater part of the passage. I have had but two chances. The ship ran in four consecutive days 1275 miles ; and the next run was 3375 miles in 12 days. These were but moderate chances. I was 31 days to the equator and carried skysails 65 days ; set them on leaving Liverpool and never shortened them for 35 days. I crossed the equator in 26° 30′, and went to 53° 30 S., but found no strong winds. I think if I had gone to 58° S. I would have had wind enough : but the crew were insufficiently clothed and about one half disabled, together with the first mate. At any rate we have beaten all and every one of the ships that sailed with us, and also the famous English clipper *Gauntlet* 10 days on the passage, although the *Sovereign of the Seas* was loaded down to 23½ feet.

Sovereign of the Seas' passage was, in fact, an exceedingly good one, considering all things, but there was not much glory attached to beating the little *Gauntlet*, which only measured 693 tons register and was built of iron.

The *Sovereign of the Seas* sailed from Melbourne with the mails and a very large consignment of gold dust; but amongst her crew she had shipped some old lags, who attempted a mutiny in order to seize the ship and get away with the gold. However, Captain Warner succeeded in suppressing these rascals without bloodshed and kept them in irons for the rest of the passage.

The *Sovereign of the Seas* made the splendid time of 68 days between Melbourne and Liverpool; but after this one voyage for the Black Ball she seems to have returned to her original owners, who put her into the Shanghai trade for a voyage or two before selling her to a Hamburg firm.

Best Outward Passages for 1853-4, Anchorage to Anchorage.

Ship.	Port from	Date Left.	Date Arrived Melbourne.	Dys.
Try	Bristol	Oct. 12, '52	Jan. 12, '53	92
Alipore	London	,, 16, ,,	,, 19, ,,	95
Marian Moore ..	Liverpool	Nov. 15, ,,	Feb. 15, ,,	92
Kent	London	Jan. 27, '53	Apl. 20, ,,	83
Eagle	Liverpool	Feb. 22, ,,	May 13, ,,	80
Marco Polo ..	,,	Mar. 14, ,,	,, 29, ,,	76
Bothnia	,,	,, 5, ,,	June 3, ,,	90
Ganges	London	,, 23, ,,	,, 22, ,,	91
Osmanli	Liverpool	Apl. 16, ,,	July 4, ,,	79
Indian Queen ..	,,	May 17, ,,	Aug. 8, ,,	82
Gibson Craig ..	London	June 4, ,,	,, 22, ,,	79
Star of the East ..	Liverpool	July 7, ,,	Sept. 23, ,,	78
Statesman ..	S'thampton	,, 10, ,,	Oct. 5, ,,	87
Tasmania ..	Liverpool	,, 23, ,,	,, 23, ,,	92
Mobile ..	,,	Aug. 16, ,,	Nov. 16, ,,	92
Sovereign of the Seas	,,	Sept. 7, ,,	,, 26, ,,	80
Chimera	,,	,, 17, ,,	Dec. 17, ,,	92
Nereus	,,	Oct. 5, ,,	,, 24, ,,	80
Flying Dragon ..	London	,, 14, ,,	,, 30, ,,	77
Kent	,,	,, 26, ,,	Jan. 12, '54	78
Marco Polo ..	Liverpool	Nov. 8, ,,	,, 31, ,,	84
Salem	,,	Dec. 7, ,,	Feb. 28, ,,	83
Essex	,,	,, 9, ,,	Mar. 12, ,,	92
Marlborough ..	London	Jan. 1, '54	,, 19, ,,	77
Indian Queen ..	Liverpool	,, 29, ,,	Apl. 21, ,,	84
Crest of the Wave	,,	Feb. 14, ,,	,, 28, ,,	73

1854—The Year of the Big Ships.

The result of *Sovereign of the Seas'* visit to Liverpool and that of her builder and designer Donald Mackay was a further order to America and Nova Scotia for still bigger ships.

In fact, Donald Mackay returned to Boston with James Baines' commission to build the famous quartette, *Lightning, Champion of the Seas, James Baines* and *Donald Mackay*, which were shortly to astonish the world. Against these the White Star Line put forward the equally big *White Star* and *Red Jacket*, two vessels which both in strength, beauty and speed were worthy to be ranked on equal terms with the great Black Ballers.

Only two wooden ships were ever launched in England which could compare in size with these six giants. One of these was the ill-fated *Schomberg* and the other the beautiful *Sobraon*, which, however, had iron frames and was not launched until the palmy days of the gold rush were over. Both came from the famous yard of Hall, of Aberdeen. *Schomberg* was, of course, wrecked on her maiden passage, but *Sobraon*, though never as hard sailed as the great Black Ball and White Star ships, made equally good passages, and being built of the finest Malabar teak retained her speed right up to the end of her long and successful career.

In comparing the measurements of the American built, Nova Scotian built and Aberdeen built ships the most noticeable point is the greater beam of the Nova Scotians and the greater length of the British. This is well shown by the following table :—

American Built	*Lightning*	5.54	beams to length.	
	Red Jacket	5.54	,,	,,
	Champion of the Seas ..	5.55	,,	,,
	James Baines	5.70	,,	,,
	Donald Mackay	5.72	,,	,,
British Built	*Schomberg*	5.82	,,	,,
	Sobraon	6.80	,,	,,
Nova Scotian Built	*Marco Polo*	4.86	,,	,,
	White Star	4.84	,,	,,

Carrying On.

Perhaps no ships ever sailed the seas which held on to their canvas longer than these great Black Ball and White Star clippers; and yet the carrying away of spars and sails, which was so common an occurrence with the earlier American clippers and also with the early British iron clippers, was quite rare on these big emigrant ships.

There is no difficulty, however, in finding reasons for their freedom from dismasting and heavy casualties aloft, their designers and builders had learnt something by the dismastings and constant losses of spars which overtook their earlier ships, and thus no ships were more scientifically stayed than these big ships, at the same time in their outfit we find hemp rigging and wooden spars in their highest state of efficiency. Strength of gear had for some time been one of the chief problems that a clipper ship builder had to contend with, and in the rigging of these six famous ships we see this problem finally mastered.

Topsails, topgallant sails and even royals were diagonally roped from clew to earing. The rope used for standing rigging was the very best procurable and of immense thickness; for instance, *Lightning's* lower rigging, fore and main stays and backstays were of 11½ inch Russian hemp; whilst in regard to spars, here are the diameters in inches of some of *James Baines'* masts and yards:—

Mainmast	42	inches in diameter.
Main topmast ..	21	,, ,,
Main topgallant mast..	16	,, ,,
Main royal mast ..	14	,, ,,
Mainyard	26	,, ,,
Main topsail yard ..	21	,, ,,
Main skysail yard ..	8	,, ,,

Advantages of a Light Load Line and High Side.

But added to their greater strength aloft these great clippers had another advantage over their older sisters in the Californian trade.

. They sailed on a lighter load line and showed a higher side. Four or five hundred emigrants made them dry and buoyant instead of wet and hard mouthed. Besides being very easy in a sea-way, these big emigrant clippers were extraordinarily steady ships without any tendency to heavy quick rolling. This is easily proved from their logs, for one constantly reads that their passengers were able to enjoy dancing on the poop when the ships were running 15 and 16 knots before the strong gales and big seas of easting weather.

Speaking at a dinner given in Melbourne in honour of Captain Enright, Mr. Alexander Young, a veteran voyager to and from the Antipodes, who had just travelled out in the *Lightning*, remarked:—"I have much pleasure in adding my slight testimony to her well-earned fame by stating that she is the driest and easiest ship I have ever sailed in. I assure you, ladies and gentlemen, that we scarcely shipped a bucketful of water all the passage, and when going 16 knots an hour there was scarcely any more motion than we feel at the present moment."

And here are other proofs of the *Lightning's* steadiness taken from the *Lightning Gazette*, a newspaper published on board:—

9th February, 1855.—14 knots upon a bowline with the yards braced sharp up and while going at this extraordinary rate she is as dry as possible, seldom shipping a spoonful of water. During the greater part of the day the carpenter was employed on a stage below the fore chains, where he worked as easily as if it had been calm.

18th March, 1857.—The wind increases a little towards evening and we make 15 to 17 knots an hour, yet the ship is so steady that we danced on the poop with the greatest ease (Lat. 42° 34' S., Long. 17° 04' W.)

21st February, 1855.—During this time the ship was going 16 knots an hour and in the saloon the motion was so slight that we thought she had only a light breeze.

Examples of Carrying Sail.

Two or three quotations also from the log books and shipboard newspapers may be of interest to show the power of these ships to carry sail in heavy weather and strong winds.

Here are two days from the log of the *James Baines* when running her easting down in 1856 :—

16th June.—Lat. 43° 39′ S., Long. 101° E. ; Bar. 29.80°. Wind. S.W. to W.S.W.   Commences with fresh breezes and squalls of sleet, 8 a.m., more moderate.   Noon, sighted a ship ahead; at 1 p.m. was alongside of her and at 2 p.m. she was out of sight astern.   *James Baines* was going 17 knots with main skysail set, the *Libertas*, for such was her name, was under double-reefed topsails.

18th June.—Lat. 42° 47′ S., Long. 115° 54′ E.   Bar. 29.20°. Wind, W. to S.W.   First part breeze freshening.   At 6 p.m. wind S.W. and freshening.   At 8.30 p.m. in all starboard studding sails ; ship going 21 knots with main skysail set.   Midnight, fresh gale and fine clear night.   8 a.m., wind and weather the same.   Noon, less wind attended with snow squalls.   Distance 420 miles.

Then in the *Lightning Gazette* I find the following entries :—

15th January, 1855.—Lat. 39° 42′ N., Long. 19° 25′ E.   Wind, S.S.E., strong breezes and cloudy, with occasional squalls and showers ; the ship going 13 knots close-hauled.   In the morning we passed a ship outward bound with topgallant sails in and exchanged colours with a Swedish brig homeward bound—this vessel was under close-reefed topsails, while we were carrying three royals and main skysail.

26th February, 1855.—Lat. 45° 48′ S. ; Long., 16° 55′ E.   Wind, N.N.W., course, S.E.   Another wet uncomfortable day ; thick mist and small rain.   The barometer had been falling for a day or two back and went down half an inch last night.   The change took place at 4 p.m., when the wind suddenly shifted to the west and soon afterwards to S.W., from whence it blew hard with squalls and occasional showers of hail and snow.   At 8 p.m. it backed again to west, where it remained all night, blowing a fresh gale, the ship running 16 and occasionally 18 knots per hour with main skysail and topgallant studding sails set.

27th February, 1855.—Lat. 46° 22′ S., Long. 26° 15′ E.   Wind, west, course S.E.   All last night it blew a fresh gale with heavy squalls and occasional showers of hail and snow, the sea running high.   From noon yesterday till noon to-day, we ran down 9 degrees and 20 miles of longitude and 34 miles of latitude, making 390 geographical miles or 450 English miles direct course in the 24 hours, giving an average of 16¼ knots or 18⅞ statute miles per hour. During 6 hours in the morning the ship logged 18 knots per hour with royals, main skysail and topgallant studding sails set, the wind blowing a fresh gale from the westward.

21st October, 1855.—Lat. 36° 4' S., Long. 24° 52' W. During the afternoon the wind chopped round and blew strongly from the S.W. At 5 p.m. sighted a large ship on our weather quarter, sailing under double-reefed topsails and we apprehend they must have taken us for the *Flying Dutchman* seen occasionally in these latitudes, for notwithstanding the strong breeze we could be observed carrying our skysails with studding sails 'low and aloft.

14th March, 1857.—Lat. 34° 47' S., Long. 35° 06' W. The breeze a splendid one. A barque on the port beam about 3, homeward bound. The wind was as fair for her as wind could be, yet she had no royals set. We formed a striking contrast to her, for we—on a wind— had all sail set up to main skysail.

20th March, 1857.—Lat. 43° S., Long. 0° 55' E. We have made during the last 47 hours the greatest run that perhaps ship ever made, yet all the time we have carried our main skysail and all sorts and conditions of studding sails.

Extraordinary 24-hour Runs.

I have quoted the above passages to show the way in which a Black Baller could carry sail either with a fresh favouring gale or in a strong head wind. This is sufficiently astonishing in itself, but what amazes most present day sailors and compels many of them to be incredulous are such statements as the much quoted one concerning *James Baines*—"Ship going 21 knots with main skysail set."

This and other log book statements have been looked upon by many as far-fetched exaggerations, but, after careful study of the subject, during which I have pricked off the different voyages on a track chart, I have come to the conclusion that these amazing performances were in no way a stretching of the imagination.

To begin with, I will give the main arguments advanced against them by the sceptics.

The late Mr. J. N. Barry, writing in an Australian paper, remarks:—

Where American records are concerned much caution must be observed in taking their feats of speed for granted. Our cousins had a canny fashion of, no matter where they might be sailing, always reckoning 60 miles to a degree of longitude whilst doing their easting, so that a day's run of, say, 240 miles upon a parellel of 45°, would by this means give the distance covered as exactly 100 miles in excess of what it should be.

Another nautical writer remarks:—

The skippers of many of the celebrated Black Ball clippers were not above adopting this mode of calculation, viz., 60 miles to a degree of longitude, but while it gave some wonderful results for a single 24 hours, it did not as a matter of fact make their passages any more rapid.

And I have had letters scoffing at the Black Ball records, remarking that their skippers were a leery lot and provided "palatable pabulum for the proud passengers."

I will now try and show that these arguments were altogether too sweeping, and if they may possibly have applied to certain individuals, they are by no means fair to the greater number of the skippers.

In the first place, not one of the Black Ball or White Star ships was commanded by an American, and though the accusation was levelled at Americans, it was evidently done in the belief that the American built Australian clippers were commanded by Americans.

In the second place, such men as Anthony Enright, of the *Lightning*, James Nicol Forbes, of the *Marco Polo*, Charles McDonald, of the *James Baines*, Sam Reid, of the *Red Jacket*, Captain Pryce, R.N.R., of the *Donald Mackay*, and Alexander Newlands, of the *Champion of the Seas*, were known and respected all over the world as leading men in their profession, occupying a position in the Mercantile Marine which would correspond with that of Orient and P. & O. commanders nowadays, whilst their performances were very much more widely known, thus such elementary cheating as giving 60 miles to a degree in the roaring forties would have been exposed at once.

The greatest 24-hour run ever accomplished by a sailing ship was one of 436 nautical miles made by the *Lightning* when crossing the Atlantic on her maiden passage. The second greatest run was also made by the *Lightning*. This was 430 miles when running her easting down bound out to Australia in 1857, and on the following day her run was 360. This wonderful performance drew the following letter from Captain Enright to his passengers, and I think it will dispose of the 60 miles to a degree accusation, at any rate as far as the *Lightning* and her commander are concerned :—

21st March, 1857.

LADIES AND GENTLEMEN,— I cannot help informing you of the extraordinary run we have made during the last 48 hours—or rather allowing for change of time, 46 hours and 48 minutes. During this time we have run, by thoroughly good and trustworthy observation, no less than 790 knots or 920 statute miles, being an average of nearly 17 knots or more than 19½ statute miles per hour. Yesterday our noble ship made no less than 430 knots amounting to an average during the 24 (23½) hours of more than 18 knots. Our change of longitude has amounted to 18 degrees, each degree being equal to 44 miles.

I firmly believe this to be the greatest performance a sailing ship has ever accomplished.

I hope this information will in some degree compensate you for the inconvenience which the heavy weather has occasioned you.

And I remain, LADIES AND GENTLEMEN,

Very faithfully yours,

A. ENRIGHT, *Commander.*

If further proof is wanted that Captain Enright did not allow 60 miles to a degree, but only 44 as he states to his passengers, here are the noon positions found by observation, not account only, from which the runs can be verified on the chart.

March 18, Lat. 42° 34′ S., Long. 17° 04′ W.
  19, ,, 43° 0′ S., ,, 7° 17′ W.
  20, ,, 43° 0′ S., ,, 0° 55′ E.

The following is a list of all runs of 400 miles and over, which I have been able to verify.

March 1, 1854.—*Lightning* 436 miles.
March 19, 1857.— ,, 430 ,,
February 6, 1855.—*James Baines* 423 miles.
February 27, 1855.—*Donald Mackay* 421 miles
June 18, 1856.—*James Baines* 420 miles.
February 27, 1854.—*Red Jacket* 413 miles.
January 27, 1855.—*James Baines* 407 miles.
July 6, 1854.—*Red Jacket* 400 miles.

All these performances were made running east, making the day's work under 24 hours.

Several other ships claimed runs of over 400 miles, but I have not included these as I have not sufficient particulars to verify them.

Marco Polo is supposed to have done a run of 428 miles under Captain McDonald on 7th January, 1854, and *Shalimar* 420 miles in 1855 on her first passage to Australia, under Captain Robertson. With this general account of their powers I must now return to a more detailed description of the giant clippers themselves.

The "Lightning."

The *Lightning* was built by Donald Mackay to the order of James Baines in the winter of 1853-4 at a cost of £80,000, and on her arrival in Liverpool was furnished and decorated below at a further cost of £2000.

"LIGHTNING."

From a painting.

[To face page 60.

Her measurements were:—

Tonnage (builders)	2096 tons.
(register)	1468 ,,
(burthen)	3500 ,,
Length	244 feet.
Beam	44 ,,
Depth	23 ,,
Dead rise at half-floor 20 inches.	

Her poop was 92 feet long and her saloon 86 feet, whilst she had 8 feet under the beams in her 'tween decks, a most unusual height for those days.

With regard to design she was one of the sharpest ships ever launched. Her model is thus described by Captain H. H. Clark:—"She had long, concave water-lines and at her load displacement line a cord from her cut-water to just abaft the fore rigging showed a concavity of 16 inches. Her stem raked boldly forward, the lines of the bow gradually becoming convex and blending with the sheer line and cut-water, while the only ornament was a beautiful full-length figure of a young woman holding a golden thunderbolt in her outstretched hand, the flowing white drapery of her graceful form and her streaming hair completing the fair and noble outline of the bow.

"The after-body was long and clean, though fuller than the bow, while the stern was semi-elliptical in form, with the plank sheer moulding for its base, and was ornamented with gilded carved work, though this really added nothing to the beauty of the strong sweeping outline of her hull."

The *Lightning's* spar and rigging measurements were tremendous:—

Mainmast, deck to truck	.. 164 feet.
Foremast ,, ,, ...	.. 151 ,,
Mizenmast ,, ,, ...	.. 115 ,,
Mainyard ,, ,, ...	.. 95 ,,
Lower stunsail booms	.. 65 ,,

She spread 13,000 yards of canvas when under all plain sail. Donald Mackay had her rigged as a three skysail yard ship, but later Messrs. James Baines fitted her with a moonsail on the main by lengthening the skysail mast. This was also done in the case of *James Baines*. And these two ships had the proud distinction of being perhaps the only two ships afloat which regularly crossed a moonsail yard.

The *Lightning* was provided with iron water tanks holding 36,000 gallons of water—a novelty at that date. And in various other ways her accommodation for passengers was an improvement on anything attempted before.

The great Bully Forbes was sent out to Boston to superintend her outfit and take command of her, and he was lucky in finding a valuable friend and adviser in Captain Lauchlan Mackay, who made the trip to Liverpool in her as builders' representative.

The " Red Jacket."

The *Red Jacket*, *Lightning's* great rival, was designed by Samuel A. Pook, of Boston, the well-known designer of *Game-cock*, *Surprise*, *Northern Light*, *Ocean Telegraph*, *Herald of the Morning*, and other famous clipper ships. She was built by George Thomas at Rockland, Maine, for Messrs. Seacomb & Taylor, and only took the water a few days before the *Lightning*.

Her measurements were:—

Tonnage (registered)	..	..	2460 tons.
(burthen)	..	..	5000 ,,
Length	..	..	.. 260 feet.
Beam	..	..	.. 44 ,,
Depth	..	..	.. 26 ,,

Though her bow and stern were very sharp and

"RED JACKET."

From an old lithograph.

[To face page 63.

beautifully modelled and she had concave bow lines, she was not so extreme a ship as the *Lightning*.

Donald Mackay's ships were chiefly distinguished for their powerful workmanlike appearance rather than for delicate beauty—they showed strength rugged and unmistakable, but the *Red Jacket's* strength was more disguised under graceful curves; for instance, she had the graceful arched stem and clipper bow of a China ship, whereas *Lightning's* stem was almost straight, with only a very slight curve in it.

Red Jacket was not named after Tommy Atkins, but after a great Indian chief, and her figure-head was a beautiful representation of this warrior in all the magnificence of feather head-dress and beaded buckskins.

Race across the Atlantic between "Lightning" and "Red Jacket."

The *Lightning* loaded at Constitution Wharf, Boston, and sailed for Liverpool on 18th February, 1854, whilst the *Red Jacket* sailed from New York on the following day, and great interest was shown in shipping circles as to which should make the best passage across the Atlantic.

In the end these two magnificent clippers arrived in Liverpool on the same day, 4th March, their exact times being:—

Red Jacket—Sandy Hook to Rock Light 13 days 1 hour.
Lightning—Boston Light to Rock Light 13 days 19½ hours.

Their 24-hour runs opened the eyes of the packet ship commanders and in fact the whole world.

The *Red Jacket* put up runs of 413, 374, 371, 343, and 300 against the *Lightning's* 436, 328, 312 and 306, thus there was little to choose between the two vessels on this point.

The *Boston Daily Atlas* of 18th February, 1854, thus describes the *Lightning's* departure from Boston :—

At 2 o'clock the *Lightning* hove her anchor up, and at 3 o'clock discharged her pilot off Boston Light.   She went down in tow of the steamer *Rescue*, Captain Hennessy, and was piloted by Mr. E. G. Martin.

Before the steamer left her, she set her head sails, and fore and mizen topsails, and had a moderate breeze from W. to S.W.   She appeared to go at the rate of 6 knots under this canvas, though she draws 22 feet of water and has only 23 feet depth of hold.

We have seen many vessels pass through the water, but never saw one which disturbed it less.   Not a ripple curled before her cut-water, nor did the water break at a single place along her sides.   She left a wake as straight as an arrow and this was the only mark of her progress. There was a slight swell, and as she rose we could see the arc of her forefoot rise gently over the seas as she increased her speed.   At 5 p.m., two hours after the pilot left her, the outer telegraph station reported her 30 miles east of Boston Light with all drawing sails set and going along like a steam boat.

And the following extract from her log book was published in the *Liverpool Albion* on her arrival.

			Distance.	
Feb. 19	Wind,	W.S.W. and N.W. moderate	200 miles.	
20	,,	N.N.E. and N.E. strong breezes with snow	328	,,
21	,,	E.S.E. with snow storms	145	,,
22	,,	E.S.E., a gale with high cross sea and rain	114	,,
23	,,	N., strong gales to E.S.E.; ends moderate	110	..
24	,,	S.E., moderate	312	,,
25	,,	E.S.E. and S.E., fresh breezes with thick weather	285	,,
26	,,	W.S.W., moderate	295	,,
27	,,	W.N.W. ,, ...	260	,,
28	,,	W. and N.W., steady breezes	306	,,
March 1	,,	South. Strong gales ; bore away for the North Channel ; carried away the fore topsail and lost jib ; hove the log several times and found the ship going through the water at the rate of 18 to 18½ knots ; lee rail under water and rigging slack	436	,,
2	,,	South, first part moderate, latter part light and calm.		
3	,,	Light winds and calms.		
8	,,	Light S.E. winds and calms; at 7 a.m. off Great Orme's Head. 12 noon off the N.W. lightship.		

On 28th February at noon she was in Lat. 52° 38′ N., Long. 22° 45′ W., and her run of 436 nautical miles from that position to her noon position on 1st March gives her the greatest day's work ever accomplished, to the best of my belief, by a sailing ship. The 1st March entry "Wind south—bore away for the North Channel," has misled some nautical critics, who have plotted her as being up with Rathlin Island when she bore away, without noticing the direction of the wind. The log is rather ambiguously worded, but her run of 436 miles puts her some 80 miles west of Achill Head— and she then bore away north, bringing the wind on the starboard quarter. If she had been off Rathlin Island she would have had to bring the wind on the starboard bow for the course through the North Channel.

Captain Charles McDonald always hoped to get a day's run of 500 miles out of the *James Baines*,.and firmly believed she could do it; but he never succeeded in beating the *Lightning's* records.

The *Red Jacket*, which was under the command of Captain Asa Eldridge, of American packet ship fame, had strong winds from S.E. to W.S.W. with rain, snow and hail. As with *Lightning*, the first half of her passage was the slowest half and for the first seven days she could only average 182 miles a day. But with practically the same weather, it is interesting to compare the performances of the two vessels as they approached the Irish Coast. *Red Jacket's* last six runs were 219, 413, 374, 843, 800, and 371, giving a total of 2020 and an average of 336.

The only vessel that has ever beaten this six-day run is the famous *Cutty Sark*, which in 1876, before her wings were clipped, ran 2163 miles in six days in the roaring forties, when outward bound to Sydney.

D

"Red Jacket's" First Voyage to Australia.

At Liverpool Captain Eldridge handed over his command to Captain Samuel Reid, who managed to get the *Red Jacket* away for Australia, as one of the White Star regular packets, 10 days ahead of Captain Forbes. The *Red Jacket* sailed on 4th May, 1854, one day behind a new Nova Scotian built Black Ball packet named the *Mermaid*.

On the 10th May the two ships were off Oporto, and kept close to each other as far as Teneriffe; the N.E. trades were poor and it was a light weather passage to the line, which was crossed on 29th May by the *Red Jacket*, the *Mermaid* being then in 1° north.

From this point the *Red Jacket*, steering a more westerly course, had light and variable winds, whilst the *Mermaid* was better treated and reached the latitude of the Cape five days ahead, and still held better winds, being actually 1397 miles ahead of the *Red Jacket* on 15th June. *Red Jacket*, indeed, did not really get going until 26th June, but from that date her log is so remarkable that I give it below.

The *Red Jacket* was in 40° S., 14° E., before there was any need to touch her topgallant sheets, and Captain Reid was evidently determined to find wind somehow, with the result that, in spite of it being the depth of winter, he was not deterred from standing far to the southward on a Great Circle course. He was rewarded by all the wind he could desire, but so great was the cold that the ship was put down by the head by the frozen spindrift which covered her to the mainmast in an icy mantle.

Her log from 26th June, when she first began to feel the benefit of the westerlies, was as follows :—

Date.	Lat.	Long.	Weather	Dist.
June 26	48 06S	34 44E	Var. and stiff rain and sleet.	315
27	50 06	42 19	Wind N.W., fresh and squally with hail, very cold weather.	330
28	50 54	49 16	Wind W.N.W., squalls with hail showers.	263
29	50 34	56 34	Wind N.N.W., squalls, entire fore part of ship covered with ice.	286
30	52 03	63 50	Wind N.N.W., fresh with hail squalls ; very cold, air 19°.	287
July 1	51 39	71 21	Wind N.N.W., fresh, with hail squalls, latter part light, air 19°.	286
2	50 29	72 26	Wind S.W., first part calm, latter part heavy gales and heavy sea.	
3	50 12	80 30	Wind W.S.W., first part heavy gales, latter part fresh breezes, high sea, freezing.	312
4	49 25	88 30	Wind variable, fresh gales and heavy sea, freezing, rain and sleet.	300
5	49 13	95 00	Wind N.N.W., first part light and heavy rain, latter stiff, with heavy squalls.	288
6	48 38	104 15	Wind W.N.W., strong gales and squalls, heavy sea.	400
7	47 25	112 44	Wind variable in strength and direction.	299
8	46 38	119 44	Wind N.N.W., stiff and squalls, with rain.	350
9	45 09	129 18	Wind N.N.W., strong and squally, with rain.	357
10	42 42	134 38	Wind N.N.W., fine weather.	334
11	40 36	139 35	Wind N.W., heavy squalls and rain.	245
12			Wind N.N.W., fine weather. Made King's Island at 10.50 p.m., crossed bar at 11.50 p.m.	300

Red Jacket made the passage from Rock Light to Port Phillip Heads in 69 days 11 hours 15 minutes; passage under sail 67 days 13 hours, total distance run 13,880 miles.

The *Mermaid*, which gained such an advantage over the *Red Jacket* in the earlier part of the passage, ran her easting down a good deal further to the northward, and did not arrive till the 17th July, having made a passage of 74½ days.

Red Jacket set sail on her homeward passage on 3rd August. She was not in very good trim this time, being too light and very much down by the stern, however, she still continued to show her quality, constantly logging 17 or 18 knots in fresh breezes and 14 and 15 knots when close-hauled   Only once on the homeward passage were her topsails close-reefed and only once did she ship any water. This was on the 31st August in a heavy squall with foresail and fore and main topgallant sails set.

She rounded the Horn on the 23rd August, only 20 days out, her week's work averaging out as follows:

> 1st week 231 miles per day.
> 2nd „   307   „   „
> 3rd „   254   „   „

But on the day after she had rounded the Horn, she had a narrow escape of being embayed by ice, and one of her passengers gave the following account of her danger to the newspapers:—"On the morning of 24th August, I was roused out of sleep by the noise of shortening sail and the look-out singing out land. Ice had been seen some time before, but the solid masses had been supposed in the dark to be land. On getting out I found we were in smooth water and large masses of ice floating about us. As the day broke, we found ourselves sailing along a lake of water not unlike a canal. The ice seemed to extend on every side in solid fields as far as the eye could reach without any prospect of getting out, so that we had to follow the channel. All sail was clewed up except the topsails, and as there was a good breeze we proceeded along at about 4 or 5 knots. Our situation at this time seemed most appalling, as we appeared to be getting further into the ice, so that by 10 or 11 o'clock we were almost making up our minds to remain for weeks in this fearful situation.

"About noon the captain and second mate, who had been on the fore topsail yard all the morning, discovered clear sea again, to gain which we had to force a passage through dense masses of ice. It was here she sustained the principal damage to her stem and copper. We soon got clear and the rest of the day we saw no traces of ice and were very thankful we had got off so easily. But to our dismay at 8 p.m. we again fell in with it. The ship was put about and sail shortened for the night and we ran back to the clear water in which we had been sailing. At daybreak sail was made and at 7 a.m. we came up to the ice. At first it was only large pans much melted, the water having all the appearance of brine and being quite thick round them. Afterwards large masses of icebergs presented themselves. In grinding the ship through these, great difficulty was experienced—very large bergs were also interspersed and visible all round.

"This day we cleared it again about noon. Icebergs were still, however, seen both near and in the distance; their appearance was most grand, the largest being thought to be about 2 miles in circumference and 100 feet high. It was passed about 4 or 5 miles distant on our starboard and lee side

"We hove to again at night. Next day, Saturday, was for the most part a dead calm and we were carried back with the current. There was not a breath of wind; a clear sky and beautiful weather, only the air sharp. Icebergs were, however, still seen. The next day, Sunday, we passed a number more, which were the last ice seen. One of these was most grand, being about 200 feet high. We cleared it on our port or windward side about a mile or less distant. The weather during this period was clear and fine. Indeed, the day before encountering the ice was beautiful, a fine light breeze which heightened towards evening and sea smooth. We were running close-hauled 14 knots an hour steadily during the night. The sun had set a deep crimson behind a bank of clouds over against Cape Horn.''

Red Jacket's next three weeks' runs averaged:—

4th week	..	205 miles per day.	
5th week	..	237 ,, ,,	(Mostly light breezes, squalls and rain.)
6th week	..	224 ,, ,,	(Easterly winds.)

The line was crossed on 13th September, the *Red Jacket* having run 10,243 miles in 42 days, an average of 244 per day. She now had every hope of beating the record, but, alas, from here on she had nothing but calms and light head winds which drove her across into 43° W. and she was 31½ days from the line to port, reaching Liverpool on 15th October, after a passage of 73 days. This was considered an extraordinary performance, when allowance was made for the light weather experienced after crossing the line. During one whole week in the doldrums she averaged under 100 miles per day, and the two following weeks she only averaged 142 and 106 miles respectively.

The whole voyage, however, had been a wonderfully fast one. She had made the trip, out and home, in 5 months 10 days and 22½ hours, and had actually circumnavigated the globe in 62 days 22 hours, between 11th June and 2nd September, running 15,991 miles in that time.

On her homeward passage she ran 14,863 miles, her

greatest day's work being 376 miles and her average 202¼ miles per day.

She brought home gold dust and sovereigns to the value of £208,044. She sailed this voyage under the American flag, being only chartered by the White Star Line, but on her return to Liverpool Messrs. Pilkington & Wilson bought her for the sum of £30,000.

The "Lightning's" First Voyage to Australia.

The *Lightning*, with the famous Bully Forbes in command and the almost equally famous Bully Bragg as mate, left Liverpool on the 14th May for Melbourne. But unlike the *Red Jacket*, she had a light weather passage out, her topgallant sails being carried the whole way. She crossed the line 25 days out and took 30 days running from the meridian of the Cape to Port Phillip Heads, arriving off Sandridge Pier on the afternoon of 31st July, 77 days from Liverpool, her best runs being 348, 332, 329, 311, and 300.

On the morning of the 20th August she left her anchorage at Melbourne in company with the *Mermaid*, having gold dust on board to the value of £1,000,000. The tug dropped her off the Heads at 4 p.m., and by the following noon she had done 268 knots. At 4 a.m. on the 24th she passed a large ship supposed to be the *Mermaid*, and at 10 p.m. on the same day passed the Auckland Islands. From here she had fresh westerly and south-westerly winds, seldom logging less than 14 and frequently 18½ and 19 knots per hour. Forbes carried on in the most daring manner, and on the *Lightning's* arrival at Liverpool her passengers told weird stories of Bully Forbes keeping his station at the break of the poop with a pistol in each hand in order to prevent his scared crew from letting go the royal halliards.

By 28th August the ship was in 57° 20′ S., but at 11 p.m. on this day a violent squall from the S.W. carried away the fore topmast stunsail boom, and a moment later the fore topmast went over the side, the fore royal, fore topgallant sail and fore topsail being blown out of the bolt ropes at the same instant.

For the next four days the ship was kept under easy canvas whilst a new fore topmast was got aloft and the other damage made good. However, in spite of this delay the ship averaged 300 miles from 1st September to the 8th, when Cape Horn bore N.W., distant 50 miles at 3 a.m.; *Lightning's* actual time from the Heads to the Horn was 19 days 1 hour, a record. For the next three days she had the wind ahead at N.E., but on the 13th it came out of the south again strong, and her runs on the 13th and 14th were 351 and 354 miles respectively. Then from the 15th to the 20th with light head winds again, she could only average 6 to 7 knots an hour. On the 20th September she was in Lat. 29° 13′ S., Long. 31° 40′ W. Light N.E. and N.N.E. winds still held right up to the line. On the 28th she passed Pernambuco, 6 miles off, and at 9 a.m. on 30th September she crossed the equator in Long. 34° 30′ W., being only a little over 40 days mean time from Port Phillip, which, considering the poor winds met with after rounding the Horn, was a wonderful performance.

For the first five days after crossing the line she had the usual doldrums with torrents of rain and made little or no progress. On 5th October a gentle N.E. trade was picked up in 10° N., 34° W., which held until the 10th when she was in 30° N., 37° W. On the 11th and 12th she had moderate S.E. winds, being in the latitude

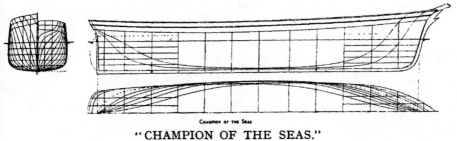

"CHAMPION OF THE SEAS."

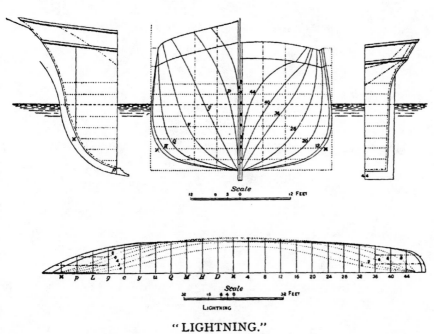

"LIGHTNING."

[*To face page* 73.

of St. Michael's at noon on the 12th. For the next week she had nothing but very light N.E. and E.N.E. winds, but at 10 p.m. on the 19th when in 46° 15′ N., 28° W., a strong northerly breeze sprang up which held until she reached port.

She was off the Old Head of Kinsale at 4 a.m. on 22nd October, passed Minehead at 10 a.m., the Tuskar at 3.30 p.m., and Holyhead Light at 8.30 p.m. A pilot was picked up off Point Lynas at 10.30 p.m., who kept her under easy sail through the night, waiting for enough water to take her over the bar. The *Lightning* anchored in the Mersey at 9.30 a.m. on 23rd October; her actual time being 64 days 3 hours 10 minutes, a record, which, I believe, has never been broken.

The *Lightning* brought answers to letters sent out in the *Great Britain* which left Liverpool on 13th June, thus making a course of post of only 132 days. The *Lightning's* round voyage, including 20 days in port, was only 5 months 8 days and 21 hours.

"Champion of the Seas."

Whilst the *Red Jacket* and *Lightning* were astonishing the world, Donald Mackay was building the *Champion of the Seas* and *James Baines* for the Black Ball Line. He was given a free hand, and the new vessels were intended to be more perfect than anything he had hitherto attempted.

The *Champion of the Seas* was launched in April, 1854, and, owing to the monster four-master *Great Republic* being cut down a deck, claimed the honour of being the largest ship in the world until the *James Baines* eclipsed her.

Her hull measurements were as follows:—

Tonnage (builders' measurement)	2447 tons.
„ (registered)	1947 „
Length of keel	238 feet.
„ between perpendiculars	252 „
Fore rake	14 „
Extreme beam	45½ „
Depth	29 „
Dead rise at half-floor	18 inches.
Sheer	4½ „
Concavity of load line forward	2½ „

In strength of construction she was a considerable improvement on the *Lightning*. Her ends were as long but not quite so sharp or concave and were considered to be more harmoniously designed. She had an upright sternpost and her stern was semi-elliptical and ornamented with the Australian coat-of-arms. Her figurehead was a life-like representation of the old-time shellback and was an object of interest wherever she went.

It is thus described by Captain Clark:—"One of the most striking figure-heads was the tall square-built sailor, with dark curly hair and bronzed clean-shaven face, who stood at the bow of the *Champion of the Seas*. A black belt with a massive brass buckle supported his white trousers, which were as tight about the hips as the skin of an eel and had wide, bell-shaped bottoms that almost hid his black polished pumps. He wore a loose-fitting blue and white checked shirt with wide rolling collar and black handkerchief of ample size, tied in the most rakish of square knots with long flowing ends. But perhaps the most impressive of this mariner's togs were his dark-blue jacket and the shiny tarpaulin hat which he waved aloft in the grip of his brawny tattooed right hand."

The *Champion of the Seas* had her greatest beam at the centre of the load displacement line, and, like the *Lightning*, she was fuller aft than forward. Her deck houses and cabin arrangements were also on the same plan as those of the *Lightning*, viz., a topgallant foc's'le for the crew; a house, 50 feet long, abaft the foremast, for petty officers, galleys and second class passengers; a small house, 16 feet square, contained the chief mate's quarters and sheltered the first class companion, whilst a large wheel-house astern had a smoking-room on one side and the captain's cabin on the other.

The following details of her construction, taken from an American paper, may be of interest to present day wood shipwrights:—"Her entire frame was of seasoned white oak and all her hooks, pointers and knees were of the same wood, her planking and ceiling being of hard pine, and she was square fastened throughout and butt and bilge bolted with copper. The keel was of rock maple in two depths, each 16 inches square. The floor timbers were moulded 21 inches on the keel and sided from 12 to 13 inches, and over them were four tiers of midship keelsons, each 16 inches square, and on each side of these were two depths of sister keelsons of the same size, the whole scarphed and keyed and fastened with $1\frac{3}{4}$ inch bolting. The whole frame, fore and aft, was diagonally cross-braced with iron, 5 inches wide, $\frac{7}{8}$ of an inch thick and 38 feet long. These braces were bolted through every frame and through every intersection; were let into the timbers and ceiling and extended from the first futtocks to the top timbers. All the waterways as well as the keelsons and ceiling were scarphed and bolted in the most substantial style. The upper deck was of white pine $3\frac{1}{2}$ inches thick and the other decks of hard pine of the same substance. Her ends were almost filled with massive hooks and pointers. The hooks in the between decks were beamed and kneed and fastened through all. Her garboards were 9 by 15 inches, the next strake 8 by 14, the third 7 by 14; the bottom planking 5 inches thick, the wales 6 by 7 and the waist 4½ inches thick, the whole finished smooth as joiner work and strongly fastened.''

The *Champion of the Seas* had about the same sail area and spar measurements as the *Lightning*. Her masts and bowsprit were built of hard pine and the masts were 74 and 63 feet apart. The foremast raked ¼ inch to the foot, the main ⅜ and the mizen 1 inch. When she left the builders her working suit of sails consisted of 12,500 yards of American cotton, 18 inches in width.

She was of course painted the regulation Black Ball colours, black outside and white inside, with blue waterways. Her masts white, mastheads and yards black, and stunsail booms bright with black ends. Captain Alexander Newlands was sent out from Liverpool to superintend her outfit and take command, the lighting and ventilation below being carried out according to his designs. On her completion the *Champion of the Seas* was towed to New York by the famous Boston tug *R. B. Forbes* and from thence came across to Liverpool in the month of June in 16 days.

She left Liverpool on her first voyage to Australia on 11th October, 1854, and arrived out in 72 days, coming home again in 84, thus proving herself quite up to the standard of the famous Black Ball Line, and from that date she was always a favourite ship.

" JAMES BAINES."

From a painting by Captain D. O. Robertson, late commander of ship " Lightning."

[To face page 77.

The "James Baines."

The *Champion of the Seas* was closely followed by the *James Baines*, considered by most sailormen to have been the finest and fastest of the great Mackay quartette. When she loaded troops for India in 1857 and was inspected by Queen Victoria at Portsmouth, the Queen remarked that she did not know she possessed such a splendid ship in her Mercantile Marine.

When she first arrived in Liverpool a well-known Liverpool shipowner wrote to a Boston paper:—" You want to know what professional men say about the ship *James Baines*? Her unrivalled passage, of course, brought her prominently before the public and she has already been visited by many of the most eminent mechanics in the country. She is so strongly built, so finely finished and is of so beautiful a model that even envy cannot prompt a fault against her. On all hands she has been praised as the most perfect sailing ship that ever entered the river Mersey."

Donald Mackay never built two ships exactly alike, and the *James Baines* was of slightly fuller design than the *Lightning* and yet sharper and longer in the bow than the *Champion of the Seas*.

Her chief measurements were:—

Registered tonnage (American)	..	..	..	2525$\frac{11}{16}$ tons.
,, ,, (British) ..	..	..	..	2275 ,,
Length over all	..	..	..	266 feet.
,, between perpendiculars ..	..	..	..	226 ,,
Beam	..	..	..	44$\frac{1}{2}$,,
Depth of hold	..	..	..	29 ,,
Dead rise at half-floor	..	..	..	18 inches.

The following extracts are taken from an account of the *James Baines* given in the *Boston Atlas* at the time of her launch:—" She has a long, rakish, sharp bow with slightly concave lines below, but convex above, and it is ornamented with a bust of her namesake, which was carved in Liverpool and which is said by those who know the original to be an excellent likeness. It is blended with the cut-water, is relieved with gilded carved work and forms a neat and appropriate ornament to the bow. She is planked flush to the covering board, has a bold and buoyant sheer, graduated her whole length, rising gracefully at the ends, particularly forward; and every moulding is fair and harmonises finely with the planking and her general outline. Her stern is rounded, and although she has a full poop deck, her afterbody surpasses in neatness that of any vessel her talented builder has yet produced.

"Our most eminent mechanics consider her stern perfect. It is rounded below the line of the plank sheer, is fashioned above in an easy curve, and only shows a few inches of rise above the outline of the monkey rail: and as this rise is painted white and the rest of the hull black, when viewed broadside on, her sheer appears a continuous line along her entire length. Her stern is ornamented with carved representations of the great globe itself, between the arms of Great Britain and the United States, surrounded with fancy work, has carved and gilded drops between the cabin windows and her name above all, the whole tastefully gilded and painted. Her bulwarks are built solid and are surmounted by a monkey rail, which is panelled inside, and their whole height above the deck is about 6 feet, varying of course towards the ends.

"She has a full topgallant foc's'le, which extends to the foremast and is fitted for the accommodation of her crew; and abaft the foremast a large house, which contains spacious galleys, several staterooms, storerooms, an iceroom and shelters a staircase which leads to the decks below. She has a full poop deck, between 7 and 8 feet high, under which is the cabin for female passengers and before it a large house which contains the dining saloon and other apartments. The outline of the poop and the house is protected by rails, on turned stanchions, and the enclosure forms a spacious and beautiful promenade deck. She has also a small house aft, which shelters the helmsman in a recess, protects the entrance to the captain's cabin, is also a smoking room for passengers and answers a variety of other purposes.

" The captain's cabin and sleeping room are on the starboard side and communicate with the wheelhouse on deck, so that it will not be necessary for him to enter the cabin set apart for female passengers. Besides these the cabin contains 11 spacious staterooms, a bath-room and other useful apartments.

" The dining saloon is 35 feet long by 15 feet wide; the entrance to the deck from the saloon is $2\frac{1}{2}$ feet wide and extends across the house, with a door on each side, and opposite the midship door of the saloon is the pantry, which is spacious and fitted up in superior style. In the front of the saloon house are the staterooms of the first and second officers, and the windows of these rooms are of stained glass and have the ship's name in them. The staircase in the after part of the saloon leads to the main deck, where are the gentlemen's sleeping apart-ments, 24 in all, each stateroom having two berths. The deck before the gentlemen's sleeping cabin has three large ports for cargo opposite the hatchways, one on each side, and square ports suitable for staterooms along the sides. The lower decks are ventilated amid-ships with trunk skylights which pass through the house forward as well as the cabin and saloon aft. The height between each of the decks is 7½ feet. The ascent from the quarter-deck to the poop consists of two staircases, built into the front of the poop. She is very heavily sparred and will spread about 13,000 yards of canvas in a single suit of sails. Her mastheads and yards are black; the lower masts, from the truss bands to the fiferails, are bright and varnished, their hoops white and the tops and down to the truss band are also white. She has iron caps and is rigged in nearly the same style as the *Champion of the Seas.* Her bulwarks and houses are painted white and her waterways blue, and in this style she is also painted below."

Captain McDonald left the *Marco Polo* in order to take charge of the *James Baines*. She sailed from Boston on 12th September, 1854, and the following is the log of her record run across the Atlantic:—

Sept. 12—At noon parted with steam boat and pilot. Wind, S.W., light.

13—Lat. 42° 10' N., Long. 66° 33' W. Distance 225 miles. Light airs and calms, increasing in the evening to brisk winds and clear weather.

14—Lat. 40° 18' N., Long. 62° 45' W. Distance 238 miles. Light breezes and clear.

15—Lat. 42° 26' N., Long. 59° 53' W. Distance 218 miles. Strong breezes at S.S.W.

16—Lat. 43° 15' N., Long. 53° 9' W. Distance 305 miles. Strong gales from S.S.W. to N.W.

17—Lat. 44° 54' N., Long. 48° 48' W. Distance 280 miles. Strong breezes from N.W. 4 a.m., passed several vessels fishing.

18—Lat. 45° 42' N., Long. 44° 16' W. Distance 198 miles. Light breezes and hazy weather. 10 a.m., brisk breezes and cloudy, wind west.

19—Lat. 47° 22' N., Long. 36° 42' W. Distance 342 miles. Strong breezes and squally.

20—Lat. 48° 39' N., Long. 33° 12' W. Distance 200 miles. Light breezes and hazy. Variable.

21—Lat. 49° 34' N., Long. 28° 38' W. Distance 230 miles. Light breezes and clear . Wind, S.W.

22—Lat. 50° 12′ N., Long. 21° 00′ W.   Distance 291 miles.
    Brisk S.S.W. winds and cloudy weather.   Passed several
    sail standing eastward.
23—Lat. 50° 37′ N., Long. 13° 39′ W.   Distance 337 miles.
    Strong breezes and cloudy weather   Wind, S.W.
24—Strong breezes and gloomy weather.   At 6 a.m. made the
    land and at 8 a.m. passed Cork.   Distance 296 miles.
    Passed Tuskar at 3 p.m., and Holyhead at 9 p.m.
Time 12 days 6 hours from Boston Light to Rock Light.

It will be seen that the *James Baines* had her share of light breezes, and Captain McDonald believed that he could have made the passage in eight days with strong winds. Running up Channel the wind was strong and fair and very squally, the vessel sometimes making 20 knots an hour between points.

At Liverpool the *James Baines* was fitted and furnished for passengers by Messrs. James H. Beal and brother. And her cabin fittings are described as being of "almost lavish splendour," with innumerable pilasters and mirrors.

I also note the following in a Liverpool account:— "Before the mainmast there are three gallows frames, upon which her spare boats are stowed, bottom up, and over the sides she carries quarter boats, suspended in iron davits. She has copper-chambered pumps, six capstans, a crab-winch on the foc's'le, a patent wind-lass, Crane's self-acting chain stoppers, a patent steering apparatus and a large variety of other improvements of the most modern kind."

Record Voyage of "James Baines" to Australia.

The *James Baines* sailed for Melbourne on 9th December, 1854, and broke the record by arriving out in 63 days. Captain McDonald wrote the following account of the passage to his owners:—

"I have great pleasure in announcing the arrival

of the *James Baines* in Hobson's Bay at 8 p.m. on 12th February, making a run of 63 days 18 hours 15 minutes mean time from passing the Rock till the anchor was down in Hobson's Bay. On leaving Liverpool I had strong head winds to contend with. The 7th day from Liverpool-I touched off St. Ives Head; the 10th day I had to tack off Cape St. Vincent and stood to the N.W. In 19° N. in the middle of the trade winds, I got the wind at S.S.E., got to leeward of Cape San Roque, and was 18 hours in beating round. I experienced nothing but light northerly winds all the way across. Sighted Cape Otway on the 54th day from Liverpool; main skysail off the ship only three days from Liverpool to this port. The greatest distance run in 24 hours was 423 miles, that with main skysail and stunsails set. Had I only had the ordinary run of winds I would have made the voyage in 55 days.''

The *James Baines* took out 700 passengers (80 in the first class) 1400 tons of cargo and 350 sacks containing over 180,000 letters and newspapers. By her mail contract she was bound to deliver these in 65 days under penalty. Amongst her live stock were a bullock, 75 sheep, 86 pigs, and 100 dozen of fowls and ducks.

This passage of the *James Baines* showed her splendid capabilities both in light head winds and strong fair winds, for after a succession of light head winds she was reported in 3° N., 29° W., on the 29th December, only 19 days out, whilst in the boisterous gales of the roaring forties she made the following splendid 24-hour runs in about a 23½-hour day.

Friday, Jan. 26—Lat. 48° 02′ S., Long. 50° 46′ E.   Distance 391 miles.
        27—Lat. 48° 56′ S., Long. 60° 46′ E.   ,,   407   ,,
   Feb. 6—Lat. 50° 09′ S., Long. 123° 40′ E.   ,,   423`   ,,

This magnificent run showed 10′ difference of latitude

"DONALD MACKAY."

Entering Port Phillip Heads, 20th December, 1866.

[To face page 99

and 10° 40′ difference of longitude, her position at noon on 5th February being 50° 19′ S., 113° E.

Leaving Melbourne on the 12th March, 1855, the *James Baines* made the run home in 69½ days, having completed the voyage to Melbourne and back in 133 days under sail.

Black Ball captains were celebrated for their daring navigation and McDonald was no exception in this respect. His passengers declared that the *James Baines* was nearly ashore three times whilst tacking off the coast of Ireland under a heavy press of sail, and that when McDonald put her round off the Mizenhead the rocks were so close that a stone could have been thrown ashore from her decks. It was a lee shore, and if she had missed stays she must have been lost. But as McDonald said, when remonstrated with for taking such risks, it was a case of " we have to make a good passage."

The "Donald Mackay."

The *Donald Mackay*, last of the famous Mackay quartette, was for many years the largest sailing ship in the world, her measurements being:—

Registered tonnage	.. 2408 tons.
Gross ,, ...	.. 2486 ,,
Net ,, ...	.. 1616 ,,
Length of keel	.. 257.9 feet.
Length between perpendiculars	.. 266 ,,
Breadth	.. 46.3 ,,
Depth	.. 29.5 ,,
Dead rise at half-floor	.. 18 inches.
Mainyard	.. 100 feet.
Sail area	.. 17,000 yds.

A novelty in her sail plan was Forbes' patent double topsail yards. These came out before Howe's, and differed from them in having the topmasts fidded abaft the lower masts.

Donald Mackay was said to have the heaviest main-mast out of Liverpool. It was a built mast of pitch-pine, heavily banded with iron, weighing close on 20 tons. She was, of course, a three-decker; and as a figure-head she had a Highlander dressed in the tartan of the Mackays. In design she took after the *Champion of the Seas*, being not so sharp-ended as the *Lightning* or *James Baines*. Captain Warner left the *Sovereign of the Seas* to take her, and superintended her fitting out.

Leaving Boston on 21st February, 1855, she made Cape Clear only 12 days out. On 27th February her log records:—'' First part a strong gale from N.W.; middle part blowing a hurricane from W.N.W., ship scudding under topsails and foresail at the rate of 18 knots; latter part still blowing from W.N.W. with heavy hail squalls and very high sea running.''

Under these conditions she made a run of 421 miles in the 24 hours. She made the Fastnet Rock on 6th March, distant one mile, it blowing a gale from S.E. to E.N.E., her run for the day being 299 miles. But in he Channel her passage was spoilt by strong easterly winds, and she did not receive her pilot off Point Lynas until Saturday, the 10th.

Donald Mackay himself came over in the ship, and on his arrival expressed himself highly satisfied with her. She was at once put on the berth for Melbourne, but did not leave Liverpool until 6th June, and thus had a light weather passage south, being spoken on 14th July in 12° S., 88 days out. She arrived in Port Phillip on 26th August, 81 days out. She left Melbourne again on 8rd October, arriving in Liverpool on 28th December,

"WHITE STAR."

From an old lithograph.

[To face page 85.

1855, 86 days out, and bringing 104,000 ounces of gold consigned to the Bank of France.

Donald Mackay's times on the Australian run, though never very remarkable, were very consistent, her average for six consecutive outward passages being 88 days. And I find her making a passage out to Hobson's Bay in 1867 in 84 days. She once took 1000 troops from Portsmouth to Mauritius in 70 days.

"Blue Jacket," "White Star" and "Shalimar."

Three other magnificent ships were built on the other side of the Atlantic for the Liverpool-Melbourne emigrant trade in 1854. These were the *Blue Jacket*, *White Star* and *Shalimar*.

The *Blue Jacket* came from the well-known yard of R. E. Jackson in East Boston, the other two ships being Nova Scotian built. The *Blue Jacket* arrived in the Mersey on 20th October, 1854, having made the run from Boston, land to land, in 12 days 10 hours; the *Shalimar* arrived about the same time, and the *White Star* reached Liverpool on 1st December, 15 days out from St. John's in spite of strong head winds. She was timber laden and drawing 22½ feet of water. The *Blue Jacket* on her arrival was bought by James John Frost, of London, and put on the berth for Melbourne as one of the Fox Line of packets, the other two being owned by the White Star Line.

In looking at old pictures and prints of these American built ships, several points in their construction seem to have been common to all, such as the semi-elliptical stern, the bowsprit built into the sheer, the large wheel-house aft, etc.; their figure-heads, also, were generally most elaborate full-length figures and did not grow out of the bow in the graceful way of the British-built. but seemed to be plastered upon it. And from *Marco Polo* to *Donald Mackay*, these soft-wood clippers had more the appearance of strength and power than of grace and beauty, though the famous *Red Jacket* was an exception, being an extremely taking ship to the eye.

Blue Jacket, however, was of the powerful type, and extremely like the Mackay ships in appearance. She was designed to stow a large cargo, having a full midship section, but her bow was long and sharp enough.

Her chief measurements were :—

Length of keel	..	..	..	..	.. 205 feet.
Length between perpendiculars		..	..	.. 220 ,,
Length over all	..	..	..	..	.. 235 ,,
Beam ..	..	..	..	..	.. 41.6 ,,
Depth of hold ..	..	..	..	..	.. 24 ,,
Registered tonnage	..	..	..	..	.. 1790 tons.

Her poop was 80 feet long and 7 feet high, and she had 8 feet of height between decks. She had the usual accommodation arrangements, two points only being perhaps worth noting; the first was a line of plate glass portholes running the length of her 'tween decks, and the second was an iron water tank to hold 7000 gallons.

Blue Jacket sailed for Melbourne on 6th March, 1855, in charge of Captain Underwood, and made a magnificent run out of 69 days. She further distinguished herself at a later date by making the homeward run in 69 days.

Shalimar, the smallest ship of the three, measured 1557 tons register ; 195.8 feet length ; 35.2 feet beam ; and 23 feet depth. She sailed for Hobson's Bay on 23rd November, 1854, was off Cape Northumberland in 67 days, but owing to head winds took another 10 days to reach her port. She came home in 75 days, her whole voyage, including 45 days in port, only occupying 6 months and 14 days. The newspaper report of her passage out states that she ran 420 miles in the 24 hours on one occasion, although unfortunately it gives no particulars.

The most celebrated of these three ships was the *White Star*, which had the distinction of being the largest clipper built by Wright, of New Brunswick, her measurements being:—

Registered tonnage	..	..	..	..	..	2339 tons
Length over all	..	..	..	..	..	288 feet
Length of keel ..	..	..	..	..	..	213.3 ..
Beam ..	..	..	..	..	..	44 ..
Depth ..	..	..	..	..	..	28.1 ..

The *White Star* soon proved herself to be one of the fastest ships afloat. On her first voyage she did nothing out of the way, being 79 days out and 88 days home. But in 1856 she went out in 75 days (67 days land to land), and came home in 76 days, beating the auxiliary *Royal Charter* by 10 days from port to port. In 1858, she went out in 72 days, this being the best White Star passage of the year; whilst on 25th February, 1860, she left Melbourne and made her number off Cape Clear in 65 days. In 1860 she went out in 69 days, running 8306 miles in 10 days between the Cape and Melbourne.

The Wreck of the "Schomberg."

We now come to the unfortunate *Schomberg*, the only wooden ship ever built in a British yard that could in any way compare with the big Boston and Nova Scotian built ships in size.

In 1854, James Baines was so impressed by the success of the little Aberdeen tea clippers, that he gave Hall an order for a monster emigrant clipper of 2600 tons. Unfortunately, Hall had had no experience in the building of emigrant ships and the *Schomberg* was more of a copy of Mackay's clippers than Hall's own beautiful little ships. The *Schomberg* cost when ready for sea £43,103 or £18 17s. 6d. per ton. She measured :—

Tonnage (builder's measurement)	2600 tons.
,, (for payment of dues)	2492 ,,
,, (registered)	2284 ,,
Length over all	288 ,,
Length between perpendiculars	262 ,,
Beam	45 ,,
Depth of hold	29.2 ,,

She had three skins, two of diagonal planking, and one fore and aft, the whole fastened together with screw-threaded hard-wood trunnels—a novelty in shipbuilding. She was specially heavily rigged, her mainmast weighing 15 tons, being a pitch-pine spar 110 feet in length and 42 inches in diameter. Her mainyard was 110 feet long. She crossed three skysail yards, but no moonsail.

Captain Forbes, as commodore of the Black Ball, was shifted into her from the *Lightning*, and great hopes were entertained that she would lower the record to Australia.

On 6th October, 1855, she was hauled through the pier heads amidst the cheers of a patriotic crowd of sightseers, with the boast of "Sixty days to Melbourne" flying from her signal halliards. The passage was one of light and moderate winds. *Schomberg* was 28 days to the line and 55 days to the Greenwich meridian. Running her easting down she averaged 6 degrees daily to 180° E., her greatest speed being 15½ knots and her best run 368 miles. She made the land off Cape Bridgewater at 1 p.m. on Xmas day, the wind being fresh at E.S.E. On 27th December after two days' tacking, with the wind still blowing fresh from ahead, Forbes went about at noon when 4 miles off shore and tacked out; at 6 p.m. he tacked in again. At about

10.30 p.m., the land being faintly visible, the wind gradually died away. It was a moonlight night. Forbes was playing cards in the saloon when the mate came down and reported that the ship was getting rather close in under the land and suggested going about. As luck would have it, Forbes was losing and, being a bit out of temper, insisted on playing another rubber of whist before tacking ship, and the danger point had been overstripped when at 11 o'clock he came on deck and gave the order to 'bout ship.

As there was next to no wind and a current running 3 to 4 knots to the westward, the *Schomberg* refused to come round. Forbes next tried to wear her, with the result that the ship slid up on to a sandbank 35 miles west of Cape Otway. On sounding round the ship it was found that she was stuck fast in 4 fathoms of water. Sail was kept on her in the hopes of it pulling her off into deep water again.

Forbes, on being told that the ship was hard aground, said angrily:—"Let her go to Hell, and tell me when she is on the beach," and at once went below.

Henry Cooper Keen, the mate, then took charge, and finding that the *Schomberg* was only being hove further in by the swell and current, clewed up all sail, let go the starboard anchor and lowered the boats. And it was subsequently proved at the inquiry afterwards that it was chiefly due to the chief officer and a first class passenger, a civil engineer of Belfast named Millar, that all the passengers were safely disembarked and put aboard the steamer *Queen*, which hove in sight on the following morning.

All efforts to save the ship failed and she presently went to pieces. Forbes at the inquiry was acquitted of all blame for the stranding, the sandbank being uncharted, but at a mass meeting of his passengers in the Mechanics' Institute, Melbourne, he was very severely censured. Many of them declared that he was so disgusted with the slowness of the passage that he let the ship go ashore on purpose. Others complained of his tyranny during the voyage and even made worse allegations against his morality and that of the ship's doctor; altogether the affair was a pretty scandal and Forbes never obtained another command in the Black Ball Line.

The Best Outward Passages—Liverpool to Melbourne, 1854-5.

Ship.	Captain.	Date Left.	Date Arrived.	Days. Out.
		1854		
Red Jacket	Sam Reid	May 4	July 12	67
Mermaid	Devy	,, 3	,, 17	74
Miles Barton	Kelly	,, 4	,, 22	78
Lightning	J. N. Forbes	,, 14	,, 31	76
Marco Polo	Wild	July 22	Oct. 25	95
Arabian	Bannatyne	Aug. 19	Nov. 13	86
Morning Star	—	Sept. 6	,, 20	75
Champion of the Seas	Newlands	Oct. 11	Dec. 22	72
			1855	
Indian Queen	McKirdie	Nov. 12	Jan. 31	80
Shalimar	Robertson	,, 23	Feb. 7	76
James Baines	McDonald	Dec. 10	Feb. 12	64
		1855		
Lightning	A. Enright	Jan. 6	Mar. 20	73
Blue Jacket	Underwood	Mar. 6	May 13	69
Marco Polo	Clarke	April 6	June 26	82
White Star	Kerr	,, 30	July 18	79
Oliver Lang	Manning	May 5	,, 31	87
Arabian	Bannatyne	,, 21	Aug. 13	84
Donald Mackay	Warner	June 6	,, 26	81
Champion of the Seas	McKirdy	July 5	Sept. 26	83
Shalimar	Robertson	,, 20	Oct. 16	88
James Baines	McDonald	Aug. 5	,, 23	79
Emma	—	,, 21	Nov. 17	88
Lightning	A. Enright	Sept. 5	,, 25	81
Red Jacket	Milward	,, 20	Dec. 4	75
Invincible	—	,, 30	,, 18	79

1855-1857—Captain Anthony Enright and the "Lightning."

When Forbes was given the *Schomberg*, James Baines offered the command of the *Lightning* to Captain Anthony Enright, who had earned a great reputation as a passage maker in the tea clipper *Chrysolite*. At the same time the White Star Line asked Enright to take over the *Red Jacket*, and it was only after considerable deliberation that he decided to take the *Lightning*, first demanding a salary of £1000 a year. The Black Ball Line replied that it was a great deal more than they had ever previously given to their captains, but eventually they agreed to his terms rather than lose such a good man.

Captain Enright had the *Lightning* for four voyages, from January, 1855, to August, 1857, and proved himself perhaps the most popular and successful captain under the famous house-flag; indeed, under him the *Lightning* became a very favourite ship with passengers.

Enright was a very religious man, a Puritan of the old type yet no bigot; a stern disciplinarian, the men before the mast knew that he was sure to give them a square deal, impartial and just, and fair treatment for good service, and for that reason never gave him trouble, whilst in controlling his passengers and keeping a happy ship in spite of the trials of such long passages and crowded quarters, he showed the most wonderful tact and gift for ruling men. This gift of tact was perhaps more desirable in the captain of an emigrant ship than in any other walk of life, especially in the days of the gold rush when the emigrants represented every nationality, every creed, every class and every trade ; and the *Lightning*, under Enright, was as good an example of the best-run first-class emigrant ships as can be found. I therefore intend to give as good a picture of life aboard the *Lightning* during 1855-7 as I possibly can with the material at my command.

Captain Enright's Regulations.

First of all I will give a list of Enright's regulations for preserving order amongst his passengers, which were always posted up in prominent places about the ship.

RULES OF THE *LIGHTNING*.

1st. No smoking or naked light allowed below.

2nd. All lights, except the hatchway lights, to be put out by 10 p.m.

3rd. No Congreve matches to be used in the berths or on the lower deck.

4th. Cleanliness and decorum to be strictly observed at all times.

5th. Every place below to be well cleaned every day after breakfast, for the inspection of the surgeon and chief officer.

6th. All bedding to be on deck twice a week.

7th. The 'tween deck passengers to appoint constables to preserve order and see these rules are strictly observed.

8th. The constables are to keep watch in their respective compartments for their own safety and that of their families ; trim the lamps ; report all misdemeanours, for which they will receive a glass of grog or a cup of coffee every morning.

9th. Second cabin passengers are not allowed on the windward side of the vessel ; but can promenade at all hours on the leeward side.

10th. Passengers must not upon any account open the 'tween deck ports without my express permission : a violation of this rule may be attended with serious consequences, and will, in any case, be severely punished.

11th. Dancing and promenading on the poop from 7 till 9 p.m., when all passengers may enjoy themselves, but not abaft the mizen mast. The promenaders are not in any way to interrupt the dancers, but will be expected to promenade in parts of the poop where dancing is not being carried on.

12th. On account of the overcrowded state of the poop and to satisfy all parties, third class passengers are only allowed on the quarter-deck from 7 till 9 in the evening.

13th. The use of the private staircase (into the saloon) is strictly prohibited after 11 at night.

14th. No person allowed to speak to the officers of the watch whilst on duty : nor to any of the quartermasters, whilst at the wheel

15th. All parties not complying with these rules will be liable to have a part of their provisions deducted as a punishment. as the commander and officers may think fit

ANTHONY ENRIGHT, *Commander*

The Passengers on the ''Lightning.''

Perhaps a few details regarding the number and kind of passengers, for which these rules were framed, may now be of interest.

In 1855 the *Lightning* took out 47 saloon, 53 second cabin, 20 intermediate and 253 steerage passengers, her crew numbering 87; total of souls on board—495.

In 1856 her purser gave the following details of the outward bound passengers :—

Saloon—Adults 39 ; children 12 :	.. Total	**51**
'Tween deck—Married adults male	..	..	42
,, ,, female	..	..	55
Single ,, male	..	..	184
,, ,, female	..	..	33
children	..	..	47
infants	..	..	7
crew	..	..	85
Number of souls on board		**504**

On the homeward passage the numbers were naturally very much less, and women were not so numerous.

In 1855 the *Lightning* brought home 51 saloon, 123 second cabin and 80 intermediate ; total—254. On her second voyage that year, owing to the accident to her false bow when outward bound, she could only muster 80 passengers.

In 1856 her homeward bound passengers consisted of—

Saloon—Adults 31 ; children 3 ;	.. Total	34
'Tween decks—Married adults male	..	..	10
,, ,, female	..	..	10
Single ,, male	..	..	114
,, ,, female	..	..	1
children	..	..	6
infants	..	..	4
crew	..	..	77
	Total all told	..	256

All Europe sailed from Liverpool to the Australian goldfields, so that all nationalities were to be found in a Black Baller's foc's'le.

I find the following account in the *Lightning Gazette*, the newspaper published on board, of 1855:—"Here in the steerage we find there are many nations, including Jews, Germans and French; the largest number, however, being English with a few Irish and Scots. Here are all ages and not all, but many, trades and occupations. Here are some more or less successful diggers, who had returned to their native land to gratify a feeling of love and affection; or it may be vanity; and who are now returning to settle in the land of promise."

The homeward bound passengers were just as mixed if only half as numerous—thus the *Gazette* when homeward bound in 1856:—

The passengers generally are a very mixed community, English and French, American and German, Italian and Pole, young and old, merry and sad, the open-hearted and the reserved, the enterprising merchant and the adventurous gold digger, artizan and mechanic, soldier and sailor, prosperous husbands returning to escort their wives and families to the Colony, and the disappointed man, cheered alone by the magic influence of once again beholding home.

And under the heading of "The Gent Afloat," I find a very amusing description of the adventurer of the times aboard ship, and though it is rather long, it is such a vivid little study of a type of character, only too common in the snobbish mid-Victorian era, that I cannot resist giving it in full.

The Gent Afloat.

"This class of individual is to be found in great abundance in every clipper ship community. He is easily known, more easily detected. He is a man of vast importance when first he steps aboard; makes no advances; keeps aloof; is evidently selecting, with great caution, those with whom he dare associate without compromising his connections. After a little time, however, he—with a condescending grace, which cannot be too highly extolled—relaxes slightly his vigorous demeanour, and smiles upon the *very* young men of known good family (of course), occasionally honours them with his arm and promenades the deck for half an hour—is very careful during the peregrination to recount his latest adventures at home—the parting dinners Captain Allalie and Colonel Gammon would insist on giving him; the ballet dancer, who forsook an Earl for his advances and embraces; the prima donna who would insist on rehearsing her role before him as she entertained so high an opinion of his musical criticism and abilities. The borough he might have gone in for at the last election, with the Duke of Sarum's interest, but that his *own* family objected on the score of difference in political opinions, and the positive certainty that in a few years his great talents and eloquence must command the most independent seat in the House.

"He is of an average height and features, with the exception of a protruding chin, which gives to the mouth a horrible grin; an eyeglass of course; luxuriant hair and whiskers, redolent of macassar. He apes the gait of a military man; wears a frock coat terribly inclined to the third and fourth letters of the alphabet; a waistcoat of the most approved and fashionable cut; trowsers of the loudest plaid style about two to the pair, with very ragged bottoms and straps, the latter article proving a very useful adjunct when the supply of socks falls short; a shirt with miniature cartoons after Raphael or a correct likeness of the last murderer and the last ballet dancer printed upon it; a necktie of the *striking stripe* pattern, to make him smart. His whole appearance is indicative of a worn-out Stultz. His hands are covered with a variety of rings, from the enamelled and delicately wrought diamond to the massive and substantial signet bearing his crest. An immense watch chain (bearing a striking resemblance to the ship's cable) with an abundance of charms attached completes the *tout ensemble* of the outer man. His wardrobe is somewhat limited—but this he accounts for by—'D—n those agents, the rascals have put my trunks marked "wanted on the voyage" in the hold, and left out those "not wanted," isn't it annoying? Could you lend me a few shirts until they're got at? ' He is decidedly great at the borrowing dodge. Of course his cigars, tobacco and all the little comforts for the journey are in his trunks in the hold. But the way he solicits a loan of the required articles is irresistible. His natural grace (or impudence, we don't know which) defies refusal. But at last even that—as all things good or bad will—palls and borrowing becomes a more difficult art. Friends shirk him, acquaintances avoid him, and long before the end of the journey 'the Gent Afloat' is known and scouted as a penniless, reckless adventurer void alike of honour or honesty.''

Shipboard Newspapers.

This account of an adventurer of the fifties came out of the *Lightning Gazette*, a paper published weekly aboard the ship.

Realising the importance of keeping such a mixed collection of passengers amused Messrs. James Baines put a printing press aboard each of their ships and thus the issue of the shipboard newspaper was something always to be eagerly looked forward to on Saturdays. In many an English and Australian home there are no doubt still to be found treasured, stained and tattered, copies of these ships' newspapers. I have myself handled volumes of the *Lightning Gazette*, the *Eagle Herald*, the *Royal Charter Times* and coming down to more modern days, the *Loch Torridon Journal* and other Loch Line papers.

The printer of these ship newspapers was usually a paid member of the crew, but the editor and sub-editor were elected by the passengers, the captain, of course, acting not only as a frequent contributor but also as a censor—no matter of a controversial sort either religious, political or otherwise being ever allowed to appear in the news sheet of Captain Enright's ship.

The Ship's Notice Board.

The ship's official newspaper sometimes had to contend against rival productions, promoted by private enterprise, but its chief rival was the ship's notice board, which was a stout one, being no less than the mainmast.

Here are a few notices, gathered haphazard from the *Lightning's* mainmast.

E

CLOTHING SOLD BY THE PURSER

Cigars, 2d. each ¦ per hundred		£0	12	0
Do. Havannah .. .. each		0	0	4
Canvas trowsers		0	3	6
Kersey drawers		0	3	6
Mits		0	1	0
Oilskin trowsers		0	5	6
Oilskin coats		0	7	6
Pilot cloth coats		0	5	0
Pilot cloth trowsers		0	12	0
Blue serge shirts		0	5	0
Regatta shirts (printed fronts)		0	3	6
Black alpaca coats		0	12	0
Felt hats		0	3	0
Sou'westers		0	2	0
Black glazed hats		0	4	0
Guernsey frocks		0	8	6
Scotch caps		0	2	0
Knives		0	1	6

Apply to C. T. RENNY, *Purser.*

RAFFLES.

To be raffled for—
On Thursday next, June 7, at 2 o'clock,
A Splendid Model of the *Lightning,*
By 40 members, at 5/- each.
Application for shares to be made at the printing office.

HEALTH OFFICE

WANTED.

Swabbers to assist at the force pump and relieve two saloon passengers, who work with indefatigable zeal.

Application to be made to Dr. Colquhoun and Mr. Winter at 5 a.m. any morning.

The above is capital exercise, strongly recommended.

WANTED.

A washerwoman—one accustomed to get up gentlemen's linen preferred. Apply to Mr. NECK, *Chief Steward.*

FOR SALE.

Opossum Rugs. Apply to MR. FYSH, second cabin tween decks.

FOUND.

By the Boatswain of this ship, a coat with a pair of pincers in the pocket. The owner can have the same by paying expenses.

AUCTION.

On Wednesday next, at 2 p.m., a Public Auction will be held on the poop, when a large and well selected assortment of merchandise will be submitted to public competition by —

CHARLES ROBIN, *Auctioneer.*

Auctioneer's Address—No. 5 After Saloon Stateroom.

Riddles and Epigrams, so - numerous in the *Gazette*, were not, however, to be found on the ship's notice board. The riddles are mostly very feeble, many of them making great play with the ship's name, thus:—

Why is the Commander of our ship like the electric wire ?   *Ans.*—Because he is a Lightning conductor.

But there is a rather more interesting one of the times:—

Why is a scolding wife like American steamers ?   *Ans.*—Because she is fond of blowing up.

The epigrams are better, as follows:—

Upon seeing a lady filling a gentleman's pipe on board the *Lightning*—

" I would that ladies' hands might find
Something worthier to stuff
Nor give to those who are inclined
An opportunity to puff "

and—

Upon seeing a young lady printing the *Lightning Gazette* :—

" An angel form in earthly mould
Upon my ink has shed a blessing,
And manly hearts to others cold
Cannot resist when she is *pressing*."

The Ship's Band and Concerts, etc.

Perhaps the most important method of keeping an emigrant ship's passengers amused was by means of the ship's band, especially in those days when dancing was so popular, that even in bad weather the poops of these ships were always crowded with dancers every evening.

Of course the bands provided were not quite on a par with those of present day leviathans crossing the Atlantic; the *Lightning*, for instance, rejoiced in the good old-fashioned German band, which used to be such an institution in the London streets and is now practically extinct.   This band consisted of six musicians, and besides playing selections and accompaniments at the concerts, supplied the music for the daily dancing.

In those days the polka was the great dance, the valse had not yet come into fashion and was not very well known, and instead of the romping lancers the stately quadrille was the order of the day.

I find a set of instructions showing a sailor how to dance a quadrille in one of the numbers of the *Lightning Gazette*.   It is rather too long to quote, but the following figure shows the gist of it:—" Heave ahead and pass your adversary yardarm to yardarm: regain your berth on the other tack in the same order: take your station in a line with your partner, back and fill, face on your heel and bring up with your partner: she then manœuvres ahead and heaves all aback, fills and shoots ahead again and pays off alongside: you then make sail in company until stern on with the other line: make a stern board and cast her off to shift for herself: regain your berth by the best means possible and let go your anchor.''

Looking over the old concert programmes, I find that negro melodies (now called coon songs) were even then very popular, amongst which figured " Nelly Bligh,'' " Poor Old Joe,'' " Stop dat Knockin','': " Oh ! Carry Me Back'' and others. The rest of the programmes were generally filled up with the old familiar Scots and Irish folk-songs, some well-known

English choruses, the usual sentimental ditty, and amongst the sailor songs I find "A Life on the Ocean Wave," "Cheer, Boys, Cheer," "I'm Afloat," "The Pride of the Ocean" and "The Death of Nelson." Concerts were generally pretty numerous during a passage. As a rule each class had its own; then, to end up, a "Grand Monster Concert" was organised, in which the talents of saloon, house on deck, and steerage were pitted against one another.

Other diversions of this kind were plays of the class of "Bombastes Furioso"; mock trials, with the invariable verdict of guilty on the wretched culprit and the sentence of "champagne all round," and of course debating, choral and other societies.

Then there were the usual high jinks crossing the line; and such occasions as the Queen's Birthday, the "Captain's Wedding Day," etc., were celebrated by " a cold collation of the most sumptuous order" in the saloon and many speeches.

A Bill of Fare on the "Lightning."

In the first cabin the living on these big clippers seems to have been uncommonly good for such a length of time at sea. Here is the dinner menu of 14th January, 1855, on the *Lightning*, when a week out from Liverpool.

BILL OF FARE.

Soups—Vermicelli and macaroni.

Fish—Cod and oyster sauce.

Meats—Roast beef, boeuf a la mode, boiled mutton, roast veal, boiled turkey and oyster sauce, roast goose, roast fowl, boiled fowl, minced escallops, veal and ham pie, haricot mutton, ham.

Sweets—Plum pudding, rice pudding, roll pudding, tarts, orange fritters, small pastry.

Dessert—Oranges, almonds, Barcelona raisins, figs, etc.

Wines—Champagne, sparkling hock.

St. Valentine's Day.

Captain Enright was very fertile in raising a new amusement directly his passengers began to show signs of boredom. His favourite dodge was to appoint a St. Valentine's Day, when a letter box was placed in front of the poop and twice during the day the darkey steward, Richard, who was evidently a great character, came round and delivered the Valentines as postman. He was always dressed up for the occasion in some extraordinarily fantastic costume of his own invention— and his antics and fun, quite as much as the contents of his postbag, kept the ship in roars of laughter and most successfully dissipated all signs of boredom and discontent.   Here is one account of his doings:—

Richard, the coloured steward, made a first-rate walker, dressed in the tip-top style of St. Martins-le-Grand, with gold-laced hat, yellow collar and cuffs to his coat and white tops to his boots : he acted the part of Cupid's messenger to admiration and drew down thunders of applause.   There was a second delivery in the afternoon on the poop, when Richard again made his appearance dressed in full general's uniform.

And it goes on to say:—

The Valentines, which were very numerous, contained the usual amount of bitters and sweet, flattering verses and lovers' vows; some amusing hits at marked propensities and a few rather broad hints at infirmities and habits were all taken in good part and the day passed off most pleasantly.

And here is one of the Valentines which Captain Enright received:—

To
Captain Go-ahead Enright, A1,
Ship " Flash of Lightning,"
who never cracks on, and is supposed to have
at no time seen a moonsail.
It is currently reported that he lays to
and turns in when it blows a gale.
N.B.—No certain address, but always to be found
ON DUTY.

Other Amusements at Sea.

During the time of the Crimea, if there happened to be a soldier or two aboard, a corps of volunteers was raised and drilled daily. A parade in bad weather was a great source of amusement to the onlookers, if not so pleasant for the performers.

In the fine weather deck games such as quoits, shovel board and deck billiards were as popular as they are nowadays, but I find no mention of sports, cock-fighting or ship cricket.

Below draughts, whist, chess, backgammon and dominoes all had many devotees; and on the homeward passage nap, poker, blackjack, eucre and other gambling games robbed many a returning digger of his pile and sometimes led to such trouble that the captain had to interfere.

Under captains of Enright's stamp, there was very little disorder and the sailing ships seem to have carried a much happier crowd than the auxiliary steamers.

The ill-fated *Royal Charter's* passage home in the summer of 1856 presents an example of a badly run and disciplined ship. The food was bad, everyone had a growl about something, drunken riots occurred constantly, fighting in which even the crew and stewards took a part was of almost daily occurrence, and excessive gambling ruined scores of returning diggers on the lower deck. I am glad to say that I can find no such instance of disorder and lack of discipline amongst the ships which relied upon sail power alone.

Best Homeward Passages, 1855-56.

The honours for the year 1855 were, however, taken by the Duthie built Aberdeen clipper *Ballarat*, 718 tons, owned by Duncan Dunbar, which went out to Sydney in under 70 days, and came home Melbourne to Liverpool in 69 days with 110,000 ounces on board. The *Ocean Chief*, Captain Tobin, was a Black Baller on her second voyage. On her previous passage home in the autumn of 1854 she made the run in 86 days, during which she was embayed by ice for three days in the Southern Ocean, had the unusual experience of being becalmed for three days off the Horn and finally had N.E. winds from 18° N. to soundings.

Ship.	Port from	Date Left	Gold on Board	Date Arrived	D'ys Out.
		1855		1855	
Oliver Lang ..	Sydney	Jan. 3		Mar. 20	76
James Baines ..	Melbourne	Mar. 11	40,000 oz.	May 20	69
Indian Queen ..	Hobart	,, 17		June 5	78
Shalimar	Melbourne	,, 24	42,000 oz.	,, 5	75
Lightning	,,	Apl. 11	69,000 oz.	,, 29	79
Ocean Chief ..	Sydney	June 3		Aug. 26	84
Marco Polo ..	Melbourne	July 26	125,000 oz.	Oct. 20	86
White Star·	,,	Aug. 31	80.000 oz.	Nov. 27	88
Donald Mackay	,,	Oct. 3		Dec. 28	86
				1856	
Champion of the Sea	,,	,, 27		Jan. 25	90
Lightning	,,	Dec. 27	12,000 oz.	Mar. 23	86
		1856			
Red Jacket ..	,,	Jan 12		Apl. 8	86

The *Oliver Lang*, 1236 tons, was called after her designer, being a British built ship from the famous Deptford yard.

Best Outward Passages 1855-56, Liverpool to Melbourne.

I have failed to point out before that the Black Ballers always sailed on the 5th of the month from Liverpool, and the White Star on the 20th; it thus becomes an easy matter to pick out the ships of the rival lines.

At such a time it is only natural to find *Golden* a

favourite part of a ship's name. *Golden Era, Golden City, Golden Eagle, Golden Light, Golden State, Golden West, Golden Age,* and *Golden Gate* were all down-east clippers, built for the Californian gold rush.

Ship	Date Left	Date Arrived	Days Out.
	1855	1856	
Ocean Chief	Dec. 7	Jan. 25	80
Mermaid	,, 21	Feb. 10	82
	1856		
Oliver Lang	Jan. 7	April 3	87
Champion of the Seas ..	March 8	June 1	85
James Baines	April 7	,, 24	78
Mindoro	,, 22	July 13	82
Lightning	May 6	,, 14	69
Red Jacket	,, 20	Aug. 13	85
Golden Era	June 20	Sept. 9	81
Morning Light	July 6	,, 17	73
Mermaid	,, 22	Oct. 17	87
Ocean Chief	Aug. 5	,, 19	75
White Star	,, 21	Nov. 5	76
Marco Polo	Sept. 5	Dec. 2	89

The *Morning Light* was a monster New Brunswick built ship, registering 2377 tons. She was on her first voyage and must not be confused with the American clipper of that name, owned by Glidden & Williams, of Boston, and built by Toby & Littlefield, of Portsmouth, N.H., a ship of half her size.

The "James Baines" Overdue!

In the autumn of 1856 there was tremendous sensation in Liverpool, when the famous *James Baines*, considered by many to be the fastest ship in the world, was posted as overdue when homeward bound. All sorts of rumours spread like wildfire, and as the weeks went by and no definite information was obtained from incoming ships, something like consternation began to reign in shipping circles.

The *James Baines* sailed from Melbourne at 1 p.m. on 7th August, 1856, passing through the Heads the following morning. On the 9th she made her best run, 356 miles, royals and skysails being set part of the time, the wind fair but squally. She made one more good run, of 340 miles, and then was held up by light airs and calms all the way to the Horn; here she encountered heavy gales, snowstorms and high cross seas. She was 36 days to the pitch of the Horn; then from 26th September to 8th November another spell of light and baffling winds delayed her passage, and she was 65 days from Port Phillip to the line.

On the 30th October, her great rival the *Lightning*, which had sailed from Melbourne just three weeks behind her, hove in sight, and the two ships were in company for a week. The meeting of the two Black Ballers is joyfully recorded in the *Lightning Gazette*, as follows:—

Thursday, 30th October.—Lat. 29° 03′ N., Long 33° 14′ W. Distance 131 miles. Wind more easterly; 7 a.m. tacked ship to N.N.W. A large ship in sight went about at same time, ahead of us. During forenoon Captain Enright expressed himself confident that she was the *James Baines*. Great excitement and numerous conjectures, bets, etc. One thing certain, that she sailed almost as fast as ourselves, and her rigging and sails were similar to those of the *Baines*. By sunset we had both weathered and gained on our companion.

Friday, 31st October.—Lat. 30° 31′ N., Long. 35° 15′ W. Distance 137 miles. All night light airs, and early dawn showed us our friend much nearer. At 8 a.m., she at last responded to our signals by hoisting the " Black Ball " at the mizen ! and a burgee at the gaff, with her name—*James Baines* ! Great excitement spread throughout the ship, and the conversation was divided between sympathy for all on board our unfortunate predecessor and conjectures as to the cause of her detainment. All day we were watching her every movement; now she gains, now we near her ; now she " comes up " and now " falls off." About 2 p.m., we were evidently nearer than in the morning. A conversation *a la* Marryat. The *Baines* informed us that her passengers were all well, asked for our longitude, if any news, etc. Captain Enright invited Captain McDonald to dine, but he did not respond. At 5 a.m., still light airs, *James Baines* distant 1½ miles

Saturday, 1st November.—Lat. 31° 12′ N., Long. 36° W. Distance 56 miles. During Friday evening, about 8 o'clock, the wind being still very light, we passed to windward of the unfortunate *James Baines*; so closely that we could hear the people on board cheering, and most vociferously did some of our passengers reply, with the addition of a profuse supply of chaff : such as amiable offers to take them in tow, a most commendable solicitude as to their stock of " lime juice," very considerate promises to " say they were coming " on arrival at Liverpool, etc. All night the wind was light and baffling. At 2 a.m. it suddenly chopped round to the N.W., and the ship was put on the port tack. At 4, she was put about again. At 6.30, tacked ship to eastward, light airs and variable. The *James Baines* about 6 miles to leeward, a little brig on lee bow—which had been in company all Friday, and a barque on lee quarter. At 9, the brig, having put about, stood up towards us, and passing close to leeward, showed the Hambro ensign with private number 350. We once more tacked ship and stood to the northward and westward, the others following our example, and the breeze freshening, we all started on a race. The barque hoisted her ensign and number and proved to be the *Cid*, which we passed on the 29th ultimo. The brig soon after bore away to his " chum " to leeward, and they had a quiet little race to themselves, in which the barque appeared to be the victor.

The clipper sisters were now once more pitted against each other : the far famed *Lightning*, with concave lines and breadth of bilge, in our opinion the worthy Donald's brightest idea, and the champion—the ship of 21 knots' notoriety—the *James Baines*.

In light winds or airs we had crept by him, now, as the breeze freshens, as the white crest appears on the short toppling sea, as we lift and dive to the heavy northerly roll and all favours the long powerful ship. What do we behold ? The little brig and barque going astern, of course. Aye, but what else do we see ? Oh, ye Liverpool owners ! *et tu*, Donald, who thought to improve on the *Lightning* ; tell it not " on 'Change," publish it not in the streets of Liverpool. What do we see ? Hull down, courses and topsails below the horizon at 2 p.m., five hours from the start, the *James Baines* just discernible from the deck : at the very lowest computation we have beaten her at the rate of 1¼ knots per hour. At sundown she is barely visible from the mizen topgallant crosstrees. It was generally supposed on board that her copper must have been much worn and rough or we never could have beaten so rapidly a ship of such noble appearance and well-known sailing qualities.

Sunday, 2nd November.—Lat. 32° 57′ N., Long. 37° 37′ W. Distance 134 miles. Another day of light winds, heading us off to N.N.W. still. Evening, a little more wind, ship going about 7 knots.

Monday, 3rd November.—Lat. 34° 41′ N., Long. 38° 28′ W. Distance 113 miles. In the middle watch wind backed to the N.E. and fell light again. At 8, improvement again and by noon we lay N.E. by N., the best we have done for some days, but only going from 4½ to 5 knots. A ship coming up astern, supposed to be the *James Baines*, bringing up a fair wind.

Tuesday, 4th November.—Lat. 35° 47′ N., Long. 38° 28′ W. Distance 66 miles. Commences with very light airs from the north, our ship on the port tack. Our friend *James Baines* again in sight astern.

And this was the last the *Lightning* saw of the *James Baines* though the two ships arrived in the Mersey within 24 hours of each other, the *Lightning* leading. Both anchored in the river on 20th November, the *Lightning* being 84 days out, and the *James Baines* 105 days.

The following comparison between the two passages is interesting, as it shows that the two ships took the same number of days from the equator to Liverpool, viz., 40 days :—

Points Between	James Baines		Lightning	
	Days	Date Passed	Days	Date Passed
Melbourne to Cape Horn	36	Sept. 12	24	Sept. 1
Cape Horn to equator	29	Oct. 11	20	Oct 9
Equator to Western Isles	28	Nov. 8	29	Nov. 7
Western Isles to Liverpool	12	Nov. 20	11	Nov. 20

Best 24-hours' run　　　　356 miles　　　　377 miles.

The *James Baines* was simply unlucky in having a very light weather passage. Donald Mackay's ships were never light weather flyers, in spite of setting every kind of light weather kite, from tiny "bulldog," as they called the moonsail on the main, down to the lowest watersail, that barely cleared the wave crests.

Whilst we are comparing the speeds of *James Baines* and *Lightning*. it is only fair to do so in heavy weather as well as light. I therefore give below the logs of their best week's work on their respective outward passages in 1856. Here it will be seen the *James Baines* just has the best of it. I have taken the remarks for *Lightning's* run from the *Lightning Gazette*, not the ship's log.

BEST WEEK'S RUN BY *James Baines*, LIVERPOOL TO MELBOURNE, MAY, 1856.

25th May.—Lat. 37° 40' S., Long. 3° 28' E.   Distance 328 miles. Winds, S.S.W., S.W. This day begins with heavy gale and heavy squalls. I have never before experienced such a heavy gale with so high a barometer. At 4 p.m. double-reefed main topsail and cross-jack. Midnight, similar wind and weather, heavy sea, ship labouring very heavily and shipping great quantities of water. Noon, very heavy sea; sun obscured.

26th May.—Lat. 38° 38' S., Long. 10° 0' E.   Distance 320 miles. Winds, S.W., W.S.W. P.M., begins with strong gale and heavy sea, squalls and showers of rain, dark, gloomy weather. Midnight, gale decreasing, reefs out of courses, and set staysails. At 4 a.m., still moderating, out all reefs, set royals and skysail; 8 a.m., set all starboard studding sails. Noon, gentle breeze, fine clear weather; wind westering all the time and sea going down.

27th May.—Lat. 40° 2' S., Long. 17° 41' E.   Distance 384 miles. winds, W.S.W., S.W. Fine gentle breeze and fine clear weather, all sail set. Midnight, same wind and weather. A.M., breeze freshening and heavy black clouds driving up from S.W. Noon, same wind and weather.

28th May—Lat. 42° 44' S., Long. 25° 48' E.   Distance 404 miles. Winds, W.S.W., west. P.M., begins with brisk gale and occasional heavy squalls accompanied with heavy rain. At 4 p.m., handed small sails and double-reefed fore and mizen courses. Midnight, still increasing. Noon, as previously.

29th May.—Lat. 44° 15' S., Long. 30° 51' E.   Distance 240 miles. Winds west. First part strong gales and fine clear weather, heavy sea, ship rolling. Midnight, less wind, sea going down, set all small sails. At 4 a.m.. set all starboard studding sails. Noon, light breeze, dark gloomy weather.

30th May.—Lat. 46° 16' S., Long. 36° 56' E.   Distance 300 miles. Winds, W.N.W., W.S.W., S.S.W. First part light breezes and dark gloomy weather. 8 p.m., sky clearing and breeze increasing, barometer falling. Midnight, fresh gales, took in royal and skysail studding sails; 8 a.m. heavy snow squall; took in topgallant studding sails. Noon fresh gales and clear weather with snow showers and squalls

31th May.—Lat. 46° 52' S., Long. 43° 54'. E.   Distance 300 miles. Winds, W.N.W., W.S.W., S.S.W.   First part fresh breeze and squalls. 10 p.m., ran through between Petit and Grande, Prince Edward Islands. Midnight, dark with snow squalls.   Noon, as at midnight.

BEST WEEK'S RUN BY *Lightning*, LIVERPOOL TO MELBOURNE, JUNE-JULY, 1856.

28th June.—Lat. 44° 25' S., Long. 42° 58' E.   Distance 232 miles. Winds westerly.   P.M., snow squalls, wind increasing.   Preparations were made for shortening sail by taking in the lighter canvas. This was not accomplished before the mizen royal and mizen topmast staysail were torn to pieces.   Between 5 and 6 p.m. the conflict raged most furiously.   Reefs were taken in the topsails and these with the exception of the foresail were all the canvas set.

29th June.—Lat. 43° 36' S., Long. 50° 07' E.   Distance 312 miles. Winds westerly.   The gale of yesterday abated the intensity of its fury about midnight, we have set more sail though the wind blows stiff.

30th June.—Lat. 44° 02' S., Long. 56° 35' E.   Distance 281 miles. Winds westerly.   The weather has been excessively cold, dark and cloudy.   The heavy sea running caused the ship to roll heavily.

1st July.—Lat. 44° 39' S., Long. 63° 27' E.   Distance 298 miles. Wind westerly.   Fine at first, then cloudy with showers of snow.

2nd July.—Lat. 45° 07' S., Long. 70° 55' E.   Distance 319 miles. Wind westerly.   Wind still fresh and fair.

3rd July.—Lat. 45° 07' S., Long. 79° 55' E.   Distance 382 miles. Wind westerly.   Her run to-day has been only once surpassed since she floated.   She indeed seemed to fly through the water like a seabird on the wing, causing one of our passengers, who knows something of navigation, to remark that it was skating, not sailing.

4th July.—Lat. 45° 07' S., Long. 88° 30' E.   Distance 364 miles. Wind westerly.   Still favoured with the propitious breeze.   Our week's run is the best we have done yet and the best the *Lightning* has ever accomplished.

It will be seen from the above log extracts that the *James Baines* ran 2276 and the *Lightning* 2188 miles in the week.

The "James Baines," "Champion of the Seas," and "Lightning" race out to India with Troops in the Time of the Mutiny.

In 1857, the *James Baines* regained her reputation, coming home in 75 days against the *Lightning's* 82 days.

Both ships, together with the *Champion of the Seas*, were at once taken up by the Government, and sent round to Portsmouth to load troops for India, on account of the Mutiny. It was confidently believed that the great Black Ballers would lower the record to Calcutta and the importance of getting the troops out as quickly as possible, was, of course, very great at such a crisis.

After being carefully prepared for the voyage, the *James Baines* and *Champion of the Seas* sailed from Portsmouth at the beginning of August. Before sailing the *James Baines* was inspected by the Queen, when she is stated to have remarked that she did not know she had such a fine ship in her Dominions.

On the 17th August the two ships were met by the homeward bound *Oneida*, and reported to be making great progress. Both ships were under a cloud of canvas—the *James Baines* had 34 sails set, including 3 skysails, moonsail and sky stunsails—and presented a splendid appearance as they surged by, their rails red with the jackets of the cheering troops. Unfortunately for the hopes of countless anxious hearts, the two Black Ballers reached the Bay of Bengal at the worst season of the year, and as they had not been built to ghost along in catspaws and zephyrs like the tea clippers, their progress up the Bay was very slow.

Both ships arrived off the Sandheads on the same day, the *James Baines* being 101 days out and the *Champion of the Seas* 103. This was a disappointing performance. The *Lightning* did not sail till the end of August. Owing to the illness of his wife, Captain Enright was obliged to give up his command, and was succeeded by Captain Byrne. On 24th August, the day before her departure from Gravesend, a dinner was given to Captain Enright aboard his old ship, at which several well-known public men, amongst whom was Mr. Benjamin Disraeli, paid their tribute to the world famous sea captain.

The *Lightning* made a better passage than her sisters, being off the Hooghly, 87 days out.

The Burning of the "James Baines."

After their trooping, the *Lightning* and *Champion of the Seas* returned to the Australian run, but her Calcutta voyage proved the death of the famous *James Baines*.

She loaded the usual cargo of jute, rice, linseed and cow hides in the Hooghly, and arrived back in Liverpool in April, 1858. She was hauled into the Huskisson Dock and discharging commenced. The 'tween decks were emptied, and on the 21st April the lower hatches were taken off in the presence of the surveyors, when there appeared no sign of anything wrong. But on the following morning smoke was noticed issuing from her hold, and a fire which started in the main hold soon destroyed her. The following account of her end I have taken from the *Illustrated London News* :—

The fire burst out on Thursday morning, 22nd April, 1858. Although the engines were brought into play as rapidly as possible, there was no visible effect produced; and four or five times the firemen, whilst endeavouring to penetrate the interior of the vessel so as to get at the seat of the fire, were driven back by the density of the smoke. It then became necessary to cut away the spars, rigging, stays, etc., which was done promptly and after some time it was deemed advisable to scuttle the ship as the exertions from the deck to extinguish the fire seemed unavailing. There was plenty of water in the dock at the time, but at the receding of the tide the vessel grounded and the fire seemed to have run through the entire length of the ship, for the smoke burst out of all parts and baffled every exertion. In the forenoon the masts were an anxiety, their fall being anticipated, and in the afternoon this happened, the main mast and mizen mast falling with terrific crashes upon the quay and in their descent destroying the roofs of two sheds. At 9 o'clock at night the inner shell of the hull, for nearly the whole length of the vessel, was rapidly burning, the flames rising with fury between the ribs, which had connected the outer and inner hull, the intervening spaces being to the spectators like so many flues; and iron bolts, released by the flames, were dropping one after the other into the hold, where in the fore part of the ship, particularly the uppermost portion of the cargo, was being fast consumed.

At first great alarm was felt for the neighbouring shipping, several of the steamers of the Cunard fleet being in the same dock, but no material damage was sustained by them, and they, with others, were as soon as possible removed out of harm's way.

The value of the *James Baines* and cargo is estimated at £170,000. The vessel became a complete wreck, looking, according to one account, like a huge cinder in the Huskisson Dock; and very little of the cargo was saved.

The loss of this magnificent ship was considered as a national disaster. Since that date thousands and thousands of people have boarded the *James Baines* without knowing it, for the old Liverpool Landing Stage was none other than the wreck of this celebrated clipper.

America Sells her Clippers to Great Britain.

When the great financial depression fell upon America in 1857 and was followed four years later by the Civil War, James Baines seized the opportunity to buy American clippers cheap and many other British firms followed his example. Mr. George Crowshaw, the American shipbroker in London, negotiated the sales and working arrangements. I have given a list in the Appendix of the best known of these ships, which put up the last fight for the sailing ship built of wood. Their day in the Australian trade was a short one; and they soon found iron passenger clippers in the lists against them, even to flying their own house-flag. And in their last days we find the Black Ball and White Star Lines chartering fine iron ships such as the *Sam Cearns*, *Cornwallis* and *Ellen Stuart*.

Notes on the later American-built Passenger Ships.

Space does not admit of more than a few lines on the best known of these later clippers.

The *Southern Empire* was an old three-decker Atlantic packet ship, and so was the, Mackay-built *Chariot of Fame*, which is credited with a run out to Melbourne of 67 days. There has lately been a reunion in New Zealand of the passengers who came out to Maoriland in that ship.

The *Invincible* was said to be the tallest ship sailing out of Liverpool. She was a White Star clipper and made some very fast passages.

The *Empress of the Seas*, No. 1, was also a very fast ship. On 1st June, 1861, she left Liverpool, and arrived in Melbourne on 6th August, 66½ days out.

The *Neptune's Car*, another big ship, is notable for a very different reason; for in 1857, when still under the Stars and Stripes, she was navigated for 52 days by the captain's wife. Captain Patten had placed his mate under arrest for incompetence and insubordination; then whilst the ship was off the Horn beating to the westward, Captain Patten himself became entirely blind. The second mate was no navigator. In this dilemma Mrs. Patten, who was only 24 years of age, took command of the ship and navigated her successfully from the Horn into Frisco Bay.

Golden Age was the ship which claimed to have run 22 knots in the hour with current to help her.

The *Royal Dane* was a well-known ship in the London River when she was commanded by Captain Bolt. She also was a big three-decker.

The *Florence Nightingale* was celebrated for her looks.

"BLUE JACKET."

"ROYAL DANE."

[To face page 114.

A curious incident happened anent the *Mistress of the Seas*; a passenger brought an action against the ship because he was ducked during the ceremony of crossing the line and the captain was fined £100.

The *Sunda* was a very fine fast ship, and made some fine passages under the famous Bully Bragg.

Black Ballers in the Queensland Emigrant Trade.

Besides some smaller Nova Scotia built ships such as the *Conway, Wansfell, Utopia* and *David MacIver*, some of the best of the later Black Ballers were engaged in the Queensland emigration trade in the late sixties and early seventies.

The *Flying Cloud* and the *Sunda* once had a great race out to Moreton Bay, in which the *Sunda* beat the *Flying Cloud* by 18 miles in a 4-day run which averaged 16 knots; this was the voyage in which *Flying Cloud's* boat was capsized between Brisbane and the anchorage, the second mate and all in her being drowned.

In 1870 I find the following passages to Queensland:

Young Australia, Captain James Cooper, 241 passengers left London, 17th May—arrived Brisbane 25th August—100 days out.

Flying Cloud, Captain Owen, 385 passengers left Liverpool, 4th June—arrived Hervey's Bay 30th August—87 days out.

Royal Dane, Captain D. R. Bolt, 497 passengers left London, 30th July—arrived Rockhampton 19th November—112 days out.

"Sunda" and "Empress of the Seas" Carry Sheep to New Zealand.

In the early days of the gold excitement, the emigrant ships rushed out and home, but in the sixties we find them making short intermediate passages; for instance, the *Sunda* and *Empress of the Seas* one year transported thousands of sheep from Australia to New Zealand, each ship making two trips between Port

Phillip and Port Chalmers, with several thousands of sheep on board each trip.

The Gold Rush to Gabriel's Gully in 1862.

In 1862 several ships were hurried across with diggers from Melbourne to Port Chalmers for the gold rush to Gabriel's Gully. Money ran like water in Port Chalmers in those days, and as usual the gold miners were a pretty uproarious crowd. The *Lightning*, which was commanded at that date by Captain Tom Robertson, the marine painter, made a special trip with 900 diggers on board, and they gave Captain Robertson so much trouble that he put into the Bluff and landed a number of them there. The *Blue Jacket*, also, took a load of this troublesome cargo.

After Life and End of the Liverpool Emigrant Clippers.

A favourite round in the latter days of the Liverpool soft-wood clippers was from Melbourne across to Auckland and from there over to the Chincas to load guano. From this the survivors gradually descended to the Quebec timber trade. By the early seventies I find *Marco Polo*, *Red Jacket*, *Ben Nevis*, and other well-known ships already staggering to and fro across the Atlantic between the Mersey and the St. Lawrence, whilst in June, 1874, the *Flying Cloud* got ashore on the New Brunswick coast, when making for St. John's, and was so strained that she was compelled to discharge her cargo and go on the slip for repairs. Here misfortune again overcame the grand old ship, for she took fire and was so gutted that she was sold for breaking up.

It is curious how many of the old American-built soft-wood ships were destroyed by fire, their number

" LIGHTNING," on Fire at Geelong.

[*To face page* 117.

Including the *James Baines*, *Lightning*, *Empress of the Seas No. 1*, *Blue Jacket No. 1*, *Ocean Chief*, *Fiery Star*, and second *Sovereign of the Seas*.

The Burning of "Lightning".

The *Lightning* was burnt on 31st October, 1869, whilst alongside the pier at Geelong loading wool, and she already had 4000 bales of wool on board when the fire was discovered at 1.30 in the morning in her fore hold. From the first the ship seemed to be doomed, and it was feared that the wharf might catch fire. She had an anchor out ahead, and an attempt was made to heave her clear of the pier, but the flames soon drove the crew from the windlass; however, on the mooring lines being cast off, she drifted clear, and swung to her anchor, the whole fore part of the ship being now in flames. The foremast, which was an iron one, melted in its step owing to the heat and soon went over the side. An attempt was made to scuttle her by the desperate means of bombarding her from two 32-pounders, and to a modern gunner the result was astounding to say the least of it, for at only 300 yards range most of the rounds missed the *Lightning* altogether, whilst the few that hit her did more harm than good by giving the wind access to the fire and thereby increasing its fury. After burning all day, the famous old ship sank at sundown.

The cause of the fire on the *Lightning* was agreed to be spontaneous combustion. A very different reason was given for the burning of the second *Sovereign of the Seas*. This ship had just arrived in Sydney with emigrants in 1861 and was discharging at Campbell's Wharf when the fire broke out, and at the coroner's investigation the jury found "that the ship *Sovereign of the Seas* was wilfully, maliciously and feloniously set on fire on the 10th September, and that there was sufficient evidence to commit one of the ship's sailors, then in custody of the water police, on the charge.'' The Sydney fire brigade fought the flames for a whole day without avail; then half a dozen ship's carpenters attempted to scuttle her, but all in vain, and she was left to her fate.

The *Ocean Chief*, which was burnt at the Bluff, New Zealand, was also said to have been set on fire by her crew.

The first *Empress of the Seas* was burnt at Queenscliff on the 19th December, 1861, three months after the *Sovereign of the Seas* had been set on fire at Sydney.

"Blue Jacket's" Figure-head.

The first *Blue Jacket* left Lyttelton, N.Z., homeward bound, and was abandoned on fire off the Falkland Isles on 9th March, 1869. Nearly two years later, on 8th December, 1871, to be exact, *Blue Jacket's* figure-head was found washed up on the shore of Rottnest Island, off Fremantle, Western Australia. Part of it was charred by fire, but there was no mistaking the identity of the figure-head, which was described as ''a man from the waist up, in old sailor's costume, a blue jacket with yellow buttons, the jacket open in the front, no waistcoat, loose shirt, and large knotted handkerchief round the neck; with a broad belt and large square buckle and cutlass hilt at the side. On either side of the figure-head was a scroll, saying:— 'Keep a sharp lookout!' ''

The Loss of the "Fiery Star."

On 1st April, 1865, the *Fiery Star* left Moreton Bay for London. On the 19th one of the men reported a strong smell of smoke in the foc's'le—this soon burst forth in volumes and a fire was located in the lower hold. The captain, named Yule, immediately had all hatchways battened down and ventilation pipes blocked up. The ship was running free, 400 miles from Chatham Island. A few days before a heavy sea had made matchwood of two of the boats, so the westerlies were evidently blowing strong.

On the 20th a steam pump was rigged down the fore hatchway, and wetted sails were fastened over all scuttles and vents in the deck. But the fire continued to gain, and at 6 p.m. it burst through the port bow and waterways. The four remaining boats were at once provisioned and got over the side. Seeing that there was not room for everybody in the boats, Mr. Sargeant the chief officer, 4 A.B.'s and 13 apprentices agreed to stand by the ship—the remainder of the passengers and crew, to the number of 78, leaving in the boats under the captain.

As soon as the boats had left, Mr. Sargeant renewed every effort to subdue the fire, and at the same time altered his course to get into the track of other ships. Then for 21 days he and his gallant band fought the flames and the numerous gales of those regions. Finally on 11th May, when the foremast was almost burnt through and tottering, a ship called the *Dauntless* hove in sight and took the mate and his worn-out crew off the doomed *Fiery Star*.

For their gallantry in remaining behind, Mr. Sargeant and his men were presented with £160 by the people of Auckland, New Zealand, and right well they deserved it, for in all the glorious history of our Mercantile Marine fewer brave acts have ever been recorded.

Some Famous Coal Hulks.

Many an old Black Baller ended her days as a coal hulk. Even the winter North Atlantic could not down the *Red Jacket* and *Donald Mackay*, and eventually *Red Jacket* went to Cape Verd and *Donald Mackay* to Madeira as coal hulks. How many of the Union-Castle passengers knew, when they cast their eyes pityingly or perhaps disdainfully on the grimy looking hulk floating a cable's length or so away from their spotless liner, that they were looking upon a crack passenger ship of their grandfather's day.

Light Brigade was a coal hulk at Gibraltar for many years, having as a companion the famous *Three Brothers*.

The *Golden South*, after lying in Kerosene Bay, Port Jackson, for about twenty years with her holds full of coal, was burnt through sparks from the old reformatory ship *Vernon* falling upon her decks. The burning of the two ships lit up the hills for miles round, and many an old time Sydney-sider will remember the spectacle.

Loss of the "Young Australia."

The *Young Australia*, after ten years' successful trading between England and Brisbane, was wrecked on the north point of Moreton Island on 31st May, 1872, when homeward bound, just four and a half hours after leaving her anchorage off the pilot station. Whilst the ship was in the act of going about, the wind fell calm and the heavy easterly swell and southerly current set the ship towards the rocks. The anchor was let go too late, and the heavy swell hove the ship broadside on to the rocks. With some difficulty the passengers were got ashore; and before night, owing to the way in which the heavy swell was grinding the ship on the rocks, it was deemed advisable for the crew to abandon her.

"LIGHT BRIGADE."

"YOUNG AUSTRALIA."

[To face page 120.

By the 6th June the wreck had broken in half and was full of water, and on the 7th it was sold by auction in Brisbane, and after some brisk bidding was knocked down to a Mr. Martin for the sum of £7100.

The *Champion of the Seas* foundered off the Horn when homeward bound in 1877.

The *White Star* was wrecked in 1883.

Southern Empire fell a victim to the North Atlantic in 1874.

Royal Dane was wrecked on the coast of Chile when homeward bound with guano in 1877.

The *Morning Star* foundered on a passage from Samarang to U.K. in 1879.

The *Shalimar* was bought by the Swiss and the *Morning Light* by the Germans, who renamed her *J. M. Wendt.*

The *Queen of the Colonies* was wrecked off Ushant in 1874, when bound from Java to Falmouth.

The *Legion of Honour* went ashore on the Tripoli coast in 1876, after changing her flag.

The Fate of "Marco Polo."

The *Marco Polo* in her old age was owned by Wilson & Blain, of South Shields; then the Norwegians bought her. After years in the Quebec timber trade, she was piled up on Cape Cavendish, Prince Edward Island, in August, 1883, and on the 6th her cargo of pitch-pine and the famous old ship herself were sold by auction and only fetched £600.

And so we come to the end of a short but wonderful period in the "History of Sail."—*Sic transit gloria mundi*

PART II.—"THE WOOL CLIPPERS."

(*Wood and Composite Ships*).

With tallow casks all dunnaged tight, with tiers on tiers of bales,
With cargo crammed from hatch to hatch, she's racing for the sales;
A clipper barque, a model ship, a "flyer" through and through,
O skipper bluff! O skipper brave! I would I went with you!

—G. J. BRADY.

The Carriers of the Golden Fleece.

IF it was the discovery of gold that founded Australia's fortune, the Golden Fleece and the Wheat Sheaf have set it upon a rock.

It was the gold fever that swept the great tide of emigration in the direction of the Southern Cross and carried the star of the Liverpool shipowners upon its flood, but that star began to set as soon as the output of alluvial gold began to diminish, as soon, indeed, as the great soft-wood clippers of the Black Ball and White Star began to grow water-soaked and strained, for their prosperity may be said to have ended with the sixties and had scarcely a longer run than the classification of their ships. But the percentage of emigrants landed by these ships, who stuck for any time to the elusive hunt for gold, was very small; and the greater number of the gold seeking emigrants eventually settled and worked on the homesteads and great runs of the interior, with the natural result that there was a large and steady increase in the output of wool, hides, tallow, wheat and other land products.

The huge Liverpool emigrant ships, however, were

122

not fitted for the economical transport of these products to their central market in London. They were too big for one thing, for, in those early days, wool and tallow dribbled into the big ports in small amounts; also the repair bills of these soft-wood clippers were an ever increasing item to put against their freight receipts.

Thus it came about that the wonderful American-built ships dropped out of the running. But their London rivals, the beautiful British-built hard-wood ships of half their size, having no heavy repair bills, being splendidly built of that imperishable wood teak, and being able to fill up their small holds quickly, continued to carry passengers outward and wool homeward until supplanted in their turn by the magnificent iron clippers of the Clyde, Liverpool and Aberdeen.

The London Wool Sales.

These were the days when great races home from Australia took place—not only did ship race against ship, but it was the aim and object of every skipper to get his ship home in time for the first wool sales in London. And in the wool trade, unlike the custom in the tea trade, the fastest ships were loaded last— the pride of place—that of being the last ship to leave an Australasian port for the London wool sales being reserved for that which was considered the fastest ship in the trade.

In the eighties, when the tea trade was entirely in the hands of the steamers, this pride of place in Sydney was always kept for Willis' famous clipper, *Cutty Sark*, no other ship, either wood or iron built, being able to rival her passages both out and home in the wool trade.

The London wool sales took place in January, February and March, and the lists of the first sales

were closed as soon as a sufficient number of cargoes
had arrived or been reported in the Channel. Thus
it was the aim of every skipper to get reported as soon
as possible after reaching the Channel, as the cargoes
of ships reported in the Channel by noon on the opening
day of the sales were included in the sale lists. Whereas
if a captain missed the sales, his cargo would have
to be warehoused for perhaps two or three months
until the next sales, thus involving extra expenses
such as warehouse charges, loss of interest, etc., not
to speak of the possibility of a fall in the price of wool.

In those days signal stations were not as numerous
on our coasts as they are now, and so wool clippers
on arriving in the Channel kept a specially sharp look-
out for fishing smacks or pilot cutters to take their
reports on shore. Occasionally the captains of the
late-starting, crack ships were promised substantial
cheques if they caught the sales and truly it was money
well earned.

The Lost Art of the Stevedore.

In the present days of steam, steel and water
ballast, stevedoring is no longer the fine art which
it used to be in the days of masts and yards, clipper
keels and oak frames.

As every sailor knows, no two ships are alike, even
when built from the same moulds; and though this
is the case with every water-borne vessel, it is
specially noticeable with that almost living thing—
the sailing ship. Not only does every sailing ship
have its own character as regards its stability, but
its character often changes with age, etc., and no
tables can give the exact way in which its cargo should
be loaded as regards weights and trim. The hand

books on the subject give rough, general rules, but the captain of a ship, from his own first hand knowledge of his ship's peculiarities, would always give careful instructions to the stevedore as to how he wanted the weights of the cargo placed or distributed.

So first of all the old time stevedore had to load his ship in accordance with her own particular character and the wishes of her captain. Next he had to be an expert packer, especially with a wooden ship with a hold cut up by big oak frames and knees. No space was wasted. There is an old story told of a stevedore loading the little Tasmanian barque *Harriet McGregor*, who sang out to his mate on the wharf. " Sling us down a box of pickles, Bill!" Then the stevedore had all sorts of goods in a general cargo, some of which could not be stowed near each other, such as soda, which melts at sea and destroys cottons, etc. Also washed wool, leather, flour or wheat would be damaged if stowed with tallow and greasy wool. Other goods could only be stowed in the hatches, such as cases of glass, whilst wine and spirits had to be stowed aft to be out of the way of the crew.

Instances have been known also of ships coming home from Australia with their iron masts packed full of bullocks' horns, shank and knuckle bones, which were more generally used for broken stowage.

An amusing case with regard to bullocks' horns and knuckle bones happened on one of Carmichael's ships, through the mate signing the bills of lading without examining them. He signed for so many horns, so many shank bones and so many knuckle bones loose. On arrival in London the consignee sent a lighter for the horns, and intimated that he wanted the shank bones delivered entirely separate from the knuckle bones. Carmichael's got out of it by some very plain speaking, the mate's receipts proving that a fraud had been attempted.

Bags of pearl shell were generally used in Sydney to fill up cargo near the hatches; and I find in July, 1868, that the *Jerusalem*, (Captain Largie) shipped 9 tons of mother-of-pearl shell at Melbourne in small casks and 8-foot cases.

Below are specimens of early cargoes home from Australia in the sixties, with port charges, pilotage dues, etc.

The ship *Omar Pasha*, Captain Thomas Henry, belonging to Messrs. G. Thompson, Sons & Co., of Aberdeen, took in at Melbourne, in October, 1864:—

3550 bales of wool,	20 tons spelter,
14,000 hides,	4000 ounces of gold
80 casks of tallow,	

and 12 cabin passengers. With the above she drew 19 ft. aft and 18 ft. 9 in. forward, her best trim at sea. The ballast of stones, spelter and hides was estimated at 480 tons. The wool was screwed in; and the dunnage, stones and horns, was 12 inches thick in the bottom and 15 inches in the bilges. Port charges were 1s. per ton ; pilotage in £28 18s. 6d.; out £28 18s. 6d.

The ship *Transatlantic*, Captain Philip, belonging to Messrs. G. Thompson, Junr., & Co., of London, took in at Sydney, June, 1864 :—

1360 bales of wool,	300 bags and 40 cases Kauri gum,
135 casks of tallow,	50 tons of iron bark timber,
5300 hides,	

She had no ballast. Dunnage wood in the bottom 9 inches, bilges 12 inches, one treenail between the wool and the sides. So laden, she drew 14½ ft. aft, 14 ft. forward. Her best sea trim was 6 inches by the stern. Port charges at Sydney, customs entry and shipping office £4 4s.; pilotage out 4d. per ton; the same in.

The ship *Queen of Nations*, Captain Thomas Mitchell, belonging to Messrs. G. Thompson & Co., left Sydney on 21st September, 1865, loaded with:—

484 bales of wool,	2602 ingots and plates of copper,
44 bales of cotton,	62 tons of gum,
1037 casks of cocoanut oil,	9452 hides.
219 casks of tallow,	

For ballast she had 30 tons of kentledge; dunnage, treenails and bones, 12 inches in the bottom, 18 in the bilges and 6 in the sides. The hides were laid from two beams abaft the foremast to the mizen mast; oil on the hides, with a tier of tallow between; the wool, cotton, gum, etc., in the 'tween decks. Her best trim was 9 inches by the stern. So laden she drew 18 ft. forward and 18½ ft. aft. Pilotage in £14 2s.; out £14 2s.

The *Murray*, under the command of Captain J. Legoe, belonging to Anderson's Orient Line, left Adelaide in December, 1863, loaded with:—

3182 bales of wool,	35 boxes silver lead ore,
19,522 ingots of copper,	15 bales of leather,
1590 bags of silver lead ore,	277 calf skins,
473 bags of copper ore,	1150 horns,
16 cases and 10 casks of wine.	

She had a full complement of passengers, who occupied 250 tons of cargo space. So laden she drew 15½ ft. forward and 16 ft. 2 in. aft, her best draught for sailing being 15 ft. forward and 15 ft. 8 in. aft. Port charges, harbour dues and light and tonnage dues £28 11s. 6d.; pilotage in and out £17.

Screwing Wool.

As every sailorman knows, wool is screwed into a ship's hold like cotton; and a good captain in the old days would see that his ship was jammed so tight with bales that one would think her seams would open—indeed wood and composite ships always used to have their decks and topsides well caulked before loading wool. As showing how much the amount of wool loaded depended upon the captain, Captain Woodget used to get 1000 bales more into the *Cutty Sark* than his predecessor. He made a habit of spending most of the day in the ship's hold and thought nothing of having a tier or half longer pulled down and restowed if he was not satisfied with the number of bales got in.

You can dunnage casks o' tallow; you can handle hides an' horn;
You can carry frozen mutton; you can lumber sacks o' corn;
But the queerest kind o' cargo that you've got to haul and pull
Is Australia's "staple product"—is her God-abandoned wool.
For it's greasy an' it's stinkin', an' them awkward, ugly bales
Must be jammed as close as herrings in a ship afore she sails.
For it's twist the screw and turn it,
And the bit you get you earn it;
You can take the tip from me, sir, that it's anything but play
When you're layin' on the screw,
When you're draggin' on the screw,
In the summer, under hatches, in the middle o' the day.

So sings the Australian sailor's poet Brady.

In the sixties the bales of wool were pressed on shore by hydraulic power, then lashed with manila or New Zealand hemp, or hoop iron, at the ship's expense. The bales were generally pressed on their flats, but sometimes, for the sake of stowage, on their ends, when they were called "dumps." They had to be stowed immediately after being pressed, as if left for any time, especially in the sun, the wool would swell and carry away the lashings. There were from 8 to 12 lashings for each package of Sydney wool, which were called single dumps, doubles, trebles and fourbles, according to the number lashed together, trebles being the most common.

"LOCH LINE"
AITKEN, LILBURN & C?

AITKEN, LILBURN & C?

A. & J. CARMICHAEL.

T. STEPHENS & SONS.

"LONDON LINE,"
BETHEL, GWYN & C?

WATSON BROTHERS.

D. ROSE & C?

ALEX. NICOL & C?

HINE BROTHERS.

NEW ZEALAND SHIP C?

SHAW, SAVILL & C?

ALBION SHIPPING C?

The actual loading of a wool cargo was a slowish process, and sometimes attended with danger to the stowers if great care was not used, as wool bales have great elasticity. A description of the uses of screws, sampson posts, trunk planks, toms, shores, etc., would, I fear, be so technical as to be wearisome.

One of the chief dangers in a wool cargo is spontaneous combustion. This caused the end of several fine ships, such as the *Fiery Star* and the new Orient liner *Aurora*. Spontaneous combustion was likely to happen if the bales were wet or damp, either when loaded or through contact with other damp cargo, dunnage, ballast or even sweating water tanks. Often enough the wool got a wetting on its way to the ship, and though possibly afterwards sun-dried on the outside of the bales, so that to all appearances it was perfectly dry, was really damp inside and very inflammable. Some Australian wool growers contended that the practice of clipping sheep in the morning when the fleeces were heavy with dew was a cause of spontaneous combustion.

Wool, of course, being a very light cargo, requires stiffening, but hides, tallow, etc., were generally used as deadweight, also copper ore. A ship with a wool cargo was reckoned to require two-thirds of the ballast necessary when in ballast only. Wool freights in the early days were 1d. per lb., and gradually fell to a farthing per lb.—this was for washed wool: the freight for greasy wool, which had not been cleaned and was therefore heavier than washed wool, being about 25% less.

The Aberdeen White Star Line.

Amongst the pioneers of the trade with the Colonies George Thompson, of the Aberdeen Clipper Line, known to generations of Australians as the

F

Aberdeen White Star Line, holds a foremost place. The history of this celebrated firm dates back to the year 1825, when its first representative, a clipper brig of 116 tons named the *Childe Harold,* was sent afloat.

It may safely be said that from that hour the Aberdeen White Star Line has never looked back. From the first it earned a reputation for enterprise and good management. Amongst its fleet were numbered some of the earliest clipper ships built in the United Kingdom, ships whose records were worthy to rank with those of the celebrated Black Ball and White Star Lines; and which in their liberal upkeep had little to learn from even such aristocrats of the sea as the Blackwall frigates.

Until the discovery of gold, the green clippers ran regularly to Sydney, but when all the world began to take ship for Melbourne, the port of the gold region, it was only natural that some of the Aberdeen White Star ships should be put on the Melbourne run, and from that date the little flyers from Aberdeen were as well known in Hobson's Bay as Sydney Cove.

The ships were all built in the yard of Walter Hood, of Aberdeen, in whose business Messrs. Thompson held a large interest, and were all designed by Walter Hood with the exception of the celebrated *Thermopylae.*

George Thompson, who founded the line, was joined, in 1850, by his son-in-law the late Sir William Henderson, and later on Mr. Thompson's sons, Stephen, George and Cornelius, came by turns into the partnership.

The following is a complete list of the wood and composite ships of the Aberdeen White Star fleet, dating from 1842:—

List of the Wood and Composite Ships of the Aberdeen White Star Fleet.

1842	Neptune,	wood ship	..	343 tons.
1842	Prince of Wales	,, ,,	..	582 ,,
1846	Oliver Cromwell	,, ,,	..	530 ,,
1846	Phoenician	,, ,,	..	530 ,,
1849	John Bunyan	,, ,,	..	470 ,,
1850	Centurion	,, ,,	..	639 ,,
1852	Woolloomoolloo	,, ,,	..	627 ,,
1852	Walter Hood	,, ,,	..	936 ,,
1853	Maid of Judah	,, ,,	..	756 ,,
1854	Omar Pasha	,, ,,	..	1124 ,,
1855	Star of Peace	,, ,,	..	1113 ,,
1856	Wave of Life	,, ,,	..	887 ,,
1857	Damascus	,, ,,	..	964 ,,
1857	Transatlantic	,, ,,	..	614 ,,
1858	Moravian	,, ,,	..	996 ,,
1860	Strathdon	,, ,,	..	1011 ,,
1861	Queen of Nations	,, ,,	..	872 ,,
1862	Kosciusko	,, ,,	..	1192 ,,
1864	Nineveh	,, ,,	..	1174 ,,
1864	Ethiopian	,, ,,	..	839 ,,
1865	George Thompson	,, ,,	..	1128 ,,
1866	Christiana Thompson	,, ,,	..	1079 ,,
1866	Harlaw	,, ,,	..	894 ,,
1867	Thyatira	comp. ship	..	962 ,,
1867	Jerusalem	wood ship	..	901 ,,
1868	Thermopylae	comp. ship	..	948 ,,
1868	Ascalon	wood ship	..	938 ,,
1869	Centurion	comp. ship	..	965 ,,
1870	Aviemore	wood ship	..	1091 ,,

No ships that ever sailed the seas presented a finer appearance than these little flyers. They were always beautifully kept and were easily noticeable amongst other ships for their smartness: indeed, when lying in Sydney Harbour or Hobson's Bay with their yards squared to a nicety, their green sides* with gilt streak and scroll work at bow and stern glistening in the sun, their figure-heads, masts, spars and blocks all painted

* The green with which the Aberdeen White Star ships were painted was a composite paint always known as Aberdeen green.

white and every rope's end flemish-coiled on snow-white decks, they were the admiration of all who saw them.

> There's a jaunty White Star Liner, and her decks are scrubbed and
>   clean
> And her tall white spars are spotless, and her hull is painted green.
> Don't you smell the smoky stingo? Ech! ye'll ken the Gaelic lingo
> Of the porridge-eating person who was shipped in Aberdeen.
> —BRADY.

From the first to the last they were hard-sailed ships, and some of the fastest were often sent across to China for a home cargo of tea, though the *Thermopylae* was the only *bona-fide* tea clipper in the fleet.

On the outward passage, whether to Sydney or Melbourne, they generally carried a few first-class passengers, but it was only during the very height of the gold rush that their 'tween decks were given up to a live freight.

The " Phoenician."

The first of the Aberdeen White Star fleet to make a reputation for speed was the celebrated *Phoenician*, under the command of one of the best known passage makers of the day, Captain Sproat.

Her dimensions were :—

Length of cut keel	.. ..	122 feet
Rake of stem	.. ..	25 ,,
Rake of sternpost	.. ..	7 ,,
Extreme breadth	.. ..	27 feet 5 inches.
Depth of hold	.. ..	19 ,, 1 ,,
Registered tonnage (old)	..	526 tons.
,, ,, (new)	..	478 ,,
Deadweight capacity	.. ..	780 ,,

Her first three voyages were considered extraordinarily good for those days.

1849-50 London to Sydney 90 days—Sydney to London 88 days.
1850-51   ,,   ,,   96 ,,   ,,   ,,   103 ,,
1851-52   ,,   ,,   90 ,,   ,,   ,,   83 ,,

The *John Bunyan* in 1850 made the run home from Shanghai in 99 days, which, even though she had a favourable monsoon, was a very fine performance.

The *Walter Hood* on her maiden voyage under the command of Captain Sproat made the passage out to Australia in 80 days, and the account given in the papers remarks:—"Her sailing qualities may be judged from the fact of her having run during four several days 320 miles each 24 hours."

The *Maid of Judah* had the honour of taking out the Royal Mint to Sydney in 1853. Her dimensions are interesting to compare with those of the *Phoenician*, so I give them :—

Length of keel	..	..	..	160 feet.
Length over all	..	..	..	190 ,,
Beam	..	..	..	..	31 ,,
Depth of hold ..	..	..	..	19 ,,

The *Queen of Nations*, under Captain Donald, went from Plymouth to Melbourne in 87 and 84 days; but the fastest of these earlier clippers was the well-known *Star of Peace*, which made four consecutive passages to Sydney of 77, 77, 79, and 79 days under the redoubtable Captain Sproat.

I remember seeing a picture of this fine clipper, representing her off the Eddystone when homeward bound. She was a very rakish looking craft with long overhangs and carried a heavy press of sail, which included double topsails, skysails, main and mizen sky staysails and also three-cornered moonsails stretching to the truck of each mast.

The *Ethiopian*, on her first voyage to Melbourne, went out in 68 days under Captain William Edward. She sailed her last voyage under the British flag in 1886. She was then rigged as a barque, and on her passage home from Sydney had a remarkable race with the iron *Orontes*, belonging to the same owners. The two vessels cast off their tugs together outside Sydney Heads, sighted each other off the Horn, were becalmed together in the doldrums, spoke the same ship off the Western Isles; and when the chops of the Channel were reached, the *Ethiopian* was hove to taking soundings in a fog, when the *Orontes* came up under her stern within hailing distance. Finally the *Ethiopian* got into the East India Docks one tide ahead of the *Orontes*, thus winning the race and a considerable sum in wagers.

The Lucky " Nineveh."

The *Nineveh*, built the same year as the *Ethiopian*, was an extremely lucky ship in her freights and passengers and made a great deal of money. Old Stephen Thompson was so pleased that he gave Captain Barnet a banquet at the Holborn Restaurant, and all through the dinner kept toasting "the lucky *Nineveh*."

The " Jerusalem."

These wooden clippers were often very tender coming home with wool, as the following reminiscence given by Coates in his *Good Old Days of Shipping* will show:—"Apropos of *Jerusalem*, I remember a most exciting race with the large American ship *Iroquois*. We were homeward bound from the Colonies, flying light and very crank, a not uncommon condition with a wool cargo. The Yank was first sighted on our quarter, the wind being quarterly, blowing moderately, though squally at times.

"Whilst the wind remained so the *Iroquois* had no chance, but when it freshened the *Jerusalem* heeled over to such an extent that it necessitated sail being taken in. Soon the American was ploughing along to leeward carrying her three topgallant sails and whole mainsail and going as steady as a die, whilst the *Jerusalem* was flying along with fore and main lower topgallants and reefed mainsail, but heeling over to such a degree that one could barely stand upright, the water roaring up through the lee scuppers, and during the squalls lipping in over the rail.

"In a short time the topgallant sails and mainsail were handed and preparations made to reef the fore topsail. By this time, however, the *Iroquois* had just passed the beam, when, apparently, her skipper, satisfied to have passed us, snugged his ship down to three reefed topsails and we shortly after lost sight of her in a blinding squall."

And Coates goes on to say:—"To see this ship when moderately light was a great pleasure, her lines were the perfection of symmetry. In one day I remember 324 miles being got out of this ship; she was one of the first to carry double topgallant yards."

As a matter of fact, the *Jerusalem* was generally considered the fastest ship in the fleet next to *Thermopylae*. She made several very good passages from China in the seventies of under 110 days. Captain Crutchley, in his book *My Life at Sea*, gives an instance of her speed, in describing how she raced ahead of the tea clipper *Omba*, both ships being bound up the Channel with a strong beam wind. On this occasion, however, it was the *Omba* which was the tender ship, as she could not carry her royals though the *Jerusalem* had all plain sail set.

The *Thyatira*, Thompson's first composite ship, was also a very ticklish vessel to handle when wool-laden. On her maiden voyage she went out to Melbourne in

77 days, but took 96 days to get home, during which passage she gave her officers much anxiety owing to her extreme tenderness.

Captain Mark Breach's First Encounter with his Owner.

Captain Mark Breach, one of the best known of the Aberdeen White Star captains, entered the employ of the firm as second mate on the newly launched *Thyatira*. The *Thyatira* was on the berth for Melbourne when he joined her. On his second day aboard he was superintending the stowage of cargo in the hold, when old Stephen Thompson came down to have a look round. The *Thyatira's* owner happened to be smoking a fine meerschaum pipe, and young Breach, being completely ignorant of the identity of the visitor, immediately went up to him and informed him in no uncertain language that his lighted pipe was dead against all rules and regulations. Mr. Thompson, without disclosing his identity, at once apologised and returned his pipe to its case. Presently when the visitor had departed, the mate asked Mr. Breach what he had been talking to Mr. Thompson about. And one may well imagine that the new second mate was somewhat scared when he learnt that it was his owner to whom he had been laying down the law. However, the mate comforted him by telling him that Stephen Thompson had been very pleased and prophesied that he would be a good servant to the company.

Mark Breach afterwards served as mate of the *Miltiades*, then commanded the *Jerusalem*, *Aviemore*, and finally the famous *Patriarch*.

The *Thyatira* was a very favourite ship and made some very good passages. She and the *Jerusalem* both loaded tea home from China on more than one occasion, and made passages of under 110 days in the N.E. monsoon.

The "Thermopylae."

Thermopylae's career I have already dealt with fully in the *China Clippers*. Her sail plan was cut down twice in her old age, thus taking off a good deal of her speed in light weather, but even then there were not many vessels which could give her the go-by, either in light or heavy weather.

The "Centurion."

The second *Centurion* was launched in the spring of 1869, and measured :—Length 208 ft.; beam 35 ft.; depth 21 ft. Captain Mitchell overlooked her building and was her first commander. She was a very fast ship and he always hoped to beat the *Thermopylae* with her, but never succeeded.

On her first voyage she went out to Sydney in 69 days. It was a light weather passage and she never started the sheets of her main topgallant sail the whole way. She is stated to have made 360, 348 and 356 miles in three successive days running down her easting, but I have been unable to verify these runs. Captain Mitchell died on her second voyage just before reaching the Channel homeward bound She also made some creditable tea passages, but was mostly kept in the Sydney trade. In 1871 she went out in 77 days and in 1872 in 78 days.

The "Aviemore."

The *Aviemore* was the last of the wooden ships, and at the date of her launch, the first iron ship built for Thompsons, the celebrated *Patriarch*, had already proved herself such a success as to put all idea of building any but iron ships in the future out of the question.

The Fate of the Early White Star Clippers.

The first *Centurion* ended her days as a total loss in 1866.

The *Walter Hood* was wrecked near Jervis Bay Lighthouse, New South Wales, on 27th April, 1870, when bound from London to Sydney with general cargo, her captain and 12 men being drowned.

The *Woolloomoolloo* ended her days under the Spanish flag and was wrecked in 1885.

The *Maid of Judah* was sold to Cowlislaw Bros., of Sydney, in 1870. In December, 1879, she left Sydney for Shanghai, coal-laden, with Captain Webb in command, and the following June was condemned and broken up at Amoy.

The *Omar Pasha* was burnt at sea in 1869, when homeward bound from Brisbane, wool-laden.

The celebrated *Star of Peace*, after being run for some years by Burns, Philp & Co., of Sydney, was converted into a hulk at Thursday Island, being only broken up in 1895.

The *Wave of Life* was sold to Brazil, and sailed as the *Ida* until 1891, when she was renamed *Henriquita*. Finally she was condemned and broken up in March, 1897.

The *Damascus* was bought by the Norwegians, who changed her name to *Magnolia*. On 1st September, 1893, she stranded at Bersimis and became a total loss.

The *Transatlantic* was rebuilt in 1876; in 1878 she was owned by J. L. Ugland, of Arendal; and on 15th

October, 1899, when bound to Stettin from Mobile, she foundered in the Atlantic.

The *Moravian* was sold to J. E. Ives, of Sydney, and ended her days as a hulk, being broken up at Sydney in March, 1895.

The *Strathdon*, under the name of *Zwerver*, did many years' service with the Peruvian flag at her gaff end. She was broken up in 1888.

The *Queen of Nations* was wrecked near Woolloagong, New South Wales, on 31st May, 1881, when bound out to Sydney. All hands were saved except one.

The *Kosciusko*, like the *Maid of Judah*, was bought by Cowlislaw Bros., being broken up at Canton in 1899.

The *Nineveh* was bought by Goodlet & Smith, of Sydney. She was abandoned in the North Pacific in February, 1896.

The *Ethiopian* was sold to the Norwegians. In October, 1894, when bound from St. Thomas to Cork, she was abandoned near the Western Isles. She was afterwards picked up 15 miles from Fayal and towed into St. Michael's, where she was condemned.

The *George Thompson* passed through the hands of A. Nicol & Co., of Aberdeen, and J. Banfield, of Sydney, to the Chileans. On 13th June, 1902, she was wrecked at Carlemapu.

The *Christiana Thompson* went to the Norwegians and was renamed *Beatrice Lines*. She was wrecked near Umra in Norway on 7th October, 1899.

The *Harlaw* was wrecked at Hongkong in 1878.

The *Jerusalem*, like many of the others, was converted into a barque in her old age. In 1887 she was bought by the Norwegians. On 28th October, 1893. she left New Brunswick for London with a cargo of pitch-pine and resin and never arrived, the usual end of timber droghers on the stormy North Atlantic.

The *Thyatira* was bought by J. W. Woodside & Co., of Belfast, in 1894. In July, 1896, when bound from London to Rio with general cargo, she was wrecked at Pontal da Barra.

The *Ascalon* was bought by Trinder, Anderson & Co. in 1881. They ran her for nine years and then sold her to the Norwegians. She was wrecked on 7th February, 1907, at Annalong, when bound from Runcorn to Moss.

The second *Centurion* left Sydney for Newcastle, N.S.W., on 17th January, 1887; at 1.30 a.m. whilst off the Heads, the tug's line carried away: the ship drifted on to the North Head, struck and then sank in 18 fathoms, barely giving her crew 15 minutes to get clear.

The *Aviemore* was bought by the Norwegians. In October, 1910, she left Sandejford for the South Shetland where she was converted into a floating oil refinery. Later she was resold to the Norwegians, and I have a snapshot of her taken in Bristol in 1915, rigged as a barque with a stump bowsprit.

Duthie's Ships.

Another well-known Aberdeen firm which was a pioneer in the Australian trade was Duthies. They were builders as well as owners. The original William Duthie started his shipbuilding business over 100 years ago. Besides owning many of the ships he built, he was also a large timber merchant, and kept some vessels in the North American timber trade. He was also one of the first to send ships to the Chinchas and Peru for guano. He eventually turned over his shipbuilding business to his brothers John and Alexander, but retained his interest in some of the ships.

The first of Duthie's ships of which I have any record is the *Jane Pirie*, of 427 tons, built in 1847 for the Calcutta trade and commanded by a well-known skipper of those days, Captain James Booth.

The next vessel to be launched by Duthie was the *Brilliant* in 1850. She measured 555 tons, and, commanded by Captain Murray and sailing under Duthie's house-flag, she became a very popular passenger clipper in the time of the gold rush. On her first outward passage she went from London to Melbourne in 87 days, and this was about her average. She generally loaded wool for the London market at Geelong, and made the homeward run in under 90 days.

Few ships came home from the Antipodes in those days without gold dust on board; and the *Brilliant* on one occasion brought home 7 tons of gold, giving Captain Murray an anxious time until he had it safely handed over to the Bank of England. After a dozen years as a first class passenger and wool clipper the *Brilliant* was debased to the guano and nitrate trades, being finally lost at sea when homeward bound from Callao with a cargo of guano.

The next of Duthie's ships was the *James Booth*, of 636 tons, named after the celebrated captain. She was launched in 1851 for the Calcutta trade.

In 1852 Duthie built the *Ballarat*, 713 tons, for the great shipowner Duncan Dunbar. The *Ballarat* distinguished herself by coming home from Melbourne in 69 days in 1855. All these early ships had the famous Aberdeen clipper bow and painted ports, and ably maintained the high reputation of the Aberdeen clipper.

In the sixties Messrs. Duthie launched the following

well-known wool clippers, all called after various members of the family :—

1862	*William Duthie*	wood ship	..	..	968	tons.
1863	*Martha Birnie*	,,	,,	..	.:	832	,,
1864	*John Duthie*	,,	,,	..	..	1031	,,
1867	*Alexander Duthie*	,,	,,	..	..	1159	,,
1868	*Ann Duthie*	,,	,,	..	..	994	,,

The ships were all three skysail yarders, and good passage makers; they were kept almost entirely in the Sydney trade, and must have made good dividends in those early days. The *John Duthie* on one occasion made £5000 freight for the wool passage home. Her commander at that time was Captain Levi, a very well-known character, who always offered a glass of Scotch and an apple to any visitor who came aboard his ship.

The next Duthie ship was the *Abergeldie*, of 1152 tons. She was their first ship with iron in her composition, having iron beams. She was launched in 1869, the same year as the *Windsor Castle*, a beautiful little wood ship of 979 tons, which Duthie built for Donaldson Rose. This *Windsor Castle* must not be confused with Green's Blackwall frigate of the same name. For some years both ships were trading to Sydney, and one year there was more than a little confusion owing to the two *Windsor Castles* arriving out on the same day. Duthie's *Windsor Castle* made many fine passages both out and home, her best known commander being Captain Fernie. After being sold her name was changed to *Lumberman's Lassie*, and under this name she was for many years a well-known Colonial trader, and finally a coal hulk

Passages of Aberdeen Ships to Sydney, 1872-1873.

The best passage made out to Sydney between these dates was that of the iron tea clipper *Halloween* on her maiden voyage.   She left the Thames on 1st July, 1872, crossed the line in 27° W. on the 20th, 19 days out, crossed the meridian of the Cape on 10th August, 40 days out, ran her easting down in 42° and **arrived in Sydney on 8th September, 69 days out.**

Another very famous Aberdeen ship, the *Star of Peace*, left London, 21st September, 1873, and arrived at Melbourne on 16th December, 86 days out.

This little table will perhaps give a good idea of the usual passages made by the wood and composite built ships.

Ship	Sailed	Crossed Equator	in Long.	Crossed Meridian of Cape	Ran Easting Down in Lat.	Arrived	D'ys Out
	1872						
Thyatira ..	Feb. 23	Mar. 20	22 W	April 25	42 S	May 23	89
Ann Duthie ..	Mar. 5	,, 25	27	—	48	,, 24	80
Ascalon ..	,, 5	April 2	23	April 30	41	June 7	94
Maid of Judah	,, 21	,, 18	22	May 21	—	,, 23	94
Centurion ..	April 18	May 10	22	June 8	39	July 5	78
John Duthie	June 4	June 30	27	July 28	42	Aug. 29	86
Strathdon ..	July 8	Aug. 14	26	Sept. 9	45	Oct. 25	109
William Duthie	,, 16	,, 17	27	,, 15	44	,, 31	107
Ethiopian ..	,, 25	,, 29	21	—	—	,, 31	98
	1873						
Harlaw ..	Feb. 5	Feb. 25	23	Mar. 22	45	April 29	83
Nineveh ..	,, 11	Mar. 8	21	April 3	44	May 1	79
Aviemore ..	Mar. 14	,, 29	23	May 28	45	June 4	82
Abergeldie ..	July 7	—	—	Sept. 1	42	Oct. 2	87

The South Australian Trade.

During the sixties and seventies, when Sydney and Melbourne were filling their harbours with the finest ships in the British Mercantile Marine, Adelaide, in a smaller way, was carrying on an ever increasing trade of her own, in which some very smart little clippers were making very good money and putting up sailing records which could well bear comparison with those made by the more powerful clippers sailing to Hobson's Bay and Port Jackson.

From the early fifties South Australia had been sending wool home in exchange for general cargoes from London.

This trade was in the hands of two or three well-run firms, such as the Orient, Devitt & Moore and Elder. These firms owned some beautiful little composite ships, which up till now have received scant notice in the annals of our Mercantile Marine. These little clippers, most of them well under 1000 tons register, were driven as hard as any Black Ball or White Star crack, and this without the incentive of publicity.

Their captains, however, were always in keen rivalry and put a high value on their reputations as desperate sail carriers. They made little of weather that would have scared men who commanded ships of three times the tonnage of the little Adelaide clippers, and they were not afraid of a little water on deck—indeed, when running down the easting, their ships were more like half-tide rocks than merchant vessels, being swept from end to end by every roaring sea; and even in only a fresh breeze their decks were hidden by a curtain of spray.

It was a common saying that they took a dive on leaving the tropics, came up to breathe at the Cape and did not reappear again till off Cape Borda. A South Australian trader prided himself on carrying a main topgallant sail when other ships were snugged down to reefed topsails; and he considered that he had made a bad passage if he was not up with Cape Borda in 70 days. Indeed he usually began to look for the Australian coast about the 60th day out, and if he was at sea for much longer than that without raising the land would begin to think that he had overrun his distance and got into the Gulf of St. Vincent.

It is not surprising, therefore, that the crews of these vessels rarely knew what it was to have a dry shirt on their backs, and usually had had more than enough of it by the time they were off Kangaroo Island; thus it was the general thing for them to run on arrival.

The late Mr. Barry wrote the following interesting account of the usual homeward bound crew on a South Australian wool clipper:—"They loaded some of the golden fleece at the Port and the rest perhaps at Port Augusta at the head of Spencer's Gulf. There one could see at times quite a clump of pretty little clippers lying in the stream between the mangrove-clad shores, waiting for the camel trains to come in from Pekina and Coonatto and Mount Remarkable. Much rivalry there was too between the ships, as to which should get her hatches battened down first, complete her crew and clear away for the February wool sales. And men in those days were not always easy to procure, for the long, cold Cape Horn passage and the prospect of shipping again out of London at 50s. per month were not very tempting experiences. Thus it often happened crews ran in Port Adelaide and 'runners' or temporary hands, just shipped for the trip, had to be engaged to take the vessel round to Port Augusta. These returning by the *Penola* or the *Royal Shepherd* or the *Aldinga* left the shipmasters to trust in providence for men to work the vessels home. But, now and again, bushmen coming down country for a spree at 'the Port', a mere hamlet, consisting then mainly of gnats, sand and galvanized iron, would be induced, once their money was gone, to sign articles for the trip home. Men who had never thought to use the sea again. bullock drovers, boundary riders, shepherds and station hands of every description were thus often found on board the clippers of the composite wool fleet.   Many of them had not been to sea for years; but before they had got the smell of ice in their nostrils all the old tricks of the craft came back to them and better crowds no skipper could wish for, if at times apt to be a little intolerant and careless of discipline, with the liberal life of the bush so close behind them.

"A hard experience, too, it generally proved for them, quite unprovided as they (for the most part) were with a sea-going outfit of any description and dependent on the often scantily supplied slop chest.   And many a time when washing along the decks in icy Cape Horn seas or hoisting the frozen canvas aloft, while hail and rain pelted and soaked them, poorly fed, poorly clad, the merest sport of the bitter southern weather, they regretted with oaths deep and sincere their snug bunks and ' all night in' of the far away bush stations, where tempests troubled them not and the loud command of 'all hands' was unknown.   Nor, as a rule, London Town once reached, did they lose any time in looking for a ship bound to some part of the country they had so foolishly left."

The Orient Line.

Of the firms which were chiefly instrumental in exploiting the South Australian trade first mention should perhaps be made of the Orient Line of clippers, the forerunners of the present Orient Line of steamers.

The Orient Line was originally started by James Thompson & Co., who had a number of small ships and barques trading to the West Indies, then Mr. James Anderson joined the firm and eventually became head partner, upon which the name was changed to Anderson, Anderson & Co.

The first of the firm's Australian ships was the *Orient* and this vessel gave her name to the line.

The Orient Line were nothing if not enterprising. Most of their vessels were built in the Nelson Docks, Rotherhithe, to the designs of Mr. Bilbe. Mr. Bilbe was a designer of great ability and he and Mr. Perry, an old shipmaster, were the working partners of the Nelson Dock, which consisted of a dry dock and a building yard, owned by Anderson, Anderson & Co. Mr. James Anderson had a wonderful knowledge of everything pertaining to ships and their business, and like many an old-fashioned shipowner took a practical interest in his ships, and nothing either in their design, construction or management was undertaken without his approval.

Messrs. Bilbe & Perry built one of the earliest composite clippers, the *Red Riding Hood*. She was launched in 1857 some six years before the first of the composite tea clippers. They also went in for iron ships at an early date, their first iron ship, the *White Eagle*, being built as far back as 1855. But owing chiefly to a very ill-advised strike of shipwrights, the Thames builders found themselves unable to compete with the North in iron shipbuilding and the Clyde took the trade which should have belonged to the Thames. Thus 1866 saw the last of the Thames composites to be built in the Nelson Dock when *Argonaut* was launched for the Adelaide trade.

However, Messrs. Anderson, Anderson & Co. meant to have the fastest ships procurable, and gave Hall, of Aberdeen, Steel, of Greenock and the Sunderland shipyards each a chance to turn them out a flyer.

The " Orient."

The *Orient*, the pioneer of the line, was launched at Rotherhithe in 1853, and measured:—

Registered tonnage .. .. ⁍	1033 tons.
Length	184.4 feet.
Beam	31.7 ,,
Depth	21.1 ,,

She was built to participate in the gold boom to Melbourne, and was fitted to carry passengers under a poop 61 feet long. However she was not destined to start life on the Australian run, for she had barely been launched before she was taken up by the Government for the transport of troops to the Crimea. At the landing at Alma in September, 1854, she was transport No. 78, carrying the 88th Connaught Rangers. She managed to ride out the gale of the 14th November, 1854, off Balaclava, in which 34 of the Allied ships were wrecked and over 1000 lives lost. And in October, 1855, we find her acting as a hospital ship during the expedition against Kinburn and Odessa. In 1856 she returned to London and was then put on the berth for Adelaide. She sailed from Plymouth under Captain A. Lawrence on the 5th July, 1856, with a full passenger list, and hence forward was a favourite passenger ship in the South Australian trade.

"Orient's" Outward Passages.

The following table gives her time out for twenty-one voyages under the Orient flag. She generally took about 95 days coming home *via* the Cape, calling in at Capetown and St. Helena, as it was the custom with ships carrying passengers.

"ORIENT."

Arriving at Gibraltar with Troops from the Crimea.

From a lithograph.

[To face page 193.]

Date.	Captain.	Date Left London.		Date Left Plymouth.		Date Arrd. Port Adelaide.		Days Out.
1856	A. Lawrence	June	28	July	5	Sept.	24	81
1857	,,	,,	28	,,	2	,,	22	82
1858	,,	,,	28	,,	4	,,	18	76
1859	,,	,,	28	,,	2	,,	23	83
1860	,,	May	29	June	5	Aug.	24	80
1861	,,	,,	26	,,	1	,,	20	80
1862	Harris	,,	27	,,	2	,,	24	83
1863	,,	—		May	1	July	12	73
1864	,,	May	29	June	2	Aug.	22	81
1865	,,	April	29	May	4	July	20	77
1866	,,	Sept,	10	Sept.	16	Nov.	27	72
1868	R. de Steiger	Oct.	31	Nov.	6	Jan.	26	81
1869	,,	Aug.	29	Sept.	1	Nov.	24	84
1870	,,	Sept.	17	,,	22	Dec.	17	86
1871	,,	Aug.	28	,,	2	Nov.	27	86
1872	W. H. Mitchell	Nov.	4	Nov.	7	Jan.	27	81
1873	,,	Sept.	28	—		Dec.	16	79
1874	,,	July	25	Downs	27	Oct.	19	84
1875	,,	,,	22	Downs	25	,,	16	83
1876	M. Haffner	,,	23	—		,,	11	80
1877	,,	Aug.	21	—		Dec.	3	104

"Orient" Nearly Destroyed by Fire.

On 3rd November, 1861, the *Orient* left Adelaide
with 2600 bales of wool, some copper ore and several
passengers.   Touching at the Cape she left Table Bay
on 18th December.   On the morning of 2nd January,
smoke was observed to be rising from the fore hatch.
Captain Lawrence at once had the lower deck hatches
lifted fore and aft, but there was no smoke in the hold,
which seemed to prove that the fire was confined to
the 'tween decks.   The hands were turned to breaking
out cargo, but were driven from the fore hold after
getting to the third beam aft of the hatchway.   The
mainsail was then hauled up and the fore hatches put
on to prevent a current of air.   The main hatchway
was then opened and an attempt made to break out the

cargo from that hatch, but again the crew were driven back. The hatches were next battened down and every aperture closed. The carpenter was then ordered to bore holes in the deck. He started in the galley and gradually worked forward until he was over the seat of the fire. On this being found the fire engine, condensing engine and every other means was brought into use for pouring water below; and as fast as it went down it was sucked up again by the ship's pumps. The deck ports and scupper holes, also, were closed and the deck itself kept some inches deep in water.

Whilst the crew fought the fire, the passengers, under the direction of the bosun, provisioned and lowered the boats and streamed them astern. At 5 p.m. dense smoke began to issue from the scuttle under the fore chains, the woodwork was charred, and the glass bull's-eye melted. The scuttles were immediately plugged and the deck cut through at this place. The result was startling. Smoke and flames burst out in volumes. All night long the crew kept doggedly at the pumps and fire engine. Next day the women passengers were all transferred to a Dutch ship which stood by the burning *Orient*. At last the fire was smothered and on the 5th January the *Orient* arrived at Ascension, where a large portion of the cargo was taken out and examined. She was temporarily repaired and then proceeded, and arrived safely in the London River.

Twelve of her timbers were so charred that they had to be replaced, together with the planking of the main deck as far aft as the main hatch. The saving of this ship was a very fine performance and the underwriters presented Captain Lawrence with a piece of plate worth £100, and also £800 for himself, officers and crew. The steadiness and discipline of both passengers and crew were worthy of all praise, and undoubtedly saved the ship.

The "Orient" delivers her Carpenter's Chest to the "Lammermuir" in Mid-Ocean.

In 1872 the *Orient* was diagonally sheathed, and Captain Mitchell took command of her.

In 1873 the *Orient* was just about to leave London for Adelaide, when old John Willis, with his frock-coat flying open and his white hat on the back of his head, came aboard and said to Captain Mitchell: " The carpenter of my *Lammermuir* has left his tool chest and tools behind; will you take them out to Adelaide and deliver them to him."

" No," replied Captain Mitchell, who was a skipper of the good old sort, " but I will take them and deliver them before I reach the line."

The *Lammermuir* had sailed some 10 days before on the 12th of September to be exact. Old John Willis immediately offered to bet Captain Mitchell £5 that he would not be as good as his word. The bet was accepted and the *Orient* sailed on 28th September. In 5° N. a ship was sighted ahead and overhauled. It turned out to be the *Lammermuir*. Signals were exchanged, and a boat put over with the chest on board, and the *Lammermuir's* carpenter duly received his tools as Captain Mitchell had promised. The two ships then parted company and the *Orient* eventually arrived at Adelaide on the 16th December, 79 days out, the *Lammermuir* arriving six days later.

It was a great triumph, and the apprentices of the *Orient* composed a pumping chanty to the tune of

"Marching through Georgia" to commemorate it, the first verse of which ran as follows:—

> The *Lammermuir* left London, boys,
> A fortnight's start she'd got,
> She was bound to Adelaide,
> Her passage to be short,
> But the *Orient* overhauled her
> Before halfway she'd got
> As we were sailing to Australia.

In 1879 the *Orient* was sold to Cox Bros., of Waterford, and she was still afloat quite recently as a coal hulk at Gibraltar.

The Little "Heather Bell."

In 1855 Hall, of Aberdeen, built the little *Heather Bell* for Brown & Co., from whom the Orient Line bought her. Her measurements were—

Registered tonnage		..	..	479	tons.
Length	..	..	..	..	155	feet.
Beam ..	..	..	..	..	28.5	,,
Depth ..	..	..	..	..	17.5	,,

She was not one of the South Australian traders, however, but ran regularly to Sydney and Melbourne. She made herself famous by a wonderful run home from Melbourne under Captain William Harmsworth. She left Port Phillip Heads on 15th October, 1856, with a strong easterly wind and took the route down the West Coast of Tasmania. In spite of five days of easterly gales, she made the passage to the Horn in 26 days. The record for this run was made by the *Lightning* in 1854, being 19 days. *Heather Bell* ran from the Horn to the line in 21 days. This was a record, and considered such a remarkable performance that it was pricked off on old South Atlantic charts. And so far as I know, it has only been twice beaten, once by the *Cutty Sark* and once by the *Thomas Stephens*. *Heather*

Bell made the land at Start Point 20 days from the line, thus making a passage of 67 days. Her best 24-hour run was 330 miles, and her best week's work was 1885 miles. Of course she had great luck with her winds, but, even so, she proved herself a very speedy little ship.

Heather Bell had a long life of 39 years, and was finally broken up at Balmain, Sydney, in 1894.

The " Murray."

Another Adelaide passenger ship belonging to Anderson was the *Murray*. She was built by Hall, of Aberdeen, in 1861, being the last Orient liner to be built entirely of wood. Her measurements were:—

Registered tonnage	..	..	903	tons.
Length of keel	..	..	..	180	feet.
Beam	..	..	..	..	33.3	,,
Depth	..	..	..	..	20.8	,,

She had a long floor with sharp ends, and, whilst fitted with every convenience for passengers, she carried a very large cargo on a very small draught.

The *Murray* was considered a fast ship, her best day's run being 325 miles, but I can best show her capabilities as to speed by recalling a race which she sailed with the well-known Blackwall frigate *Hotspur*.

The two ships, as was usual with passengers on board, had called in at Capetown ; and they left Table Bay together. Then with stunsails set alow and aloft they were 11 days in company running down to St. Helena. In 26° N. they again met and were six days in company, finally they made the Channel within a day of each other, the *Hotspur* leading.

Regarding this race, the late Captain Whall, who was on board the *Hotspur*, says of the run to St. Helena:

" The wind was steady, and the two ships seemed so nearly matched that for hours together our bearings did not alter."

Under the well-known Captain Legoe, the *Murray* made the following fine passages out from Plymouth :—

1861 Left Plymouth, July 26, arrived Adelaide Oct. 16—82 days out.
1862 „   „   „ 13, „   „   Sept. 30—79 „
1863 „   „   „ 15, „   „   Sept. 26—73 „
                                (68 days to the Borda).
1864 Left Plymouth, Aug. 5, arrived Adelaide Oct. 21—77 days out.

The Orient Composite Clippers.

It was during the sixties that the Orient Line came to be known in Australia for the remarkable speed of its beautiful little composite clippers, consisting of :—

Date Built	Ship	Tonnage	Builders.
1863	*Coonatto*	633	Bilbe, of London
1864	*Goolwa*	717	Hall, of Aberdeen
1864	*Borealis*	920	Bilbe, of London
1865	*Darra*	999	Hall, of Aberdeen
1865	*Yatala*	1127	Bilbe, of London
1866	*Argonant*	1073	„ „

The *Coonatto's* measurements were—Length 160 ft. 2 in.; beam 29 ft.; depth 18 ft. 7 in. She was an out and out clipper with very fine lines, but like most of Bilbe's ships—very wet. However this may in part be put down to the hard-driving of her skipper, Begg, a Highlander, who never spared her and made some very smart passages out and home. Her best run to the Semaphore Lightship was 66 days, and she once did a 70-day passage out after broaching to off St. Paul's Island and losing both helmsmen and the wheel itself overboard. This famous little ship stranded on Beachy Head in 1876.

" PEKINA " and " COONATTO," at Port Adelaide, 1867.

" JOHN DUTHIE," at Circular Quay, Sydney.

[To face page 154.

The *Darra* also went out to Adelaide in under 70 days, on which occasion her captain wrote home that she "dived off the Cape and came up to blow off the Leeuwin."

" Yatala."

Probably the fastest of the six was the fine passenger clipper *Yatala*, which the redoubtable Captain Legoe left the *Murray* to command. The record from London to Adelaide, pilot to pilot, 65 days, was shared by the *Yatala* and Devitt & Moore's clipper *City of Adelaide* until the famous *Torrens* beat it.

Unfortunately, *Yatala* came to an early end, and the following are the times of her outward passages during her short existence :—

Date.	Left Plymouth	Arrived Adelaide.	Days Out
1865	Aug.　4	Oct.　27	84
1866	,,　2	,,　14	73
1867	,,　10	,,　15	66
1868	July　9	Sept.　24	77
1869	Aug.　7	Oct.　23	77
1870	,,　11	,,　26	76
1871	July　6	,,　2	88

On 18th December, 1871, *Yatala* left Adelaide in company with the Elder Line clipper, *Beltana*, which she led to the Horn by a day　The *Beltana* arrived safely after a tedious light weather run from the line, but the *Yatala* got ashore near Cape Gris-Nez on 27th March, 1872, when almost in sight of home. Her wool cargo was nearly all saved, but the ship herself became a total loss.

Of the other Orient composites, the *Goolwa* disappeared from the Register in 1880, but *Borealis* and *Argonaut* lasted some years longer.

The " Beltana," and Captain Richard Angel.

The *Beltana*, which raced the *Yatala* in 1871-2, was a composite clipper, belonging to A. L. Elder & Co., a well-known firm in the Adelaide trade and the agents for the celebrated *Torrens*. Built by Laing, of Sunderland, in 1869, the *Beltana* measured:—

Registered tonnage	..	..	..	..	734 tons.
Length	..	..	..	..	172.5 feet.
Beam	..	..	..	..	33.6 ,,
Depth	..	..	..	..	19.2 ,,

She was a beautiful little ship, a fine sea boat with a good turn of speed. In 1872, when running her easting down, she did a day's work of 335 miles under foresail, three lower topsails and fore topmast staysail. She made her reputation as a heeler under Captain Richard Angel, a sail carrier of the most determined character, as the following anecdote will prove.

The *Beltana* was rounding the Horn, homeward bound and reeling along before a heavy westerly gale under topgallant sails, when a vessel was sighted ahead, head-reaching under three close-reefed topsails, though bound the same way as the *Beltana*. Angel, to show his contempt of such caution, immediately bore down on the stranger, and passing ahead of him, put his helm down and brought his yards on the back-stays. As the *Beltana* came up to the wind, she lay right down until the amazed crew of the stranger could almost see her keel, and momentarily expected to see her capsize or her masts go overboard. But the little ship bore this harsh treatment in the bravest manner, and, though her rail was fathoms deep in the scud to leeward, never stranded a ropeyarn. Having crossed the stranger's bows, Angel rounded to close under her stern, then squared his yards and raced ahead again. This

" TORRENS."

" TORRENS " at Port Adelaide.

[To face page 157.

manoeuvre of " sailing round a vessel" was not one that most men would care to attempt in Cape Horn weather.

Indeed, hardly was the *Beltana* on her course again before Angel's trembling mate approached his captain with a request to be allowed to shorten sail, only to be met by the scornful order of:—"Get the royals on her; and then, if you can't find anything else to set, go below and ask Mrs. Angel to lend you her petticoat." Such an order was worthy of Bully Forbes himself.

Captain Richard Angel lost the command of the *Beltana* on the voyage that she raced the *Yatala*. On his passage out he ran the *Beltana* ashore on Kangaroo Island, but got her off and did not report the accident. He loaded wool at Port Augusta, but on getting to sea the ship leaked so much that he had to take her in to Port Adelaide. Here the wool was discharged, and the *Beltana* hauled up on the slip and repaired, whilst Angel got his dismissal and a Captain Blanch took his place. *Beltana* caught fire when loading wool in Port Lyttelton, and her end was one of the biggest ship fires in New Zealand.

The Wonderful "Torrens."

Of other ships managed by Elder & Co., the most noteworthy were the *Glen Osmond*, *Collingrove* and *Torrens*. Of these the *Torrens* requires special mention, as she was without doubt one of the most successful ships ever built, besides being one of the fastest, and for many years she was the favourite passenger ship to Adelaide. She was built in 1875 by James Laing, of Sunderland, and launched in October of that year, her chief measurements being:—

Registered tonnage	..	..	..	..	1276 tons.
Length	..	..	..	..	222.1 feet.
Beam	..	..	..	..	38.1 ,,
Depth	..	..	..	..	21.5 ,,

She was composite built with teak planking and was specially designed for carrying passengers, having a poop 80 feet long.

A beautifully modelled ship and a splendid sea boat, she was very heavily sparred and crossed a main skysail yard. She was also one of the last ships to hold on to fore topmast stunsails; indeed for years she was the only ship with stunsail booms aloft in the Australian trade.

Regarding her capabilities as a sea boat, in easting weather she would drive along as dry as a bone, making 300 miles a day without wetting her decks. But it was in light winds that she showed up best, her ghosting powers being quite extraordinary. The flap of her sails sent her along 2 or 3 knots, and in light airs she was accustomed to pass other clippers as if they were at anchor.

Commander Harry Shrubsole, R.N.R., in a letter to the *Nautical Magazine*, gives the following interesting reminiscences of her wonderful speed.

Some items of one of her passages are worth noting. Crossed the equator in 15 days from Plymouth; arrived off Semaphore, Port Adelaide, 61 days from Plymouth. The last two days were employed in beating up the Gulf from the western end of Kangaroo Island, I forget the name of the point we made, so 59 days could easily be counted as the passage.

We sighted the *Jennie Harkness*, obviously American, at daylight right ahead in the S.E. trades; at noon we were alongside her, and our Foo-Foo band played "Yankee-Doodle" as we passed her. She had Jimmy Greens and water-sails, flying jib topsails and what not aloft, and we slid by her as if she was—well—sailing slowly, as she undoubtedly was, compared to our speed. We passed a large ship running the easting down. She was under upper topgallant sails, whilst we were under upper topsails with weather upper and lower stunsails set. The old ship was never driven; she did not need it, neither would she stand it. But she sailed rings round anything sighted. To sight a ship to windward and ahead, on a wind, was to ensure the tautening of the weather braces, an order to sail a bit finer and to see her passing ahead

and to windward of that ship by the early afternoon. We did this
with a four-master, the *Amazon*, and I bear a scar on my eyebrow
to-day in memory of that ship—merely a small argument about her
name. In the case of the *Jennie Harkness*, I was the "leadin' 'and"
of the Foo-Foo band and can picture the incident now in all its features.

Captain H. R. Angel, who had previously commanded
the *Glen Osmond* and *Collingrove*, was the chief owner
of the *Torrens*, and had a great say in her design; and
after overlooking her building he took her from the
stocks and commanded her for 15 voyages. Under
him she was a wonderfully lucky ship and a great
deal of the credit for her success undoubtedly belonged
to Captain Angel.

Her biggest run in the 24 hours was 336 miles; and
her fastest speed through the water by the log was 14
knots. Her average for 15 outward passages under
Captain Angel was 74 days from Plymouth to the
Semaphore, Port Adelaide. Captain Angel always
brought her into the St. Vincent's Gulf *via* the Backstairs Passage, east of Kangaroo Island, instead of
through Investigators' Straits. On the homeward
passage he always took the Cape route, for the benefit
of his passengers, calling in at Capetown, St. Helena
and Ascension.

To show the extraordinary way in which luck clung
to the *Torrens* as long as Captain H. R. Angel commanded her, I will give the following instance, given
me by Captain Angel himself.

On a certain homeward passage, the lamp oil ran
short or was lost through some mismanagement. This
caused Captain Angel to grow very anxious as the
Torrens approached the mouth of the English Channel,
in whose narrow crowded waters lights are naturally
of the utmost importance. But before soundings were
reached a barrel was passed, floating on the water.

Angel at once hove his ship to and lowered a boat, picked the barrel up and took it aboard—and, on being opened, it was found to contain oil.

As commodore of the Elder Line, Captain Angel flew a white flag with red crescent and stars at the masthead of the *Torrens*, instead of the ordinary house-flag with red ground, white crescent and stars.

In the autumn of 1890 Captain Angel retired from the sea and handed over the *Torrens* to Captain Cope. With the change of captain, the *Torrens* luck deserted her. On her first passage out under her new commander the *Torrens* lost her foremast and main topmast in 6° N., 27° W., and put into Pernambuco to refit; and before she was refitted she caught fire. However, the fire was put out, she was remasted and she eventually reached Adelaide 179 days out.

Whilst Captain Cope had her, the *Torrens* had the honour of having Joseph Conrad as mate for a voyage. This was in 1893, and Conrad made two important literary friendships whilst on the *Torrens*, for W. H. Jacques made the voyage in her and Galsworthy was a passenger from Adelaide to Capetown.

In 1896 Captain F. Angel, the son of Captain H. R. Angel, took over the command of the *Torrens*, and again the Goddess of Fortune objected to the change. On his third voyage, young Angel ran foul of an iceberg in the Southern Ocean; and with her bow stove in and partially dismasted, the *Torrens* managed to struggle into Adelaide, for the second time in her career over 100 days out.

Her last passage, also, under the British flag was a disastrous one. She left Adelaide on 23rd April, 1903, and before she was clear of Kangaroo island a storm burst on her and she had difficulty in clawing off the land. Then when she got down to the Cape latitudes another heavy gale forced her back towards Mauritius. However, at last she got into Table Bay. She had little cargo from Adelaide on board, and as no cargo was offering at Capetown, she went on to St. Helena, and took in a load of explosives for the British Government—ammunition, etc., returning from the Boer war. But even when the Thames tug had got her hawser, the dangers of this passage were not over, for whilst the *Torrens* was in tow a vessel tried to pass ahead of her, between her and the tug, and was cut down and sunk by the sharp forefoot of the famous clipper. When the collision was seen to be unavoidable there was almost a panic on the *Torrens*, owing to her cargo of explosives. However nothing happened, the *Torrens* was uninjured and Captain Angel was not held to blame.

But old Captain Angel had had enough of it—her cost for repairs since he had given her up had come to more than her original cost to build; and he sold her to the Italians.

"'Torrens'" Outward Passages.

When inspecting *Torrens'* wonderful times, two things in her favour must be remembered, firstly that she sailed from England at the most favourable time in the year, and secondly that, carrying passengers, she was always in perfect trim. On the other hand, everything was done to make the passengers comfortable, especially as many of them were invalids or consumptives going for the benefit of the voyage, thus she was never driven as she might have been.

With the change of ownership as with the change of skippers, evil luck again struck the celebrated old

G

ship, for the Italians soon ran her ashore and after getting her off again sent her to Genoa to be broken up. But when the Genoese shipbreakers saw the beauty of her model and construction, they went to the expense of repairing her, only to again bump her on the rocks. This time she was towed back to Genoa for good and all, and was broken up in 1910.

Captain.	Date Left London.	Date Left Plymouth	Date Arrived Adelaide	Days Out.
H. R. Angel	Dec. 8, 1875	Dec. 12, 1875	Mar. 7, 1876	85
,,	Oct. 26, 1876	Oct. 29, 1876	Jan. 18, 1877	81
.	,, 27, 1877	Nov. 4, 1877	,, 11, 1878	68
,,	,, 26, 1878	,, 2, 1878	,, 18, 1879	77
,,	,, 26, 1879	Oct. 30, 1879	,, 8, 1880	70
,,	,, 28, 1880	Nov. 2, 1880	,, 6, 1881	65
,,	,, 27, 1881	Oct. 29, 1881	,, 8, 1882	71
,,	,, 26, 1882	,, 29, 1882	,, 16, 1883	79
,,	,, 27, 1883	,, 29, 1883	,, 7, 1884	70
,,	,, 26, 1884	Nov. 2, 1884	,, 25, 1885	84
,,	,, 27, 1885	,, 1, 1885	,, 8, 1886	68
,,	,, 28, 1886	,, 2, 1886	,, 15, 1887	74
,,	,, 27, 1887	,, 8, 1887	,, 14, 1888	67
,,	,, 27, 1888	,, 1, 1888	,, 14, 1889	74
,,	,, 30, 1889	,, 7, 1889	,, 26, 1890	80
W. H. Cope	,, 29, 1890	Dismasted	April 26, 1891	179
,,	—	Nov. 25, 1891	Feb. 28, 1892	95
,,	Oct. 25, 1892	—	Jan. 30, 1893	97
.	Nov. 3, 1893	—	,, 26, 1894	84
,,	Oct. 14, 1894	—	,, 13, 1895	91
,,	Sept. 18, 1895	—	Dec. 6, 1895	79
F. Angel	Oct. 26, 1896	Left Downs Oct. 28	Jan. 11, 1897	75
,,	,, 30, 1897	—	,, 15, 1898	77
,,	.. 25, 1898	Struck Iceberg	Feb. 5, 1899	103
,,	,, 31, 1899	—	Feb. 5, 1900	97
,,	.. 27, 1900	Left Downs Oct. 30	Jan. 20, 1901	82
,,	,, 24, 1901	—	Feb. 2, 1902	101
,,	,, 26, 1902	—	Jan. 17, 1903	83

The *Torrens*, with the exception of the Lochs, was the last sailing ship to carry passengers. As a composite ship, built specially for passengers, she had no rival except Devitt & Moore's celebrated *Sobraon*.

" SOBRAON."

" SOBRAON."

To face page 168.

The Great "Sobraon."

The *Sobraon* was built by Messrs. Hall, of Aberdeen, to the order of Lowther, Maxton & Co., the tea clipper owners, and launched in November, 1866. She was the largest composite ship ever built, being constructed of solid teak with iron beams and frames; she was copper fastened and classed 16 years A1.

Her measurements were:—

Registered tonnage	..	..	..	..	2131 tons.
Burthen	..	..	..	..	3500 ,,
Length over all	..	..	..	..	317 feet.
Length between perpendiculars	..	..	272 ,,
Beam	..	..	..	..	..	40 ,,
Depth of hold	..	..	..	..	27 ,,

Her lower masts were of wrought iron, and her topmasts and lower yards on each mast of steel. On her first two voyages she carried skysails, but these were found to make her rather crank and so were done away with. In the eighties she followed the fashion and was fitted with double topgallant yards on her fore and main masts. With all sail set, she had a spread of just 2 acres of canvas.

Mr. A. G. Elmslie, who served in her for 11 years under his father, from apprentice to chief officer, gave me the following account of her sailing qualities :—

A glance at the perfect lines of the ship in dry dock would be quite sufficient to show there was nothing to stop her going through the water, and I can honestly say that during my 11 years I never saw any other sailing ship pass her in a breeze either on a wind or before it. The fact of the *Sobraon* being first intended for an auxiliary steamer and having the two stern posts, the space between which was filled up with solid timber. gave her a perfect run. and her bows were as fine as any yacht's. Runs of over 300 knots when running down the easting were frequent. On one occasion over 1000 knots were covered in three days and over 2000 in a week. 340 knots in the 24 hours was the best run made. I have seen over 16 knots reeled off by the log. This was with the wind some 2 or 3 points on the quarter, which was her best sailing point. On a wind and sailing within 5½ points, she could do her 7 to 8 knots good.

On her first five voyages from 1866 to 1871, *Sobraon* sailed to Sydney, and after that, from 1872 to 1891, to Melbourne, always returning *via* the Cape of Good Hope instead of the Horn.

Her fastest trip to Sydney was 73 days and to Melbourne 68 days. On the latter passage she sighted Cape Otway on the morning of the 60th day out, but then had light variable winds, which spoilt what promised to be a 61-day passage.

Most of her outward passages were between 70 and 80 days, but it must be remembered that she was never driven hard out of consideration for her passengers, or there is little doubt that she would have gone near to lowering the golden cock at *Thermopylae's* masthead. On her first voyage to Sydney in 1866-7, she went out in 75 days and came home in 78.

Lowther & Maxton only owned her for a few years, and from the first she loaded as one of Devitt & Moore's monthly line of packets to Australia, the latter firm buying her outright about 1870.

On her maiden voyage the *Sobraon* was commanded by Captain Kyle. In 1867 he was succeeded by Lieut. J. A. Elmslie, R.N.R., who had her for the rest of her active career, from 1867 to 1891, a period of 24 years.

Captain Elmslie commenced his career in 1842 and for several years traded out to India and China and later to Australia in the well-known London ships *La Hogue* and *Parramatta*. Prior to taking the *Sobraon*, he commanded the ill-fated *Cospatrick*, from 1863 to 1867, his brother, who was afterwards lost in her in 1873, succeeding him in the command of that ship.

Captain Elmslie's name was so closely and for so long associated with that of the *Sobraon*, that passengers were no doubt as much attracted by the one as by the other. In fact there were many instances in which they booked their passages solely on account of the name of the commander. Whilst being a strict disciplinarian and respected by all who sailed under him, he was, at the same time, kindness itself and laid himself out on every occasion to study the interests of his passengers. The fact that the *Sobraon* never had anything approaching a serious loss of spars or sails may be safely put down to his never ceasing attention to the ship and the weather. He was always about, and his keen sense of watchfulness and duty readily imparted itself to his officers and crew.

Captain Elmslie was elected a Younger Brother of the Trinity House on 1st September, 1868, and he would have been elected an Elder Brother many years before his death had he been eligible, but the fact of his never having served in steam barred him.

No greater proof of the popularity of the *Sobraon* and her captain can be given than the length of time both officers and men stayed in her. James Cameron, who was foreman shipwright at the building of the *Sobraon*, served as carpenter on her during the whole time that the ship was afloat—service 1866-1891.

Thomas Willoughby, formerly with Captain Elmslie in *Cospatrick*, from 1864 to 1867, transferred with his captain to the *Sobraon* and served throughout, first as butcher and later as chief steward—service 1866-1891.

James Farrance served 16 years as A.B. and boatswain. Thomas Routledge served 10 years as sailmaker.

This length of service on the part of her petty officers is, I should think, easily a record.

And amongst well-known seamen who learnt their craft in the *Sobraon* were—

Captain R. Hoare, apprentice to chief officer, 1872-1882 (a commander in the Orient Line and Elder Brother of Trinity House).

Captain F. Northey, apprentice to chief officer, 1867-1869, and 1874-1882 (afterwards commanded the *John Rennie*).

Captain A. E. Baker, apprentice to chief officer, 1887 (afterwards commander in the P. & O.)

Captain Elmslie also had his first and second sons with him. C. T. Elmslie, the eldest, as apprentice before going into the P. & O. and Captain A. G. Elmslie from apprentice to chief officer, 11 years from 1880 to 1891.

The *Sobraon's* crew usually consisted of captain, 4 officers, 8 apprentices, carpenter, sailmaker, boatswain, engineer, 2 boatswain's mates, 26 A.B.'s, 4 O.S.'s, 2 boys, 16 stewards and 2 stewardesses — total all told=69.

Only one voyage was made in each year, the sailing date from London always being the latter end of September and from Australia early in February.

From her immense carrying capacity, the cargo was invariably a good source of revenue. Owing to her regular sailings there was never any difficulty in getting a full hold, and this applied especially to the homeward run, when her cargo consisted chiefly of wool and wheat. It was, however, as a crack passenger ship to Australia that the *Sobraon* was most celebrated as she never formed one of the fleet which raced home to be in time for the February wool sales. Indeed, on the homeward run she usually touched at Capetown and always at St. Helena, these breaks in the passage being very popular with passengers.

At St. Helena the ship made a regular stay of about

three days, and this visit was as much looked forward to by the inhabitants of the island as by the *Sobraon's* passengers. As a rule about 100 tons of cargo, consisting of flour, corn, preserved meat, etc., were landed there and occasionally a few bullocks were taken there from Capetown. Whilst the *Sobraon* lay at St. Helena, the passengers roamed the Island, climbed the 699 steps to the barracks, visited Longwood and Napoleon's tomb and generally enjoyed themselves. Captain Elmslie also made a habit of giving a fancy dress ball on board before leaving, to which all the *elite* of the Island were asked.

Sobraon's passenger accommodation was unequalled for a sailing ship. She only had a short poop, but her first class saloon reached from right aft to within 20 feet of the foremast, and was 200 feet in length. The second class saloon took up the remaining space in the 'tween decks, with the exception of 20 feet in the eyes of the ship, which was bulkheaded off as a store room and sail locker.

The number of first class passengers on the outward trip averaged close on 90, with 40 in the second saloon. There were generally a few less coming home. Owing to the good accommodation and to the fact that the voyages were timed for the finest climatic conditions, there were always a fair number of invalids booked and a good many of them made the round voyage. And there were many instances, also, of marvellous cures aboard the *Sobraon.*

In her early days she took many notable people out to Australia. Lord and Lady Belmore and their suite went out in her, the former to take up the Governorship of New South Wales. It was on this voyage that the Duke of Edinburgh was in Sydney whilst the *Sobraon* lay there ; and it was at his request that she was made the flagship at the Sydney Regatta. Captain Elmslie had the honour of entertaining and being entertained by the Duke on several occasions, and on his return passage brought home numerous cases of curios collected by the Duke whilst in the East.

On the next voyage the *Sobraon* took out Mr. Ducane, the new Governor of Tasmania, and his suite.

Fresh food was obviously a necessity for the class of passenger carried, and the following live-stock were carried on each passage—8 bullocks, 90 sheep, 50 pigs, 3 cows for milking and over 300 geese, fowls and ducks. Fresh water and plenty of it was always procurable—a large condenser running every alternate day ; there was an ice chamber, also, in which several tons of ice were stored.

The *Sobraon* came through her 25 years' active service with singularly little damage at the hands of the elements.

On making the African coast on the homeward run, she had the usual narrow shaves from being dismasted, which are experienced by all west-bound ships in that locality. The wind shifts from N.W. to S.W. in squalls accompanied by the most terrific thunder and lightning at this dreaded spot, and it is almost impossible for a close-hauled ship to avoid getting caught aback.

The most serious storm experienced by the *Sobraon* was in 1889, when running her easting down. She was a little to the north of the Crozets, and it began to breeze up on a Sunday morning. The glass gave every indication of a real snorter, and by 4 p.m. had tumbled down to 27.75. By that time the *Sobraon* had been shortened down to foresail, lower fore topsail, upper fore topsail reefed, main lower topsail and fore topmast staysail. The shift from N.W. to S.W. came at 5 o'clock, and the yards were hardly round before the foresail went and in a few moments there was nothing left of it. The sea was running in mountainous ridges, and with the foresail gone threatened every moment to poop her badly. It was too late to heave to and the ship was kept away before it. After four hours' battling and over 30 men aloft a brand new foresail was bent and set reefed. This was hardly done before the fore upper topsail blew away. However, with the foresail reefed and two lower topsails the *Sobraon* fled before the blast like a startled deer. The squalls every few minutes were terrific and in spite of such short canvas the *Sobraon* was making over 14 knots an hour.

The sea was all the time running higher and higher and breaking aboard in the most alarming fashion. During the night the greater portion of the bulwarks on the port side was carried away ; a boat in davits, hanging 22 feet above the water, was filled by a sea and disappeared, the davits breaking short off : the main skylight over the saloon was washed away and tons of water found its way below before the open space could be covered over. The amount of water in the saloon at this time can be imagined when passengers were actually being washed off their feet. On deck there were many narrow escapes of men being washed overboard, the broken bulwarks being a great source of danger. The mate and three of the men were washed from the main fiferail to the break of the poop, and, after being dashed up against the heavy boarding which had been put up to protect the fore end of the poop, managed to save themselves by the life-lines which had been stretched across. The forward deck house which held the galley and engine room was almost demolished and everything moveable in it was washed over the side.

The storm continued at its height from the Sunday afternoon until Wednesday morning. The passengers, who had been battened down for three days, were in a sorry plight owing to the quantities of water that had got below and the catering for them under such conditions proved very difficult. As is usually the case after such a storm, the wind subsided very much quicker than the sea, and for a few hours on the Wednesday night, the wind having dropped completely and the ship losing way, the rolling was terrific. Fortunately everything held aloft in spite of the great strain on the masts during these few hours.

On two occasions the *Sobraon* had narrow escapes of getting ashore when making the Channel in thick weather. On her first voyage, after several days without sights and when it was calculated that the ship was in the chops of the Channel, several fishing boats were met, and, on asking his position, the captain found that he was heading up the Bristol Channel. Several of the passengers availed themselves of the opportunity of going ashore in the fishing boats, and, landing on the Devonshire coast, reached London several days before the ship.

On the homeward passage in 1888 it came on very thick after Land's End had been sighted. The *Sobraon* stood on for some 24 hours and then suddenly the fog lifted and disclosed the land inside Portland Bill dead ahead and under a mile distant. The wind was easterly and light, and the *Sobraon* close-hauled on the starboard tack; however, she came round in time and stood off, thus escaping destruction by the narrowest margin.

The *Sobraon* had two escapes from being burnt at sea. The first was on the outward passage in 1884. A little water had been making in the vicinity of the main hatch and the carpenter went below one morning to try to discover where it was coming in. Amongst the cargo in the square of the hatch and around it were several crates of bottles packed in straw. In climbing over these the carpenter dropped the light he was carrying and inside of a minute the straw was alight and the flames darting out in every direction. Luckily the ship carried a quantity of fire extinguishers, and with these and the hoses from two pumps the fire was got under in about 20 minutes. Had there been the slightest delay the fire must have spread to the other cargo, and there being no means of getting at it nothing could have saved the ship.

The second instance occurred in the tropics when outward bound in 1888. A quantity of oil and some 90 tons of coal were down in the fore peak, which was only separated from the cargo in the fore hold by a wooden bulkhead. By spontaneous combustion apparently the coal caught alight, and one morning smoke was discovered coming out of the hatch. All hands were at once started getting the coal up, but as the hatch was only 4 feet by 8 feet this proved an extremely slow job. After 20 tons had been got on deck, the smoke had become so thick and the heat so intense that the hose had to be resorted to. However, this conquered the fire in about half an hour. Luckily the burning part of the coal had been well away from the bulkhead or the consequences must have been more serious.

There was only one person lost overboard off the *Sobraon* in her whole career, but this was a particularly distressing case. The following account of it was given to me by Captain A. G. Elmslie :—

"In about latitude 35° S. and longitude 5° W., one Sunday evening early in November, 1883, we were bowling along at a good 13 knots with the wind on the starboard quarter and royals set, being outward bound to Australia. I was third mate and keeping the first watch. Four bells had just been struck when I noticed a lady passenger come up on the poop and walk aft, sitting down on the weather side of the wheel box and close to the man at the wheel. About five minutes later the quartermaster cried out:—' My God! she's overboard! '

" I rushed aft, and with the quartermaster tried to get hold of the girl, who was then hanging on to the lower rail outside, but before we could get her she let go and dropped into the water. Although only a few seconds had elapsed since the quartermaster had let the wheel go, the ship was up in the wind and nearly aback.

" After telling the midshipman to throw some life-buoys over and the fourth officer to get the boat ready, I sang out:—' Man overboard! Let go your royal and topgallant halliards! '

" Fortunately the men were handy and the yards came down before we were flat aback. By this time the captain and other officers and all hands were on deck. Owing to the pace the ship was still going through the water, together with the strong wind blowing, it was necessary to let the topsails come down also.

" With the courses and lower topsails alone set, she soon lost way sufficiently to allow the boat being lowered, which by that time had been manned. Only four minutes elapsed between the girl going over the side and the boat being in the water, but in this short space of time the ship had travelled a good half mile and quite far enough to make the search a most difficult one, especially seeing that the night was intensely dark and a heavy sea running. The search was kept up for some four hours and only abandoned then through the danger of keeping the boat in the water, for she was several times nearly swamped. Needless to say, on such a night, and the probabilities being that the girl was drowned at once, no sign was seen of her. Two of the life-buoys were afterwards picked up by another ship. The reason of the suicide, for such it undoubtedly was, remained a mystery. The girl had no relations with her and no one on board could throw any light on the matter.''

On another occasion the ship was going some 5 knots in the tropics when an apprentice fell overboard during the forenoon watch. It was quite 20 minutes before the boat reached him, but he was found swimming along quite composed, having unlaced and taken his heavy boots off and slung them round his neck, as their weight was less felt there and he did not want to lose them.

Another of *Sobraon's* apprentices was even still more cool-headed. This one fell off the footrope of the mainyard, being one of 30 hands aloft stowing the mainsail. Luckily he was well in to the quarter of the yard and so fell on the deck. If he had gone overboard there would have been little chance of picking him up. The fall was one of 58 feet and he fell within 3 feet of the second mate. The latter naturally expected to find him dead, but he recovered consciousness within an hour, and was about again a month later quite recovered. He declared that as soon as he felt himself falling he made himself as rigid as possible, brought his head and legs together and protected the former with his arms ; and he landed in that position on his side. He was a big fellow, being over 6 feet in height and weighing 14 stones.

Another marvellous escape from aloft was that of a man who was helping to stow the main upper topsail. This man suddenly lost his hold and came down spread-eagle fashion. He dropped on to the main rigging and carried away 7 ratlins of 27 thread stuff, then landed on the rail without breaking a bone. This was in 1886, and the *Sobraon* was just making Plymouth. The man was taken to hospital and recovered in a few days. As soon as he came out of hospital, he claimed damages from the ship, declaring that a grummet on the jackstay had given away ; but it was easily proved that nothing went and the man had simply lost his hold.

But all falls from aloft on the *Sobraon* were not so fortunate as these two. A young ordinary seaman once fell from the mizen topgallant rigging with fatal consequences. The crossjack had just been hauled up and the mizen topgallant sail clewed up, and the hands were sent aloft to make the sails fast. This man, with three others, being first aloft, went up to stow the topgallant sail. Suddenly the men on the crossjack footropes heard an agonising cry and a form whizzed past them, struck the spanker gaff and then fell on the deckhouse. The poor fellow broke his spine amongst other injuries and died almost immediately.

On still another occasion, when the *Sobraon* was again coming into Plymouth, a man working in the main futtock rigging lost his hold and fell on deck right in the midst of a crowd of passengers. There were close on 100 people standing about at the time and it was extraordinary that he fell on no one—he just touched a lady on the shoulder and bruised her a little—but was of course horribly smashed up himself and killed instantly. The shock to the crowd of passengers standing round may easily be imagined.

There were two curious cases of somnambulism amongst the passengers of the *Sobraon*. The first was a Church of England clergyman and he was most methodical in his movements. He invariably appeared on deck about midnight and would first of all go up on the poop and peer into the compass ; and then, after strolling the deck for a few minutes, would go below to the small saloon aft where prayers were held by him on that voyage. Here he would go over the service to an imaginary congregation, after which he would return to his berth and turn in. In the early days of the voyage he was spoken to about his sleep walking, and, at his own request, was locked into his cabin one night. The result was that when he found that he could not get out for his sleep walk, he worked himself into a fury of rage and began smashing things in his cabin. At last the door had to be opened for fear that he would do himself some damage and after a great deal of coaxing he was got back to bed. For some days after this, however, he was in a pretty bad way and no further attempt was made to stop him walking in his sleep.

The second case was of a young man who generally appeared on deck for about an hour each night. On one occasion the officer of the watch, thinking that he was too close to the side of the ship and fearing that he might get on the rail or fall overboard, touched him with a view to getting him away. The somnambulist at once grappled with the mate and was only mastered after over a quarter of an hour's desperate struggle.

As on an ordinary occasion the mate in question could probably have accounted for three men of the somnambulist's build and physique, the incident goes to prove that sleep walkers, if interfered with, are possessed temporarily of a madman's strength.

On her last trip the *Sobraon* arrived at Melbourne about mid-December, 1891, and after discharging took in sufficient ballast to take her round to Sydney. Here she was sold to the New South Wales Government, who turned her into a reformatory ship, and for the next twenty years she lay moored in Sydney harbour. In 1911 she was handed over to the Federal Government to be converted into a training ship for boys entering the Australian Navy. On being put into dry dock for survey, it was found that, in spite of her age, she was as sound as a bell.

Messrs. Devitt & Moore.

In *Sobraon* Messrs. Devitt & Moore undoubtedly had possessed one of the finest passenger sailing ships ever launched ; this firm, indeed, possessed a very keen eye where ships were concerned. The two partners started as shipbrokers, and loaded ships for the Australian trade as far back as 1836. They always loaded on commission, and I believe the first ships for which they did business belonged to Robert Brooks, afterwards the well-known M.P. for Weymouth. But the most famous shipowner who gave Devitt & Moore his ships to load was Duncan Dunbar. And on the death of Dunbar in 1862 Devitt & Moore acquired an interest in several of his best ships, notably the wonderful old *La Hogue*, one of the favourite passenger ships to Sydney in her day and celebrated for her huge figure-head and single mizen topsail.

Shortly before his death Duncan Dunbar had commissioned Laing, of Sunderland, to build him a 1000-ton frigate-built passenger ship, to be called the *Dunbar Castle*. This ship, afterwards known as the " Last of the Dunbars " was launched in 1866, and sailed regularly in Devitt & Moore's list of passenger ships to Australia.

The *La Hogue*, by the way, was built by Pile, of Sunderland, and measured 1331 tons, being one of the largest frigate-built ships ever launched.

Devitt & Moore kept her in the Sydney trade, and so popular was she with the Australians that they would wait weeks and often months on purpose to sail in her.

In 1866, Laing, of Sunderland, launched the equally well-known and popular frigate-built liner *Parramatta*, of 1521 tons, for Devitt & Moore's Sydney passenger trade. These two ships do not properly come within the scope of this book and I shall give a more detailed account of them in the next book of this series, which will deal specially with these frigate-built Blackwallers.

Few shipowners can escape scot-free from disaster, and the firm's greatest loss was when their new ship, the *Queen of the Thames*, considered by many to be the finest ship that ever left the London River, was lost off the Cape on her first homeward bound passage from Melbourne.

With *La Hogue* and *Parramatta* in the Sydney trade and *Sobraon* in the Melbourne trade, the house-flag was well known throughout Victoria and New South Wales. Nor was it less well known in South Australia; indeed Devitt & Moore's ships were amongst the pioneers in the passenger and wool trade of Adelaide.

" City of Adelaide " and " South Australian."

In the Adelaide trade, the beautiful little composite ships of Devitt & Moore rivalled those of the Orient and Elder Lines. Of these little clippers the best known passenger ships were the *City of Adelaide* and *South Australian*.

The *City of Adelaide* was launched in 1864 from Pile's yard, her measurements being:—

Registered tonnage ..	..	..	..	791	tons.
Length	..	..	..	..	176.8	feet.
Breadth	..	..	..	..	33.2	,,
Depth	..	..	..	..	18.8	,,

She was a very fast little ship with a 65-day run from London to Adelaide to her credit.

The *South Australian* came out in 1868, also from Pile's yard, and measured :—

Registered tonnage ..	..	..	..	1040	tons.
Length	..	..	..	..	201	feet.
Breadth	..	..	..	..	36	,,
Depth	..	..	..	..	20.1	,.

She had a poop 80 ft. long, and was classed 17 years A1. Though not as fast a ship as the smaller *City of Adelaide*, she was a very fine sea boat with very comfortable accommodation for first and second class passengers.

She was commanded by Captain David Bruce, who with his three sons was very well known in the Adelaide trade. Old David Bruce was one of the good old breed of sea dog—a sturdy, weather-beaten, grey-whiskered Scot. He always dressed in black broadcloth, topped by a straw hat and puggaree. He possessed a merry wit—also a lame leg, which had been crushed by a run-away cask during a storm. His three sons served their time under him, and the commands of the *City of Adelaide* and *South Australian* seem to have been taken in turn by each member of the Bruce family.

"CITY OF ADELAIDE."

David Bruce, Commander.

From an old lithograph.

"SOUTH AUSTRALIAN."

From an old lithograph.

[*To face page* 178.

South Australian was occasionally seen in Melbourne,
but the *City of Adelaide* was always in the South Australian trade, and usually loaded wool at Port Augusta.
Both ships were still running in the late eighties.

The Speedy Little " St. Vincent."

Messrs. Devitt & Moore always considered that
the little *St. Vincent,* launched in 1865 by Pile, of
Sunderland, was the fastest ship they ever owned.   Her
measurements were :--

Registered tonnage ..	..	..	..	892	tons.
Length ..	..	..	..	190	feet.
Breadth ..	..	..	..	35	,,
Depth ..	..	..	..	18.9	,,

She was also composite built, with a 68-ft. poop
and 36-ft. foc's'le. With hard driving skippers, like
J. Bissit and J. Barrett, she had as bad a reputation
amongst foremast hands as the Orient flyers in the
matter of wetness. However, she was such a beautifully modelled ship that she came to no harm in spite
of generally travelling through the water instead of
over it. But no hard driven ship comes through the
westerlies year after year without a scratch, and one
occasionally comes across such entries as the following
in her log books :—

27th October, 1878.—Struck by a heavy squall, sustained severe
damage to spars, losing bowsprit, headgear, etc.

She was not often over the 80 days going out, and her
times coming home would have been as good, if she
had not come *via* the Cape and St. Helena like most
South Australian traders ; nevertheless she was usually
home in under 90 days. In spite of being hard driven
for most of her life the *St. Vincent* was still afloat in
1905 as a Norwegian barque under the name of *Axel.*

" Pekina " and " Hawkesbury."

Messrs. Devitt & Moore owned two other well-known clippers, built of wood. These were *Pekina*, 770 tons, built by Smith, of Aberdeen, in 1865 ; *Hawkesbury*, 1120 tons, built by Pile, of Sunderland, in 1868.

The *Pekina* was in the South Australian trade, but the *Hawkesbury* always ran to Sydney. Though she had many fine passages to her credit, the *Hawkesbury's* chief claim to fame was her reputation for being the wettest ship in the wool trade. She was composite built, but the *Pekina* was all wood.

Messrs. Devitt & Moore sold the *Pekina* in 1880, but the *Hawkesbury* was still in the Sydney trade in the late eighties.

Mr. T. B. Walker.

Messrs. Devitt & Moore, as shipbrokers, had many fine ships figuring in their books, notably *Mermerus* and *Thessalus*, and at odd times others of Carmichael's fleet. They were also brokers for Mr. T. B. Walker's speedy little barques in the Tasmanian and Brisbane trades. These sailed under the Devitt & Moore house-flag, and Mr. Walker occupied a room and his clerk a desk in their office.

Mr. T. B. Walker was a very prominent man amongst London shipowners and for many years was chairman of Lloyd's Register. He was a shipmaster of the old school and took a great pride in his ships, and kept them up in most liberal fashion. One of his customs was to keep officers and apprentices on board whilst the ships were at home, an old pensioned cook going into the galley and acting as shipkeeper. Thus the Walker apprentices had a most valuable training in docking and undocking, shifting ship, refitting rigging, bending and unbending sail, etc., and a further result of this custom was that these pretty little barques were kept in such good order whilst at home that they came to be known as the West India Dock yachts.

Mr. Walker lived at Hackney and later at Snaresbrook, and he used to arrive at the docks punctually at 9.30 every morning. By this time the decks of all the Walker clippers in port had been washed down, the ropes Flemish coiled, the brass polished and everything was in order for his inspection. And everything had to be in perfect order, for he had an eye like a hawk and nothing escaped him : the least thing wrong or out of order and he was sure to detect it. His captains used to assemble together to meet him and make a daily report on their ships. After Mr. Walker had made his inspection it was the long-established custom for his captains to conduct him to the West India Dock Station, where he entrained for his day's work in the City. In the spring when most of the ships were home, this procession of Mr. Walker and his captains from the docks to the station was a well-known sight of the neighbourhood and was referred to as " Mr. T. B. Walker and his satellites."

Walker's Clipper Barques.

Mr. T. B. Walker's long connection with the Tasmanian trade began in 1851-2 when he despatched the brig *Arnon*, of 338 tons register, to Launceston. She was commanded by Captain Benjamin Fowler, a brother-in-law of Mr. Walker's ; she arrived out of season and lay in port for some months waiting for the following season's wool, during which time Captain Fowler married a daughter of Captain William Nielley (late 40th Regiment), of Rostella, East Tamar, Launceston, and by so doing set an example which was followed by quite a number of Walker's skippers and officers. To name only a few, I may mention Captain Barwood, who succeeded Fowler in the *Arnon* and is, I believe, still living in Tasmania ; Captain Wittingham, who was lost in the *Lanoma* ; Captain Smith, of the *Westbury* ; and Captain Brown, of the *Corinth*. To return to the *Arnon*, on her return trip besides wool, she carried the mails and a large shipment of gold.

On his arrival home Captain Fowler transferred to Walker's new barque, the *Henry Reed*, of 495 tons, and finally commanded the *Alfred Hawley*, another new barque of 420 tons. Captain Fowler retired early from the sea and settled down in his native town, Scarborough, where he took a great interest in municipal and local affairs, becoming in turn Alderman and Mayor, and lived to a good old age, being greatly respected and esteemed by his fellow townsmen.

In the early sixties Walker kept three ships in the Launceston trade, the *Durnstan*, *Fugitive* and first *Westbury*, all small wooden barques. He also had ships in the Queensland trade ; most of his ships were built by Pile, of Sunderland, as the following list of his later ships will show :—

Date Built.	Ship.	Description	Tons.	Builders.
1863	*Arab Steed*	wood barque	635	Pile, of Sunderland,
1866	*Araunah*	,, ,,	448	Gardner ,,
1867	*Westbury*	iron ,,	493	Pile ,.
1868	*Decapolis*	,, ,,	632	,, ,,
1869	*Berean*	comp. ,,	526	,, ,,
1870	*Corinth*	,, ,,	614	,, ,,
1873	*Barossa*	iron ship	968	,, ,,
1876	*Lanoma*	,, barque	665	Austin ,,

Captain JOHN WYRILL, of "Berean."

"BEREAN."

From a painting in possession of the late Captain John Wyrill.

[*To face page* 183.

The beautiful little "Berean."

The best known, as well as the fastest, of all Walker's barques was the beautiful little *Berean*. She was built by Pile, of Sunderland, on similar lines to the tea clippers *Maitland* and *Undine*, and was launched in August, 1869. She was a 19-year A1 ship, and so fine was the shipwright's workmanship that when she was 18 years old and due for remetalling, Mr. Spencer, Lloyd's senior surveyor, who was superintending the work, asked Captain Wyrill when she was last caulked, to which he got the reply :—" On the stocks before launching." Mr. Spencer could hardly believe this surprising statement ; he had the seams of the topsides put to the severest test, but was obliged to admit that they could not be improved, his opinion being shared by the master caulker. And the *Berean* continued to the end of her career without being recaulked ; even after years of carrying heavy ice cargoes when owned by Norwegians, it was not deemed necessary to touch her seams.

Her registered measurements were :—

Net tonnage ..	..	..	..	..	526	tons.
Gross tonnage	..	..	..	..	542	,,
Under deck	..	..	..	..	506	,,
Length	..	..	..	..	160.5	feet.
Breadth	..	..	..	..	30.2	,,
Depth	..	..	..	..	17.2	,,

She had a raised quarterdeck 43 feet long. This was laid with New Zealand Kauri pine planking, 4 inches wide, extending the full length without a butt, and what is more without a knot. All the deck fittings, houses, fiferails, skylights and topgallant bulwarks were of selected teak, the bulwarks being panelled with fretwork designs. The boats also were of polished teak ; in fact, the only bit of painted wood about the decks was the longboat chocks. Even the bunk boards and lining of the foc's'le were of teak.

The *Berean* carried skysails for many years, and the following are her spar measurements :—

Spars.	Foremast.	Mainmast.	Mizen mast.
	ft.	ft.	ft
Mast (deck to truck)	112	116	93
Lower mast (deck to cap)	50	54	50
Doublings	12	12	9
Topmast	38	38	29
Doublings	6.6	6.6	—
Topgallant, royal and skysail masts	42.6	42.6	23
Lower yard	62	62	—
Lower topsail yard	55	55	—
Upper topsail yard	50	50	—
Topgallant yard	40	40	—
Royal yard	30	30	—
Skysail yard	23	23	—
Spanker boom	—	—	44.6
Spanker gaff	—	—	44
Bowsprit and jibboom	48		

Berean's best point of sailing was with a whole sail breeze and smooth water, the wind quarterly or 2 points abaft the beam. Her best run in the 24 hours was 315 miles. She was, of course, too small and hardly powerful enough to equal the larger iron clippers when running down the easting, but in moderate weather there were not many ships which could show her their sterns. The following sailing records will give some idea of her powers :—

Equator to the Channel	..	..	..	17 days.
First 4 passages out averaged	..	..		77 „
First 4 passages home averaged	..	..		84 „

In sailing round the world from 30° S., 20° W., to 30° S., 20° W., her yearly average was from 80 to 85 days, her quickest circle of the globe being 76 days.

Her best outward passage to Launceston was :—

> 71 days pilot to pilot.
> 68 days land to land.

In 1881-2 she ran from Launceston to the Lizard in 79 days. During her first 14 voyages, all her passages were under 90 days. She generally left the West India Docks in May and was back in the Thames about the following March.

Captain John Wyrill.

Captain John Wyrill, who, I am glad to say, is still hale and hearty, took *Berean* from the stocks and only left her when she changed her flag. He is one of the few sailors left of the good old sort, for he has the distinction of never having served in a steamship. Coming from one of the foremost seafaring families in Scarborough, Captain Wyrill went to sea as far back as 1850 ; his apprenticeship indentures were for seven years, but he was an acting second mate within three years of his going to sea.

His first command in T. B. Walker's ships came about in rather a curious way. He was appointed to command a ship, belonging to Mr. Hodgson Smith, the father of Scarborough's present harbourmaster, in place of a captain who was ill. This ship lay in a South Coast port, but on Captain Wyrill arriving there to take up his command he found that the sick skipper had recovered and sailed on his voyage. Mr. Smith thereupon introduced him to Mr. T. B. Walker and his brother Henry Walker, who, by the way, were natives of Scarborough. Through them he obtained command of a ship called the *Lady Stanley*, his next command was the *Asphodel*, then the *Velocidade*, which he left to take the *Berean*.

Captain Wyrill circumnavigated the globe no less than 36 times, and was 44 years in command of sailing ships, for 42 of which he was in the Tasmanian trade. Indeed no history of Tasmania's rise to her present prosperity and importance would be complete without some mention of the *Berean* and her commander. And when it was known in Launceston that Captain Wyrill was leaving Tasmania homeward bound for the last time, with the intention of retiring from the sea, a meeting and public send-off was arranged and a purse of sovereigns and an illuminated address were presented to the veteran captain by the Mayor of the town after several eulogistic speeches, in which Captain Wyrill was referred to " as one of the most popular men ever connected with the shipping of Launceston." Like many another sailing ship captain, Captain Wyrill was no mean surgeon and the setting of broken limbs at sea held no terrors for him. He once made a very good job of his second mate's broken arm.

The *Berean* was so free from accidents at sea that after she had been afloat some years the underwriters at Lloyd's offered to insure her at a specially reduced premium. Her most serious misfortune, whilst under Captain Wyrill, occurred whilst she was towing up to the docks from Gravesend. A large ship ahead suddenly took the ground and the *Berean* was unable to clear her, the collision costing her a new bowsprit, besides damages to figure-head and cutwater. Her narrowest escape from shipwreck was owing to a wrong light in 1888 in no less a place than the Channel. *Fairplay*, in criticising the misdeeds of Trinity House, gives the following account of the incident :—

The *Berean*, Captain Wyrill, left London for the Colonies in the fall of last year. Before sailing the captain received from the Board

of Barnacles notice that the light on St. Catherine's, Isle of Wight, was
to be altered in October from a fixed oil light to an electric flash with
intervals of about five seconds. The captain, like a prudent man,
entered this on his chart, so that it should not be overlooked. Before
he left the Colonies, another notice of the inpending change was given
him, and he was well armed with timely advice. He made his homeward
voyage, and calculated he was off the Channel. He had not been able
to get an observation for three days, but he felt sure of his position,
and he shaped a course right up Channel for Beachy Head. A strong
S.W. wind was blowing, and the weather was thick and dirty. When
he judged he had run his distance to Portland, he bore up a little for
the English land to catch St. Catherine's light, and word was given to
look out for the bright electric flash. No such light was visible and the
vessel was still kept away. Presently a dim light was seen 2 points on
the starboard bow. At first this light looked green and was taken to be
the starboard light of an approaching ship, and the helm was starboarded
a little to give more room. A little time showed that idea to be wrong,
and eyes were still strained to catch St. Catherine's with no result. Then
the light seen was taken for a steamer's masthead light, but that notion
did not do, and it was quite clear that the light, let it be what it might,
was a fixed shore light. Over went the lead, and the soundings showed
the shore to be handy, but what shore ? Or what part of the shore ?
Clearly not off St. Catherine's, because according to notice given there
could be no fixed light there.

The course and soundings would have agreed with the French shore
in the neighbourhood of Cape La Hogue. Something had to be done,
and quickly. The light was getting clearer but no land could be seen.
If the vessel was on the French coast it would be fatal to haul her wind,
if on the English coast it would be destruction to bear up. What was
to be done ? Over went the lead again. Twelve fathoms. That was
enough, thank you. There was too much sea on to stay the ship in a
hurry, so the captain wore her round and stood off on the port tack to
get back where he came from. The compass soon showed that the
flood tide was setting the vessel in by the light, and there was nothing
for it but to wear again and get out past the light on the old course, if
it could be done. The captain took the wheel, and calling to the crew
to pull hard if ever they pulled in their lives, sent her round again. It
was hit or miss, but the vessel was smart, and was smartly handled. She
came round like a duck and just managed to go clear of the light, which
after all, turned out to be St. Catherine's. It had never been altered.

The " Berean's " Races.

In her 27 years of sailing out to the Antipodes
and home, the *Berean* had many a contest with clippers

twice her size, in which she gave a very good account
of herself.

Captain Wyrill gave a very interesting description of
three of these encounters in the *Nautical Magazine* a
few years ago, and I do not think I can do better than
quote his own words.   He writes :—

Coming home from Tasmania in the *Berean* early in 1870, about the
equator and nearing the tedious " variables," alias " doldrums,"
alias " horse latitudes," we overhauled the clipper ship *Yosemite*, from
San Francisco for United Kingdom for orders.   Her captain signalled
for permission to come on board, and a prompt reply of welcome went
up.   The captain reported himself tired and restless, that he was
racing home with two or three ships, and was anxious to know what
vessels we had spoken.   My list was produced, but none of his com-
petitors was in it.   After a pleasant visit the captain returned to his
ship giving me the names of two of his antagonists.

Berean gradually crept away from *Yosemite*, and in about two days
she had dipped below the horizon, but was still visible from aloft.   By
this time we were coming up with two ships, which, by their spread
of stunsails, water-sails, Jimmy Greens, etc., were evidently in a great
hurry.   In exchanging signals they proved to be the two vessels racing
the *Yosemite*, viz., ship *Lady Blomfield* and barque *Cerastes* ; the latter
was slightly ahead.   We passed within hail of the *Lady Blomfield*, and
when I reported the *Yosemite* not far astern the cap'ain was greatly
excited.   Throwing up his cap, he exclaimed, " Go and tell the other
ship there is a bet of £100 between them."

A hand went aloft and pointed out the *Yosemite* astern.   Shortly
after we sailed alongside the *Cerastes*, but the captain took the news of
the racer's proximity very calmly and seemed to be surprised she was
so near.   We gradually got away from these two ships and saw no more
of them.   On arrival in the English Channel I sent a report ashore
which appeared in the *Shipping Gazette*, and I found considerable
interest was being taken in this race.   I was interviewed by *Yosemite's*
agents as to my opinion which ship would win.   Two or three days
after *Berean* arrived in London *Cerastes* reached Queenstown, and
was the winner of that race.

In 1893, homeward bound from Tasmania to London, Lat. 19° S.,
Long. 22° W., *Berean* fell in with Geo. Thompson's Aberdeen White
Star clipper *Samuel Plimsoll* from Sydney to London ; strong S.E. trade
wind, squally.   At daylight the two ships were exactly abeam of each
other, and throughout the day neither could gain an inch.   (The old
man of the *Samuel Plimsoll* stamped up and down his poop all day in a

very excited state of mind and kept exclaiming, " A little thing like that hanging on to me like a flea and I cannot shake her off.") The royals were frequently lowered during the squalls and hoisted again when they had passed. *Samuel Plimsoll* steering slightly more easterly, the two ships gradually closed, and if the respective courses had been continued must have collided. *Berean*, being the windward ship, was bound to give way, so at sundown she was shaken up in the wind and the *Samuel Plimsoll* allowed to pass ahead. At daylight next day, the Aberdeen clipper was well out to windward and slightly ahead, and in that bearing the ships parted, seeing no more of each other.

Unfortunately, in the chops of the Channel, *Berean* was surrounded with a fleet of herring nets, some of which clung to her the rest of the passage impeding her speed. *Samuel Plimsoll* arrived at Gravesend an hour or two ahead, but being too early in the tide had to anchor. *Berean*, being of lighter draught, passed her and was first in dock. But for the detention through fouling the nets, in all probability these two ships would have reached Gravesend together after a race of 6000 miles.

In 1895, when outward bound to Tasmania and in the doldrums north of the equator, *Berean* fell in with the four-master Loch liner *Loch Carron*, bound to Adelaide. The two ships after a chat with signals parted on opposite tacks and did not sight each other again until crossing the Great Bight of Australia, when at lunch one day the welcome cry of " Sail-ho ! " was heard. Going on deck the chief officer and myself naturally looked ahead for the stranger, but a ship on our starboard quarter was pointed out. *Berean* was steering due east for Tasmania with the wind right aft, the worst point for fine-lined ships, head sails all becalmed ; the *Loch Carron* hauling up for Adelaide was carrying the wind 2 or 3 points on the quarter, all sails drawing, and was gaining on the *Berean*. When she got into our wake she kept off on the same course as if intending to speak, but finding she could not gain on that course hauled to again, crossing astern, and with the difference in the courses the two ships were soon out of sight of each other. The picture of the *Loch Carron* as she sheered away under all sail, scattering the feathery foam from her bows, still lives, forming one of the series of mental photographs an old sailor naturally collects.

Another still more interesting meeting was with the famous *Thermopylae*. Both ships were outward bound, and the *Thermopylae* overhauled and passed the *Berean* to the southward of the Cape, the weather being unsettled, and the *Thermopylae*, being able to bear more sail than the little *Berean*, soon went out of sight ahead. Nevertheless she only passed Cape Otway

17 hours ahead of the *Berean*, so Captain Wyrill was not quite broken-hearted.

On another occasion the *Berean*, when outward bound, crossed the southern tropic in company with Green's *Melbourne* (afterwards the well-known cadet ship *Macquarie*) and the little barque arrived in Launceston two or three days before the big iron ship arrived in Hobson's Bay.

Again, when homeward bound, the *Berean* was passed off the Falkland Isles in a strong breeze by Green's fast Blackwall frigate *Windsor Castle*, nevertheless the *Windsor Castle* docked in London four days later than the *Berean*.

All the above trials of speed were with vessels very much larger and more powerful than Mr. Walker's clipper barque, but the *Berean* once had a very interesting race round the world with another well-known barque, the little *Harriet McGregor*, of 331 tons, belonging to Hobart. The two ships left Tasmania together, and the *Berean* arrived at Gravesend, 90 days out, beating the *Harriet McGregor* by a week. On the return passage, the *Harriet McGregor* was loaded first and got away about nine days ahead of *Berean*, but again Walker's clipper got in ahead of her, this time by one day only, after making the run to Launceston in 77 days.

" Berean " as an Ice Carrier.

Mr. T. B. Walker died in 1894, and all his ships were sold two years later.

Berean went to the Norwegians and was employed for the next 14 years carrying ice from Norway to the Thames. Captain Wyrill took over the *Eden Holme* and some of his old hands went with him. He was hauling into the London Dock after his first voyage to Tasmania in the *Eden Holme*, when the poor little *Berean* under her new flag was hauling out ; and the change for the worse in the old ship was so marked that one of her old crew remarked to Captain Wyrill with tears in his eyes :—'' There she is, sir, but she looks very different from what she was when *we* had her.'' Nevertheless, though uncared for, the *Berean* still continued to make good regular passages, and was a constant visitor to the Regent's Canal Dock. But in 1910 she was run into by a foreign steamer below Gravesend, when inward bound from Langesund, and was towed ashore in a sinking condition. This was the end of her active career, for she was now condemned, and after being patched up went to Falmouth as a hulk. I saw her there not many years before the war, and the marks of the thoroughbred were still plain to be seen.

Loss of the '' Corinth.''

The *Corinth*, Walker's only other composite ship, was lost by spontaneous combustion.

In the year 1890 she sailed from Launceston, in the wake of the *Berean*, with a cargo of wool and skins, under command of Captain Littler. When she was a week out and about 900 miles S.E. of New Zealand, signs of fire in the hold were discovered early on a Sunday morning. Prompt measures to fight the fire were at once taken, everything was battened down, holes were cut in the deck, through which the hose was led and the wool bales were soused with water ; nevertheless the fire gained rapidly and at 10 o'clock the same night the ship had to be abandoned. The crew got safely away in two boats and headed for the New Zealand coast, but with little hope of making the land against the stormy weather of the prevailing westerly winds.

After they had been five days and nights adrift, the smoke of a steamer was sighted about sundown ; then darkness set in. The provisions had become soaked in salt water but the shipwrecked crew had managed to keep a few rockets dry, and these were sent up one after the other in the hope of attracting the attention of the steamer. At last only one rocket remained, and after some discussion as to whether to risk it or keep it for a future occasion, it also was fired and was seen from the bridge of the approaching vessel. However, she showed no signs of having seen it in the way of an answering rocket or flare, so one can imagine the relief of the shipwrecked crew when her masthead and later her side lights were seen, steering end on for the boats. The steamer proved to be the *Fifeshire*, homeward bound from New Zealand, and she took the *Corinth* castaways right on to London.

A description of Walker's iron barques will be found at the end of Part III.

The Little " Ethel."

Perhaps the most familiar ship to old City men was the little *Ethel*, which under the command of Captain A. Ross ran for years with the utmost regularity between London and Tasmania, and when in the Thames always moored at Hayes Wharf, London Bridge. She was a composite barque of 556 tons and was built in 1866 by Pile, of Sunderland, and owned by Fenwick & Co., of London.

The Hobart Barque " Harriet McGregor."

A still smaller ship than the *Ethel* in the Tasmanian trade was the smart little *Harriet McGregor*, which had the " round the world " race with *Berean*. A. McGregor who built her was also her owner.

She was built at Hobart in 1871, and measured:—

Registered tonnage	..	..	..	..	331	tons.
Length	..	..	..	..	134.2	feet.
Beam	..	..	..	..	27.6	,,
Depth	..	..	..	..	15.9	,,

This little ship for year after year did the following annual round with the regularity of a clock. On Christmas day she left Hobart for London, loaded with wool and sperm oil. She returned to Hobart from London with general cargo at 40s. and often more. Then she ran across to Mauritius from Hobart with coal, and returned with a cargo of sugar, in time to get away on her usual sailing day for London.

The Fremantle Barques " Charlotte Padbury " and " Helena Mena."

In the early days the Fremantle wool trade, including that of the Ashburton River and Sharks Bay, was all carried in the holds of fast clipper barques, such as Walker's *Westbury*, *Decapolis* and *Corinth*, and well worthy to be ranked with these were the *Charlotte Padbury* and *Helena Mena*, both of which were well known and much admired in the London River for many years.

The *Charlotte Padbury* was a wood barque of 640 tons, she was built at Falmouth in 1874 for W. Padbury, of Fremantle. '

The *Helena Mena* was a composite barque of 673 tons, and was built by Thomson, of Sunderland, in 1876, for J. Wilson, of London.

The *Charlotte Padbury* was wrecked in April, 1903, and the *Helena Mena* was sold to the French for £1275 in 1898.

H

These were two of the last of the wood and composite clippers, for by the early seventies every shipowner, however conservative, found himself compelled to go in for iron ships, if he was to compete sucessfully in the world's freight market.

PART III.—"THE IRON CLIPPERS."

Fill us with wool till we're nigh overflowing,
Send us away when strong breezes are blowing,
    And we'll show all the others the road.
The tug boat is coming for us in the morn,
We'll drive her like blazes from here to the Horn,
    For the main royal shall never be stowed.—

J. St. A. Jewell.

The Introduction of Iron in Shipbuilding.

IT was the introduction of iron, as the chief material for the building of ships, that contributed more than anything else to the supremacy of the British Mercantile Marine.

Iron killed the competition of our American cousins, who, as long as wood was the chief factor, were able to give us a hard fight as to which should lead the world in shipbuilding. Yes, it was the advent of iron, more than the North and South War, more than the sinkings of the *Alabama*, more than any slump in freights or foolish shipping legislation on the part of the United States, and more even than our adoption of Free Trade, which made the British nation the carriers of the world.

Many people think, and they have been fostered in their belief by the good old conservative wood and hemp sailor, that iron also sounded the knell of the sailing ship. This is, of course, to a certain degree true, yet sail continued to flourish for 50 years after the advent of iron, and up to the late nineties no finer ships had ever been built or sailed than the iron clippers from the Clyde and other British shipyards.

It was the deterioration of the man before the mast which the advent of steam brought about, and the cutting of freights induced by coal, the cry for bigger ships and more luxury, and also, that soulless modern institution, the company manager, which drove sailing ships down and down in the trade of the world ; these and the growing desire for mechanical speed, which have invaded almost every department of life, killed the windjammer.

But in iron, as in wood, sail had a zenith to reach before the decline set in, and through the last half of the nineteenth century the ports of the world were crowded with magnificent iron full-rigged ships and barques, such as it would have been hard to improve upon with all our new knowledge of wind pressure, streamlines, and least resistance curves.

The Drawbacks and Advantages of Iron.

Like everything else iron had its drawbacks as well as its advantages. At first its effect upon the deviation of the compass caused many a stranding and many a disastrous shipwreck. Then too, though an iron ship can be driven into a head sea in a way no dare-devil of a Yankee driver would have dared to attempt with his soft-wood clipper, iron has not the buoyancy of wood, and the sight of a modern four-poster's main deck when running before the westerlies would have made a Black Ball skipper rub his eyes with astonishment. As a preventative of weed and barnacles, no anti-fouling has yet been discovered which can compete with copper, and thus an iron hull, especially if it had been long in certain well-known localities, was ever a handicap to a vessel's speed through the water. Iron ships have never been able to equal their wooden sisters in light winds, and this chiefly owing to the trouble of foul bottoms.

The three chief advantages of an iron ship were firstly, that her hull would stand unlimited driving, especially into a head sea; secondly, she had more room for cargo than a wooden ship of the same size; and thirdly, she was safer from that dreaded scourge at sea—fire.

Increase in the Size of Ships.

The chief change brought about by iron has been the increase in the size of ships. The old-style ship-owner held that a very big ship was a very big mistake.

When the *Jason*, a 1500-ton ship, went out to Calcutta at the beginning of the seventies, Patrick Keith, of Gladstone, Wyllie & Co., wrote to the Carmichaels, her owners, saying that she was far too big a ship for the Indian trade, and that Smith's smart little 1000-ton "Cities" were quite large enough. Yet on her last voyage to the Hooghly, 20 years later, the *Jason* was by far the smallest deep-water sailing ship in the port of Calcutta.

The difficulty of working wood in big sizes kept down the tonnage in the old days, but with the introduction of iron this difficulty was at once removed. And iron masts and yards in the place of Oregon pine, and wire in the place of the tremendous hemp shrouds, solved the problem of rigging strain—thus, with sail as with steam, the first result from the use of iron was the steady increase in individual tonnage.

Sail Plan Alterations.

Iron masts and wire stays caused a big change in the sail plan of the full-rigged ship. The increased strength led at first to a certain amount of over-masting as well as over-carrying of sail, with the result that many a new clipper was dismasted on her maiden voyage. 1874 was a specially disastrous year in this way. No less than seven ships lost their masts bound out to Australia, and the *Loch Ard* was twice a victim. It was her maiden voyage, and she lost her " gossamer," as Joseph Conrad poetically calls it, before she had cleared the land. She put back to the Clyde and refitted, only to again lose her masts running the easting down. About this date also a great number of iron ships were posted as missing, notably the *Africa, Asia, Loch Laggan* (ex-*America*), *Cairo* and *Great Queensland*. No doubt some of these losses were due to dismasting.

It was not only that the ships were tremendously lofty, but their yards became squarer and squarer, until it was found that stunsails were a luxury. In fact, partly for this reason and partly owing to the competition of steam and the resulting need for economy, flying kites of all descriptions were given up and by the early eighties even a fore topmast stunsail was looked upon as a curiosity.

The lesson of rigging strain had to be learnt with the iron clippers, just as it had had to be with the early wood clippers, but it was not long before the seas were crowded by perfectly sparred iron ships. Specially worthy of mention for perfection of sail plan were Carmichael's beautiful main skysail clippers, such as the *Golden Fleece, Jason, Mermerus, Thessalus, Argonaut* and others.

Double topsail yards were followed before very long by double topgallant yards, then came the eclipse, and the seas became covered with stump topgallant mast horrors and that pathetic sight, the full rig ship masquerading as a barque.

I give a mainyard table, which may be of interest as showing the development of width in sail plans.

MAINYARD TABLE.

Length of Mainy'd in feet	Ship	Tonnage	Date Built	Description.
120	*Great Republic* ..	3357	1853	American 4-mast barque
108	*British Ambassador*	1794	1873	British iron "jute" clipper
102	*Preussen*	5081	1902	German 5-mast ship, nitrate clipper
100	*Royal Sovereign* ..	1637*	1637	Brit. 1st rate man-of-war
,,	*Daylight*	3756	1902	Brit. steel 4-mast barque. Oil tank
,,	*James Baines* ..	2515	1854	"Black Ball" pass. clipper
,,	*Donald Mackay* ..	2598	1855	,, ,, ,,
96	*Prince Royal* ..	1187*	1610	Brit. 1st rate man-of-war
,,	*Glory of the Seas* ..	2103	1869	Amer. "C. Horn" clipper
95	*Lightning*	2084	1854	"Black Ball" pass. clipper
,,	*Champion of the Seas*	2448	1854	,, ,, ,,
,,	*Royal Charter* ..	3000	1855	Brit. full-rigged auxiliary
,,	*Roanoke*	3559	1892	Amer. wood 4-mast barque
94	*Shenandoah* ..	3258	1890	,, ,, ,,
92	*Dirigo*	3005	1894	American steel 4-mast barque (British design)
90	*Challenge*	2006†	1851	American wood clipper
,,	*Sovereign of the Seas*	2421†	1852	,, ,, ,,
89	*Star of the East* ..	1219	1853	New Bruns. wood clipper
88	*Mermerus* ..	1671	1872	Brit. iron "wool" clipper
,,	*Loch Torridon* ..	2000	1881	Brit. iron 4-mast barque
84	*Ben Voirlich* ..	1474	1873	Brit iron "wool" clipper
,,	*Loch Maree* ..	1581	,,	,, ,, ,,
,,	*Port Jackson* ..	2132	1882	British iron 4-mast barque
82	*Cimba* ..	1174	1878	British iron "wool" clipper
,,	*Flying Cloud* ..	1793†	1851	American wood clipper
81	*Salamis*	1079	1875	British iron "wool" clipper
,,	*Witch of the Wave*	1500†	1851	American wood clipper
80	*60-gun ship* ..	1500*	1800	Brit. 4th rate man-of-war
,,	*Thermopylae* ..	948	1868	British tea clipper
,,	*Typhoon*	1610†	1851	American wood clipper
79	*Dreadnought* ..	1413†	1853	Amer. Atlan. packet ship
78	*Cutty Sark* ..	921	1869	British tea clipper
,,	*Hallowe'en* ..	920	1870	British iron tea clipper
,,	*Surprise*	1361†	1850	American wood clipper
75	*Roscius*	1100†	1836	Amer. Atlan. packet ship
74	*Norman Court* ..	834	1869	British tea clipper
72	*Ariel*	852	1865	,, ,, ,,

*Old.   †American.   ε

The "Ironsides," First Iron Sailing Ship.

The first vessel to be constructed of iron was launched in 1838, and appropriately named the *Ironsides*. She was built at Liverpool by Messrs. Jackson, Gordon & Co., and in appearance differed very little from wooden ships of that date. She was very short, with heavy stern and low bow, out of which cocked an extremely long bowsprit and jibboom, whilst her masts in contrast to her hull seemed to rake the heavens. However she was the pioneer of the new material and at one time her picture was a common sight in shop windows. It is doubtful if she was altogether a success, and iron ships were still a rarity 20 years later.

The "Martaban."

In 1853, an iron sailing ship was launched from the yard of John Scott, of Greenock, with intercostal plates and stringers. This was the *Martaban*, of 743 tons register, built for the well-known firm of Carmichael. Her specifications were the product of the brains of Matthew Orr, brother-in-law of the first Thomas Carmichael, and of John Ferguson, who was afterwards a member of Barclay, Curle & Co., the famous shipbuilders. The *Martaban* was classed nine years A1 at Lloyd's, being rated equal to a nine years wooden ship.

At that time Lloyd's had no rules or class for iron ships, so they retained *Martaban's* original specification as a basis for their rules concerning iron ships. That the *Martaban* was a success is proved by the fact that she received £4 a ton for a cargo of coffee and cotton from Bombay to Havre, and was offered a Diplomé d'Honneur at the local exposition for delivery of her cargo in perfect condition.

Mr. THOMAS CARMICHAEL, of A. & J. Carmichael.

[To face page 200.

Iron Ships in the Australian Trade.

It was in the Australian trade that the iron passenger ship was to be seen in her perfection. She succeeded the great Liverpool clippers and the little Blackwall frigates, and she was as beautiful and perfect as any of her wooden sisters.

In the sixties, seventies and even eighties thousands of emigrants were carried from the Old Country to Australia and New Zealand in these magnificent iron clippers. They also took out blood stock of every description from racehorses to pedigree bulls and rams; and a nice time some of these animals must have had when the clippers were carrying on running their easting down.

Most of the ships raced home again with wool for the London sales, but a few, notably Heap's fine ships, went on from Australia to India and Burma, generally with a load of walers for the army in India. In the Bay of Bengal they either loaded jute home from Calcutta or rice from Rangoon. Messrs. J. Heap & Sons were rice millers, and their ships took the firm's rice home.

In the seventies and eighties these beautiful clippers were a never-ending interest in the London River, the Mersey, the Clyde and the great ports of the Antipodes. In Sydney landsmen made special Sunday excursions to Circular Quay to see the ships, and it was the same with the other ports in the days of masts and yards. Every Australian, whether native-born or new chum, kept a tender corner in his heart for the tall ships which had had so much to do with the development of his country. The Sydney-side native, indeed, not only took a pride in the regular traders to the port, but knew them intimately, and could generally be relied on to name an incoming clipper correctly long before she had reached the anchorage.

The New South Dock.

A visit to the docks of the London River is only made nowadays from dire necessity. Their charm has entirely departed. Instead of a forest of spars, nothing now shows above the warehouse roofs but the soot-covered, stumpy masts, blunt-nosed derricks, and squat funnels of a few steamers. Truly the glory of the docks has departed for ever, and only the sentiment remains. Joseph Conrad, in his delightful *Mirror of the Sea*, thus describes the New South Dock in the days of the iron wool clipper:—

To a man who has never seen the extraordinary nobility, strength, and grace that the devoted generations of shipbuilders have evolved from some pure nooks of their simple souls, the sight that could be seen five-and-twenty years ago of a large fleet of clippers moored along the north side of the New South Dock was an inspiring spectacle. Then there was a quarter of a mile of them, from the iron dockyard gates guarded by policemen, in a long, forest-like perspective of masts, moored two and two to many stout wooden jetties. Their spars dwarfed with their loftiness the corrugated iron sheds, their jibbooms extended far over the shore, their white and gold figure-heads, almost dazzling in their purity, overhung the straight, long quay above the mud and dirt of the wharfside, with the busy figures of groups and single men moving to and fro, restless and grimy under their soaring immobility.

I have a photograph of the South Dock just as it is depicted by Conrad, showing the long row of lean, knife-like cut-waters, surmounted by their spotless figure-heads, and with their bowsprits stabbing the sheds opposite, whilst the masts and yards criss-cross the dull grey of the London sky.

The Builders of the Iron Wool Clippers.

Before proceeding to the ships themselves, I must not omit to say a few words about the men who built these splendid iron sailing ships.

The London River, partly owing to an ill-advised strike and partly owing to its distance from the raw material in comparison to the northern ports, entirely lost its shipbuilding business in the latter half of the nineteenth century; and the builders of the iron wool clipper were pretty evenly distributed over the Clyde, the Mersey and Aberdeen. Once more, as with the tea clippers, there was a keen rivalry between Glasgow and Aberdeen, and it is difficult to say which carried the day, for both cities were represented by countless beautiful ships. Duthie, Hall and Hood had, however, to contend with more than twice their number of Clydeside rivals. If I were asked to give my humble opinion, I should award the palm to Messrs. Barclay, Curle & Co. for producing the most perfect iron ships that ever sailed the seas. They built many of the best "Lochs," such as *Loch Maree*, and the four-posters *Lochs Torridon*, *Carron* and *Broom*. They were responsible for the whole of Carmichael's splendid fleet, and the two famous "Bens"—*Voirlich* and *Cruachan* —emanated from their drawing lofts.

Thomson, of Glasgow, built some half-dozen "Lochs," his masterpiece being the *Loch Garry*. The rest of the Loch Line were divided amongst Lawrie, Inglis, Henderson, and Connell. Duthie's finest ship was the *Brilliant*. Hall built the well-known *Port Jackson*, whilst Hood was the originator of all the Aberdeen White Star ships and also built the smart little *Cimba*.

Heap's ships were mostly built by Evans, of Liverpool; and Potter, of Liverpool, produced the two well-known London ships, *Thomas Stephens* and *Old Kensington*. Of the other London owned ships, *Hesperus* and *Harbinger* worthily upheld the name of Steele, while Pile, of Sunderland, was represented by *Rodney*.

I must now turn to the ships themselves, and, taking them in order of date, will begin with that famous veteran the *Darling Downs*.

The " Darling Downs."

She was one of that numerous fleet of ships, the converted from steam to sail, about which one could make a largish book without much trouble. And she was one of the most successful of the lot. She was built as far back as 1852 and sailed under the flag of the General Screw Steamship Company, as the *Calcutta*, an auxiliary steamer with a 300 horse-power engine. Like nearly all early steamship businesses the General Screw S.S. Co. did not remain solvent very long, their ships were sold and were promptly converted into sailing ships, and in many cases renamed.

As a sailing ship, the *Darling Downs* was a very favourite passenger ship to Sydney. Like all converted steamers she was a very fast sailer, and made very good and regular passages. After a prosperous career as a Sydney trader, she was finally run into and sunk off the Nore in 1887.

" City of Agra " and " Sam Mendel."

These two early iron ships were both exceedingly fast and made many a good passage to the Colonies. *City of Agra* once landed her passengers in Melbourne when only 65 days out from the Tuskar ; on another occasion she passed Port Phillip Heads on her way to Queensland, when 63 days out; and she made the run out to Lyttelton, New Zealand, in 71 days.

In 1881, when commanded by Captain Young, she left Gravesend on 25th May, took her departure from the

"DARLING DOWNS."

"ANTIOPE."

Photo by Captain Schutze, Sydney.

[To face page 204.

Lizard on the 29th, and crossed the equator on 17th June in 27° W., 19 days from soundings. Between the N.E. and S.E. trades, she had very squally variables and lost her fore topgallant mast. She crossed the meridian of the Cape on 11th July and ran her easting down in 39° and 40° S., making a very steady average, as her best run was only 270 miles, and she crossed the Leeuwin meridian on 30th July, signalled the Otway on 5th August and arrived in Hobson's Bay the following day, only 69 days out from the Lizard.

Sam Mendel is known for her 68-day run from London to Port Chalmers in 1876. On another occasion, whilst racing one of the "Cities" to New Zealand, she lost her foremast, and I have a photograph of her as she appeared under jury rig.

Both ships lived to a ripe old age.

The *City of Agra* was wrecked on Cape Sable on the 31st March, 1907, when on a passage from New York to Bridgewater. The *Sam Mendel*, after being twice sold and twice renamed, the first time *Charlonus* and secondly *Hannah*, was at last condemned and broken up in June, 1909. Thus it will be seen that *City of Arga* was afloat 47 years and *Sam Mendel* 48 years, which speaks volumes for the good workmanship of their builders.

"Dharwar."

The *Dharwar*, which was one of Harland & Wolff's finest productions, originally belonged to the Indian "Iron Ship Company." Though the company made money in the early sixties, a slump in freights brought it into the hands of the Receiver after a very short existence. The *Dharwar* sailed for England in 1868, and on her arrival was bought by John Willis, who always had an eagle eye for a good ship. He fitted her for emigrants and during the seventies she was usually carrying passengers outward; later she became a favourite Sydney trader, and when loading at Circular Quay was usually to be seen on the cross berth opposite the old Paragon Hotel. A beautifully built ship, with teakwood decks, the *Dharwar* was also a very consistent performer, and made a good name for herself under Captain Freebody. Before settling down in the Australian trade, Captain Freebody took her to Calcutta sometimes for a Dundee jute cargo, he also took her across the Pacific, and made a very fine passage from Frisco to Liverpool in 1872-3 of 97 days. As late as 1902 I find the old ship arriving at Fremantle on 24th May, 80 days out from Barry. Willis eventually sold her to the Swedes, who sent her to the ship-breakers in 1909, after 45 years of service.

The Strange Career of " Antiope."

The *Antiope* was one of the earliest of Joseph Heap's ships, and, like all his others, had a name which no sailor could possibly pronounce correctly. Indeed when she came out many an old salt shook his head over such a name. Who ever heard of a ship called the "Anti-hope" coming to any good? However she upset the predictions of the evil prophets by being one of the luckiest ships ever launched, and at the present day must be one of the oldest ships afloat.

She was Heap's fourth ship, I believe; her sister ship, the *Marpesia*, having been launched from Reid's yard four months before her. The first ship of Heap's "Thames and Mersey Line" was the little *Hippolyta*, of 853 tons, built as far back as 1856. Then came the *Eurynome*, of 1847 tons, built at Whitehaven in 1862.

[To face page 206.

" ANTIOPE."

She had an unenviable reputation for small collisions, so was generally known as the " You're into me."

For some years the Thames and Mersey Line was managed by Thompson, May & Co., of Water Street, Liverpool. The ships carried emigrants and general cargo from Liverpool to Melbourne, then crossing to the Bay of Bengal, often with walers to Madras or Calcutta, they came home from Rangoon with Heap's rice. They generally sailed from Liverpool on the 10th of each month. In the early eighties the line was bought by Mr. Beazley to start his son, and was henceforth known as the Australian Shipping Company, managed by Gracie, Beazley & Co.

The *Antiope* made her best passage in 1868, running out to Melbourne under Captain Withers in 68 days, and but for being hung up on the line for 10 days would have gone near to breaking the record.

After Beazley sold her she was for some years in the South American trade. Then during the Russo-Japanese war she was captured by the Japanese whilst under Russian colours. The Japs sold her to Mr. J. J. R. Matheson, of Ladysmith, British Columbia, and for a short while she was in the timber trade. The world war found her lying in a New Zealand port, doing duty as a coal hulk for the Paparoa Coal Co. Here the Otago Rolling Mills bought her at a stiff price, and like many another old sailing ship, she came out of her retirement with a new set of wings in order to brave the German submarines and keep the old Red Duster flying.

In 1916, she got ashore on the coast when making for Bluff Harbour in a gale of wind, and there she lay on her side in the wash of the tide for 96 days. At last, with tonnage pretty near worth its weight in gold, an attempt was made to float her. For this purpose a large steam trawler, fitted with pumps to throw 10,000 gallons a minute, was brought down to this most southerly port in the Empire. No progress, however, was made until a journalist named Bannerman, with the inquisitiveness of his kind, got down into the *Antiope's* fore peak by means of a rope ladder and discovered the chief leak. Then, with mats over the bow, the pumps slowly overcame the water, the *Antiope* righted and finally floated. She was then towed round to Port Chalmers, docked, repaired and once more fitted for sea. From Port Chalmers she ran across to Newcastle, N.S.W., in ballast, making the trip in the good time of 12 days. Here she loaded coal for Valparaiso, after refusing a £9000 freight to the United Kingdom. Again she made a good passage. From Chile she went up to San Francisco. And she is still earning money at the wonderful age of 54 years.

"Theophane."

The *Theophane* was probably the fastest of all Heap's ships, and was built on sharper lines than the *Antiope* or *Marpesia*. On her maiden passage—the abstract log of which I give in the Appendix—she went out to Hobson's Bay under Captain Follett in 66 days.

Her first 12 passages to Melbourne were 66, 75, 75, 70 80, 73, 73, 82, 73, 75, 79 and 77 days, giving an average of 75 days, this being from the Channel.

On the 11th December, 1891, she sailed from Newcastle, N.S.W., with a cargo of coal for Valparaiso, and was never heard of again.

Messrs. Aitken & Lilburn and the Loch Line of Glasgow.

The best known line of sailing ships running to Australia since the use of iron shipbuilding has undoubtedly been the famous Loch Line of Glasgow.

" THEOPHANE."

" DHARWAR."

[*To face page* 208.

It was started in 1867 by two young men who had been in the employ of Patrick Henderson & Co.—these were William Aitken and James Lilburn. In the old days it was the custom for owners to make a daily visit to intending shippers; this was Aitken's part of the work and he continued to make a practice of it long after other owners had given it up. Lilburn superintended the loading and despatching of their ships, and so great was his practical knowledge and so keen his interest that it is no exaggeration to say that no ships were better kept up than the Loch liners. All over the world the Loch Line clippers were held up by seamen as examples of what well run and comfortable ships should be. A keen yachtsman and a one-time Commodore of the Royal Northern Yacht Club, Mr. Lilburn was a man who not only thoroughly understood ships but loved them for their own sake. And it is under such owners that sailors consider themselves lucky to serve.

The ships carried first, second and third class passengers outwards, and when steam began to cut in they still held on until they were the last of all the sailing ships to continue carrying passengers. Many an invalid or consumptive has gained fresh vigour and untold benefit from a voyage to the Antipodes in a Loch liner.

The saloon fares charged were:—£40 to Adelaide and Melbourne, £42 to Sydney, £76 for the round trip out and home.

The "Clan Ranald," "Ben Nevis" and "Loch Awe."

Messrs. Aitken & Lilburn commenced business by chartering the *Clan Ranald*, *Ben Nevis* and *Loch*

Awe. The *Clan Ranald* they eventually bought and renamed the *Loch Rannoch*.

Captain Bully Martin, who was afterwards one of the best known skippers in the Loch Line, superintended the building of the *Clan Ranald*, and took command of her for the first few years of her existence.

Bully Martin was a great personality amongst sailing ship skippers.   He was a driver of the old type, and stories referring to Bully Forbes are often mixed up with those referring to Bully Martin.   He nevertheless was such a consummate seaman that in 45 years' service as master he never cost the underwriters a penny, and only lost a couple of men, one through a fall from aloft and one from being washed overboard. He is said to have hated passengers.   He served his time in Allan's beautiful little Transatlantic sailing ships—his first ship being the *Caledonia*, a full-rigged ship carrying royals and stunsails though only of 390 tons.   She was commanded by Captain Wylie, who was afterwards marine superintendent of the Allan Line. After passing for mate, he obtained the berth in the 900-ton iron ship *Shandon*, which was fitted with patent reefing gear for topgallant sails, topsails and courses. She made three voyages a season to Montreal and in the winter ran to the Southern States for cotton.   After four years as mate, he obtained command of the *Eden-dale*, belonging to the same owners, Messrs. W. Kidston & Son, of Glasgow.   His next command was the *Lord Clyde*, which he left for the *Clan Ranald*. He commanded her for two or three voyages and then went to Watson Bros., commanding the *Ben Venue, Ben Voirlich* and *Ben Cruachan* in turn, after which he returned to the Loch Line, and after having the *Loch Ness* and *Loch Long*, commanded the *Loch Broom* until he retired from the sea in 1907, the very year, curiously enough, that Messrs. Aitken & Lilburn sold his first ship in their employ.

On 22nd February, 1907, the *Loch Rannoch* left Melbourne under Captain Morrison with the usual cargo of wool, hides and tallow for Hull, at which port she arrived on 8th June, 106 days out. After discharging she returned to Glasgow, and was then sold to the Norwegians. In November, 1910, she was again sold to the Germans, and has since been broken up.

The *Ben Nevis* after making her maiden voyage under charter to Aitken & Lilburn became one of Watson's passenger ships to Australia. On 14th July, 1897, when bound to Dunedin from Glasgow, she unexpectedly appeared in Hobson's Bay, having put in to repair damages which had taken place 12 days before in the Southern Ocean. It appeared that she had been swept from stem to stern by a tremendous wave; two of the crew had been taken overboard along with everything movable on the main deck; besides which the break of the poop had been burst in and the interior so gutted that her officers had nothing but the clothes they stood up in. The repairs cost £3000.

In 1898 the *Ben Nevis* was sold to the Norwegians and renamed *Astoria*. On 24th January, 1912, she was abandoned, dismasted, in the Atlantic, after being set on fire, her crew being taken off by the steamer Dungeness and landed at Penzance.

The *Loch Awe* is known for her record passage to Auckland, New Zealand, under Captain Weir.

> Gravesend to Auckland 73 days.
> Pilot to pilot   69 days.

As far as I know this record still holds good.

Captain Weir was a great driver, and the *Loch Awe*

came into Auckland with everything washed off her decks, including hen coops, spare spars and all her boats. She was carrying emigrants who had had a terrible time, having been battened down for days on end. On her arrival she was delayed a week, as she had reached Auckland before her papers, the mails in those days coming *via* Panama to New Zealand.

The Famous "Patriarch"—First Iron Ship of the Aberdeen White Star Line.

In 1869 the Aberdeen White Star Line gave their first order for an iron clipper ship, the result of which was the famous *Patriarch*. George Thompson was only contented with the very best, and *Patriach* was no exception to his rule. Built of the best iron plating at a cost of £24,000, she was considered the finest iron ship in the world when she first came out. She had a poop 90 feet long, under which extended a magnificent saloon. In her rigging plan she was a long way in advance of her times. Her topmasts and lower masts were in one, and her topgallant masts were telescopic, fitting into the topmasts ; and in the seventies she was fitted with double topgallant yards on fore and main, whilst she still carried stunsails in the eighties when most ships had discarded them.

As a sea boat she proved herself on numberless occasions, notably in the Indian cyclone of 1892, which she weathered out with only the loss of a lifeboat, whilst the fine Loch liner, *Loch Vennachar*, was totally dismasted 70 miles away. She possessed that very rare quality in iron vessels—dryness. And during her life of 29 years under the Red Ensign she never had a serious accident and never made a bad passage.

Patriarch's best 24 hours' run was 366 miles, and

"PATRIARCH."

Photo by Hull & Co., Sydney.

[To face page 212.

her best week's run was 2060 miles, her main royal being set the whole time.

Patriarch was no doubt lucky in her captains : Captain Pile took her from the stocks until 1876, Captain Plater had her ten voyages from 1877 to 1887, Captain Allan from 1887 to 1890, and Captain Mark Breach took her until she was sold in 1898, during which time, he says, that she never stranded a ropeyarn.

Patriarch's maiden voyage was almost as much of a record as *Thermopylae's*, each passage being the best ever made by an iron ship at that date.   On her outward passage with 40 passengers and a large general cargo, she arrived in Sydney on 10th February, 1870, only 67 days from pilot to pilot, and 74 anchorage to anchorage.   And on the homeward run she went from Sydney Heads to the West India Dock in 69 days.   This was an extraordinary performance, as anything under 90 days is very good for an iron ship on the homeward passage.

After this the *Patriarch* was one of the most regular ships in the Sydney trade.   She was never much over 80 days going out, and though she never repeated her maiden performance coming home her passages were most consistent and she only twice ran into three figures in over 20 passages from Sydney.

In 1897-8 the good old ship sailed her last voyage under the Red Ensign—a round of London, Sydney, Newcastle, N.S.W., Manila and home in 13 months. On his arrival Captain Mark Breach was horrified to find that his beloved ship had been sold to the Norwegians for a paltry £3150, and on 1st November, 1898, he hauled down the celebrated house-flag and handed her over to her new owners.

For another 14 years she washed about the seas,

unkempt, bare of paint and forgotten. Of her passages in this condition, I have picked out a couple at random :—

1908	Monte Video to Port Victoria (Make)	64 days.
1910	Bantjar (Java) to Delegoa Bay	57 days.

On Christmas Day, 1911, she left Algoa Bay for a Gulf port, and on 23rd February, 1912, got ashore on Cape Corrientes, south of the River Plate, and became a total loss.

The " Thomas Stephens."

The *Thomas Stephens* was one of the best known ships of her day. When she came out she was considered the most up-to-date and perfectly appointed passenger sailing ship ever built on the Mersey. She was intended for the old Black Ball Line, but never actually sailed under the famous flag, but sailed as one of the London Line of Australian Packets (Bethell & Co.). She was owned by Thomas Stephens & Sons, of London. Captain Richards, the well-known commander of the *Donald Mackay*, superintended her building and fitting out and eventually left the *Donald Mackay* to command her.

The *Thomas Stephens* soon proved herself one of the fastest iron ships afloat, and a very successful ship financially. She was beautifully sparred, crossing three skysail yards, and was a very lofty ship—one of the tallest ships, indeed, that ever sailed either from the Mersey or the Thames; and she carried all her stunsails well into the eighties. At first she was fitted with single topgallant yards, but followed the fashion for double topgallant yards before she had been afloat many years.

She was launched in July, 1869, and left Liverpool on 24th September, with a full passenger list for Melbourne, arriving out on 15th December in 82 days.

"THOMAS STEPHENS."

From a painting by F. B. Spencer ; lent by Messrs. Thomas Stephens & Sons.

On her second voyage she left Liverpool on 9th September, 1870, and anchored in Hobson's Bay on 21st November, 73 days, port to port. After this she always sailed from London as one of the London Line of Packets, along with her great rival *The Tweed*. And for her third voyage, I find the following advertisement in the *Times* of 5th October, 1871.

MELBOURNE—LONDON LINE OF PACKETS.

THOMAS STEPHENS.

R. RICHARDS (so well and favourably known when in command of the *Donald Mackay* and *Great Victoria*), commander. This superb clipper, 1507 tons registered, of the highest class at Lloyd's, and owned by Messrs. Thomas Stephens & Sons, is one of the finest specimens of marine architecture afloat, and made her last passage in 64 days. Constructed specially for the Australian passenger trade. Her spacious full poop saloon is fitted with bathrooms, cabin furniture, bedding, and every convenience. The second and third cabins are most comfortable. Carries a surgeon.—Bethell & Co., Cowper's Court, Cornhill, E.C.

Thomas Stephens left London on 26th October, 1871, for Melbourne, her great antagonist *The Tweed* sailing for Sydney about the same date. She crossed the line on 20th November in long. 29° 57′ W., making 12 knots with the S.E. trade blowing steadily from S.E. by S. Her best run was 315 miles in a 23½-hour day when running down her easting. This was from Saturday, 9th December to Sunday, 10th December, and her log book gives the following details :—

SATURDAY, 9th December, 1871.—Lat. 44° 50′ S,, long. 20° 34′ E Courses S.E. by E. ½ E., S. by E., S.E. by E. ½ E., S.S.E., S.E. Winds E.N.E., E. by N., variable, west. A.M., strong wind and squally, logging 10 knots. 11 a.m., heavy squalls, handed topgallant sails, crossjack, spanker and outer jib. P.M., squally with heavy rain. 4 p.m., set main topgallant sail. 9 p.m., wind veering into westward; set fore topgallant sail and main topgallant staysail. Midnight, logging 16 knots during last four hours

SUNDAY, 10th December, 1871.—Lat. 44° 48′ S., long 27° 57′ E. Courses S.E. ½ E., S.E. Winds west, N.W. Distance 315 miles. A.M.

heavy gale, high cross sea; ship labouring and straining heavily; decks at times completely flooded fore and aft. 1 a.m., main topgallant staysail stay carried away. 7 a.m., continuation of gale, logging 16 knots Heavy sea struck ship on starboard quarter, washing starboard lifeboat out of davits, completely flooding main deck and washing away main hatch-house. 9.30 a.m., gale moderating, made all plain sail, still logging 16 knots. P.M., moderate with high cross sea; decks completely flooded; have logged 16 knots during last 16 hours.

On Friday, 29th December, the westerlies were so strong that the *Thomas Stephens* had to be hove to for 4½ hours, the gale being preceded by six hours' calm with fog; the log reads as follows :—

FRIDAY, 29th December, 1871.—Lat. by acc. 45° 21' S., long. 129° 7' E. Courses N.E., E.N.E., E. by S., N.N W., N.E. Winds variable, calm, N.W., west. A.M., light variable airs, thick foggy weather. Watch hauling up cable. 10 a.m. strong breeze, dull cloudy weather, logging 12 knots. 3.30 p.m., strong gale, handed topgallant sails. 4 p.m., gale still increasing, handed upper topsails, courses and jib. Brought ship to the wind under lower topsails. Heavy sea running; decks completely flooded. 8.30 p.m., wind veering into S.W. Wore ship off before the wind. 10 p.m., set foresail and upper fore topsails, logging 10 knots.

On Saturday, 30th December, the gale still continued and the log book records :—

Lat. by acc. 43° 57' S., long. 134° 27' E. Courses N.E., N.E ¼ N. Winds W.S.W. A.M., strong gale, high sea. Shipping a quantity of water over all, logging 13 knots. 4 a.m., set upper main and mizen topsails. 7 a.m., set topgallant sails, weather moderating, logging 12 knots. 10 a.m., heavy sea. Decks at times completely flooded. P.M., strong gale and heavy sea. Shipping a quantity of water over all, logging 13 knots. 10 p.m., gale increasing. Handed fore and mizen topgallant sails, logging 14 knots. 10.30 p.m., handed main topgallant and mizen topsail. Midnight, strong gale and high sea; have logged 14 knots during last six hours.

On Tuesday, 2nd January, 1872, Cape Otway bore north, distant 2 leagues; at 7 a.m. the pilot came on board and took charge, and at 1 p.m. the *Thomas Stephens* came to anchor in Hobson's Bay, 66 days out from her Channel pilot. From Melbourne she went across to Calcutta in 45 days, with walers on board, and loaded jute home, the usual round of first-class ships in the seventies.

During her long and successful career she usually loaded outwards to Melbourne or Sydney; but in 1879 on her twelfth voyage she went out to Otago, and on her thirteenth left Liverpool on 29th April and arrived at Rangoon on 21st July, 83 days out.

In 1881 she went out to San Francisco in 124 days from Holyhead, and coming home to Falmouth in 98 days. Except for an occasional run to Frisco, Calcutta or Rangoon, she was kept regularly in the Sydney trade during the eighties and nineties.

The following is a list of her best sailing records:—

16 knots for 16 successive hours, 10th December, 1871, in 44° 48′ S., 28° 7′ E. 1000 miles in 70 hours.

16 days (the record) from Cape Horn to the line, under Captain Robertson.

1870	Liverpool to Hobson's Bay;	Sept. 9 to Nov. 21	.. 73 days
1871-2	London to Hobson's Bay;	Oct. 26 to Jan. 2	.. 68 ,,
1872	Melbourne to Calcutta;	Feb. 1 to March 17	.. 45 ,,
1872-3	Lizard to Hobson's Bay;	Dec. 4 to Feb. 11	.. 69 ,,
1873	Ushant ,, ,,	Sept. 3 to Nov. 8	.. 66 ,,
1874-5	Lizard ,, ,,	Nov. 22 to Jan. 31	.. 70 ,,
1876	Lizard ,, ,,	Aug. 7 to Oct. 24	.. 78 ,,
1877	Tuskar ,, ,,	Aug. 12 to Oct. 27	.. 76 ,,
1878	Plymouth ,, ,,	June 15 to Aug. 31	.. 77 ,,
1880	Liverpool to Rangoon;	April 29 to July 21	.. 83 ,,
1880-1	Frisco to Queenstown;	Nov. 8 to Feb. 18	.. 99 ,,
1881	Holyhead to Frisco;	Jan. 12 to May 16	.. 124 ,,
1882	Frisco to Falmouth;	June 7 to Sept. 13	.. 98 ,,
1882-3	London to Sydney;	Nov. 8 to Jan. 22	.. 75 ,,
1885	Antwerp to Sydney;	July 25 to Oct. 20	.. 87 ,,
1886	London to Sydney;	May 29 to Aug. 16	.. 79 ,,

In the later eighties her passages began to slow up for two very good reasons: firstly her sail plan was cut down; and secondly her captain, owing to a very nervous wife being with him, made no attempt to drive her.

Captain Richards had her through the seventies, except for two voyages in 1874-5 when Captain Bloomfield had her, then Captain Archibald Robertson commanded her for half a dozen voyages, he was followed by Captain W. Cross, then Captains Cutler, Davis and Belding took her in turn.

The *Thomas Stephens* was a lucky ship and kept singularly free of trouble; indeed she had no serious mishap until July, 1893, when she got well battered by a severe gale in 52° S., 130° W., whilst homeward bound from Melbourne with wheat. Her bulwarks were carried away from the fore rigging to abaft the main rigging on the starboard side and her main deck was swept clean. She put into Callao for repairs, but she was not leaking and her cargo was found to be undamaged.

On her following voyage she got into more serious trouble in battling to get to the westward of Cape Stiff. She sailed from Barry on 27th December, 1894, and was partially dismasted off the pitch of the Horn. Put back to the Falklands, arriving in Stanley harbour on 28th February, 1895. Captain Belding, however, refused to agree to the extortionate demands of the Stanley shipwrights, and sailed for Capetown under jury rig, arriving there 14th May, 1895. Here he refitted, and leaving Table Bay on 22nd June arrived at Esquimalt by the eastern route on 24th September.

This unfortunate voyage terminated her career under the Red Ensign, for on her arrival home in 1896 the *Thomas Stephens* was sold to the Portuguese Government. The Portuguese have a singularly shrewd eye for a ship; and in this year they bought at breaking up prices three of the finest and fastest ships ever built, namely the *Thomas Stephens, Cutty Sark* and *Thermopylae*.

Captain Belding was retained to sail the *Thomas Stephens* to the Tagus under her new flag. He had a Portuguese crew, and the passage was not without incident, for a fire broke out on board and it was chiefly owing to Captain Belding's personal bravery that it was extinguished. Indeed so pleased were the Portuguese with his behaviour that they presented him with a service of plate and a Portuguese Order, at the same time asking him to continue in command. For many years after this the *Thomas Stephens* served as a naval training ship in the Tagus in conjunction with the *Thermopylae*. She survived the famous tea clipper, however, and many a British naval officer has probably been aboard the famous old ship without realising that, disguised under the name of *Pero d'Alemgucr*, floated one of the crack Australian passenger ships of the seventies.

The Great War found her lying a hulk in the Tagus. The Portuguese fitted her out when tonnage began to get scarce in 1915, and sent her across to America. On her return passage to Lisbon in January, 1916, she was posted as missing—possibly a Hun torpedo sent her to the bottom—and that terrible word " missing " may be hiding some awful tragedy or glorious heroism. Anyhow her name goes on the " Ships' Roll of Honour in the Great War," along with more than one of her sisters in the Australian trade.

The First Six Ships of the Loch Line.

Messrs. Aitken & Lilburn started their venture with six splendid ships, of 1200 tons each, all built during 1869-70. These were the *Loch Katrine*, *Loch Earn*, *Loch Lomond* and *Loch Levcn*, all built by Lawrie, of Glasgow, and the *Loch Ness* and *Loch Tay*, built by Barclay, Curle & Co.

At first it had been intended to name the ships after clans, but the Clan Line registered first, and so at the start the "Lochs" were advertised as the "Clyde Line of Clipper Packets."

The *Loch Katrine* was the first ship away. She arrived in Hobson's Bay under Captain M'Callum, on 20th December, 1869, 81 days out from Glasgow. The *Loch Ness*, Captain Meiklejohn, arrived on 13th January, 1870; the *Loch Tay*, Captain Alex. Scott, on 12th February, 1870; the *Loch Earn*, Captain W. Robertson, on 31st March, 1870; the *Loch Lomond*, Captain Grey, R.N.R., on 26th May, 1870; and the *Loch Leven*, Captain Branscombe, on 19th August, 1870.

Of the six clippers, the *Loch Tay* made the best passage out, being only 73 days, anchorage to anchorage. Running her easting down, her best week's run was over 2000 miles, and she averaged 285 miles a day for nine consecutive days. Stunsails and large crews were carried by the Loch clippers right up to the end of the seventies; and the following passages under these conditions will show their speed capabilities :—

TUSKAR TO CAPE OTWAY.

Loch Katrine	.. 74 days	*Loch Earn*	..	63 days
Loch Ness	.. 68 ,,	*Loch Lomond*	..	76 ,,
Loch Tay	.. 67 ..	*Loch Leven*	..	68 ,,

Their average, pilot to pilot, 69½ days; port to port, 77 days.

Four of these ships lived to a good old age, whilst the other two came to early and tragic ends.

When sailing ship freights began to fall, the *Lochs Katrine, Tay, Ness* and *Lomond* were converted into barques, but in, spite of losing the yards on the mizen, they continued to make good passages right into the twentieth century.

The *Loch Katrine* made her best passage in 1893, from the Channel to Melbourne in 71 days.

In 1907 she was nearly lost running her easting down when bound out to Australia. It was blowing hard from the S.W., and a heavy sea broke aboard, tearing up the standard compass and washing it into the scuppers, besides smashing up a lifeboat and floating the gig out of its chocks. The next roller came right over the stern, crumpling up the wheel and binnacle and breaking in the cabin skylight. The men at the wheel were washed away, and the ship broached to, filling her main deck to the rail. All hands were called to save the ship, and as usual in such cases, it meant risking life and limb to venture along the flooded main deck and man the braces. However Captain Anderson managed to get his ship off before the wind and by the following night a jury wheel of capstan bars had been lashed on to the remains of the old wheel.

Three years later, in 1910, the *Loch Katrine* was dismasted off Cape Howe. After a perilous trip of three days, a boat in charge of her mate was picked up near the land by a Swedish steamer, and a tug was sent out from Sydney, which found the disabled ship and towed her into Port Jackson. The *Loch Katrine* was then sold in Australia, and for some years earned a living carrying coal round the coast. So far as I know she is still afloat

The fastest of these six ships, in my opinion, was the *Loch Ness*. In 1874-5 she beat the time of her maiden voyage by going out to Melbourne in 67 days. The following voyage she went out in 74 days; but what is more astonishing is the time of her passages, in her old age when cut down, rigged as a barque and with small and indifferent crews

Under these conditions she made the following five runs home from either Melbourne or Adelaide:—1893, 85 days; 1894, 87 days; 1895, 85 days; 1899, 90 days; 1900, 91 days; and she finished her active career by two splendid passages. In 1906 she came home from Melbourne to Hull, laden with wool and wheat, in 79 days; and on 20th May, 1907, she left the Tail of the Bank for Adelaide, crossed the equator 28 days out, passed the Cape meridian on 9th July, and arrived at the Semaphore anchorage on 4th August, 76 days out. On 16th June when in lat. 3° N. she fell in with a 9-knot tramp steamer bound to the southward; and the two ships were constantly in company for 2000 miles, and it was not until they were south of lat. 30° S. that the steamer saw the last of the old *Loch Ness*.

Running her easting down the *Loch Ness* averaged 245 knots for 18 consecutive days, her best day's work being just under 300 miles. Captain M. Heddle, who had previously commanded the *Loch Rannoch*, was in charge of the *Loch Ness* and deserved great credit for this fine performance as a wind up to the old clipper's career. The *Loch Ness* was sold in Adelaide along with her sister ship, the *Loch Tay*, and the celebrated pair are ending their days together as coal hulks for the N.D.L. Co. at Adelaide.

There was probably not much to choose between the two sister ships in point of speed, though *Loch Ness* had slightly the better record. *Loch Tay*, however, had many fine runs to her credit. For many years she brought wool home from Geelong, her passages being most consistent and rarely being much over 90 days.

The *Loch Earn* became world-notorious by her fatal collision with the French Transatlantic mail steamer

Ville du Havre. On 21st November, 1873, on a bright starlight night, the Loch liner struck the steamer right amidships, cutting her down to the water's edge. The *Ville du Havre* sank in 12 minutes, and Captain Robertson of the *Loch Earn* was only able to save 26 of her passengers and 61 of the crew, 226 souls in all going down in the Frenchman. The following day the American packet ship *Tremountain* was fallen in with, and Captain Robertson transferred the survivors to her and they were landed at Cardiff. Two days later the *Loch Earn*, being fatally injured by the collision, also sank, Captain Robertson and his crew being rescued by a passing ship.

The *Loch Lomond,* which in her palmy days under Commander Grey, R.N.R., was known as the Scotch man-of-war owing to her smart appearance, was a steady going ship without any very special records to her credit. In May, 1908, she was sold to the Union S.S.Co. of New Zealand to be converted into a coal hulk. Loading a cargo of coal at Newcastle, N.S.W., she left there on 16th July, 1908, bound for Lyttelton, N.Z., under Captain J. Thomson. But time went by and she never arrived, and in due course she was posted as missing. The only trace of her that was ever found was a life-buoy which was picked up on the New Hebrides.

The *Loch Leven* came to a sudden end on her second voyage. On 22nd October, 1871, she left Geelong for London with 6523 bales of wool on board, valued at £154,000. Two days later she stranded on King's Island and became a total loss. All her crew got ashore safely, but Captain Branscombe ventured back in a surf boat to rescue the ship's papers. The boat capsized and the captain was drowned.

King's Island—A Death Trap for Ships.

King's Island, lying 80 miles S.S.W. of Port Phillip Heads, has been the cause of many a fine ship's end. Nearly 50 sailing ships, from first to last, have found a grave in the King's Island surf. A Captain Davis, who for many years carried cattle between the island, Melbourne and Tasmania in the coasting steamer *Yambacoona*, made a list some ten years ago of 36 ships known to have perished on the rocky shores of King's Island. This list, which was included with other interesting data regarding tides, currents and pilotage notes of King's Island, was used by the Hydrographic Office, Washington, U.S.A., and contains the following names :—

Neva, ...	ship	wrecked	1835
Cataraque, ..	ship	,,	1845
City of Melbourne,	ship	,,	1853 refloated
Waterwitch, ..	barque	,,	1854
Bruthen, ...	schooner	,,	,,
Elizabeth, ...	ketch	,,	1855
Whistler, ...	schooner	,,	,,
Maypole, ...	schooner	,,	1856
Katherine, ...	schooner	,,	1861
Brahmin, ...	schooner	,,	1862
Favor, ...	schooner	,,	1864
Arrow, ...	schooner	,,	1865
Dart, ...	cutter	,,	,,
Netherby, ...	schooner	,,	1866
Europa, ...	brig	,,	1868
Omagh, ...	barque	,,	,,
Helen Ann, ..	ketch	,,	,,
Loch Leven, ..	ship	,,	1871
Ocean Bridge, ..	brig	,,	,,
Martha Lovinia, ..	schooner	,,	,,
Arrow, ...	barque	,,	1873
Cape Pigeon, ..	cutter	,,	1874
British Admiral, ..	ship	,,	,,
Blencathra, ..	barque	,,	1875
Dart, ...	ketch	,,	1876

" MERMERUS " alongside.

" MILTIADES."

Photo by Captain Schutze, Sydney

[To face page 225

Flying Squirrel,	..	schooner wrecked	1876
Abrona, ..	..	barquentine ,,	1877
Mary Ann,	..	schooner ,,	1878
Anna, ..	..	barque ,,	,,
Peerless, ..	..	ketch ,,	,,
Kalahone, ..	..	barque ,,	1879
Loch Lomond,	..	schooner ,,	1891
Garfield, ..	..	schooner ,,	1897
Landisfarne,	..	ship ,,	1904 refloated
Earl of Linlithgow,	ketch	,,	,,
Clytie, ..	..	ketch ,,	1906
Shannon, ..	..	schooner ,,	,,

On many parts of King's Island's rocky shore these wrecks have been piled one on top of the other, one reef of rocks alone tearing the life out of no less than six vessels. No doubt the list is far from being complete; there was no light on King's Island in the earlier days, and this no doubt was the cause of many an unknown tragedy.

"Miltiades."

George Thompson's second iron ship was the beautiful *Miltiades*, for many years a favourite ship in the Melbourne trade. Like the *Patriarch*, she was built for the emigrant trade, and in the Australian papers was spoken of as " that mammoth clipper," though to modern eyes she would look quite small and one of the daintiest of ships. Unlike *Patriarch* she was a very wet ship, especially when running in heavy weather, but she was just as fast as the *Patriarch*, if not faster—indeed taking her average, both outward and homeward, I do not think that any ship can beat her record for an iron ship except the little *Salamis*.

Captain Perrett took her from the stocks and had her until 1885, when Captain Harry Ayling assumed command. On her first voyage she carried stunsails, but when she got home the booms were sent down and never used again.

1

Her best outward passage was made in 1873, being 70 days dock to dock, 68 days pilot to pilot. She left London on 5th May, dropped her pilot off the Start on 12th May. Had very light winds to the equator, crossed the line on 6th June in 27° 30′ W., crossed the meridian of the Cape on 24th June in 44° S. On 24th, 25th and 26th June she ran 305, 310, and 345 miles. Crossed the meridian of Cape Leeuwin on 9th July, and was off the Otway on 14th July, only 20 days from the Cape, finally anchored in Hobson's Bay on the 15th; just 39 days from the equator. On this passage her decks were lumbered up with sheep pens, and one can well imagine what an unpleasant time those sheep must have had when she was running her easting down.

In 1874 *Miltiades* was diverted from Melbourne to Wellington. Emigration to New Zealand was booming and many extra ships had to be taken up; for instance the *La Hogue* took 448 emigrants to Wellington, the fine iron Calcutta clipper *Ballochmyle* took 484 to Canterbury and the *Rooparell* 361 to Auckland.

The change was very near being the end of *Miltiades*, for she missed stays whilst beating up to Wellington and slid on to a reef. Captain Perrett immediately fired his signal guns and sent up a rocket to attract attention. Luckily for him the inter-colonial steamer had just rounded the North Heads bound in and at once went to his assistance, and after one or two failures managed to get the *Miltiades* off. It was not until many years later that the *Militades* was again seen in Maoriland, but in the early nineties she made the following fine runs home:—

1890 Lyttelton to London, February 8 to April 27   78 days
1891 Wellington to London, January 14 to April 6   82 ,,

When the Aberdeen White Star sold their ships the

Italian owners of the *Titania* bought the *Miltiades*. She was finally condemned and broken up in 1905.

Carmichael's Superb Wool Clipper "Mermerus."

This beautiful ship was one of the finest and most successful of all the iron wool clippers, and as a specimen of an iron sailing ship she could hardly be beaten, either for looks, speed or sea worthiness. Barclay, Curle never turned out a more graceful and handsome ship as looks; and like all Carmichael's, she was most beautifully sparred, crossing the main skysail yard, which was so characteristic a feature of their ships. I give her spar plan below.

SPAR PLAN OF *MERMERUS*.

Spars	Fore	Main	Mizen
Masts—deck to truck	156 feet	161 feet	135 feet
Lowermast	64 ,,	68 ,,	56 ,,
Doubling	16½ ,.	16½ ,,	14 ,,
Topmast	57 ,.	57 ,,	48 ,,
Doubling	11 ,,	11½ ,,	10 ,,
Topgallant mast	32 ,,	32 ,,	26 ,,
Royal mast	17 ,,	17½ ,,	15 ,,
Skysail mast	13½ ,,	13½ ,,	12½ ..
Lower yard ·..	87 ,,	88 ,,	73½ ,,
Lower topsail yard	74½ ,,	76 ,,	62 ,,
Upper topsail yard	73 ,,	73½ ,,	60 ,,
Lower topgallant yard	57½ ,.	60 ,,	52 ,,
Upper topgallant yard	56 ,.	56 ,,	45 ,,
Royal yard	44 ,,	44 ,,	32 ,,
Skysail yard		32 ,,	

Jibboom 72 ft.	Spanker boom 55 ft.	Spanker gaft 37 ft.

This is her original spar plan. Barclay, Curle planned her spars for three skysails, but the fore and mizen were not sent aloft. *Mermerus* had a poop 54 feet long, and a foc's'lehead 32 feet long. She carried a cargo of 10,000 bales of wool, representing the fleeces of a million sheep and worth £180,000 more or less as wool varied in price.

She never made a bad voyage under the Golden Fleece house-flag, and the regularity with which she arrived every year in time for the February wool sales caused her to receive the most out-spoken praise. On one occasion, when as usual she had arrived in time and several notable ships had missed the sales, Mr. Young, of the Australian Mortgage Land and Finance Company, greeted one of the Carmichaels in Cornhill with the heart-felt remark:—"That ship of yours is the most satisfactory ship in the wool trade."

Most of those connected with the *Mermerus* regarded her with great affection and spoke of her as a living thing. Mr. John Sanderson, a well-known Melbourne merchant, was often heard to say:—"The *Mermerus* is a wonderful ship, I can always depend on the *Mermerus*."

The Melbourne people, indeed, looked upon her as the pride of their port; and Lord Brassey, when Governor of Victoria, heard so much about her that he paid her a special visit and inspected her with the approving eye of a seaman.

Captain W. Fife commanded her until 1888, and then Captain T. G. Coles had her until she was sold to the Russians. Except for her third voyage she was always in the Melbourne trade, but in April, 1874, she went out to Sydney. On this passage she took out a dozen South Sea Island missionaries as passengers. Whilst in the North Atlantic she happened to be becalmed for a few hours, and several turtle were noticed lying asleep on the water close to her. Captain Fife, who was a great fisherman, immediately launched a boat and succeeded in capturing six of them.

The *Mermerus* duly arrived in Sydney early one morning in June after a splendid passage of 72 days. The passengers, on the morning of her arrival, were joined at breakfast by a troop of friends, who so enjoyed themselves that they all returned, sky-pilots and friends as well, to the mid-day shipboard dinner, and at its finish declared that they would all return again for supper. This was too much for Captain Fife and he plainly said so. The parsons thereupon began grumbling at his meanness, whereat the irate skipper fairly boiled over:—"You are the greediest lot I ever carried," he thundered; "on a 70-day passage you have eaten up 140 days of cabin stores and six turtle besides—and you call me a stingy Scottie. Now clear out and never let me see you again."

This voyage she did not come home with wool, but went up to Newcastle, N.S.W., and loaded coal at 24s. for San Francisco. After making the passage across the Pacific in 56 days, she loaded 2420 tons of wheat at £4 1s. 3d. for Liverpool. She finally arrived in the Mersey on the 25th May, 104 days out from Frisco. This must have been a good voyage for her owners, as the freight on the outward passage to Sydney alone came to £5000.

On her next voyage she left Liverpool Docks on 21st July, 1875, and went from the Tuskar to Melbourne in 69 days; this time she loaded wheat home.

She made her best passage out in 1876; leaving London on the 25th June, she took in gunpowder at Gravesend, and arrived in Hobson's Bay on 30th August, exactly 66 days from the Gravesend powder buoys to Melbourne. The powder was only just 66 days on board, being landed on the 67th day. She crossed the line on 17th July and the Cape meridian on 6th August. Her best homeward run was made the following year, when she was 71 days to the Lizard, and then was held up by head winds. And in

1886-7 she docked in London only 78 days out from Melbourne.

And as she grew older, her splendid average in no way deteriorated. In 1896 she went out to Melbourne in 76 days, and in 1897, her last voyage under the British flag, she went out in 77 days. She was then sold to the Russians, but they kept her going. On 4th February, 1902, she arrived at Port Adelaide from Cardiff only 78 days out, whilst in 1904 she made the best passage home from the Antipodes of the year, from Adelaide to the Wight in 69 days.

This beautiful ship came to her end at the beginning of December, 1909. She had sailed from Frederickstadt on 29th November, timber laden for Melbourne, and stranded near Christiansand in a heavy fog; she was floated again, but was found to be so damaged that it was not thought worth the money to repair her, so on 28th April, 1910, she was sold to the shipbreakers.

Devitt & Moore's "Collingwood."

Collingwood was Devitt & Moore's first venture into the Melbourne wool trade. She was one of the early Aberdeen built iron clippers, and thoroughly looked her part. Though she made no very remarkable passage, her voyages were very regular, and it was not often that she missed the wool sales. You could not wear out these early iron ships, and the *Collingwood* has the distinction of being on the " Ships' Roll of Honour in the Great War,'' being sunk by a German submarine on 12th March, 1917, whilst under Norwegian colours. The story is of the usual kind. The officers and crew of the U-boat were drunk with champagne and cognac obtained from the French ship *Jules Gommes*, which they had sunk two hours previously. The crew of the

" HESPERUS."

From a lithograph.

[To face page 230.

Collingwood were given ten minutes only to get clear of the ship. The captain, being a neutral, naturally wanted his papers examined for contraband, but the German U-boat commander sneeringly told him that there would be time enough to èxamine them when the submarine got home, and so one more was added to Germany's long list of crimes, and the famous old flyer sank beneath the waves after 45 years of honest service.

"Hesperus" and "Aurora," the First Iron Ships of the Orient Line.

In 1873-4 Robert Steele & Co., the celebrated builders and designers of some of the fastest and most beautiful tea clippers, built two magnificent iron clippers for the Orient Line. These were the *Hesperus* and *Aurora*, sister ships.

The *Aurora* unfortunately was destroyed by fire on her first homeward passage, through spontaneous combustion of her wool cargo. This occurred on 9th August, 1875, in 40° N., 35° W., and she was finally abandoned in flames with fore and mainmasts gone.

The *Hesperus*, her sister ship, is I, believe, still afloat. Steele put some wonderful workmanship into the building of these ships, everything was of the best; deck fittings were all of picked teak, with enough brass to outshine a steam yacht. Besides being a very comfortable ship for passengers, *Hesperus* soon proved herself a hard ship to keep with. But like most of the big passenger clippers of the seventies she did not race home, but made a comfortable passage *via* the Cape. This ship, in fact, was never hard driven, or she would have had many more fine passages to her credit.

She was a stiff ship in spite of a tall sail plan, and she

used to send up skysail yards in the tropics though she did not habitually carry them crossed.

Anderson, Anderson kept the *Hesperus* in the Adelaide trade until 1890, when she was bought by Devitt & Moore for Lord Brassey's training scheme.

The Brassey Cadet Training Scheme.

In the year 1890 it was felt by the late Lord Brassey, Sir Thomas Devitt and others who were interested in our Mercantile Marine, that it was time some effort was made to train apprentices on the old system of the Blackwall frigates, whereby parents by paying a larger premium could be sure that their sons learnt more seafaring than how to wash out a pig pen or clean brasswork during their four years' apprentice-ship and also could rest assured that they would receive good food and treatment. This was all the more necessary because it had gradually come to be the custom in many sailing ships to use the apprentices merely as drudges to do all the dirty work aboard, the historic ship's boy having been for many years extinct on deep water ships; at the same time very few captains gave their apprentices any instruction in navigation. The result of this was that parents were less inclined than ever to send their sons to sea.

With both steamship and sailing ships being run to the closest margin possible for the sake of economy, it was seen by those who studied the question that not only was the Mercantile Marine failing to get as good a class of officer as it should do, but also that if the condition of the apprentice was not improved there would soon be a shortage.

A great deal of the glamour of sea life had already departed. Cleaning hen coops on a close-run windjammer had little of the old romance about it, and chipping iron work on a dingy steam tramp had even less. A few firms, of which those in the wool trade were shining examples, still took a pride in their ships and did not look upon them merely as a commercial asset, and these still took trouble to train their apprentices. Beyond these and a few individual ships with conscientious captains, the apprentice was absolutely neglected, and of course the apathetic Board of Trade did nothing. The history of the Board of Trade has been mostly that of a masterly inactivity, and on the rare occasions on which it has displayed activity, it has not usually been for the benefit of the Mercantile Marine.

It was entirely owing to Lord Brassey and Mr. Devitt, as he was then, that we possess such highly trained officers as those who now command the present day liners. They set the ball rolling which was later taken up by most of the big steamship lines. Luckily for the success of the venture, Messrs. Devitt & Moore possessed two or three captains in their employ who were specially fitted for the arduous task of controlling and teaching a shipload of 30 or 40 high-spirited boys. Of such were Captains Barrett, Corner and Maitland.

The first two ships to be specially fitted to carry an extra number of big premium apprentices or cadets, as they should be called, were the famous Orient pair, *Hesperus* and *Harbinger*, which were taken over by Devitt & Moore for the purpose.

The *Hesperus* as a cadet ship made some very fine passages.

She left London on 11th September, 1891, and arrived Sydney on the 8th December 88 days out. There happened to be a gold rush up country and her crew cleared out, leaving the cadets to do everything during the four months the ship was waiting for a wool cargo. The cadets were not idle and played the usual pranks of their kind, and finally the *Hesperus* left Sydney with the three brass balls of a famous pawnbrokers in Argyle Cut dangling from the end of her jibboom before the envious eyes of the apprentices of all the ships in port.

On 11th October, 1892, she left London with Captain Barrett in command, F. W. Corner, chief officer, and Lieut. Hackman, R.N., as naval instructor. She was off the Lizard on the 13th and crossed the equator in 30° W. on 8th November. The meridian of Greenwich was crossed on 29th November in 42° S. Her best runs in easting weather were 300, 302, 319, 326 and 328 miles, whilst her best week's work were 1830, 1840 and 1898. She arrived at Melbourne on 23rd December, 71 days from the Lizard.

In the following year she again left on the 11th October and took her departure from the Lizard on 18th October. On 1st November, at 1.10 a.m., when in 26° 20′ N., 17° 56′ W., the shock of a submarine volcano made the ship tremble very much, though the surface of the water was not disturbed. The equator was crossed in 25° W. on 8th November. And on 30th November, the day before she crossed the Cape meridian, three icebergs were sighted. On 10th December with a strong north wind and smooth water, the *Hesperus* ran 363 miles in the 24 hours. This was done without the mainsail which, at 4 a.m., was badly torn whilst all hands were attempting to reef it and it had to be furled.

On 28th December at 6 p.m. the Otway was sighted during a strong southerly gale with heavy squalls; for some hours the ship was hove to whilst the gale was at its height, but on 29th December the *Hesperus* anchored in Hobson's Bay, 72 days from the Lizard.

Plan of Ships
Ben Cruachan & Ben Voirlich
Nos 237 & 238

SAIL PLAN OF " BEN CRUACHAN " AND " BEN VOIRLICH."

[To face page 284.

The *Hesperus* kept up this fine average, serving as a cadet training ship until 1899 when she was sold to the Russians, who renamed her the *Grand Duchess Maria Nikolaevna*, but continued her as a training ship in the Black Sea. As late as 1918 she was refitted by Swan & Hunter at Wallsend. She has survived the war and the Bolshevists, and not long ago could have been seen in the Liverpool Docks.

"Ben Cruachan" and "Ben Voirlich."

These two splendid sister ships were amongst the hardest driven of those in the Melbourne trade. They carried saloon, second cabin and steerage passengers out and wool home—and there was no snugging down for the convenience of the sorely tried emigrants with such skippers as Captains Bully Martin and McPetrie.

On her maiden passage, *Ben Cruachan*, under Bully Martin, left the Clyde on 5th October, 1873, passed the Tuskar light on 7th October, crossed the equator 26 days out in 24° 30′ W., crossed the meridian of the Cape on 21st November in 46° 30′ S., and running her easting down averaged 300 miles a day from the Crozets to the Leeuwin between 27th November and 6th December. On 13th December she arrived in Hobson's Bay, 67 days out from the Tuskar. This passage, however, was cast in the shade by *Ben Voirlich's* run in 1874-5 on her second voyage, and on her maiden passage *Ben Voirlich* only took two days longer from the Tuskar than her sister ship.

Ben Voirlich, on her maiden passage, left Glasgow under Captain McPetrie, on 3rd January, 1874. But she was held up at Greenock by bad weather until the 26th and did not pass the Tuskar until the 27th. From the Tuskar she had 15 days of head winds, crossing the equator on 19th February in 26° 30′ W. The Cape meridian was passed on 15th March and the Otway on 5th April. Her best work was between the 15th and 27th March, when she averaged 12½ knots. She arrived in Hobson's Bay on 6th April, 69 days out from the Tuskar.

On her second trip, *Ben Voirlich* left Gravesend on the 9th November, Plymouth on 11th November, but was held up in the mouth of the Channel over the 12th. She crossed the equator on 1st December in 31° 20′ W.; crossed the Cape meridian on 24th December, in 45° S., and ran down her easting on the parallel of 46° 30′, her best 24-hour run being 352 miles. She arrived in Port Phillip on 14th January, 64 days out from Plymouth.

From pilot to anchorage Captain McPetrie claimed to have broken *Thermoplyae's* record; and on *Thermopylae* arriving in Melbourne on 4th February, only 64 days out from the Lizards, a fine wrangle started.

It was a specially favourable season, and *Ben Voirlich* was very hard driven, indeed in the roaring forties her main deck was never free of water, and the midship house and half-deck were water-logged all the time. She possessed a very hard nut of a mate, a bald-headed man with a great red beard, who was a very fine seaman. But he had no mercy on the boys, his usual greeting to a delicate-looking first voyage apprentice being '' Have your people sent you to sea to escape funeral expenses or what ? ''

The *Ben Voirlich* had a winch just aft of her midship house, to which the fore braces were taken in the following way. The fore brace had a wire pennant with a gin block on its end. A chain was shackled to the ship's side, then led through the gin block and down again through the bulwarks to the winch and so on to the other fore brace, thus making an endless chain. It had stoppers on it on each side to keep a little slack. In bracing the yard, it took in on one side and gave out the other, and only needed two men to work it.

SPAR PLAN OF *BEN CRUACHAN* AND *BEN VOIRLICH*.

Spars	Fore	Main	Mizen
Mast—deck to trnck	139 feet	143½ feet	115 feet
Lower mast	60 ,,	64½ ,,	50½ ,,
Doubling	16 ,,	16 ,,	13½ ,,
Topmast	54½ ,,	54½ ,,	43½ ,,
Doubling	12 ,,	11½ ,,	9 ,,
Topgallant mast	30½ ,,	30½ ,,	26 ,,
Royal mast	21 ,,	21 ,,	18 ,,
Lower yard	84 ,,	84 ,,	70½ ,,
Lower topsail yard	73 ,,	73 ,,	59 ,,
Upper topsail yard	70½ ,,	70½ ,,	57 ,,
Lower topgallant yard ..	58½ ,,	58½ ,,	45 ,,
Upper topgallant yard ..	56 ,,	56 ,,	43 ,,
Royal yard	43 ,,	44 ,,	35 ,,
Jibboom 70 ft.	Spanker boom 51 ft.	Spanker gaff 36 ft.	

Though she made many good passages, she never again approached the time of her second outward passage. On her homeward passage in 1878 she broached to when running heavy to the westward of the Horn and was nearly lost. This occurred on the 18th November. A very big sea was running, and the helmsman, a Dutchman, let go the wheel from sheer fright. As the ship broached to a huge wave broke over her quarter. This avalanche of water smashed in the break of the poop, gutted the cabin, and took nine men overboard. For an hour the ship lay over on her beam ends dragging her lower yards in the water, entirely out of control. Two men who happened to be at work on the lee fore yardarm were actually washed off it. One of them was lost overboard, but the other caught the rail and lay there head downwards, being held from going further by the chain fore sheet. An apprentice managed to get to him and grab hold, but the next moment a sea swept over them, and whilst the apprentice was washed inboard, the man was never seen again. The same apprentice happened to be washed up against the winch, to which he clung like a limpet; and then, as the old white-bearded sailmaker was hurled by him in the cross wash of the sea, caught the old man and held on to him or he would have gone overboard.

The brave ship struggled gamely; three times she brought her spars to windward, and three times she was laid flat again. The whole of her topgallant rail and bulwarks were washed away, together with everything of a movable nature on the deck. At last after a whole hour of desperate fighting, they managed to get the wheel up, and the clipper slowly righted herself as she fell off and brought the wind astern.

Captain Ovenstone, who was in command at the time, spoke several ships in the Atlantic and told them of his near shave. One of these reported it to a homeward-bound steamer, the consequence was that when the *Ben Voirlich* arrived those on board found their parents and relations in a great state of mind, not knowing who had been amongst the nine victims and who was safe.

In 1885 the *Ben Voirlich* had almost as bad an experience to the southward of the Cape of Good Hope, when bound out to Melbourne under Captain Bully Martin. At 8 a.m. on the 6th August a terrific squall from W.N.W. struck the vessel and in a moment the foresail had blown to rags. By 10 a.m. it was blowing a hurricane, the ship scudding before it under fore and

"COLLINGWOOD."

"SAMUEL PLIMSOLL."

Photo lent by F. G. Layton.

[*To face page* 239.

main lower topsails. An hour later a tremendous sea pooped her, and washed away the two helmsmen and Captain Martin who was conning them. Captain Martin and the quartermaster, a man named Scott, were swept up against a hen coop, which was lashed up to the bucket rail at the break of the poop, with such force as to smash it to pieces; but it saved them from going over the side. As soon as they could pick themselves up, they made a dash for the wheel, which they found smashed in two and only hung together by its brass rim. Scott held the wheel whilst Captain Martin cleared away the broken part, which was jamming it, and they were just in time to save the ship from broaching to. The lee wheel, a foreigner, had meanwhile got into the mizen rigging and lashed himself with the turned up gear. The seas now broke over the ship in a continuous cascade, and the *Ben Voirlich* could only be worked from the poop and foc's'le-head, to which the crew succeeded in leading the braces. All that night a wild sea looted the ship. Both the standard and steering compasses were swept overboard. The port lifeboat on the skids was smashed to pulp; the topgallant bulwarks were stripped off her, and the poop ladders, harness casks, hen coops, handspikes and such like were all carried off by the tremendous sea.

As soon as daylight broke, they managed to lash up and repair the wheel; then the second class passengers were moved from the midship house to the poop, as Captain Martin feared that the house would be burst in and gutted by the seas raging aboard over the broken bulwarks. But again the *Ben Voirlich* safely weathered it out, and four weeks later dropped anchor in Hobson's Bay.

The two famous Bens were kept in the Melbourne trade until 1885. Then in 1886 both ships went to

Sydney, the *Ben Cruachan* in 90 days and the *Ben Voirlich* in 94 days. But in 1887 they bade a final good-bye to the wool trade and went into the San Francisco wheat trade. *Ben Voirlich* left London on 22nd May and arrived Frisco on 23rd September—124 days out. This was a very good run for the westward passage round the Horn.

The *Ben Cruachan* was not so fortunate. She left the Tyne on 4th May and did not arrive in San Francisco Bay until 15th October—164 days out.

The *Ben Cruachan* ended her days under the Mexican flag and was known as the *Carmela*, and I believe she still does duty as a hulk in a Mexican port.

The *Ben Voirlich* was sold to the Germans in 1891 and converted into a barque. In 1903 the Germans sold her to the Italians, who renamed her the *Cognati*. During the winter of 1908 she was badly damaged by collision with an iceberg off the Horn, but managed to make port. She can now be seen at Leith, where she is serving as a domicile for the crews of surrendered German ships. Here she lies a mast-less hulk, covered with deck-houses, but fitted below with electric light and every comfort.

These two sister ships were very evenly matched. Though not as fast as some of the iron wool clippers, they made up for it by hard driving and generally managed to get home in well under three figures.

" Samuel Plimsoll."

Famous as had been the Aberdeen White Star wooden clippers, the iron ships launched for Thompson in the seventies may almost be said to have eclipsed them. And not least of these magnificent vessels, either in speed, appearance or sea qualities was their third iron ship, the *Samuel Plimsoll*, named after a man who at that time was receiving broadside after broadside of abuse in shipping circles, yet who to-day is counted one of the greatest, if not the greatest, benefactors of our merchant seamen.

The *Samuel Plimsoll* was launched in September, 1873, and christened by Mrs. Boaden, wife of Captain Boaden, in the presence of Samuel Plimsoll, Esq. Captain Boaden left the famous *Star of Peace* in order to take *Samuel Plimsoll* from the stocks. She came out as a double topgallant yarder and was specially fitted for emigrants.

On her maiden passage she took out 180 emigrants. Leaving Plymouth on 19th November, she had poor winds and very light trades to the line, which was crossed on 11th December in 29° W. The meridian of Greenwich was crossed on 2nd January, 1874, and the Cape meridian four days later. Her best run in the 24 hours was 340 miles, and between the Leeuwin and the S.W. Cape, Tasmania, she was only four days. On the 17th January she overhauled and passed the *Alexander Duthie*, and finally arrived in Port Jackson on 1st February.

Whilst loading for London she was thus advertised in the *Sydney Morning Herald*:—

ABERDEEN CLIPPER LINE—For London.

THE SPLENDID NEW CLIPPER SHIP.

SAMUEL PLIMSOLL.

100 A1, 1444 tons. reg. R. BOADEN, late of the *Star of Peace*, commander.

This magnificent vessel has just completed the passage from Plymouth in 73 days, and having a large portion of her cargo stowed on board will leave about 7th April.

As this vessel has lofty 'tween decks and large side ports, she offers a good opportunity for intermediate passengers, of which only a limited number will be taken. Carries an experienced surgeon.

For freight or passage apply to Captain Boaden or to Montefiore, Joseph & Co. Wool received at Talbots.

From the very first *Samuel Plimsoll* proved herself a very fast ship. Her best performance was 68 days to Sydney from 190 miles W.S.W. of the Bishops, when commanded by Captain Henderson, who had been chief officer on her first two voyages, and left her to command the *Wave of Life, Moravian* and *Thermopylae*, eventually returning to her as commander in 1884.

Samuel Plimsoll's logs show that she revelled in the roaring forties. In 1876, when in 41° S., she ran 2502 miles in eight days, her daily runs being 348, 330, 301, 342, 320, 264, 340, 257. In 1883 she averaged 278 miles in 13 consecutive days, her best being 337. In 1895, when homeward bound, she ran from 49° 50′ S., 179° 05′ W., to 55° 25′ S., 79°59′ W. in 15 days, 29th November to 12th December, her daily distances being— 244, 286, 263, 259, 261, 273, 302, 290, 257, 253, 274, 264, 314, 235, 245—equalling 4020 miles.

The *Samuel Plimsoll* was in the Sydney trade until 1887; she was then transferred to the Melbourne trade. On her first passage to Melbourne, she left London 2nd March, 1888, dropped her pilot off the Start on 5th March, but was only 270 miles from the Start on the 15th owing to westerly gales; she crossed the equator 5th April, in 26° W., and averaged 218 miles a day from Trinidad to 130° E., her best run being 310 miles. She arrived in Hobson's Bay on 22nd May, 79 days from the Start. During the whole of her career under the Aberdeen house-flag, her only mishap was the carrying away of a fore topmast: and this freedom from casualties was the case with most of Thompson's green clippers.

Writing about the increase of sailing ship insurance rates in 1897, Messrs. Thompson remarked :—

Five of our sailing vessels now in the Australian trade, viz., *Aristides, Miltiades, Patriarch, Salamis* and *Samuel Plimsoll* are over 20 years of age, but they are in as good condition, by careful looking after and up-keep, as they were upon their first voyage; whilst they have a record that no general average homewards has ever been made on under-writers by any one of them since they were launched 21 to 28 years ago. (A remark which applies with equal truth to all our sailing vessels now running.) According to a reliable statement made up by the largest shippers and consignees of wool carried by our sailing ships during the last two years, we find that the claims thereon made on the underwriters, from inception of risk (which in many cases began in distant parts of the Colonies before shipment) were £149 1s. 7d., which, on 24,807 bales carried, valued at £12 per bale, came only to 1/- per cent. These figures clearly show that age does not affect the efficient carrying of cargo by vessels, built, as ours have been, of superior strength and scantlings, carefully kept up and treated in every way with a view to the safe carrying of valuable cargoes to and from Australia.

On the occasion of her only mishap a tropical squall carried away the bobstay, and down came the fore top-mast and main topgallant mast. It happened that a Yankee clipper was in company; this vessel beat up to the dismantled *Samuel Plimsoll* and sent a boat off with the message that she was bound to Australia and would gladly tranship the passengers and carry them on to their destination. This offer, Captain Simpson, who then commanded the *Samuel Plimsoll*, declined with thanks, so the American went on her way.

It was all day on until the Aberdeen flyer had fresh masts aloft, and then she settled down to make up the lost time. And nobly she did so, one week's work in the roaring forties totalling 2300 miles, and she even-tually arrived at Melbourne, 82 days out. Some days later the Yankee arrived and her captain at once went to the *Samuel Plimsoll's* agents and reported speaking her dismasted in the Atlantic, at the same time he commented on her captain's foolhardiness in not transhipping his passengers.

"Is it Captain Simpson you are referring to?" asked the agent.

"Yes," returned the Yankee.

"Wall," said the agent, imitating the American's leisurely drawl, "I guess you had better speak to him yourself. He's in the next room."

In 1899 the famous old ship caught fire in the Thames and had to be scuttled. After being raised and repaired she was sold to Savill of Billiter St., who ran her until 1902 when she was dismasted and so damaged on the passage out to Port Chalmers that they decided not to repair her. She was subsequently towed to Sydney from New Zealand at the end of a 120-fathom hawser, and later taken round to Western Australia where she · was converted into a coal hulk.

And here is a description of her as she lies at her moorings in Fremantle harbour :—

From quay to midstream buoy, and from buoy to quay, she is plucked and hauled. Occasionally she feeds a hungry tramp with coal. Abashed and ashamed of her vile uncleanliness she returns to her midstream moorings where most of her time is spent in idleness and neglect. One looks in vain for the long tapering spars and the beautiful tracery of her rigging. Stunted, unsightly derricks have replaced them. The green-painted hull is now transformed into a dull red, a composition red that cries aloud, not of beauty, but of utility. Regularly with each returning ebb and returning flood of the Swan, she swings to her moorings the composition smeared effigy of *Samuel Plimsoll*, alternately facing towards river and sea. Marine life has made of her plates a habitation and refuge; her bottom is foul with the dense green growth of years. Her costly fittings, solid brass belaying pins and highly burnished, brass-covered rails and spotless decks, where are they? Coal-gritted baskets, whips and tackles are strewn along the decks: they all proclaim her squalid and servile calling.

Amongst these old hulks, however, she is withal the most dignified looking, the graceful lines of her hull lending her an air of distinction at once apparent even to the layman. As coal hulking goes, she is perhaps the most fortunate of her class. Days pass—weeks—perhaps months, all spent in slothful idleness and neglect, whilst her more unfortunate sister hulks scarcely know a day but what they are not coal feeding some important steam-driven interloper.

" Loch Maree "—the Fastest of the Lochs.

The *Loch Maree* was also launched in September, 1873. She was an especially beautiful ship in every way and the fastest probably, of all the "Lochs," Barclay, Curle were instructed to spare no expense in making her as perfect as an iron ship could be, and she certainly came up to her owners' expectations, both in her looks, her outfit as an up-to-date passenger clipper, her speed, and her behaviour as a sea boat.

Underneath a poop of over 50 feet in length, she had her first class passenger accommodation arranged on the plan adopted in the P. & O. steamers.

She crossed three skysail yards, had a full outfit of stunsails and other flying kites, and the following spar plan will give one an approximate idea of her sail area.

SPAR PLAN OF *LOCH MAREE*.

Spars	Fore	Main	Mizen
Mast—deck to truck	148 feet.	153 feet	130 feet
Lower mast	63 ,,	68 ,,	59½ ,,
Doubling	16 ,,	16 ,,	13 ,,
Topmast	54 ,,	54 ,	44½ ,,
Doubling	11 ,,	11 ,,	9 ,,
Topgallant mast	34 ,,	34 ,.	28 ..
Doubling	6 ,,	6 .,	5 ,,
Royal and skysail masts ..	30 ,,	30 ,,	25 .,
Lower yard	84 ,,	84 ,,	69 ,,
Lower topsail yard	71 ,,	71 ,,	57 ,,
Upper topsail yard	69 ,,	68 ,,	54½ ,,
Lower topgallant yard ..	55 ,,	55 ,,	43½ ..
Upper topgallant yard ..	51 ,,	51 ,.	40 ,,
Royal yard	41 ,,	41 ,,	31½ ,,
Skysail yard	30 ,,	30 ,,	24 ,,
Jibboom 70 feet	Spanker boom 50 feet	Spanker gaff 36 feet	

Loch Maree's start in life was an unfortunate one. On 5th November, 1873, she sailed from the Clyde for

Melbourne under Captain MacCallum with a full cargo, 11 saloon and 30 second cabin passengers, and the following is an account of her maiden voyage, which was given me by one of her apprentices :—

On the tenth day out, we were bowling along sharp up on the starboard tack, near the Island of Palma in the Canary group, when a squall struck her flat aback with such violence, that in a few moments her tall masts with their clothing of well-cut canvas lay a hopeless tangle over the side. Everything above the lower masts disappeared under the magic breath of the squall. When the wreckage was finally cleared away, the driving power was limited to a foresail, a crossjack and a lower mizen topsail. The mainyard had been snapped in the centre, one half lay on the rail and the other hung by the slings, rasping and tearing with every roll. But the crippled sailer, unlike the crippled steamer, can usually make a very creditable effort for safety. A course was set for Gibraltar. Improvised canvas, mostly of the fore and aft variety, was rigged up, and in 14 days the Rock was reached in safety, To show her wonderful sailing qualities, when two days from Gibraltar, we overhauled and easily passed a 600-ton barque under royals.

Captain MacCallum watched the barque as she fell away astern, and remarked : " If I had only thought she could sail like this, I would have kept on for Australia."

The *Loch Maree* arrived at Gibraltar on the last day in November. and after being refitted sailed from the Straits on 20th January, 1874, and ran out to Melbourne in 74 days, arriving there on the 4th April, 150 days out from the Clyde.

She sailed from Melbourne homeward bound on 14th June, ten days behind the *Carlisle Castle* of Green's Blackwall Line. On the 14th day out, a sail appeared ahead at 11 in the forenoon. We were at the time swinging along with topgallant stunsails set on fore and main and a three-cornered lower stunsail.

Captain MacCallum, though Scotch, had sailed mostly in Yankee ships and was a veritable whale for " kites."

" Take in that three-cornered stunsail and set a square one," he ordered, " I want to be alongside that fellow this afternoon."

At 3 p.m. we were side by side with the *Carlisle Castle*. She flew no kites, her royal and skysail yards were down and the crossjack unbent, She was taking it easy and arrived in London three weeks after us.

On that same passage *Loch Maree* put up a remarkably fine spin from abreast of Fayal to the Downs, which distance she covered in 4½ days. On the run we overhauled a fleet of 12 schooners bound from the Azores to England, all bunched together in a radius of 3 or 4 miles. With topgallant stunsails set and everything drawing to a spanking breeze on the port quarter, we rushed through the centre of the group of fruiters, each one of whom was doing her best with topmast and lower stunsails set.

I had often listened to the tales of old sailors, portraying in vivid language the fabulous speed of these little vessels, but alongside a smart 1600 tonner, with a skipper who knew how to crack on, they cut but a sorry figure. The *Loch Maree* was doing at least 3 knots more than any of them, and in a very short time they were mere silhouettes on the skyline.

Right up the Channel the kites were carried, and when morning broke off the Isle of Wight a sail was discerned ahead, which daylight proved to be a big barquentine rigged steamer under all sail. We had evidently crept up on her unobserved in the darkness, for when the discovery was made that a windjammer was showing her paces astern, volumes of black smoke belched in sooty clouds from her two funnels, as if entering a protest against such a seeming indignity. But, in vain, she fell away in our wake as the fruit schooners had done a couple of days before.

Loch Maree's times, both out and home, from this date were generally amongst the half-dozen best of the year. Captain Grey, R.N.R., had her on her second voyage and then Captain Scott took her.

In 1878, when homeward bound from Melbourne, the Lizard was sighted on the 68th day out, but the passage was spoilt by hard easterly winds in the Channel.

In 1881, the *Loch Maree* made Port Phillip Heads on 19th July, 70 days out from the Channel. On 29th October she left Geelong homeward bound. When a day out she was spoken by the three-masted schooner *Gerfalcon* off Kent's Group, and that was the last seen of her. It is significant that another big ship, the *North American*, a transformed Anchor Line steamer, disappeared at the same time, also homeward bound from Port Phillip.

The Tragedy of the "Loch Ard."

The ill-fated *Loch Ard* was the largest vessel owned by Aitken & Lilburn until Barclay, Curle built those two splendid four-posters, the *Lochs Moidart* and *Torridon*.

Her maiden passage was one of the unluckiest on record. She lost her masts almost before she had cleared the land and put back to the Clyde to refit. She made a second start on 26th January, 1874, and again, whilst running her easting down, was badly dismasted, only the mizen lower mast and 15 feet of the mainmast being left standing. After rolling in the trough of the sea for four days of the greatest peril her crew managed to get her under a jury rig, and she took 49 days to cover the 4500 miles to Hobson's Bay, where she arrived on 24th May, 118 days from the date of her second start.

As I have already related, the year 1874 was a disastrous one for dismastings; and when the *Loch Ard* struggled into Melbourne, she found the *John Kerr* and *Cambridgeshire*, both on their maiden voyages, lying there in a similar plight to her own. Besides these ships and the *Loch Maree*, the following were also dismasted this year on their maiden passages:—*Rydal Hall, Norval, Chrysomene* and *British Admiral*. The latter was refitted in England, only to be wrecked on her second attempt, on King's Island, on 23rd May, 1874, with great loss of life.

The *Loch Ard* on her unfortunate maiden passage had been commanded by Captain Robertson, who, also, was skipper of the *Loch Earn* when she collided with the *Ville du Havre*. On her third voyage the *Loch Ard* was taken by Captain Gibb, who was a stranger to Australian waters. He married just before sailing. The *Loch Ard* left Gravesend on 2nd March, 1878. She was spoken by the *John Kerr*, Captain W. Scobie, on 9th April. But between 5 and 6 on the morning of 1st June, the day after the *John Kerr* had arrived in Hobson's Bay, the *Loch Ard* went ashore 27 miles from the Otway, at Curdies' Inlet, between Port Campbell and Moonlight Head.

Out of 52 souls on board, only two were saved, an apprentice and a passenger. About these two a romance has been woven, which would have done for Clark Russell. Tom Pearce, the apprentice, displayed such gallantry and pluck in saving the passenger, Miss Carmichael, that he became the hero of the hour in Australia. He was one of those people, however, who have the name " Jonah " attached to them by sailors, for a year later he suffered shipwreck again, in the *Loch Sunart*, which was piled up on the Skulmartin Rock, 11th January, 1879. The story goes that Tom Pearce was washed ashore and carried up in a senseless condition to the nearest house. This happened to be the home of Miss Carmichael, who fittingly nursed him back to health, with the proper story book finish that he married her. Whether this is true or not, Pearce lived to be a Royal Mail S.P. captain. He finally retired from the sea in 1908 and died on 15th December of that year.

I now commence a series of tables of outward passages to Australia. These have been compiled with as much care as possible, but slips will creep into lists of this kind, and I should be very grateful if any reader who is able to correct a date from an original abstract or private journal would write to me, so that the mistake may be set right in future editions. I have not always filled in a date, as where there was any want of proof I have preferred to leave it blank.

Besides the regular traders, I have tried to include every ship making the outward passage under 80 days, thus we find some of Smith's celebrated " Cities " and a numbher of the frigate-built Blackwallers figuring in the lists. As regards outsiders, I have had to omit several ships for want of sufficient data, but I think my lists are complete as far as the regular traders are concerned.

PASSAGES UNDER 80 DAYS TO SYDNEY IN 1873.

Ship	Departure	Crossed Equator	Crossed Cape Meridian	Passed S.W.Cape Tasmania	Arrived	Days Out
Samuel Plimsoll -	Plymouth Nov. 19	Dec. 11	Jan. 7 '74	Jan. 28 '74	Feb. 1 '74	74
Cutty Sark - -	Channel Dec. 16	Jan. 4 '74	Jan. 30 '74	Feb. 25 '74	Mar. 4 '74	78
Patriarch - -	Channel Apl. 12	May 9	June 8	June 24 (passed Ot.	June 30	79

PASSAGES UNDER 80 DAYS TO MELBOURNE IN 1873.

Ship	Departure	Crossed Equator	Crossed Cape Meridian	Passed Cape Otway	Arrived	Days Out
Miltiades - -	Start May 12	June 6	June 24		July 15	64
Thomas Stephens -	Ushant Sept. 3	Sept 24	Oct. 16	Nov. 7	Nov. 8	66
Ben Cruachan -	Tuskar Oct. 7	Nov. 2	Nov. 21		Dec. 13	67
Loch Tay -	Tuskar Sept. 6	Sept. 28	Oct. 22	Nov. 13	Nov. 14	69
Thermopylae -	Start Dec. 6	Dec. 30	Jan. 20 '74	Feb. 15 '74	Feb. 16 '74	72
Mermerus -	Lizard July 6	July 30	Aug. 19		Sept. 16	72
Sam Mendel -	Tuskar July 26	July 26			Oct. 6	72
The Tweed -	Lizard Sept. 6	Sept. 30	Oct. 25		Nov. 18	73
Marpesia -	St. Albans Oct. 17	Oct 17			Dec. 29	73
Theophane -	Tuskar Aug 30	Sept. 25	Oct. 17	Nov. 9	Nov. 12	74
Jerusalem -	Lizard June 29	July 24	Aug. 22	Sept. 14	Sept. 14	77
Strathdon -	Start Aug. 23	Sept. 21		Nov. 7	Nov. 9	78
City of Hankow -	Portland Dec. 3	Jan. 1 '74	Jan. 21 '74		Feb. 19 '74	78
Loch Lomond -	Tuskar June 25	July 23	Aug. 18	Sept. 12	Sept. 13	79

The homeward runs I have had to put in the Appendix for want of space, as this part has run to far greater length than I had contemplated at first.

The races to catch the wool sales will thus be found in Appendix F, under the heading of " The Wool Fleet.'"

Notes on Passages to Australia in 1873.

The fine passage of *Miltiades* and the maiden passages of *Samuel Plimsoll* and *Ben Cruachan* I have already described. The 66 days of *Thomas Stephens* was a very fine performance. She left Gravesend on

"LOCH GARRY."

[To face page 250.

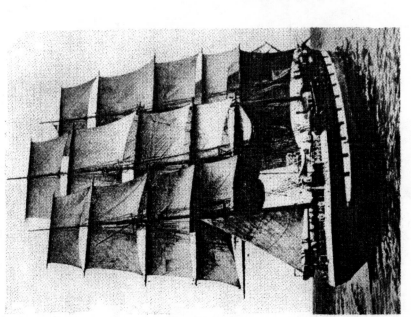

"RODNEY."

Photo lent by F. G. Layton.

30th August, with a very heavy general cargo, which put her down in the water like a sand barge. She crossed the equator in 26° 55' W. and was then forced over on to the South American coast near Pernambuco by very unfavourable S.E. trades. The meridian of Greenwich was crossed on 12th October in 44° 33' S. Her best week's work running down the easting was 2055 miles, and she would have equalled the run of *Miltiades* but for 48 hours of calm in the neighbourhood of the Otway. She arrived in Melbourne after an absence of only seven months, including nine weeks in London.

Loch Tay, which left Glasgow on 4th September under Captain Scott, also lost a day becalmed off the Otway. She crossed the equator in 29° W. and the meridian of Greenwich on 18th October in 39° S. Running the easting down she averaged 276 miles a day for 19 days, her best day's work being 336 miles.

Of the others nothing special calls for notice. *Thermopylae* left Gravesend on 2nd December, and had a light weather passage all the way, though she went as far as 47° S. in search of wind. *Cutty Sark* also was handicapped by very light winds. She ran her easting down in 40° S. with light winds and calms from the S.E. trades to Port Jackson.

This was the *Tweed's* first visit to Melbourne. This magnificent clipper was probably the tallest ship ever seen in Hobson's Bay. And wherever Captain Stuart took her she compelled admiration both for her majestic appearance and wonderful sailing performances.

Devitt & Moore's Crack Passenger Ship "Rodney."

Messrs. Devitt & Moore always considered the *Rodney* to be the fastest of their iron ships. She was also one of the finest specimens of the passenger sailing ship in its last phase.

The following account from an Australian paper of November, 1874, will give a good idea of the *Rodney's* accommodation for passengers.   It is also interesting as showing what was considered luxury in the seventies and comparing it with the present day :—

To render voyaging as easy and pleasant as possible has long engaged the attention of shipowners, but it is only of late years that it has become a special study to make the accommodations for oversea passengers not merely comfortable but absolutely luxurious.

The change in this respect since the time when only a certain amount of cabin space was provided is something akin to a transformation. The worry and bother of attending to the fitting up, as well as the extra expenditure of time and money, are now avoided, and with very little need for previous provision or preparation, the intending voyager nowadays can step on board ship and find his cabin carpeted and curtained and fitted up with almost all the accessories and appointments of a bedroom in a hotel.

An inspection of the *Rodney* will convince the most fastidious that the entire question of passenger comfort has been thought out fully and amply.   The *Rodney* is an iron clipper of beautiful model and is what is termed a 1500-ton ship.   She has been constructed specially with a view to the conveyance of passengers, and there are few sailing ships coming to the colony which have such a spacious saloon.   It measures 80 feet in length and has berthing accommodation for 60 people.   No cost has been spared in the decoration and embellishments, and yet these have not been promoted at the expense of solid and material comfort.

The cabins are 10 feet square, and a number of the sleeping berths can be drawn out so as to accommodate two people.   For each cabin there is a fixed lavatory, supplied with fresh water from a patent tap, and by the removal of a small plug in the centre of the basin, the water runs away right into the sea, so that all slopping is avoided.   The lavatory is fixed on top of a cupboard, which answers all the purposes of a little chiffoniere, being fitted up for the reception of bottles, glasses, brushes, etc.

There is also a chest of drawers in each cabin—a very great convenience—in which may be kept clothes, books, linen and many " unconsidered trifles," which generally go knocking about in ships' cabins at sea.

The windows in the cabins are large, admitting plenty of light and air, and the passengers have easy control over them. The ventilation, in fact, is all that could be desired. Good-sized looking-glasses and handy little racks for water-bottles, tumblers, combs, brushes, etc., also abound, and in other little matters the comfort of the passengers has been well cared for.

The cabins are also so arranged that two or more or even the whole of them on one side of the ship afford communication to each other without going out into the saloon, and where families are together this is very advantageous.

The bathroom occupies the space of one of the largest cabins, and hot as well as cold baths are attainable.

The saloon is lighted by two large skylights, one of them being 21 feet in length. They are emblazoned with very pretty views of Melbourne, Sydney, Adelaide, and Capetown, these being the principal ports to which Messrs. Devitt & Moore's vessels trade. There is also a piano in the saloon, by which the tedium of a voyage may be enlivened, and the tables are so constructed that they can be easily unshipped and the saloon cleared for dancing.

For gentlemen there is a capital smoking-room at the top of the companion leading from the saloon to the deck.

The accommodation in the 'tween decks for second cabin and steerage passengers is everything that could be desired, and there is quite an elaborate system adopted for ventilation.

Cooking can be done in the galley for 500 people, and there is a steam condenser, which can distil 500 gallons of water daily.

The passengers of all classes who came out in this ship on her maiden voyage here expressed themselves wonderfully well pleased with the ship and her commander, Captain A. Louttit, who has had great experience in the passenger trade.

The *Rodney's* best passage was to Sydney in 1887, when under Captain Harwood Barrett, with Captain Corner of training ship fame as his mate. On this occasion she ran from the Lizards to Sydney in 67 days, and 68 days from pilot to Sydney. Her best passage home was 77 days from Sydney to London. Her best run to Melbourne was 71 days in 1882, and to Adelaide 74 days in 1880.

The *Rodney* was sold in 1897 to the French and renamed *Gipsy*. On her previous voyage she had encountered terrible weather both out and home, and was even robbed of her figure-head by the raging sea; it was probably on account of the damage sustained on this voyage that Devitt & Moore sold her.

On the 7th December, 1901, the *Rodney* was wrecked on the Cornish coast, when homeward bound from Iquique with nitrate. The ship became a total loss but the crew were saved.

Nicol's "Romanoff."

Romanoff was Alexander Nicol's finest iron clipper until the *Cimba* came out. Nicol's ships were always good lookers, painted Aberdeen green with white masts and yards and scraped jibboom and topmasts, they fully upheld the Aberdeen reputation. *Romanoff* was a fast ship, but was overmasted with double topgallant yards and skysails, and after a few years she was severely cut down. She was a very regular Melbourne trader. She ended her days under the Norwegian flag.

Duthie's "Cairnbulg."

The *Cairnbulg* was another Aberdeen ship, but she was in the Sydney trade. She was of about the same speed as the *Romanoff*, a fine, fast, wholesome ship without any very special records to her credit.

She came to a most unusual end. After being sold to the Russians and renamed *Hellas*, she was sold by them to the Danes and called *Alexandra*. On the 26th November, 1907, she sailed from Newcastle, N.S.W., for Panama, coal laden. In April she was taken off the overdue list and posted as missing, being uninsurable at 90 guineas. The following June, one of her boats in charge of the mate, was picked up off the South American Coast. The mate then told the following

" THESSALUS."

" THESSALUS."

Photo by Hall & Co., Sydney.

[To face page 254.

extraordinary story :—On 8th May the ship was abandoned owing to her provisions running out and for no other reason—as in every other way, both in hull and gear, she was perfectly seaworthy. The position of the *Cairnbulg* when abandoned, was given as 500 miles off the South American Coast. A search expedition was at once sent out after her, but in vain. Some time afterwards she was found ashore on the rocks at Iguana Cove, Albemarle Island, with her back broken. Her insurances, hull, freight and cargo amounted to £30,000, and she was abandoned in calm weather through lack of provisions. This story is not to the credit of either her captain or her owners.

The Speedy "Thessalus."

Thessalus, Carmichael's largest three-master, was one of the finest and fastest sailing ships ever seen in Australasian waters. Though not a regular wool clipper like the *Mermerus*, she was well known both in Sydney and Melbourne. But she was also as well known in Calcutta and San Francisco, and wherever she went she always made fine passages.

Here are a few of her best :—

AUSTRALIAN PASSAGES.

1878	Start to Melbourne	67 days.
1882	London to Sydney	79 ,,
1884	Downs to Sydney	77 .,
1887	London to Sydney	79 ,,
1893	Cardiff to Sydney (*via* Capetown)	78 .,
1894	London to Sydney (*via* Capetown)	78 ,,
1896	Sydney to London	75 ,,

CALCUTTA PASSAGES.

1876	Calcutta to London	90 days
1878	Calcutta to Dundee	98 ,,
1879	Penarth Roads to Calcutta	98 .,

FRISCO AND W.C.N.A. PASSAGES.

1883	Frisco to Lizard	..	..	..	105 days.
1885	Frisco to Hull	..	..	..	125 ,,
1888	Portland, Ore., to Queenstown		..	98 ,,
1889	Frisco to Queenstown		..	..	104 ,,
1890	Swansea to Frisco ..		..	..	113 ,,
1890	Frisco to Lizard	..	..	..	109 ,,
1892	Frisco to Queenstown		..	..	101 ,,

CROSS PASSAGES.

1878	Melbourne to Calcutta	..	..	48 days
1880	Calcutta to Melbourne	..	..	49 ,,
1882	Sydney to Frisco ..	..	..	55 ,,
1884	Sydney to San Pedro	..	..	66 ,,
1884	Frisco to Newcastle, N.S.W.	..	45 ,,
1886	Newcastle, N.S.W., to Frisco	..	50 ,,

On her third voyage she encountered the cyclone of 31st October, 1876, near the Sandheads. Captain E. C. Bennett, foreseeing the approach of the cyclone, stood over to the east side of the Bay of Bengal, and considered himself lucky to escape with the loss of his topgallant masts.

Lashed on top of his main hatch, he had a large kennel containing a pack of foxhounds for the Calcutta Jackal Club. When the cyclone began, the hounds were let out of the kennel, to give them a chance to save themselves; and shortly afterwards the kennel was washed clean over the lee rail without touching it. The hounds had meanwhile disappeared and everyone thought that they must have gone overboard; but when the weather cleared they all came out, safe and sound, from under the lower foc's'le bunks, where they had taken refuge.

This cyclone wrought havoc amongst the Calcutta shipping, and cost the underwriters over £100,000. *Thessalus* was lucky to get off with a repair bill of £380.

The *Thessalus* was lucky with live freight. On her seventh voyage she took horses from Melbourne to

Calcutta and landed them all alive and in prime condition. Shortly afterwards the *Udston* arrived with
only four horses alive. She had had bad weather in the
Bay of Bengal, the horses had broken loose and in their
fright kicked each other to death. On this voyage,
Thessalus returned to Melbourne with wheat bags,
wool packs and camels. The camels also arrived in
good condition. At Melbourne she loaded wool for
London at a penny per pound.

Her best wool passage was in 1896, when she left
Sydney on the 17th October and was only 75 days to the
Start, where she signalled on 81st December. She had
left Melbourne in company with *Cimba* and *Argonaut*.
Argonaut made a long passage, but *Thessalus* and
Cimba were twice in company, concerning which
Captain Holmes of *Cimba* wrote:—

I left Sydney in company with *Thessalus* and *Argonaut*. I was
twice in company with *Thessalus* on 3rd October in 54° S., 152° W., to
5th October 54° S., 143° W., and on 25th November in 36° S., 34° W. I
came up on him in light winds, but when he got the breeze he just
romped away from me as if I was at anchor. *Thessalus* was a wonderfully fast ship. I think the German five-master *Potosi* is the only one
I have seen to touch her.

This is high praise, for Captain Holmes had a great
knowledge of ships, especially in the Australian trade,
and he had a very fast ship in *Cimba*, which on this
occasion reported at noon at the Lizard when *Thessalus*
was reporting at Start Point.

After a long and successful career *Thessalus* was sold
to the Swedes in 1905, when she was still classed 100 A1.

Notes on Passages to Australia in 1874.

1874 was *Ben Voirlich's* great year. It will be
noticed, however, that on her record passage she had
Lochs Ness and *Maree* on her heels the whole way.

K

Both Lochs had just changed their commanders, Captain Meiklejohn going to the *Loch Ness* and Captain Charles Grey succeeding Captain McCallum in *Loch Maree*. *Loch Ness* chased *Ben Voirlich* very closely all the way to the Australian Coast, her best 24-hour run being 321 miles. But *Loch Maree* dropped back in the roaring forties through no fault of her own. On 13th and 14th December she experienced a tremendous gale from east working round to S.W. with high confused sea, during which her patent steering gear was completely smashed up; and this prevented her from taking full advantage of the westerlies, as Captain Grey decided it would not be safe to go further than 42° S.

PASSAGES UNDER 80 DAYS TO SYDNEY IN 1874.

Ship	Departure		Crossed Equator	Crossed Cape Meridian	Passed S.W.Cape Tasmania	Arrived Port Jackson	Days Out
Cutty Sark - -	Start	Nov. 21	Dec. 11	Jan. 1 '75	Jan. 26 '75	Feb. 2 '75	73
Mermerus - -	Start	Apl. 14	May 8	May 29	June 24	June 27	74
Hallowe'en - -	Start	April 9	Apl. 30	May 22	June 17	June 22	74
Patriarch - -	Wight	June 8	July 2	July 26	Aug. 19 (Otway)	Aug. 24	77
Jerusalem - -	Plymouth Apl.	5	Apl. 29	May 21	June 14 (Otway)	June 22	78

PASSAGES UNDER 80 DAYS TO MELBOURNE IN 1874.

Ship	Departure		Crossed Equator	Crossed Cape Meridian	Passed Cape (Otway)	Arrived Hobson's Bay	Day Out
Thermopylae - -	Lizard	Dec. 2	Dec. 25	Jan. 14 '75		Feb. 4 '75	64
Ben Voirlich - -	Plymouth Nov. 11		Dec. 1	Dec. 24		Jan. 14 '75	64
Loch Ness - -	Tuskar	Nov. 11	Dec. 1		Jan. 16 '75	Jan. 18 '75	68
Ben Voirlich - -	Tuskar	Jan. 27	Feb. 19	Mar. 15	Apl. 5	Apl. 6	69
Thomas Stephens -	Lizard	Nov. 22	Dec. 12		Jan. 29 '75	Jan. 31 '75	70
Ben Cruachan -	Cape Clear Sept. 4		Sept. 29	Oct. 20	Nov. 13	Nov. 14	71
Romanoff - -	Lizard	Nov. 5				Jan. 16 '75	72
Theophane - -	Tuskar	Aug. 16	Sept. 12	Oct. 3		Oct. 30	75
City of Hankow -	Channel	Nov. 19				Feb. 2 '76	75
Loch Lomond -	Tuskar	Nov. 30				Feb. 14 '75	75
Loch Maree - -	Channel	Nov. 6	Dec. 1	Dec. 25	Jan. 22 '75	Jan. 23 '75	78

Cutty Sark and *Thomas Stephens* also had a great race, the famous tea clipper making the best passage of the year to Sydney.

Both ships were off the Lizards on 22nd November, and experienced very baffling winds to the equator, which *Cutty Sark* crossed in 26° W. and *Thomas Stephens* in 29° W. a day later. *Cutty Sark* was 65 days from the Lizards to S.W. Cape, Tasmania, whilst *Thomas Stephens* was 68 days to the Otway, where she was becalmed for 14 hours.

Thermopylae, with a 64-day passage from the Lizards, her best run being 348 miles, arrived just in time to defend herself, for Captain McPetrie was declaring to all and sundry that *Ben Voirlich* had broken *Thermopylae's* record, by making a better run from port to port.

The "Loch Garry."

Many experts considered the *Loch Garry* to be the finest sailing ship in the world at the date of her launch. She certainly was an example of the well-known Glasgow type at its best.

A new feature was adopted in the placing of her masts. Her mainmast was stepped right amidships, with the fore and mizen masts at equal distances from it.

Loch Garry, her sister ship *Loch Vennachar*, Green's *Carlisle Castle*, Nicol's *Romanoff* and the American ship *Manuel Laguna* were rigged in a manner peculiar to themselves. They had short topgallant masts with fidded royal and skysail masts, on which they crossed royals and skysails above double topgallant yards. When in port their upper topsail and upper topgallant yards would be half mast-headed, and with the seven yards on each mast, all squared to perfection, they presented a magnificent appearance. *Loch Garry's* first commander was Captain Andrew Black, a very fine seaman indeed. He commanded her from 1875 to 1882.

He was succeeded by Captain John Erskine, who was followed by Captain Horne.

With regard to her merits, the veteran Captain Horne, who commanded her for close on 26 years, wrote to me :—

The *Loch Garry* is a front rank ship and always will be so. She is a ship that has got no vices and when properly loaded is as gentle as a lamb. It is quite a pleasure to sail such a ship, which might be des- cribed as a 1500-ton yacht. She is not a ship of excessive speed, but with a moderately fresh breeze will maintain a speed of 10 or 11 knots without much exertion.

Loch Garry's best run under Captain Horne was on 26th December, 1892, when running her easting down in 40° S. With a N.W. wind and smooth sea she covered 334 miles. It is very possible that she exceeded this in her early days when she carried a stronger crew. She was also a good light weather ship. In 1900 she went from the South Tropic to the North Tropic in 14 days 2 hours.

The following passages of recent date will show that Captain Horne kept the *Loch Garry* moving in spite of the lack of a good crew of sailormen :—

1892 Tuskar to Cape Otway 71 dy	1903 Port Philip Heads to	
1894 Downs to Melbourne 77 ,,	Lizard .. .. 74 dy	
1895 Lizard to Melbourne 77 ,,	1904 Melbourne to Dover 77 .,	
1895 Melbourne to Prawle Pt.80 ,,	1905 Tuskar to Cape Borda 73 ,,	
1900 Melbourne to Prawle Pt.85 ,,	1905 Equator to Leuwin 36 ,,	
1901 Adelaide to C. Otway 48 hr.	(Average 240 knots)	

The following account of Captain Horne's care of his boats and system for provisioning them should be a lesson for younger masters. It is taken from the *Melbourne Herald* :—

A feature of *Loch Garry's* equipment, in which Captain Horne takes a justifiable pride, is the system for provisioning the lifeboats, should it ever be necessary to abandon the vessel. In two minutes the appren- tices can place enough provisions in the boats to last all hands 14 days. The lifeboats are on the after skids and the falls are always kept rove, In each boat are two 15-gallon breakers, which are kept full of fresh water, charged about once a month. Then in a strong wooden box, fitted with beckets, is stowed a good supply of biscuits, in protected tins. whilst in another box a number of tins of meat are packed together with the necessary opening knife. A third box contains miscellaneous articles, such as medical comforts, clothing, tobacco, a hatchet, knives and a compass. The three boxes are always kept handy in the lazarette, the provisions they contain being changed each voyage, so that the biscuits and meat are always fresh. One man can easily lift either of the boxes and the equipment is completed by the lifeboats' sails and all necessary gear being kept in a canvas bag close by. The system is simplicity itself, and Captain Horne says that he would like to see some such plan made compulsory by the B.O.T. in all ships.

The career of Captain Horne, who was the veteran skipper of the Loch Line, is worth recording. He was born in 1834, apprenticed to the sea at 15 years of age, and only retired in 1911, after 62 years at sea and 47 years in command without experiencing shipwreck, fire or collision. The motto of his life, which he always emblazoned on the cabin bulkhead, was:—''Never underrate the strength of the enemy.'' Like many another old seaman, he was not pleased with the changes brought about by steam and cut-throat competition.

Just as Captain Horne's apprenticeship finished the Crimean war broke out, and, volunteering for active service, he was appointed to the three-decker H.M.S. *Royal Albert*, the largest ship afloat. He was rated as A.B., but soon promoted to be second captain of the maintop. Sir George Tryon was a junior lieutenant on this ship. The *Royal Albert* was in the engagement against the Kinburn Forts on the north shore of the Black Sea. At the close of the war Captain Horne received the Crimean and Turkish medals and was paid off on the *Victory*. He then returned to the Merchant Service and served in 1859 as second mate of the tea clipper *Falcon* under Captain Maxton. Subsequently he was attached to Lord Elgin's embassy and placed in charge of a lorcha by Lindsay & Co., of Shanghai. As a member of Lord Elgin's staff, he was present at the taking of the Taku Forts and was on the house-boat which was towed to Tientsin by one of the gunboats; and he remained there until the treaty was signed.

After this he was 13½ years in the employ of John Allan & Sons. In 1877 he joined the Loch Line and took command of the *Loch Sloy*, leaving her to take charge of the *Loch Garry* in 1885.

The *Loch Garry* only had two severe mishaps in her long life. In August, 1880, when running under topgallant sails off the Crozets in a heavy beam sea, the weather forebrace carried away, the fore topmast went above the eyes of the rigging and took main topgallant mast with it—and *Loch Garry* was a month getting to Melbourne under jury rig. She was rigged in Geelong with Kauri pine topmasts and long topgallant masts, as shewn in the illustration. In August, 1889, she was dismasted in a furious gale to the south'ard of the Cape. To save the ship Captain Horne was obliged to jettison some 100 tons of cargo in the shape of gunpowder, hardware, whisky, bottled beer, paper, etc. The main and mizen masts carried away close to the deck, but Captain Horne succeeded in sailing his vessel 2600 miles to Mauritius, under foresail and fore lower topsail. Here the *Loch Garry* was delayed some months whilst new spars were sent out from England, and she eventually reached Melbourne on 14th February, 1890, eight months out from Glasgow. After 36 years of good service, she was sold in March, 1911, to the Italians for the scrap iron price of £1800.

"Loch Vennachar."

One of the finest and fastest of the Lochs, as well as one of the most unfortunate, was the *Loch Vennachar*, launched from Thomson's yard in August, 1875.

She was usually one of the first wool clippers to get away from Melbourne, and for many years, sailing in

"LOCH VENNACHAR."

" LOCH VENNACHAR."

Photo lent by F. G. Layton.

[*To face page* 262.

October, she made very regular passages home, her average under Captain Bennett being 86 days for 12 passages.

Her first misfortune was in 1892, when she was dismasted during a cyclone in the Southern Indian Ocean.

The following is an account of the disaster, given in the *Melbourne Argus* :—

The *Loch Vennachar* left Glasgow bound for Melbourne on 6th April, 1892, with a crew of 33 all told and 12 passengers, four of whom were ladies. All went well with the ship until she reached lat. 39° 55′ S., long. 27° 21′ E., when at 8 o'clock on the evening of 3rd June the barometer began to fall ominously and sail was promptly shortened. Darkness lifted soon after 5 o'clock in the morning and the break of day showed the terrific head seas that swept down upon the vessel, lashed by the north-east gale. (At this time both watches were aloft fighting to make the foresail fast.) Captain Bennett, who was on the poop, saw the danger of his crew and at once resolved to sacrifice the sail. He sang out to the mate to send the men aft and the hands, who had been lying out on the pitching foreyard, gained the deck in safety and reached the poop in time. As they did so, two enormous waves bore down upon the ship, which rode slowly over the first, and sank to an interminable depth in the trough at the other side. Whilst in this position the second wave came on towering halfway up the foremast, and broke on board, *filling the lower topsail 60 feet above the deck*, as it came.

Hundreds of tons of water swept over the ship in a solid mass from stem to stern, thundering inboard on the port side of the foc's'le and racing away over the main deck and over the poop, where most of the crew were standing. Every man on the poop was thrown down, and when they regained their feet they perceived that the foremast and mainmast were over the side, and the mizen topmast above their heads had disappeared. Not a man on board actually saw the spars go or even heard the crash of the breaking rigging so violent was the shock and so fierce the howling of the hurricane. The cook was washed out of his galley and swept overboard, the galley being completely gutted of everything it contained.

For nine days after her dismasting, *Loch Vennachar* lay unmanageable, rolling in the trough of the sea, whilst the gale still raged. At last with immense difficulty a jury mast was rigged forward and a sail set on the stump of the mizen mast; in this trim Captain Bennett managed to get his lame duck into Port Louis, Mauritius, after five weeks under jury rig. The ship lay in Mauritius for five months whilst new masts and spars were being sent out to her from England.   On the arrival of the masts, Captain Bennett and his crew showed their smartness by completely rerigging her in 10 days, the cost of the refit coming to £9071.

On 18th November *Loch Vennachar* at last proceeded on her voyage, and after a light weather passage arrived in Port Phillip on 22nd December 260 days out from the Clyde.   As soon as her anchor was on the ground, her crew assembled at the break of the poop and gave three ringing cheers for Captain Bennett and his officers, who had brought them safely through such a trying time. For saving his ship under such difficulties, Captain Bennett was awarded Lloyd's Medal, the Victoria Cross of the Mercantile Marine.

In November, 1901, when anchored off Thameshaven outward bound to Melbourne with general cargo, *Loch Vennachar* was run down by the steamer *Cato*.   The steamship struck her on the starboard bow, and the Loch liner went down in 40 feet of water.   All on board, however, were saved, including a parrot and a cat, the only cat to escape out of seven on the ship.

The *Loch Vennachar* lay at the bottom of the Thames for a month and was then raised.   After repairs and alterations to the value of about £17,000 were made on her, she was pronounced by experts to be as good as the day she was launched; and she once more resumed her place in the Australian trade.

About September, 1905, when bound from Glasgow to Adelaide, she came on the overdue list.   On 6th September she was spoken " all well " by the ss. *Yongala*, 160 miles west of Neptune Island.   But as the days passed and she did not arrive, grave anxiety began to be felt.   On 29th September, the ketch *Annie Witt* arrived at Adelaide, and her captain reported picking up a reel of blue printing paper 18 miles N.W. of Kangaroo Island. This paper was identified as part of *Loch Vennachar's* cargo. A search was made on Kangaroo Island and wreckage was discovered which made the disaster only too sure. It was concluded that she had run on the Young Rocks in trying to make the Backstairs Passage. Captain Hawkins, late of the *Loch Ness*, was in command, having taken her over from Captain Bennett the year before.

As if the fatal curse of Jonah had been transmitted from father to son, T. R. Pearce, a son of the twice wrecked Tom Pearce, was one of the apprentices lost in her.

"Salamis"—an Iron "Thermopylae."

Salamis, one of the most beautiful little ships ever launched and without doubt the fastest of all Thompson's iron ships, was really an enlarged *Thermopylae* in iron,.as she was built from Bernard Waymouth's lines with a few minor alterations and improvements. The following comparison of their measurements shows that *Salamis* was roughly 100 tons larger and 10 feet longer than *Thermopylae* :—

Measurements of	*Salamis* Iron Ship	*Thermopylae* Composite Ship
Registered tonnage net	1079 tons.	948 tons.
Registered tonnage gross	1130 ,,	991 ,,
,, ,, under deck	1021 ,,	927 ,,
Length	221.6 feet.	212 feet.
Breadth	36 ,,	36 ,,
Depth	21.7 ,.	20.9 ,,
Depth moulded	23.7 ,,	23.2 ,,

In *Salamis*, Thompson's were determined to have an out and out racer, and she was not fitted for passengers,

her raised quarterdeck being only 48 feet long as against
Thermopylae's 61 feet.   She had a tremendous sail
plan and of course spread a full suit of stunsails and
other flying kites.

The following spar measurements show that she set
even more canvas than *Thermopylae*, her mainyard being
a foot longer, and the other yards in proportion :—

SPAR PLAN OF *SALAMIS*.

Mainmast—deck to truck ..	150 feet.
Main lower mast	66 ,,
Main topmast	52 ,,
Main topgallant mast ..	34 ,,
Main royal mast	23 ,,
Main masthead	2 ,,
Main lower doublings	15 ,,
Main topmast doublings ..	12 ,,
Mainyard	81 ,,
Main lower topsail yard ..	72 ,,
Main upper topsail yard ..	64 ,,
Main lower topgallant yard ..	57 ,,
Main upper topgallant yard ..	49 ,,
Main royal yard	37 ,,
Jibboom	66 ,,

Messrs. Thompson, when they gave Hood the order for
Salamis, intended her for the same round as *Thermopylae*—out to Melbourne with general cargo, then
across to China and home again with tea.   But by 1875
the steamers had got a firm hold on the tea trade, and the
clippers were either being driven away into other trades
or had to content themselves with loading at a cut rate
in the N.E. monsoon; and practically only *Cutty Sark*
and *Thermopylae* were still given a chance to load the new
teas.   This was not a bright outlook for a newcomer with
her reputation all to make, and the only time *Salamis*
loaded a tea cargo home was on her second voyage when
she came home from Hong Kong in 110 days.   In 1878
she made another attempt to get a tea cargo home, but

"THOMAS STEPHENS," "CAIRNBULG," "BRILLIANT," AND
"CUTTY SARK," in Sydney Harbour.

[To face page 266.

"SALAMIS."

Photo lent by F. G. Layton.

freights were specially bad this year, and she was withdrawn from the berth at Shanghai, and finally came home with wool from Port Phillip.

As a wool clipper she set up a wonderful record; her average for 18 consecutive passages to Melbourne being 75 days pilot to pilot, and for her outward passages from 1875 to 1895 her average was 77 days. Homeward with wool, like all iron ships, she occasionally got hung up and topped the 100 days, nevertheless here she also had the best average for an iron ship, of 87 days for 18 consecutive wool passages from Melbourne to London. Her best run from London to the equator was made in 18½ days. Twice she ran from the equator to the Cape meridian in 21 days, and twice she ran her easting down from the Cape meridian to Cape Otway in 22½ days, and no less than four times in 28 days. Captain Phillip left the *Harlaw* to take the *Salamis*, and his name is associated with her during the whole of her life under the British flag.

On her maiden passage *Salamis* left London on 6th July, took her departure from the Start on the 10th, then had very buffling winds to the equator, which she crossed on 2nd August in 25° W.; the S.E. trades were very poor and she had to make a tack off the Abrolhos Rocks. The Cape meridian was crossed on 24th August in 44° S. Running her easting down, the wind was very changeable, being mostly from the south'ard, and without any steady breezes her best run was only 304 knots. She passed the Otway on 16th September and entered Port Phillip Heads the same evening, 68 days from Start Point.

On her second voyage she had a very protracted start, losing three anchors and chains in the Downs and also a man overboard during a very severe gale. She had to slip her third anchor and get underweigh in a hurry to avoid dragging ashore. After this she had to go into Plymouth to get new anchors and chains. She finally left Plymouth on 24th March, 1876, the " dead horse " being actually up the day she left Plymouth. She took her departure from the Lizard on 25th March, crossed the line on 18th April, and had light winds to the meridian of the Cape, which she crossed on 14th May in 43° S.

In 69° E. she encountered bad weather, and shipped a heavy sea whilst running under a fore topsail. This sea broke over the quarter, smashed the wheel and broke in the cabin skylight, and she had to be hove to for 14 hours whilst repairs were made. The main upper topsail had also blown away and a new one had to be bent.

She eventually made Cape Otway at 10.30 p.m. on 7th June, entering the Heads early morning of the 8th, 75 days from the Lizards. In crossing to China, she went from Sydney to Shanghai in 82 days. Failing to get a tea cargo in Shanghai, she ran down to Hong Kong through the Formosa Channel with a strong N.E. monsoon in two days and some odd hours, but, of course, she was nearly new and in ballast.

In 1878 she again tried for a tea cargo, crossing from Sydney in 43 days; after a very tempestuous passage of 88 days from London to Sydney, during which she continually had to be hove to, indeed, Captain Phillip declared that he had never met with such heavy gales during 80 years' experience, even so she was only 79 days from the Channel to Cape Otway.

She found tea freights slumping very badly at Shanghai, and was finally placed on the berth for general cargo only at 30s. per 50 cubic feet. *Salamis* left Shanghai on 26th November in company with *Thermopylae,* which was the only sailing ship to get a tea cargo for London. The two ships made the Straits of Sunda on 15th December, but were compelled to anchor off Sumatra owing to the strong N.E. current. Here they found a fleet of 37 sail all vainly trying to get past Thwart-the-way Island.

Of this fleet the first to get through was *Thermopylae* after several ineffectual attempts, but she was closely followed by her iron sister ship; clearing Java Head on 29th December after a delay of 14 days, the two sisters squared away for the S.E. trades, and left the fleet of 37 ships to wait patiently until the N.E. current slackened.

Salamis carried the trades to 32° S., and then made some fine running to the Australian Coast, her best day's work being 336 miles. On 26th January, 1879, she arrived off Port Phillip Heads and anchored off Queens-cliff to await orders. She was sent up to Sydney and loaded coal alongside the *Cutty Sark*. On 18th March *Cutty Sark* sailed for Shanghai with 1150 tons of coal, *Salamis* followed on the 20th with 1200 tons of coal. Unfortunately I have no details of the race across, except that *Salamis* made the run in 37 days. Both ships failed to get a tea cargo for the London market, and *Cutty Sark* went off to Manila, whilst *Salamis* went to Foochow, and took a tea cargo from there to Melbourne, which she reached in time to load wool home, after a very light weather passage of 64 days. After this unsatisfactory voyage *Salamis* was kept steadily in the Melbourne trade, with the exception of one passage to Sydney.

When the Aberdeen White Star sold their sailing ships, *Salamis* went to the Norwegians, who stripped the yards off her mizen mast and turned her into a barque. After several weary years of threadbare old age, the beautiful little clipper was finally wrecked on Malden Island in the South Pacific on 20th May, 1905.

The Colonial Barque "Woolláhra."

The pretty little barque, *Woollahra*, owned by Cowlislaw Bros., of Sydney, had a very fair turn of speed, and on more than one occasion showed up well against some of the crack ships in the trade.   In her later years she used to run from Newcastle, N.S.W., to Frisco with coal.   She came to her end on Tongue Point, near Cape Terawhite, New Zealand, whilst bound in ballast from Wellington to Kaipara, to load Kauri lumber for Australia.   She was wrecked about half a mile from the homestead of a sheep station, the only habitation on the coast for miles.   The captain and an ordinary seaman were drowned, the rest of her complement getting safely ashore.   She went to pieces very quickly and there was not even an odd spar or deck fitting left a few months afterwards.

"Cassiope" and "Parthenope."

Cassiope and *Parthenope* were actually sister ships though by different builders.   They were both fine fast clippers of the best Liverpool type.   *Cassiope*, however, had a short life, being lost with all hands in 1885, when bound to London with Heap's Rangoon rice, under the well-known Captain Rivers.   *Parthenope* was sold in her old age to the Italians and rechristened *Pelogrino O.* On the 31st July, 1907, she sailed with coals from Newcastle, N.S.W., for Antofagasta and never arrived.

"Trafalgar."

D. Rose & Co.'s *Trafalgar* was a very regular Sydney trader. She went to the Norwegians and was still afloat, owned in Christiania, when the war broke out.

[To face page 270.

"WOOLLAHRA."

From a painting.

PASSAGES UNDER 80 DAYS TO SYDNEY IN 1875.

Ship	Departure	Crossed Equator	Crossed Cape Meridian	Passed S.W.Cape Tasmania	Arrived	Days Out
Cutty Sark - -	Lizard Nov. 29	Dec. 21	Jan. 13 '76	Feb. 4 '76	Feb. 12 '76	75
Samuel Plimsoll -	Falmouth Aug. 8	Sept. 4	Sept. 28	Oct. 19 (Otway)	Oct. 22	75

PASSAGES UNDER 80 DAYS TO MELBOURNE IN 1875.

Ship	Departure	Crossed Equator	Crossed Cape Meridian	Passed Cape Otway	Arrived	Days Out
Thermopylae - -	Lizard Dec. 3	Dec. 24	Jan. 14 '76	Feb. 7 '76	Feb. 9 '76	68
Salamis - -	Start July 10	Aug. 2	Aug. 24	Sept. 16	Sept. 16	68
Mermerus - -	Tuskar July 27	Aug. 15		Oct. 1	Oct. 1	68
Loch Garry - -	Tuskar Nov. 8	Dec. 5	Dec. 29		Jan. 20 '76	73
City of Corinth -	Start Sept. 4	Sept. 27	Oct. 21	Nov. 16	Nov. 16	73
Loch Maree - -	Scilly Aug. 8	Sept. 5	Sept. 26		Oct. 21	74
Romanoff - -	Lizard Aug. 10	Sept. 5		Oct. 22	Oct. 23	74
Loch Vennachar -	Inistrahull Sept. 6	Oct. 10	Oct 28	Nov. 18	Nov. 19	74
Wasdale - -	Tuskar Aug. 7	Sept. 4	Sept. 26		Oct. 20	74
Moravian - -	Lizard May 26	June 22			Aug. 9	75
City of Agra - -	Start May 31	June 24			Aug. 15	76
Ben Cruachan -	Tuskar June 7	July 1	July 29		Aug. 23	77
Parthenope - -	Tuskar June 9	June 29			Aug. 25	77
Glengarry - -	Tuskar Feb. 26	Mar. 22			May 14	77
Old Kensington -	Channel Feb. 3			Apl. 21	Apl. 22	78
Loch Katrine - -	Holyhead May 7				July 25	79

Notes on Passages to Australia in 1875.

In no year were so many magnificent iron clippers launched as in 1875, and of the ships which made the passage to Melbourne in under 80 days no less than five, namely, *Salamis, Loch Garry, Loch Vennachar, Parthenope* and *Old Kensington*, were on their maiden passages. *Loch Garry's* best run in the 24 hours was 333 miles, and *Loch Vennachar* did a week's work of 2065 miles, viz., 285, 290, 320, 320, 312, 268 and 270. *Samuel Plimsoll*, with 360 emigrants on board, left Plymouth on 6th August, at 11.15 p.m.; on the same day she ran into and sank the Italian barque *Enrica*, though without damage to herself. She saved the Italian's crew and put into Falmouth to land them.

Captain Richards left the *Thomas Stephens* in order to tune up *Parthenope*. He made the latter travel, but as he returned to the *Thomas Stephens* in 1876 he evidently preferred his old clipper.

Thermopylae still maintained her wonderful reputation; on this trip she averaged 270 miles a day from 23° W. to 100° E.

The *Old Kensington* was a very fine ship with a good turn of speed, and she usually loaded home from Calcutta or San Francisco.

The *Wasdale* must not be confused with the later *Wasdale*, which was not launched until 1881. This one must have been a very fast ship, for on this passage she made five 24-hour runs over 300, her best being 332 miles.

Many well-known heelers were just over the 80 days; for instance, *Miltiades* was 81 days from the Start, *Thessalus* 83 from the Lizards, *Theophane* 83 from the Tuskar, *Cassiope* 81 from the Tuskar, *Marpesia* 83 from the Tuskar, *Thyatira* 80 from the Start, all to Melbourne, whilst *Patriarch* was 82 days from Torbay to Sydney.

Two writers to the *Nautical Magazine*, both of whom were serving on the *Cutty Sark* during her 1875-6 voyage, claim that she was 50 miles south of Melbourne on her 54th day out from the Channel, and that owing to strong head winds she was compelled to go round Australia.

As will be seen, she was 67 days from the Lizard to the S.W. Cape, Tasmania, and I fear that a mistake of ten days has been made. Captain Watson also stated in a personal letter to me that she ran 2163 miles in six

days. I have 14 years of her abstract logs, and from
what her logs tell me I consider that she was quite
capable of accomplishing such a run with a strong
steady breeze, but it is very rarely that you get such a
breeze for six days on end even in the roaring forties.
She left London on 20th November but collided with the
Somersetshire off Gravesend, and lost her main topgallant
mast, besides other damage, so that she had to put back
to refit.

"Sir Walter Raleigh."

The *Sir Walter Raleigh*, commanded by Captain
W. Purvis, was a very well-known and regular wool
clipper of the type of *Romanoff*. I do not think she
was quite in the first flight, but she was never very far
behind, and in 1880 she shared with *Ben Voirlich* the
distinction of making the best outward run of the year.

The following extracts are from *Patriarch's* log, when
homeward bound in 1878, 79 days out from Sydney.

Feb. 8.—18° 41' N., long. 38° 55' W.—Spoke the *Sir Walter Raleigh*,
Melbourne to London, 77 days out.

Feb. 9.—*Sir Walter Raleigh* still in company.

Feb. 10.—*Sir Walter Raleigh* ahead.

Feb. 11.—*Sir Walter Raleigh* dead to windward.

Feb. 12 to 16.—*Sir Walter Raleigh* still in company.

In the end *Patriarch* got home a day ahead, *Sir
Walter Raleigh* making the best passage by a day. *Sir
Walter Raleigh* was probably faster in light and moderate
winds than in strong, as I can find no very big runs to
her credit.

On the 10th November, 1888, she left Sydney for
London, wool-laden, and was wrecked near Boulogue
on 29th January, 1889, when only 80 days out and
almost in sight of home. Five of her crew were
drowned. It was a tragic end to what promised to
be the best wool passage of her career.

"Loch Fyne" and "Loch Long."

These two 1200-ton sister ships from Thomson's yard, though fine wholesome ships, were not considered quite as fast as the earlier " Lochs," though each of them put up a 75-day passage to Melbourne, *Loch Fyne* on her second voyage in 1877-8, and the *Loch Long* in 1884.

The *Loch Fyne* left Lyttelton, N.Z., on 4th May, 1883, under Captain T. H. Martin, with 15,000 bags of wheat bound for the Channel for orders and never arrived.

In January, 1903, *Loch Long* arrived in Hobson's Bay from Glasgow, commanded by Captain Strachan. From Melbourne she was sent to New Caledonia to load nickel ore. She sailed on 29th April, but failed to arrive. Portions of wreckage, however, were washed up on the Chatham Islands, which made it only too certain that she had struck on the rocks and gone down with all hands.

"Aristides "—The Aberdeen White Star Flagship.

In March, 1876, Messrs. Hood launched the beautiful passenger clipper *Aristides*, the largest of all Thompson's sailing ships. Captain R. Kemball of *Thermopylae* fame, the commodore of the Aberdeen White Star fleet, was given command of her, and she became the firm's flagship.

On her maiden voyage she sailed from London on 6th July, and arrived in Port Phillip on 18th September— 74 days out (69 days from the land). Leaving Melbourne on 28th November, she arrived in the Thames on 17th February, 81 days out, beating two such well-known clippers as *Loch Maree* and *Collingwood*, which

" ARISTIDES."

Photo by Hall & Co., Sydney.

[To face page 274.

had sailed on 27th November, by 18 days.   The Aberdeen White Star ships invariably made fine maiden
voyages.   Their captains always left port with the firm
intention of breaking the record, and they had every
help from their owners, the ships being most carefully
loaded with their Plimsoll marks well out of water.
Crews also were picked men, and gear, of course, everything of the best.

Aristides was kept on the Melbourne run until 1889,
when she went out to Sydney in 85 days.   From this
date she was kept in the Sydney trade.   She usually had
a full passenger list and being perfectly run like all the
Aberdeen ships she was a favourite both in Sydney and
Melbourne.   Captain Kemball retired in 1887, and
Captain Spalding had her until the early nineties, then
Captain Allan took her over; her last commander was
Captain Poppy, who was lost in her.

Her best 24-hour run that I have record of was 320
miles.   Her passages, both outward and homeward,
were very regular, from 78 to 88 days as a rule, but she
never beat the times of her maiden voyage.

When the Aberdeen White Star sold their sailing
ships, they refused to part with the *Aristides*, and she
remained under their flag till the end.   On 28th May,
1903, she sailed from Caleta Buena with nitrate of soda
for San Francisco and was posted as missing.   H.M.
ships *Amphion* and *Shearwater* made a search amongst
the islands on her route for the missing ship, but no
trace of her was ever found.

"Smyrna."

The *Smyrna*, which was built on fuller lines than
most of Thompson's ships, came to a tragic end, being
run into by the steamer *Moto* on 28th April, 1888, during

a thick fog off the Isle of Wight, when outward bound to Sydney, and sank with Captain Taylor and 11 of her crew.

The "Harbinger."

The *Harbinger* was built to lower the colours of the wonderful *Torrens* in the Adelaide trade, being fitted to carry a large number of passengers. Indeed she was the last sailing ship specially built and fitted for carrying passengers. In more ways than one she was a remarkable vessel, and differed in many interesting details from the stock type of Clyde-built iron clipper.

In her rigging and sail plan, she had various fittings which were peculiar to herself.

To begin with, she was the only iron ship which had the old-fashioned channels to spread the rigging: and in another way she went back many years by never bending a sail on her crossjack yard. Instead of this sail she spread a large hoisting spanker, and she always carried a main spencer or storm trysail, a sail very often seen on down east Cape Horners, who found it very useful when trying to make westing off Cape Stiff.

The famous *Cutty Sark* was fitted with a spencer yard and sail at her launch, but I doubt if she ever used it; at anyrate, Captain Woodget told me he never used it, for the simple reason that he never hove the *Cutty Sark* to in ten voyages to Australia. I have several of *Harbinger's* abstract logs and I can find no instance of her using this sail either.

Harbinger was a very lofty ship, measuring 210 feet from the water-line to her main truck, and, unlike the *Hesperus*, she always carried her skysail yards crossed. Her jibbooms were of unusual length—I say jibbooms, for outside her ordinary jibboom she carried a sliding

"HARBINGER."

"HARBINGER."

Photo lent by F. G. Layton.

[To face page 276

gunter or flying jibboom. On these she set a whole
fleet of jibs, and, as if they were not sufficient, she had
cliphooks for a storm staysail on the fore stay.

After her first voyage 600 superficial feet of canvas
were added to her square-sail area, and even so she was
not a bit over canvassed, as she was a very stiff ship
and always stood up well to a breeze.

That she did not make more remarkable passages
must be put down to the fact that, like the *Hesperus*,
she was never hard sailed; but she could do over 300
miles in the 24 hours without much pressing, and
running her easting down 340 knots in a $23\frac{1}{2}$-hour day
was about her best. Her best speed through the water,
measured by the odometer and the common log, was 16
knots.

With regard to her sea qualities, Mr. Bullen, who
served on her as second mate, speaks as follows:—" She
was to my mind one of the noblest specimens of modern
shipbuilding that ever floated. For all her huge bulk
she was as easy to handle as any 10-ton yacht--far easier
than some--and in any kind of weather her docility was
amazing. . . . She was so clean in the entrance
that you never saw a foaming spread of broken water
ahead, driven in front by the vast onset of the hull.
She parted the waves before her pleasantly, as an arrow
the air; but it needed a tempest to show her ' way ' in
its perfection. In a grand and gracious fashion, she
seemed to claim affinity with the waves, and they in
their wildest tumult met her as if they knew and loved
her. She was the only ship I ever knew or heard of
that would 'stay' under storm staysails, reefed topsails
and a reefed foresail in a gale of wind. In fact, I never
saw anything that she would not do that a ship should
do. She was so truly a child of the ocean that even a

bungler could hardly mishandle her; she would work in spite of him. And lastly, she would steer when you could hardly detect an air out of the heavens, with a sea like a mirror, and the sails hanging apparently motionless. The men used to say that she would go a knot with only the quartermaster whistling at the wheel for a wind.''

It is doubtful if a ship ever sailed the seas with more beautiful deck fittings. They were all of the finest teak, fashioned as if by a cabinetmaker and lavishly carved. In her midship house, in addition to the galley, carpenter's shop, petty officer's quarters, donkey engine and condenser, she had accommodation for 30 passengers.

Like the *Rodney*, she was fitted up with all the latest comforts and conveniences—luxuries they were considered in those robust days. On her forward deck against the midship house were lashed a splendid cowhouse, two teak wood pens to hold 30 sheep, and a number of hen coops which were crammed with poultry, ducks, and geese, the butcher being one of the most important members of her crew.

Her foc's'le had three tiers of bunks, for she carried a large crew. In 1886 I find that she hauled out of the South West India Dock with 200 passengers and a crew of 51 all told.

She did not stay very long in the Adelaide trade, but from the early eighties was a favourite passenger ship to Melbourne, her commander being Captain Daniel R. Bolt, a very experienced passenger ship commander, who had previously had the *Darling Downs*, *Royal Dane*, and *Holmsdale*. Under him without any undue hurry, she was generally between 80 and 85 days going out, and in the nineties coming home

Below will be found a typical abstract of her log when running the easting down, taken from her outward passage in 1884:—

August 31.—Lat. 38° 00′ S., long. 1° 52′ W. Dist. 242. Moderate steady S.W. wind, rain squalls. Two sail in company.

September 1.—Lat. 38° 57′ S., long. 2° 47′ E. Dist. 226. Strong, unsteady, squally S.W. to west wind, high sea, royals set.

September 2.—Lat. 39° 07′ S., long. 7° 42′ E. Dist. 230. Variable south wind, squally, heavy rollers from S.W.

September 3.—Lat. 39° 40′ S., long. 12° 49′ E. Dist. 241. Westerly wind, fresh and squally, under topgallant sails, heavy rollers.

September 4.—Lat. 40° 06′ S., long. 19° 05′ E. Dist. 288. Strong gale and high sea.

September 5.—Lat. 40° 24′ S., long. 24° 50′ E. Dist. 267. Moderate W. gale, high sea.

September 6.—Lat. 40° 49′ S., long. 30° 44′ E. Dist. 267. Gale moderating and falling to light S.S.E. wind.

September 7.—Lat. 40° 08′ S., long. 35° 15′ E. Dist. 213. South wind variable in force and direction.

September 8.—Lat. 38° 30′ S., long 36° 37′ E. Dist. 116. Variable light E. and S.E. wind.

September 9.—Lat. 40° 25′ S., long. 38° 36′ E. Dist. 148. Moderate E.S.E. gale. Sea smooth. P.M., strong N.E. wind, reduced to topsails.

September 10.—Lat. 42° 17′ S., long. 42° 18′ E. Dist. 203. Strong gale and head sea. Main upper and three lower topsails. Later, wind dropping.

September 11.—Lat. 42° 10′ S., long. 46° 41′ E. Dist. 196. Light W. wind, variable airs increasing to strong N.W. gale at midnight.

September 12.—Lat. 42° 28′ S., long. 52° 13′ E. Dist. 247. 6.30, wind shifted to west and fell light, then freshened, sea smooth.

September 13.—Lat. 42° 22′ S., long. 58° 06′ E. Dist. 262. Moderate westerly gale and high sea, royals in. Midnight, light winds.

September 14.—Lat. 42° 10′ S., long. 63° 50′ E. Dist. 253. Increasing N.W. wind.

September 15.—Lat. 41° 30′ S., long. 70° 22′ E Dist. 298. Fresh gale, cross sea from N.N.W., a sea down saloon companion ; overcast.

September 16.—Lat. 41° 30′ S., long. 77° 07′ E. Dist. 305. Fresh W.N.W. wind and moderate sea. Bar. 29.70° to 29.60°.

September 17.—Lat. 41° 15′ S., long. 84° 19′ E. Dist. 326. Strong gale and high sea. 7.30 a.m., wind shifted from N.W. to W.S.W. Bar., 30.20°.

Sept. 18.—Lat. 40° 40′ S., long. 90° 00′ E. Dist. 259. Moderate gale W.S.W. to light W. wind, 8 knots. Bar., 30.10°.

September 19.—Lat. 41° 00′ S., long. 95° 01′ E.   Dist. 228.   Moderate to light W. wind, skysails set.   Bar., 29.60°.

September 20.—Lat. 40° 30′ S., long. 100° 44′ E.   Dist. 260.   Moderate N.W. gale, thick weather, rain.

September 21.—Lat. 40° 04′ S., long. 106° 05′ E.   Dist. 248.   Moderate gale and high seas.

September 22.—Lat. 39° 28′ S., long. 111° 05′ E.   Dist. 230. Moderate S. wind, squally with rain falling to light airs.

On this passage *Harbinger* was 81 days from the Lizard to Port Phillip Heads; she had very light winds to the line, which she only crossed 31 days from the Lizard. It was, perhaps, a pity that she was not fitted with stunsails and given a chance to go, as there is no doubt that under such conditions she could have given the fastest ships in the trade a very good race.

In 1885 she took her departure from the Start with the little *Berean*, and beat that little marvel out to the Colonies by six days, being 79 days from the Start to the Quarantine Station, Port Phillip. *Harbinger's* best run on this occasion was 310 miles.

In the year 1890 *Harbinger* was bought, along with the *Hesperus*, for Devitt & Moore's cadet-training scheme. She carried a full complement of cadets until 1897, when her boys were turned over to the *Macquarie* and she was sold to the Russians for £4800, and she was still in the Register in 1905.

"Argonaut."

Carmichael's *Argonaut*, like their *Thessalus*, was not a regular wool carrier, though often seen in Sydney and Melbourne ; for some years, however, in her latter days, she was a member of the wool fleet from Sydney. She had all the good looks of a *Golden Fleece* clipper ; and the following records speak for her sailing powers:—

" ARGONAUT."

Photo by Hall & Co., Sydney.

[To face page 280.

1879-80	London to Calcutta, undocked 3.30 p.m. October 4
	Arrived Saugor Roads, Jan 4 .. .. 90 days.
	against N.E. monsoon.
1881	Calcutta to Melbourne, Jan 10-February 25 .. .. 45 days.
1881	Melbourne to London, 7th April—off Lizard, 4.30
	p.m. June 27 .. .. 81 ,,
	—docked June 30 .. · .. .. .. 84 ,,
1882	Dundee to Frisco, July 17-November 14 .. .. 120 ,,
1882	Frisco to Queenstown, January 6-April 20 .. .. 104 ,,
1883	Wifsta, Sweden, to Adelaide, July 11-October 8 .. 89 ,,
1883	Adelaide to Tegal, Java, November 15-December 13 28 ,,
1885	Liverpool to Sydney, June 14-August 31 .. .. 78 ,,
1894-5	Sydney to London, October 14-January 4 .. .. 82 ,,
1895	Dungeness to Sydney, March 13-June 4 .. .. 83 ,,
1895	Sydney to London, October 13-December 29 .. 77 ,,

Argonaut's best known commander was Captain Hunter, who was one of those who knew how to carry sail. On his wool passage home in 1896, however, he was very much out of luck, as the *Argonaut* was one of the very few ships that took over 100 days.

Captain A. Cook was her first skipper, then Captain Bonner had her in the late eighties.

Argonaut was still afloat in 1914. Under the name of *Elvira*, she flew the Portuguese flag and used the same home port, Lisbon, as the *Cutty Sark* and *Thomas Stephens*—and her round of ports was usually the same as that of *Cutty Sark*, namely—Rio Janeiro, New Orleans and Lisbon. In 1913, her name was again changed to *Argo*. The Portuguese, as in the case of the *Cutty Sark*, retained the yards on the mizen.

PASSAGES UNDER 80 DAYS TO SYDNEY IN 1876.

Ship	Departure	Crossed Equator	Crossed Cape Meridian	Passed S.W.Cape Tasmania	Arrived	Days Out
Patriarch - -	Channel June 23	July 14	Aug. 9	Aug. 30 (Otway)	Sept. 2	71
Samuel Plimsoll -	Plymouth June 2	June 28	July 19	Aug. 9	Aug. 19	78
Cutty Sark - -	Channel Oct. 23	Nov. 19	Dec. 11	Jan. 3 '77	Jan. 10 '77	79

PASSAGES UNDER 80 DAYS TO MELBOURNE IN 1876.

Ship	Departure	Crossed Equator	Crossed Cape Meridian	Passed Cape (Otway)	Arrived	Days Out
Mermerus - -	Gravesend June 25	July 17	Aug. 6		Aug. 30	66
Miltiades - -	Lizard May 12	May 30	June 25		July 21	70
Aristides - -	Start July 10	Aug. 4	Aug. 26	Sept. 17	Sept. 18	70
Old Kensington -	Channel Aug. 17				Oct. 29	73
Loch Ness - -	Scilly July 11				Sept. 21	74
Macduff - -	Channel May 18				July 31	74
Salamis - -	Lizard Mar. 25	Apl. 18	May 14	June 7	June 8	75
Theophane - -	Tuskar Aug. 12	Sept. 11			Oct. 26	75
Loch Maree -	Start June 19	July 8	Aug. 10	Sept. 2	Sept. 3	76
Cassiope -	Channel Aug. 26				Nov. 10	76
Parthenope -	Tuskar July 27				Oct. 12	77
Marpesia -	Tuskar Oct. 21				Jan. 6 '77	77
Loch Katrine -	Start May 25	June 15	July 12	Aug. 9	Aug. 10	77
Romanoff - -	Lizard July 23	July 30		Sept. 17	Sept. 18	77
Thomas Stephens -	Lizard Aug. 7	Sept. 4			Oct. 24	78

Notes on Passages to Australia in 1876.

The only new ship to make a name for herself this year was *Aristides*, but I do not think she was as fast as Thompson's earlier ships, and I much doubt if she were capable of the following week's run, made by *Samuel Plimsoll* whilst running her easting down this year in 41° S., viz., 348, 330, 301, 342, 320, 264, and 340= total 2245 miles.

Hardly any of the cracks are missing from the " under 80 day " list. The *Tweed*, with eight fine stallions on board, ran from the Start to King's Island in 77 days on her way to Sydney, but was then held up three more days by calms.

" Brilliant " and " Pericles."

Duthie's *Brilliant* and Thompson's *Pericles* were built alongside of each other and launched on the same tide; and both ships being in the Sydney trade there was naturally great rivalry between them. The two clippers proved to be very evenly matched and it is

" PERICLES."

Photo by Hall & Co., Sydney.

[To face page 282.

difficult to award the palm. *Pericles* usually took emigrants out, *Brilliant* being loaded deep with general cargo, and they both loaded wool home. The two captains, Davidson of the *Brilliant* and Largie of *Pericles*, usually had a new hat on the result of each passage. *Pericles* with her light load line generally won the hat going out, but the *Brilliant* was always very hard to beat on the homeward run, and Captain Davidson, more often than not, got his hat back again.

On her maiden passage *Brilliant* went out to Sydney in 78 days without clewing up her main royal from the Bay of Biscay to Sydney Heads. Down in the roaring forties she made three consecutive runs of 340, 345 and 338 miles by observation, a performance which I do not think any iron ship has ever beaten.

Her best homeward passage was 79 days to the Channel in 1888, but her wool passages were so regular that she was rarely allowed more than 85 days to catch the sales.

Brilliant was a specially handsome ship; painted black with a white under-body, and with a brass rail along the whole length of her topgallant bulwarks, she was always the acme of smartness, being known in Sydney as " Duthie's yacht."

Taking the average of 16 outward passages under Captain Davidson, we find *Brilliant's* record to be 85 days, her rival *Pericles* had an average of 84 days for 10 passages; this was considerably helped by a very fine run of 71 days in 1886.

In 1888 Captain John Henderson took the *Pericles* for three voyages, leaving her to take the *Samuel Plimsoll*. He took the *Pericles* across the Pacific to San Francisco and made three passages home from the Golden Gate with wheat, his first being the best, 110 days to Falmouth.

Thompson's sold *Pericles* to the Norwegians in 1904, whilst *Brilliant* was sold to the Italians in the following year. *Brilliant*, I believe, was broken up in Genoa about 10 or 12 years ago, but *Pericles*, until recently at any rate, was still washing about the seas disguised in the usual way as a barque.

"Loch Ryan."

Loch Ryan was another 1200-ton ship, a favourite size with Messrs. Aitken & Lilburn. Though she managed to make the run to Melbourne in 78 days on her maiden passage, she was not as sharp-ended as her predecessors and was more of a carrier, her passages home being more often over 100 days than under.

She was more fortunate in her old age than most of her sisters, as she was bought by the Victorian Government and turned into a boys' training ship, her name being changed to *John Murray*. For many years, until well into the late war in fact, she lay in Hobson's Bay as spick and span as ever, occasionally making short cruises under sail for training purposes.

About the middle of the war, like many another gallant old windjammer, she was fitted out and sent to sea in the face of the German submarines and was wrecked in the Pacific.

"Loch Etive," of Captain William Stuart and Joseph Conrad fame.

The *Loch Etive*, launched in November, 1877, had the honour of being commanded by Captain Stuart of Peterhead, for long the well-known skipper of the famous *Tweed*, and the still greater honour of having Mr. Joseph Conrad as one of her officers.

She also was a fuller ship and for some years Captain

"MERMERUS," in Victoria Dock, Melbourne, 1896.

"BRILLIANT."

Photo lent by Captain C. W. Davidson.

[*To face page* 284.

Stuart failed to get anything remarkable out of her, though he drove her unmercifully; but in 1892-3 she made two very good voyages.

Leaving Glasgow on 15th October, 1892, she arrived at Melbourne on Xmas Day, 70 days out from the Tail of the Bank. Loading a wool cargo, she left Melbourne on 26th January, 1893, and arrived in the London River on 29th April, 93 days out.

On her next voyage she left Glasgow at 8 p.m. on 23rd September and arrived at Adelaide 10 a.m., 12th December; towed to powder ground and discharged 20 tons of gunpowder, and berthed at the wharf same afternoon; commenced discharging on 13th, discharged 800 tons of cargo, took on board 300 tons lead spelter, towed down the river and anchored off the Semaphore on the 16th; left on the 17th, and arrived at Melbourne on the 19th. Here she discharged 750 tons, the remainder of her inward cargo, and loaded wool and sundries for Antwerp and Glasgow.

Left Melbourne Heads on 18th January—detained a week in Bass Straits by light easterly winds—passed within 3 miles of Cape Horn at noon, 15th February—crossed equator at noon, 15th March—signalled Lizard at noon, 12th April, and docked in Antwerp on 15th April, 87 days out.

Captain Stuart died at sea on his next voyage, on the morning of his birthday, 21st September, 1894, and was buried at sea some 300 miles S.W. of Queenstown, the *Loch Etive* being five days out from Glasgow. He was 63 years of age and had been 43 years a master. It was his proud boast that during the whole of his career he had never lost a man or a mast overboard. Though offered many a chance to go into steam or a larger ship, Captain Stuart preferred to remain in the *Loch Etive*. Without a doubt he was one of the most successful captains in the history of our Mercantile Marine. Many of his men sailed year after year with him, and there are men in command at the present day who originally shipped before the mast with Stuart and owed not only their sea training but their education to him. Peterhead, his native town, was very proud of Captain Stuart, as well it might be. With Viking blood in his veins, he went to sea in 1846 through the hawse hole of a Peterhead schooner in the Baltic trade, and rose to the topmost pinnacle of his profession. May the British race produce many more like him.

Loch Etive was sold to the French in 1911 for £1850.

The Wreck of "Loch Sloy."

The *Loch Sloy* was another 1200-ton Loch liner. She was Captain Horne's first ship in the Australian trade, and he left her to take over the *Loch Garry* in 1885.

In April, 1899, when on a passage to Adelaide under Captain Nichol, the *Loch Sloy* overran her distance and was wrecked on Kangaroo Island. Captain Nichol was trying to pick up Cape Borda light, but it was shut out from him by the cliffs between Cape Bedout and Cape Couldie, and the *Loch Sloy*, in the darkness of the morning of 24th April, drove on to the Brothers Rocks and became a total loss in a few moments, the heavy surf sweeping right over her. The crew and seven saloon passengers took refuge in the rigging, but one by one the masts went over the side, and the men were hurled into the breakers. The ship had struck 300 yards from the shore and only four men reached it—a passenger, two able seamen and an apprentice. None of the survivors remembered how they got ashore; they heard the crash of the masts, then felt the wreckage bumping them about in the surf, and finally found

"LOCH ETIVE."

"ARGONAUT," in the Clyde.

[To face page 286.

themselves lying wedged amongst the rocks, where the
breakers had washed them up.

The following account of their subsequent hardships
appeared in an Adelaide paper :—

The survivors endured dreadful privations before they reached a
settlement.   They had plenty of whisky, which had floated ashore
from the wreck, but for solid food they had to eat grass, dead penguins
cast up by the waves, and shellfish.   They suffered terribly through
insufficient clothing and lack of boots.   Two of them walked along the
coast until they came to the Cape Borda light.   One went inland to
May's Settlement.   The other survivor, David Kilpatrick, the passenger,
was so ill that he had to be left behind.   When search parties came back
for him he had disappeared, and it was not till a week later that a
systematic search of the island led to the discovery of his dead body a
mile and a half from the spot where the others had left him.

The Loss of Lochs "Shiel" and "Sunart."

Loch Shiel, the sister ship of *Loch Sloy,* was lost on
the Thorne Rock, Milford Haven on the 80th January,
1901.   Her master mistook the Great Castle Head lights
and got on the rocks at 8.40 p.m., the Loch liner being
bound out to Australia from Glasgow.   There was no
loss of life, however, on this occasion, half the crew
being taken out of the mizen rigging by a lifeboat, and
the other half climbing ashore on to the rocks by means
of her bowsprit.

Loch Sunart, the last three-master built for the
Loch line, was launched in January, 1878.   Her life
was a very short one, as on her second passage out to
Melbourne she was piled up on the Skulmartin Rock,
11th January, 1879.

Notes on Passages to Australia in 1877.

Loch Maree left Glasgow on 5th May, but was
held up for four days in sight of Tory Island, first by
calms and then strong S.W. winds.   Between 21° S.—

the limit of the S.E. trades—and the Cape meridian, she had ten days of strong N.W. winds, during which she logged over 300 miles a day for several days in succession.

Ben Cruachan had such favourable winds in the Channel that she carried the Channel pilot on to Madeira, where she landed him on 25th April. She made very steady running down south, for her best day's work was only 296 miles. Her sister ship, *Ben Voirlich*, on the contrary, made a run of 350 miles on 26th July in 35° 37′ S., 22° 10′ W., though she took 83 days from Achill Head to Hobson's Bay.

Pericles, with 489 emigrants on board, made a good start in her career, like all Thompson's ships. Between the 23rd and 24th November in 44° S., she ran 354 miles before what Captain Largie called a hurricane, so it is not surprising that *Brilliant* failed to catch her in spite of an average of 261 miles a day for 22 days between the Cape and Otway. *Brilliant*, however, instead of emigrants, had 4000 tons of general cargo on board.

Patriarch, who very rarely suffered damage in bad weather, took a very heavy sea over her poop during a W.N.W. gale on the 2nd September in 100° E., and lost 9 feet of her taffrail and three stanchions over the side. This sea would not have been a pleasant one for *Loch Vennachar* or *Sir Walter Raleigh*, both of which had their decks lumbered up with horse boxes full of draught stock.

Samuel Plimsoll as usual made some good running down south, her best week's work being 2050 miles.

Thermopylae was hard chased by *Cutty Sark*, in spite of a 17-day run from the Lizard to the equator. It is a pity the two ships did run their easting down on the same parallel, as they must have been neck and neck down south, but *Cutty Sark* kept in 46° S., whilst *Thermopylae* did not go higher than 44° 30' S. Both ships by the way were forced by bad weather to put back to the Downs on their first attempts to get down Channel.*

PASSAGES TO SYDNEY UNDER 80 DAYS IN 1877.

Ship	Departure	Crossed Equator	Crossed Cape Meridian	Passed S.W.Cape Tasmania	Arrived	Days Out
Cutty Sark - -	Lizard Dec. 6	Dec. 28	Jan. 18 '78	Feb.13 '78	Feb. 16'78	72
Patriarch - -	Start July 3	July 26		Sept. 12 (Otway)	Sept. 15	74
Pericles - -	Plymouth Sept. 20	Oct. 17	Nov. 7	Nov. 30	Dec. 3	74
Brilliant - -	Start Oct. 2	Oct. 31	Nov. 26	Dec. 10 (Otway)	Dec. 20	79
Samuel Plimsoll -	Plymouth June 9	July 7	July 28	Aug. 23 (Otway)	Aug. 27	79

PASSAGES TO MELBOURNE UNDER 80 DAYS IN 1877.

Ship	Departure	Crossed Equator	Crossed Cape Meridian	Passed Cape Otway	Arrived	Days Out
Loch Maree - -	Cape Clear May 13	June 3	June 24	July 19	July 19	67
Ben Cruachan -	Lizard April 17	May 13			June 23	67
Thermopylae - -	Lizard Dec. 3	Dec. 20	Jan. 17 '78	Feb. 14'78	Feb. 15'78	74
Mermerus - -	Start June 30	July 28	Aug. 19		Sept. 13	75
Miltiades - -	Start June 13	July 10	July 31		Aug. 27	75
Loch Vennachar -	Channel April 7	May 2	May 29		June 22	75
Romanoff - -	Lizard April 1	Apl. 25	May 19		June 15	75
Loch Fyne - -	Tuskar Dec. 20				Mar. 5 '78	75
Salamis - -	Start July 7	Aug. 1	Aug. 26		Sept. 21	76
Thomas Stephens -	Tuskar Aug. 12	Sept. 9	Sept. 30	Oct. 26	Oct. 27	76
Loch Ryan - -	Tuskar Mar. 6	Mar. 27	Apl. 23		May 21	76
Theophane - -	Holyhead June 30	July 30	Aug. 21		Sept. 15	77
Parthenope - -	Holyhead Aug. 17	Sept. 19	Oct. 10	Nov. 1	Nov. 2	77
Sir Walter Raleigh	Lizard July 5	July 30	Aug. 22		Sept. 20	77
Loch Garry - -	Qu'nstown July 11	Aug. 10	Sept. 2	Sept. 25	Sept. 26	77
Maulesden - -	Tuskar Mar. 4	Mar. 26	Apl. 24		May 22	79

* This passage of *Cutty Sark* has been wrongly given in my *China Clippers*. She left London for the second time on 2nd December, not the 12th, as there stated. The mistake was made in the shipping reports of the day and never corrected, and I have only lately been able to prove it.

L

" Cimba."

In April, 1878, Hood launched the beautiful little *Cimba* for A. Nicol, and with her green hull, gold scrolls and lion figure-head she was a familiar visitor to Port Jackson for close on 30 years.

An out and out wool clipper, she was very heavily rigged, her chief measurements being :—

Main lower mast	60 feet.
Fore and main yards	82 ,,
Fore and main lower topsail yards ..	76 ,,
Fore and main upper topsail yards ..	69 ,,
Fore and main lower topgallant yard ..	58 ,,
Fore and main upper topgallant yards ..	52 ,,
Fore and main royal yards	41 ,,

Her lower masts were short compared to some clippers, but her lower yards were very heavy, her fore and main yards weighing over 4 tons each.

Her first master was J. Fimister, who had her until 1895, when Captain J. W. Holmes took her over until she was sold abroad in 1906.

Under Captain Fimister her best passages were :—

1880	Channel to Sydney	..	..	..	71 days
1882	Channel to Sydney	..	..	..	82 ,,
1884	Channel to Sydney	..	..	..	79 ,,
1889	Sydney to London	..	..	..	75 ,,
1891	Sydney to Channel	..	..	..	84 ,,
1892	Channel to Sydney	..	..	..	83 ,,
1893	Sydney to Channel	..	..	..	86 ,,
1894	Channel to Sydney	..	..	..	80 ,,

On her maiden trip she left London 27th June—left Channel 2nd July, 5 days out—crossed the line 28th July. 26 days from departure— crossed Cape meridian 20th August, 49 days from departure—arrived Sydney 29th September, 89 days from departure

A curious notoriety came upon the new clipper in Sydney owing to Captain Fimister, in his eagerness to get loaded and away in good time for the wool sales, jumping *Patriarch's* loading berth at Circular Quay.

The berth was vacated by *Nineveh* on a Saturday.

" CIMBA "

Photo lent by F. G. Layton.

[To face page 290.

The port arrangements in those days allowed ships to go alongside in the order in which they had booked the berth.   On this occasion *Patriarch* had booked the berth on 18th August, *Smyrna* on 20th August, *Cairnbulg* on 9th September, *St. Lawrence* on 13th September, *Centurion* on 26th September and *Cimba* on 30th September—the day after she arrived.

On *Nineveh* sailing, *Patriarch* should have hauled alongside, but her captain had been told that as it was Saturday he need not come alongside until Monday. The *Patriarch*, being in no particular hurry as a good deal of her wool was still up country, therefore remained where she was.   Hearing of this, the enterprising Captain Fimister proceeded to hire a tug and move his ship from Smith's Wharf where she was lying to the vacant berth at Circular Quay, all ready to load the wool which was waiting for him.   He took the precaution, however, to take his shorefasts through the quay rings and aboard again.   This defiance of the harbour authorities was allowed to go unnoticed until Monday morning.   Then Captain Fimister received an order to remove his ship.   Of this he took no notice.   His action, as may be supposed, was the talk of the port, especially amongst the captains of the wool clippers. One of these skippers threatened to moor his ship in Sydney Cove, ready to be the next to jump the berth. Others complained in person to the Colonial Secretary.

On Tuesday morning Captain Bell, the harbourmaster, went in person to the *Cimba* to order her removal, but the undaunted Captain Fimister triced up his gangway ladder and threatened to throw him overboard if he attempted to gain the deck.   By this time all the legal lights of Sydney were puzzling their heads over the legal aspects of the case; Messrs. Dangar, Gedye & Co., the ship's agents, upholding the captain. Finally the Colonial Treasurer sent the President of the Marine Board an order to remove the ship. So at 6 a.m. on Wednesday morning, Captain Hixson, the assistant harbourmaster, with 20 men and half-a-dozen water police, boarded the ship, only to find that Captain Finister and his whole crew had flown after first removing every means of weighing the anchor. But a harbourmaster is not easily balked, and Captain Hixson let go the shorefasts, slipped the chain, and with the aid of a tug took the *Cimba* out and moored her at the man-of-war buoy off Fort Macquarie.

It was now time for Dangar, Gedye & Co. to take action. They immediately enlisted the help of Sir John Robertson, who moved the adjournment of the House in order that an explanation of the harbourmaster's high-handed proceedings might be given. The House was already divided into two factions over Captain Fimister's action, but the Colonial Secretary firmly upheld the Marine Board, and in the end Captain Fimister was fined 20 shillings and 5s. costs and ordered to pay £28 4s., the cost of removing the *Cimba* from the berth.

All this trouble really arose firstly through the *Patriarch's* being ahead of her cargo, and secondly owing to Circular Quay being a free berth. This was shortly afterwards rectified, but the *Patriarch* did not get away until a month after the *Cimba* for want of cargo.

In 1889, the *Cimba* made her best wool passage, as follows:—

October 22—Left Sydney.		
November 18—Passed Cape Horn	..	.. 27 days out.
December 11—Crossed the equator	..	.. 50 ,, ,,
December 25—Passed the Western Isles	..	.. 64 ,, ,,
January 3 '90—Signalled in the Channel	..	.. 73 ,, ,,
January 5—Arrived London	.. ..	.. 75 ,, ,,

Captain Holmes, who took the *Cimba* in 1895, had had a long experience in clipper ships. He had been third mate of the *Salamis*, chief mate of *Hallowe'en* and *Blackadder*, and commander of the *Lencadia*, a smart ship built for the China trade.

The Aberdeen ships were, however, very clannish, and being a stranger and not a Scot, he had his reputation all to make, the standard set being a very high one. However, he knew how to carry sail, and he managed to keep the *Cimba* moving, though she was always a tender ship requiring a master hand.

Under him, her best passages were:—

    1895 Lizard to Sydney ..   ..   .. 82 days.

Her best week's work was 1860 miles, and her best 24 hours run, made on 6th June in 39° 51′ S., 34° 54′ E., 336 miles in a fresh gale from S.W., during which the second mate was lost overboard.

Other good runs on this passage were:—300, 302, 308 and 312.

    1896 Sydney to London ..   ..   .. 78 days.

Cimba left Sydney in company with *Thessalus* and *Argonaut* on 17th October. Passed the Horn on 15th November, 29 days out—on 18th November in 51° 31′ S., 55° 47′ W., ran 316 miles, the wind blowing a strong gale from W.S.W. to W.N.W.—crossed the line on 8th December, 23 days from the Horn—passed Fayal, Western Isles, on Xmas Day, and signalled the Lizard at 1 p.m. 31st December, 75 days out.

This was really a splendid performance, for the *Thessalus*, which was really a much faster and more powerful ship, signalled the Start on 31st December at noon, whilst *Argonaut*, which was certainly quite as fast as *Cimba*, did not arrive until a month later.

    1898 Sydney to London ..   ..   .. 81 days.

Passed the Horn on 2nd November, 25 days out, having run 3422 miles in 14 days—crossed the line on 29th November, 27 days from the Horn—passed the Western Isles on 20th December, Lizard light abeam at 8 a.m. on 26th December, 79 days out.

In 1899 *Cimba* went out to Rockhampton and loaded home from Brisbane. In 1901 she went out to Sydney in 85 days, her best run being 310 miles.

By this time sailing ship freights were in a very bad way, and a profitable charter in Sydney grew more and more difficult to obtain, thus in 1905 we find her making the record passage between Callao and Iquique for a sailing ship. As this may be of interest, I give her abstract log below:—

ABSTRACT LOG OF *CIMBA* FROM CALLAO TO IQUIQUE
RECORD SAILING SHIP PASSAGE.

July 2-7 p.m. got underweigh.

	Lat.	Long.	Course.	Dist.	Wind
July 3	12° 48′S	79° 24′W	S50° W.	80mls.	S.S.E.
,, 4	14° 30′	80° 15′	S46°	150 ,,	,,
,, 5	16° 47′	81° 49′	S34°	165 ,,	,,
,, 6	19° 20′	82° 54′	S22°	165 ,,	S.E. by E.
,, 7	21° 48′	84° 17′	S28°	168 ,,	S.Easterly
,, 8	23° 52′	85° 52′	S35°	152 ,,	,,
,, 9	25° 32′	86° 34′	S21° W.	160 ,,	,,
,, 10	23° 57′	84° 41′	N47° E.	141 ,,	S.E. by S.
,, 11	23° 8′	82° 24′	N69°	135 ,,	South, S.W.
,, 12	23° 10′	81° 35′	S87°	46 ,,	N.W. Westerly
,, 13	23° 53′	78° 00′	S78°	202 ,,	W'ly to S.S.W.
,, 14	22° 42′	75° 7′	N66°	175 ,,	S.Easterly
,, 15	21° 38′	71° 00′	N75°	246 ,,	,,
,, 16	20° 57′	70° 48′	N15°	43 ,,	,,
,, 17	20° 31′	70° 22′	S11°	31 ,,	,,

(2080 miles in 14 days.)

This was *Cimba's* last voyage under the British flag ; she came home from Caleta Buena to Falmouth in 85 days, and was then sold (March, 1906) to the Norwegians owing to the death of her owner.

Under the Norwegians she made a remarkable passage from Dublin to the St. Lawrence in 14 days; lumber

was now her chief cargo and she used often to be seen
discharging firewood from the Baltic in the Aberdeen
Bay, East India Dock, where she had so often loaded
general for Sydney.

PASSAGES TO SYDNEY UNDER 80 DAYS IN 1878.

Ship	Departure	Crossed Equator	Crossed Cape Meridian	Passed S.W.Cape Tasmania	Arrived	Days Out
Loch Etive - -	Scillies Jan. 17	Feb. 6	Mar. 4	Mar. 28	Apl. 3	76
Thomas Stephens -	Plymouth June 15	July 18	Aug. 1	Aug. 21	Aug. 31	77

PASSAGES TO MELBOURNE UNDER 80 DAYS IN 1878.

Ship	Departure	Crossed Equator	Crossed Cape Meridian	Passed Cape Otway	Arrived	Days Out
Thessalus -	Lizard Mar. 7	Mar. 28	Apl. 20		May 14	68
Parthenope -	Tuskar July 7	July 31	Aug. 20		Sept. 16	71
Aristides -	Start July 3	July 27	Aug. 18		Sept. 15	74
Miltiades -	Start May 31	June 30	July 21	Aug. 13	Aug. 14	75
Loch Vennachar	Smalls July 10	Aug. 4	Aug. 29		Sept. 23	75
Old Kensington	Lizard June 5	July 2	July 24	Aug. 19	Aug. 20	76
Aviemore -	Start June 29	July 27	Aug. 18	Sept. 15	Sept. 16	79

Notes on Passages to Australia in 1878.

Thessalus was the heroine of the year, though on
her arrival in Melbourne critics declared that she was
too deeply loaded for safety.

Miltiades had a bad time running her easting down;
on more than one occasion her decks were badly swept,
and once Captain Perrett was washed off the poop on to
the main deck and had his head badly cut about.

Loch Vennachar, owing to the death of Captain
Robertson, had a new skipper in Captain J. S. Ozanne,
her late chief officer. He proved that he could carry
sail by two 24-hour runs of 325 and 311 miles.

Captain Stuart made a very good maiden passage out
to Sydney, but *Loch Etive* never had anything like the
speed of his old ship the *Tweed.*

Parthenope had the veteran Captain Grey in command· this year, and he certainly made her travel. Of the other crack ships *Salamis* was 83 and *Samuel Plimsoll* 86 days to Sydney; whilst of the Melbourne clippers *Loch Garry* was 80, *Loch Maree* 82, *Mermerus, Ben Cruachan* and *Romanoff* 83, *Sir Walter Raleigh* 84 and *Ben Voirlich* 87 days. Neither of the two tea clippers, *Cutty Sark* and *Thermopylae,* sailed for the Colonies in 1878.

"Sophocles."

The *Sophocles* was a pretty little ship, though, following the trend of the times, she was given a fuller body than Thompson's earlier ships, as she was mean to be an economical carrier rather than a record breaker.

I believe she is still afloat rigged as a barque under Italian colours.

Passages to Australia in 1879.

I have had considerable difficulty in finding any good passages to Melbourne or Sydney in 1879. It was a time of depressed freights and ships found themselves seeking cargoes in other than their regular trades. Thus we find the tea clipper *Titania* on the Melbourne run instead of going out to China. The *Thomas Stephens* tried a voyage to Otago. *Salamis* was still in the East seeking a tea cargo. *Thessalus* went to Calcutta from Penarth, whilst the poor little *Cutty Sark* had many strange and unpleasant adventures before she resumed her place in the Australian trade, which was not until 1883.

Of the other cracks *Patriarch* with 90 days, *Miltiades* with 88, *Ben Voirlich* with 87, *Loch Maree* with 94,

"SOPHOCLES."

Photo by Hall & Co., Sydney.

To face page 206.

Old Kensington with 96, *Cimba* with 91 and *Thermopylae* with 86 days all made poor passages.

The two rivals, *Brilliant* and *Pericles*, were the only ships to make Sydney in under 80 days from the Channel, and owing to *Pericles* getting ashore close to Plymouth and having to come back and dock and discharge her cargo, etc., the two ships eventually left the Lizard together.

Ship	Departure	Crossed Equator	Crossed Cape Meridian	Passed Cape Otway	Arrived Sydney	Days Out
Pericles - -	Lizard Aug. 30	Sept. 25	Oct. 17	Nov. 10	Nov. 14	76
Brilliant - -	Lizard Aug. 30	Sept. 27	Oct. 20	Nov. 12	Nov. 15	77

The best passages out to Melbourne were the following :—

Ship	Left	On	Arrived	On	Days Out
Sobraon - -	Plymouth	Oct. 3	Melbourne	Dec. 16	74
Mermerus - -	Channel	March 26	,,	June 11	77
Titania - -	,,	Feb. 21	,,	May 7	75
Aristides - -	,,	July 8	,,	Sept. 23	77
Loch Vennachar -	Clyde	July 4	,,	Sept. 23	81
Ben Cruachan -	Channel	June 5	,,	Aug. 25	81
Loch Garry - -	Clyde	June 6	,,	Aug. 27	82
Sir Walter Raleigh	Channel	June 9	,,	Aug. 30	82

PASSAGES TO SYDNEY UNDER 80 DAYS IN 1880.

Ship	Departure	Crossed Equator	Crossed Cape Meridian	Passed Tasmania	Arrived	Days Out
Cimba - -	Channel June 11	July 7	July 27		Aug. 21	72
Samuel Plimsoll -	Plymouth April 29	May 15	June 10	July 5 (Otway)	July 9	72
The Tweed - -	Lizard May 15	June 8	June 27	July 21 (S.W.Cape)	July 29	75

PASSAGES TO MELBOURNE UNDER 80 DAYS IN 1880.

Ship	Departure		Crossed Equator	Crossed Cape Meridian	Passed Cape Otway	Arrived	Days Out
Ben Voirlich -	Lizard	June 13	July 8	July 25	Aug. 17	Aug. 19	67
Sir Walter Raleigh	Start	May 17	June 10	June 30	July 22	Ju'y 23	67
Romanoff - -	Lizard	June 11	July 6	July 27	Aug. 17	Aug. 18	68
Ben Cruachan -	Lizard	April 18	May 19	May 30		June 27	70
Aristides - -	Lizard	July 27	Aug. 23	Sept. 12	Oct. 4	Oct. 5	70
Miltiades - -	Lizard	May 6	May 31	June 21	July 15	July 16	71
Loch Vennachar -	Tuskar	June 1	June 27	July 18	Aug. 12	Aug. 12	72
Loch Maree - -	Greenock	May 1	May 25	June 19		July 12	73
Mermerus - -	Dungeness	May 14				July 26	73
Salamis - -	Start	May 27	June 20	July 11		Aug. 10	75
Loch Katrine -	Clyde	Dec. 4				Feb. 17 '81	75
Theophane - -	Tuskar	Aug. 11				Oct. 27	77
Old Kensington -	Channel	April 30				July 17	78

Notes on Passages to Australia in 1880.

It will be noticed that all the ships going out in under 80 days, with exception of *Aristides*, *Loch Katrine* and *Theophane*, left the United Kingdom in April, May or June and got a good slant South. It was also a season of hard winds both in the Channel and North Atlantic and from the limits of the S.E. trades right away to the Otway and even inside the Heads.

Captain Charles Douglas, from the Blackwaller *Malabar*, took over the *Ben Voirlich* this year; and on 21st July when south of Gough Island he got 323 and 330 miles out of her in 48 hours before a hard W.S.W. gale.

On the 17th August, when in sight of Cape Schanck, *Ben Voirlich* was held up by terrific squalls from N.N.W. and N., and had to be brought to under reefed topsails. This cost her a day as she was not able to enter the Heads until the 19th, when the wind shifted to the W.N.W.

Sir Walter Raleigh made the best passage of her career. With a good run down Channel, she took her departure from the Start the day after leaving the Thames, but from the Eddystone to the line she only had two runs of over 200. However between 4th and 11th July in 42° 30′ S., she ran 2128 miles, her best day's work being only 304 miles, which meant very steady going. She also was held up off her port by strong head winds after being braced sharp up all the way from the meridian of the Leeuwin.

Romanoff had to beat down Channel and was six days from the Thames to the Lizard, and strong S.W. winds compelled her to go inside the Canaries and Cape Verdes. She crossed the equator in 21° W. She ran her easting down in 44° S., and though she had no big runs was only 21 days between the Cape meridian and the Otway.

Ben Cruachan also had tempestuous weather and easterly winds on making the Australian coast, and came into port with most of her bulwarks gone. The day after passing the Leeuwin meridian, 19th June, she had a hard gale with a very heavy beam sea. She had her fore and mizen lower topsails blown out of the bolt ropes, and carried away two topmast backstays owing to the heavy rolling.

Aristides had to beat out of the Channel against strong S.W. gales and *Miltiades* had three days of S.W. gales in the Bay of Biscay, whilst *Salamis*, which was very deeply laden with her Plimsoll mark awash, was forced down into 47° S. by hard easterly gales.

Samuel Plimsoll, with 384 emigrants on board, was only 16 days to the equator. Between the Cape and the Leeuwin she made the following fine 24-hour runs:—

June 11	..	..	.. 298	June 22	..	..	.. 291
„ 15	..	..	.. 294	„ 23	..	..	.. 308
„ 17	..	..	.. 313	„ 25	..	..	.. 314
„ 19	..	..	.. 304	„ 26	..	..	.. 300

The *Tweed* this year was commanded by Captain

White, who had had the *Blackadder*. The old ship averaged 240 miles a day from the equator to the S.W. Cape, Tasmania, her best day's work being from 8th to 9th July, when she covered 362 miles.

Loch Maree ran down her easting in 41° S. and experienced no very heavy weather, but managed to average 284 miles a day for 28 days.

Rodney went out to Adelaide in 74 days, but her passage was thrown in the shade by the wonderful *Torrens*, which arrived a few days later, only 65 days out from Plymouth.

The *Thomas Stephens* left Liverpool on 29th April and made the fine run of 83 days to Rangoon.

Passages under 80 days to Sydney in 1881.

Again only three ships made the run out to Sydney in under 80 days.

Cimba dropped her pilot in the Channel on 10th May and arrived Sydney on 24th July, 75 days out. *Samuel Plimsoll* arrived on 10th June 79 days from the Channel, and *Loch Etive* on 20th September 79 days from the Clyde.

PASSAGES TO MELBOURNE UNDER 80 DAYS IN 1881.

Ship	Departure	Crossed Equator	Crossed Cape Meridian	Passed Cape Otway	Arrived	Days Out
City of Agra - -	Lizard May 29	June 17	July 11	Aug. 5	Aug. 6	69
Theophane - ·	Tuskar June 2	June 29	July 20	Aug. 9	Aug. 10	69
Sobraon - ·	Plymouth Sept. 27				Dec. 6	70
Loch Maree - ·	S. Johns P. May 8	June 1	June 25	July 18	July 18	71
Salamis - ·	Portland April 20	May 11	June 6	June 30	July 1	72
Ben Voirlich - ·	Lizard May 2	May 25	June 21	July 13	July 15	74
Thyatira -	Start May 23	June 15	July 10		Aug. 6	75
Sir Walter Raleigh	Dartmouth May 13	June 10	July 3	July 27	July 27	75
Cassiope - ·	Tuskar July 17				Oct. 3	78
Mermerus - ·	Lizard Mar. 31	Apl. 22	May 19	June 16	June 17	78
Miltiades - ·	Channel May 4				July 22	79
Aristides - ·	Lizard June 17	July 14	Aug. 8		Sept. 6	79

" ILLAWARRA."

[*To face page* 301.

" ILLAWARRA."

Notes on Passages to Australia in 1881.

Captain Young once more showed what the old *City of Agra* could do when she got the chance. Between the N.E. and S.E. trades she lost her fore topgallant mast in a squall, otherwise the passage was without incident. Running the easting down she maintained a splendid average, as her best run was only 270. Captain Young evidently did not believe in high latitudes as he kept her in 39° and 40° S.

Theophane made a good try to beat the *City of Agra's* time; she made no less than three attempts to enter the Heads on the ebb tide, but each time the wind dropped in the rip and she was drifted back and at last was compelled to wait until the next day and come in on the flood.

Ben Voirlich again made some big runs, her best day's work being 349 miles and her best week 2100 miles.

Loch Maree had to be careful not to ship heavy water, as she had four valuable Clydesdale stallions on her main deck. *Thyatira* was in company with the little *Berean* for three days to the south'ard, parting from her eventually in 40° S., 131° E. *Berean* arrived in Launceston on 9th August, 87 days out from Prawle Point.

The Big "Illawarra."

In 1881, Devitt & Moore launched out with a real big ship, the *Illawarra*, and put her into the Sydney trade. She was not so fine lined as the earlier iron clippers, for the competition of steam and reduced freights were making good carrying capacity a necessity for a money-making ship. Nevertheless *Illawarra* had a very fair turn of speed, and her average of passages both outward and homeward was under 90 days.

She will be chiefly remembered as a cadet ship under the Brassey scheme; she succeeded the *Hesperus*, and under Captain Maitland carried premium cadets from 1899 to 1907. In that year Devitt & Moore made a contract to take 100 *Warspite* boys round the world, and as they did not consider the *Illawarra* large enough, they sold her to the Norwegians and bought the *Port Jackson*.

The Norwegians abandoned the old *Illawarra* in the North Atlantic during March, 1912, when she was on a passage from Leith to Valparaiso, her crew being taken off by the British steamer *Bengore Head*.

"Orontes."

The *Orontes*, Thompson's new ship, was also more of a deadweight carrier than a clipper. After a plodding life with no very startling adventures, she was run into and sunk on 23rd October, 1903, by the ss. *Oceana*, when almost in sight of Ostend, whither she was bound from a nitrate port.

The "Loch Torridon."

When the competition of steam began to cut badly into the Colonial trade, all the Loch three-masters except the *Loch Vennachar* and *Loch Garry*, the two finest ships in the fleet, had their yards removed from the mizen mast and were converted into barques, yet they still continued to make fine passages.

Until the eighties 1500 tons was considered a good size for a sailing ship, but the time arrived when it became necessary to have ships which possessed both large carrying capacity and speed, and every designer strove to produce a successful compromise between the two. It was soon found that full-rigged ships of 2000 tons and over were not economical ships to work, and thus it was that the four-mast barque came into being. At first many owners went in for four-mast ships, but it was soon proved that besides being more economical the four-mast barque was just as speedy.

Following the trend of the times Messrs. Aitken & Lilburn commissioned Barclay, Curle & Co. in 1881 to build them two four-mast barques of 2000 tons burden. These were the sister ships *Loch Moidart* and *Loch Torridon*; *Loch Moidart* was launched in September and *Loch Torridon* in November.

The *Loch Moidart* was only afloat nine years and was a general trader. On the 26th January, 1890, at 4 in the morning, when bound to Hamburg with nitrate from Pisagua, her look-out suddenly reported a bright light on the port bow. Five minutes later she struck on a sand bank, close to the village of Callantsoog in Northern Holland. A violent gale from the westward was blowing at the time, and only two men, one of whom was the cook, succeeded in gaining the shore alive.

Her sister ship, *Loch Torridon*, was one of the best known four-mast barques in the British Mercantile Marine, and one of the fastest.

" *Loch Torridon* is perhaps one of the most graceful and elegant models ever launched from the Glasgow yards," wrote Sir G. M. White, the Naval Architect to the Admiralty, in 1892.

In 1904 John Arthur Barry, the Australian writer, wrote of her:—" She is exceptionally lofty as to her masts, exceptionally square as to her yards. She carries nothing above a royal, but her royal yards are as long as the topgallant yards of most vessels. Her lower yards are enormous. The vessel is uncommonly well-manned with 20 hands in the foc's'le, with the usual complement of petty officers, together with three mates and four apprentices aft.   Looking forward from the break of the poop, one is struck by the immense amount of clear room on her decks, giving a visitor a sense of spaciousness and freedom in marked contrast to the often lumbered up decks of the average sailer.''

SPAR PLAN OF *LOCH TORRIDON*.

Bowsprit	25 feet.
Jibboom (outside bowsprit) ..	31 feet.
Bowsprit and jibboom (over all) ..	56 feet.

Spars .	Foremast feet	Mainmast feet	Mizen mast feet
Mast—deck to truck .. .	148	152	152
Lower mast	68	71	71
Doubling	18	18	18
Topmast	57	57	57
Doubling	7	$7\frac{1}{2}$	$7\frac{1}{2}$
Topgallant mast	27	30	28
Royal mast	$21\frac{1}{2}$	$22\frac{1}{2}$	22
Lower yard	88	88	88
Lower topsail yard	78	78	78
Upper topsail yard	74	74	74
Topgallant yard	56	56	56
Royal yard	$42\frac{1}{2}$	$42\frac{1}{2}$	$42\frac{1}{2}$

Spars of jiggermast	Length in feet
Mast—deck to truck	128
Lower mast	70
Doubling	12
Topmast	71
Spanker gaff	38
Spanker boom	46
Jaws of gaff to head of topsail	72

Her royals were 18 feet deep, measured at the bunt; and the depth of her courses was 38 feet measured at the bunt.   She also had a spencer gaff on her mizen, measuring $24\frac{1}{2}$ feet.   Thus it will be seen that, though she did not carry stunsails, she had plenty of canvas.

Loch Torridon had a poop 36 feet long, a half-deck for apprentices 16 feet long, a midship house 25 feet long, and her topgallant foc's'le measured 49 feet in length.

Sail Plan by the
LOCH MOIDART & TORRIDON
No 302 & 303

SAIL PLAN OF "LOCH MOIDART" AND "LOCH TORRIDON."

[To face page 304.

Captain Pattman, who commanded her for over 26 years, gave the following testimony to her qualities, when interviewed by the *Shipping Gazette*:—''Being perfectly sparred, the ship is easy to steer, and even in the worst weather the smallest boy on board can keep her on her course.''

Anyone who has felt how hard-mouthed the average four-mast barque can be will appreciate this quality and envy the lucky quartermasters of such a ship. On *Loch Torridon* there was certainly no excuse for bad steering, and the most strictly adhered to rule on board was that any man or boy found more than half a point off his course was at once sent away from the wheel in disgrace. There were two other factors in *Loch Torridon's* success, which she owed to her enterprising commander. Captain Pattman believed in British crews, and took the trouble to train his apprentices.

Regarding the first, he once remarked:—''Give me a Britisher everytime, drunken and bad as he is. The best crew I ever had during the past 15 years I shipped in London last summer (1907). They were all Britishers. The view I hold on this question is that the British sailing ship sailor cannot be equalled, let alone beaten. But the difficulty I have experienced is in regard to steamship A.B.'s. I shipped one of these fellows some time ago, and it turned out that he knew nothing of sailing ship ways. He could not steer, and he knew a good deal less than one of our second voyage apprentices. As compared with such a man, I say, 'Give me a foreigner who has been at sea on sailing ships for two or three years and who knows the way things are done on a sailing ship.' I find, however, that the foreigner who has been a few years in British ships becomes more insolent, more disobedient and more difficult to manage than the British sail-trained seaman."

With regard to the training of apprentices, many a good officer owes his present position to the late Captain Pattman. The *Loch Torridon* apprentices went to the wheel on their first voyage. At first they took the lee wheel, but as soon as they showed their ability they were allowed to stand their regular trick. In other matters Captain Pattman was a strong advocate of the system carried out on board the German training ships, notably the North German Lloyd.

Captain Pattman took command of *Loch Torridon* on her second voyage. Her maiden voyage was a very tragic one. She went out to Hobson's Bay from Glasgow under Captain Pinder, arriving on 27th April, 1882, 105 days out. This gave no indication of her sailing capabilities, so she was not taken up to load wool but was sent across to Calcutta to load jute. She left Calcutta on 22nd August. On 9th October, when off the Cape, she ran into a heavy gale from W.N.W. Captain Pinder hove her to on the starboard tack under close-reefed main topsail. After a bit Captain Pinder wore her round on to the port tack, but with the squalls increasing she lay down to it, dipping her starboard rail. Thereupon Captain Pinder decided to wear her back on to the starboard tack. The mate besought him not to do this without setting the foresail, but unfortunately, having been lucky once, the captain insisted, with the result that when she got off before the wind she had not enough way on her and a tremendous sea came roaring over the stern and carried overboard the master, second mate, man at the wheel, sailmaker and a boy, all being drowned. The mate also was swept away but was saved by a hitch of the main brace

CAPTAIN PATTMAN'S EARLY CAREER.

Date	Ship served in	Rig	Tons	Capacity	Remarks
1864	Woodland Lass -	Schooner	120	Boy	Southwold to Shields and back.
,,	Hearts of Oak -	Billy boy	105	Boy	Southwold to Hartlepool.
1866	Advice -	Barque	397	Apprentice	Hartlepool to Cronstad—Cronstad to London.
,,	Hearts of Oak -	Billy boy	105	Boy	Southwold to Sunderland.
,,	Hubertus -	Brig	190	O.S.	Seaham to Boulogne, London, Hamburg, Dieppe and London.
1867	Kingdom of Italy	Barque	427	O.S.	Sunderland to Aden, Tuticorin, and back to London.
1868	Callisto -	Barque	598	O.S.	London to Adelaide, Newcastle, N.S.W. and Shanghai.
,,	Maggie -	Brigantine	230	A.B	Shanghai, Yokohama, Hongkong, put back to Yokohama disabled.
1869	Lauderdale -	Ship	1174	A.B	Shanghai to Foochow and back with Chinese passengers. Shanghai to London, 153 days, put into St. Helena short of provisions, put into Spithead Captain ill and no food.
1870	Christiana Thompson	Ship	1066	A.B.	London to Sydney and back.
,,	Kingdom of Belgium	Barque	672	2nd Mate	London to Madras, wrecked in cyclone 1st May in Madras Roads.
,,	Kingdom of Fife -	Barque	497	2nd Mate	Madras to London.
1871	Ocean Beauty -	Barque	597	2nd Mate	London to Adelaide, Newcastle, N.S.W., Hongkong, Saigon and Sourabaya.
1872	County of Forfar -	Ship	999	1st Mate	Sourabaya, Rotterdam and Glasgow.
,,	,,	,,	,,	,,	Glasgow to Batavia, Sourabaya and Rotterdam.
1873-4	,,	,,	,,	,,	Glasgow to Samarang, Sourabaya and Niewe Dieppe.
1874-5	,,	,,	,,	,,	Glasgow to Samarang, Sourabaya, Bombay, Akyab and Antwerp.
1875-6	,,	,,	,,	,,	Glasgow to Sourabaya, Bombay and London.
1878	County of Cromarty	4-mast ship	1673	,,	Glasgow to Rio Janeiro, wrecked in ballast S. Rio Grande del Sul. Captain and second mate died of smallpox.
1879	County of Selkirk	4-mast ship	1865	Master	Glasgow to Calcutta and London.
1880	County of Bute -	Ship	789	,,	Cardiff to Batavia, 80 days Akyab to Antwerp.
1881	County of Selkirk	4-mast ship	1865	,,	Cardiff, Bombay, Rangoon and Liverpool.
	,,	,,	,,	,,	Liverpool to Colombo, Bombay to London.

getting round his leg.   On the following day the weather moderated, and the mate brought the ship home to Plymouth, from whence she was towed up to London.

Captain Pattman took charge of *Loch Torridon* in December, 1882, giving up the command of the four-mast ship *County of Selkirk* in order to take the Loch liner.   As a sailing ship commander of the first rank, it may perhaps be of interest to give a short outline of Captain Pattman's previous career.

From this record it will be seen that Captain Pattman had won his way to command by the time-honoured means of the hawse-hole.

In the barque *Advice* he had an experience which would have sickened most boys of the sea, and he bore the scars to his dying day.   The officers of the ship were actually prosecuted by his father for their brutality, the result being that Pattman's indentures were cancelled, the captain had his certificate cancelled and was sentenced to 18 months' hard labour, whilst the mate was given three years' hard labour.   Both were hard drinkers and uneducated men.

The brig *Hubertus*, which Pattman joined as an ordinary seaman, was a real old-fashioned Geordie collier brig.   Her skipper could neither read nor write, and Pattman acted as his clerk and did all his correspondence.   But the old man knew his way about the North Sea by smell: he only had to sniff the arming of the lead and was never wrong in naming the ship's position.   These old collier skippers always wore sleeved vests and stove-pipe hats at sea, and in the summer the Thames was often a wonderful sight when these colliers sailed up to London before a fair wind. There were often a hundred and more, brigs, schooners, and barques, all crowding up the river so closely,

"LOCH TORRIDON."
With Perforated Sails,

[To face page 398.

CAPTAIN PATTMAN.

that these old Geordie skippers, all smoking long church-wardens, would be leaning over their respective taffrails exchanging greetings and gossip. Truly 60 years have changed the London River. Yet many a man living to-day can remember the year 1866, when Pattman sailed up to London in his Geordie brig. It was the year in which the three famous tea clippers *Ariel*, *Taeping*, and *Serica* arrived in the river on the same tide. Seafaring then was far more like that of the days of Drake and the Elizabethans than it is like the seafaring of the present day.

Lauderdale was a well-known ship in the China trade, and the *Christiana Thompson* was, of course, the Aberdeen White Star liner.

On her first three voyages under Captain Pattman, *Loch Torridon* took first, second, and third class passengers out to Melbourne from Glasgow.

She left Glasgow on 2nd March, 1883, with 7 saloon, 33 steerage passengers and 12 prize stallions for Port Phillip. Passed Rothesay Bay on the 5th and the Tuskar on the 8th. Running down the easting she made 1911 miles in one week, and was only 22 days between the Cape meridian and Hobson's Bay, passing through the Heads 74 days out from the Tuskar.

At Melbourne she took on board 820 horses, 2 cows, 8 dogs, 12 sheep and 27 Chinese grooms for Calcutta. The trade in walers between Australia and Calcutta was a very lucrative one in those days. On the *Loch Torridon* a new system was adopted for taking the horses on board. They were walked from the railway trucks up gangways on to the main deck, then down other specially laid gangways through the hatchways and so into their stalls. This method proved an unqualified success and saved four days' time on the old method of slinging them aboard. The hatch gangways were left in position, and while at sea the horses were exercised on deck in batches, every horse getting 24 hours a week on deck. This would have been impossible on a ship with an incumbered deck, but here the fine clean sweep of *Loch Torridon's* main deck came in useful as a sort of training ground.

Sailing from Melbourne on 20th June, 1883, the *Loch Torridon* was unfortunate in encountering very bad weather between Cape Otway and the Leeuwin, in which she lost 27 horses and 2 Chinese grooms. She arrived in Calcutta on 1st August, 42 days out, and cleared £1250 on the trip after paying all expenses such as fittings, grooms and horse food. From Calcutta she took 103 days to London.

On the 26th May, 1884, *Loch Torridon* again left Glasgow for Melbourne with 8 saloon, 8 second class and 34 steerage passengers, and the usual Clyde cargo of pig iron, pipes, bar iron, heavy hardware, bricks, boards, ale and whisky. She put into Rothesay Bay for shelter from the weather on 30th May, and passed the Tuskar on 2nd June. Crossed the line on 1st July in 27° W. The S.E. trades were southerly and she had to beat along the Brazilian coast to 17° S. Passed the Cape meridian on 30th July in 44° S. On 10th and 11th August she logged 642 miles, was 23 days from the Cape meridian to Port Phillip, and arrived in Melbourne 23rd August, 82 days from the Tuskar. She then took coal from Newcastle, N.S.W., to Frisco, making the run across the Pacific in 58 days: and loaded a grain cargo home.

In 1885 she ran out to Melbourne from Glasgow with 58 passengers in 89 days, crossed to Frisco with Newcastle coal in 58 days, and took 49,317 bags of wheat from Frisco to Hull.

In 1886 she went out to Bombay from Cardiff with 2928 tons of coal, arriving Bombay on 14th January, 1887, 97 days out, having raced and beaten the *County of Edinburgh*.

After lying three months in Bombay, she got a freight home to Dunkirk.

In 1887 *Loch Torridon* went to Calcutta from Liverpool and then took a Calcutta cargo to New York, arriving there on 10th June, 1888, 102 days out. From New York she took case oil back to Calcutta, but at 8.15 a.m. on 1st November she stranded on Bangaduni Sand and Captain Pattman had to jettison cargo to get her off. It was proved at the inquiry that an abnormal nor'-westerly current caused by cyclonic disturbances at the south end of the Bay of Bengal had set the *Loch Torridon* in on the land. The weather had been thick for some days and Captain Pattman had no blame attached to him. Temporary repairs were made in Calcutta, and on her arrival home permanent repairs were made at Jarrow-on-Tyne.

In 1889 *Loch Torridon* again went to Calcutta, taking a brutal cargo of railway iron from Middlesboro, and came home to London.

In 1890 she went out to Calcutta from Liverpool in 87 days port to port, and took jute back to Dundee.

In 1891 *Loch Torridon* at last returned to the Australian trade, arriving in Sydney from Glasgow 94 days out. Then after lying in Sydney for five months, she loaded her first wool cargo. Amongst the magnificent fleet of 77 sailing ships, which were screwing wool into their holds for the London market, *Loch Torridon* was considered an outsider, a dark horse with her name all to make; and she thus had to wait for the last sales, and did not get away until the 27th March,

1892. Nevertheless the *Loch Torridon* made the best passage of the season and had the honour of beating all the cracks. The following is Captain Pattman's account of his passage :—

My passage home was the smartest of the wool season, 1891-2, either from Melbourne or Sydney, being 81 days to the Lizard and 83 to dock. After I left Sydney, I got down as far as Jervis Bay and there met an S.S.E. gale, which was in force for 36 hours. I went away for the north of New Zealand, which I passed on the 14th day out. I fell in with the *Liverpool* there. I was in 150° W. on 29th April, before I got a wind without any easting in it. Nothing but N.E.E. and S.E. winds prevailed up to that time.   On 14th May I rounded the Horn, 40 days out, I was nearly grey-headed at that time.   On 21st May I fell in with the *Strathdon*. We were both dodging icebergs, the *Strathdon* had been in amongst them since 18th May, but I only had 12 hours of it, which was quite enough. I left her astern in a short time.   On 3rd June I was in 0° 27′ S. lat., 60 days from Sydney, 20 from the Horn.   On 24th June I signalled at the Lizards, 21 days from the equator. I think it is a record passage from the Horn. I can hardly believe my good fortune, for I threw up the sponge when I got to the Horn, 40 days out, and made sure that the passage would run into three figures. *Loch Torridon* passed everything we saw, in fact she never sailed better with me.

I saw in the evening papers that the *Hesperus* was reported in 14° N. on 1st June. I was in 0° 27′ S. on 3rd June. The *Hesperus* docked yesterday.   She was the only one I thought had a chance with me, and I am of opinion that if I had gone south of New Zealand I should have done much better. It would have been hard lines if I could not have rounded the Snares in 14 days and been in a better position for winds as well, but I am content. I have shown that an outsider, as they looked upon the *Loch Torridon*, can show the road to their regular traders.

Ice to the South'ard.

It will be noticed from Captain Pattman's letter on his run home in 1892 that *Strathdon* and *Loch Torridon* encountered ice to the south'ard. And they were not the only ships to do so.

In the years 1892 and 1893 a tremendous drift of field ice and huge bergs, many of them over 1000 feet in

height, blocked the way of ships in the Southern Ocean,
as the following reports will show :—

1892.

April	*Cromdale*	encountered ice	1000 feet high in	46° S. 36° W.
May	*Strathdon*	,,	,,	1000	,,	,,	45 S. 25 W.
June	*County of Edinbro,,*	,,	900	,,	,,	45 S. 37 W.
Sept.	*Loch Eck*	,,	,,	1000	,,	,,	44 S. 2 W.
Oct.	*Curzon*	,,	,,	1000	,,	,,	44 S. 31 W.
Oct.	*Liverpool*	,,	,,	800	,,	,,	55 S. 94 W.

1893.

Jan.	*Loch Torridon*	encountered ice	1500 feet high in	51° S. 46° W.
Feb.	*Cutty Sark*	,,	,,	1000	,,	,,	50 S. 43 W.
Mar.	*Turakina*	,,	,,	1200	,,	,,	51 S. 47 W.
April	*Brier Holme*	,,	,,	1000	,,	,,	49 S. 51 W.
May	*Charles Racine*	,,	,,	1000	,,	,,	50 S. 52 W.

The *Cromdale* had a very exciting experience, and
Captain E. H. Andrew wrote the following account to
the secretary of the London Shipmasters' Society :—

We left Sydney on 1st March, and having run our easting down on
the parallel of 49° to 50° S., rounded the Horn on 30th March without
having seen ice, the average temperature of the water being 43° during
the whole run across.

At midnight on 1st April in 56° S., 58° 32′ W., the temperature fell
to 37¼°, this being the lowest for the voyage, but no ice was seen though
there was a suspicious glare to the southward.

At 4 a.m. on 6th April in 46° S., 36° W., a large berg was reported
right ahead, just giving us time to clear it. At 4.30 with the first signs
of daybreak, several could be distinctly seen to windward, the wind
being N.W. and the ship steering N.E. about 9 knots. At daylight,
5.20 a.m., the whole horizon to windward was a complete mass of bergs
of enormous size, with an unbroken wall at the back ; there were also
many to leeward.

I now called all hands, and after reducing speed to 7 knots sent
the hands to their stations and stood on. At 7 a.m. there was a wall
extending from a point on the lee bow to about 4 points on the lee
quarter, and at 7.30 both walls joined ahead. I sent the chief mate
aloft with a pair of glasses to find a passage out, but he reported
from the topgallant yard that the ice was unbroken ahead. Finding
myself embayed and closely beset with innumerable bergs of all shapes,
I decided to tack and try and get out the way I had come into the bay.

The cliffs were now truly grand, rising up 300 feet on either side of us, and as square and true at the edge as if just out of a joiner's shop, with the sea breaking right over the southern cliff and whirling away in a cloud of spray.

Tacked ship at 7.30 finding the utmost difficulty in keeping clear of the huge pieces strewn so thickly in the water and having on several occasions to scrape her along one to keep clear of the next.

We stood on in this way until 11 a.m., when, to my horror, the wind started to veer with every squall till I drew quite close to the southern barrier, having the extreme point a little on my lee bow. I felt sure we must go ashore without a chance of saving ourselves. Just about 11.30 the wind shifted to S.W. with a strong squall, so we squared away to the N.W. and came past the same bergs as we had seen at daybreak, the largest being about 1000 feet high, anvil shaped. At 2 p.m. we got on the N.W. side of the northern arm of the horseshoe shaped mass. It then reached from 4 points on my lee bow to as far as could be seen astern in one unbroken line.

A fact worthy of note was that at least 50 of the bergs in the bay were perfectly black, which was to be accounted for by the temperature of the water, being 51°, which had turned many over. I also think that had there been even the smallest outlet at the eastern side of this mass, the water between the barriers would not have been so thickly strewn with bergs, as the prevailing westerly gales would have driven them through and separated them. I have frequently seen ice down south, but never anything like even the smaller bergs in this group.

I also had precisely the same experience with regard to the temperature of water on our homeward passage in the *Derwent* three years ago, as we dipped up a bucket of water within half a mile of a huge berg and found no change in the temperature.

Cromdale, Strathdon, County of Edinburgh and *Curzon,* all sighted this stupendous ice barrier, and *Loch Torridon* when she spoke the *Strathdon* was on the extreme eastern end in about 25° W., whilst the *Cromdale* cleared it at the extreme western end, giving the length of the barrier from east to west about 12 degrees of longitude.

In the following year *Loch Torridon, Cutty Sark, Turakina, Brier Holme* and *Charles Racine* fell in with an equally huge field of ice, about 6 degrees of latitude further south and stretching from 52° W. to 43° W. That the two fields were the same lot of ice it is very difficult to say for certain, but it is more likely that they were quite separate from each other.

Here is *Loch Torridon's* account of the 1893 ice as given to the *Shipping Gazette* :—

Loch Torridon reports that on 17th January, 1893, in lat. 52° 50′ S., long. 46° W., she sighted two large icebergs to the eastward. On the 19th in 50° 50′ S., 46° W., she passed between numerous immense bergs, ranging in size from ¼ to 3 miles in length, and from 500 to 1000 feet high. At 3.30 p.m. on same date she saw an immense continent of ice ahead with apparently no open water. Passing to the eastward she had the south end abeam at 4 p.m. and the north end at 9.30 a.m. As the ship had been sailing 9 knots an hour during this time, steering a N. 11° E. course, this would give the length, north and south, of this mass to be about 50 miles.

How far it extended to the westward was not known, but from aloft, as as far as the eye could see, nothing but ice was visible. Numerous large bergs were to the eastward of the barrier, through which *Loch Torridon* threaded her way, besides vast quantities of detached pieces of ice and small bergs.

Numerous bays and indentations were noticed in the continent of ice, with bergs and detached ice in the bays cracking against each other and turning over. *Loch Torridon* had sleet and fine snow all night and intense cold. Numberless bergs were passed until 8 a.m. on the 20th, when an iceberg was abeam to the eastward at least 3 miles long and 1500 feet high.

The following was the famous *Cutty Sark's* experience. I have taken it from Captain Woodget's private journal:—

Wednesday, 8th February.—Lat. 50° 08′ S., long. 46° 41′ W., course N. 50° E., distance 150 miles. Gentle S.W. breeze and fine. 6·0 a.m., foggy; 6.30, fog lifted and we found ourselves surrounded by icebergs; 8 a.m., foggy again; ice ahead, in fact there was ice all round. As soon as we cleared one berg another would be reported. You could hear the sea roaring on them and through them, the ice cracking sometimes like thunder, at other times like cannon, and often like a sharp rifle report, and yet could not see them.

At 1 p.m. the top of an iceberg was seen which one could hardly believe was ice, it looked like a streak of dark cloud. Then we could see the ice a few feet down, but we could not see the bottom. It was up at an angle of 45 degrees, we were only about 1000 feet off, so it would be 1000 feet high, it had a circular top but we could not see the ends.

A few minutes later another was under the bows, we only cleared it by a few feet.   It was about 100 feet high and flat-topped.   Just as we were passing the corner there was a sharp report that made you jump, as if it was breaking in two.

Found another on the other side quite close, and a few minutes later saw the long ridge of ice almost ahead.   Kept off, and then another came in sight on the other bow.   We were too near it to keep away, but I felt sure that it was no part of the big one—as we were passing this the point of the big one came in sight, the fog cleared and we passed in between them, there being not more than 400 feet between them. When we had cleared the big one, I saw its north end and took bearings. After sailing 8 miles I took other bearings and found that the east side was 19 miles long; and we could not see the end of the side we sailed along.   We sailed about 6 miles alongside of it, water now quite smooth. Before noon the water was quite lumpy from all ways.   After we had cleared the passage by about 3 or 4 miles, it cleared up astern and what a sight it was! Nothing but icebergs through the passage and on the south side of the passage (for the south berg was only about ½ mile long north and south, same height as the big berg.   I expect it had not long broken off.)   There was nothing but a sea of ice astern, and another large flat-topped iceberg, which as far as you could see extended like land, it must have been 20 miles long or more.

After we were through, there was nothing but small ice from small pieces to bergs 100 feet long.   Also there was one about a mile long covered with what looked like pumice stone or lumps of tallow.

"Loch Torridon's" Voyages, 1892-1908.

Notwithstanding her fine wool passage in 1892, *Loch Torridon* could not find a cargo in London and was obliged to leave the Thames in ballast.   With only 350 tons of flints and a quantity of " London rubbish " as stiffening, she sailed in magnificent style.

She left Gravesend on 30th July, 1892—was off Start Point, 31st July—crossed the equator, 19th August, 20 days out—lost S.E. trades in 22° S., 29th August—crossed the Cape meridian, 14th September, 46 days out—made Moonlight Island, 7th October, 69 days out.

Loch Torridon's best week's work was 2119 knots; she ran down her easting in 43° S. and made the following consecutive runs in the 24 hours— 303, 290, 288, 272, 285, 270, 327 and 341 miles.

Her passage worked out at 69 days pilot to pilot, 73 days port to port. This would have been still better if she had not had to battle against a " dead muzzler " for the last week of the passage. She cleared for London on 30th November, 1892, and after her encounter with the ice arrived in the Thames 96 days out.

Again she left London in ballast. This time she was sent up to Frederickstadt, where she loaded 940 pieces of timber and 400 tons of pig iron for Melbourne. Again she made a fine run out.

She sailed on 14th June, 1893, from Frederickstadt. Had strong head winds in the North Sea:—

Passed Dover, 20th June—passed Ushant 24th June—passed Cape Finisterre, 29th June—crossed the line, 23rd July—crossed Cape meridian in 42° S., 17th August.

In lat. 46° S., long. 86° E., *Loch Torridon* was caught in an unusually heavy gale with a tremendous cross sea, the barometer touching 28.83°. However, she came through it without damage, Captain Pattman using oil with good effect. *Loch Torridon* passed through Port Phillip Heads at 11.30 p.m. on 9th September, 87 days from Frederickstadt and 77 days from Ushant. At the time this was a record passage from Norway to Melbourne.

Loch Torridon cleared for London on 20th November, 1893, with a cargo consisting of 8498 bales of wool, 329 bales of sheepskins, 1250 old rails, 2 casks arsenic, 657 packages of tallow, 11 packages of books, 2000 bags of wheat, 11 bales of fur skins, 12 bales of hair, 1942 bags of peas, 118 hides, 351 pigs, horns, etc., 100 bales of scrolls. She dropped her pilot on the 30th and reached London on 6th March, 96 days out.

In 1894 she loaded coke and railway iron at Barry for Port Pirrie and made the run out in 72 days, her best week's work being 1914 miles and her best 24 hours 327 miles.

She left Barry at 6 p.m. on 18th May—crossed the equator, 23 days out—crossed the Cape meridian on 30th June—crossed the meridian of Cape Leeuwin on 20th July—sighted Cape Borda 10 p.m., 27th July— passed Wedge Island at 1 a m., 28th July, in a strong westerly gale and anchored at 1 p.m. on 30th July.

From Port Pirrie she went up to Melbourne and loaded another cargo of wool, wheat and hides; and leaving Melbourne on 20th December arrived in the Thames on 21st March, 1895.

In 1895, owing to the falling off in the export trade to Victoria, which sailing ships were, of course, the first to feel, *Loch Torridon* was compelled to accept a charter for Cape Town. Leaving London 6th July, she reached Table Bay on 30th August, 55 days out. Here she was visited and greatly admired by Lord Brassey. From Africa she went to Australia, but owing to the severe drought, like many another clipper that year, she failed to get a wool cargo and so was compelled to go across to the coast of South America for a homeward freight. It was on this occasion that she had the famous race to Valparaiso with the well-known four-mast ship *Wendur*. The vessels left Newcastle, N.S.W., in company on 1st January, 1896, and though neither sighted the other during the passage, they made a magnificent race of it. *Wendur* picked up her pilot off Cape Coronilla at 6 p.m. on 29th January, and reached the anchorage at 8 p.m., after a record passage of 29 days.

Loch Torridon was held up by fog and calm at the entrance to the Bay and did not arrive until six hours later. The previous best passage was 32 days, which had been made two years before. Many bets had been

"LOCH TORRIDON."

Photo lent by late Captain Pattman.

[To face page 318.

made on this race, as both ships were noted in the Colonies for their sailing qualities. *Wendur*, indeed, was one of the finest ships in the British Mercantile Marine, and under Captain Frank Whiston had made many a splendid passage and, curiously enough, had once before shown *Loch Torridon* the road by running from Frederickstadt to Melbourne in 81 days, before which *Loch Torridon's* run had been considered the record.

In the run to Valparaiso *Wendur's* best day's work was 330 miles with a moderate N.W. wind and heavy southerly swell in 54° S., 128° W. The next day she ran 310 miles, and three days later 320 miles, the wind strong at N.W. with heavy sea; her log remarks that she lost her boats, pigstye, goats, etc., on this day, so Captain Whiston was driving her.

Loch Torridon loaded at Tocopilla for Hamburg, and was 93 days coming home, a poor passage, her bottom was probably foul. On 6th July her decks were badly swept off the Horn and she had a big repair bill when she arrived in Glasgow from Hamburg.

In 1896-7 she went out to Adelaide from Glasgow in 71 days and then crossed from Newcastle, N.S.W., to Frisco in 46 days. She left Newcastle on 15th April in company with the four-mast ship *Thistle* and the Norwegian ship *Hiawatha*. Both these vessels were dropped hull down to leeward on the first day out. Going through the Islands continuous bad weather was met with; Captain Pattman never had his yards off the backstays until 35° N. and had difficulty in weathering Fiji; nevertheless on 31st May *Loch Torridon* came flying through the Golden Gate in front of a N.Wly. gale, and anchored in the Bay at 10 p.m.

Hiawatha took 62 days, *Thistle* 79 days, and two

other ships, the American barque *Topgallant* 100 days and the *Cressington* 106 days. Besides beating these, *Loch Torridon* passed no less than ten vessels which had sailed from Newcastle before her. Loading grain at Port Costa, *Loch Torridon* sailed on 23rd July, and arrived at Falmouth on 13th November, 1897, 113 days out. Captain Pattman stated that owing to the foulness of her bottom his ship was not sailing her best and he was disappointed with his passage.

Other passages home from Frisco that year were :—

Musselcrag	arrived Queenstown	.. 110	days out.
Lord Templeton	,, ,,	.. 111	,,
Sierra Cadena	.. ,,	.. 114	,,
Andelana	,, ..	.. 114	,,
Dominion	,, ,,	.. 117	,,
Gifford ..	arrived Liverpool	.. 118	,,
Crown of Denmark	,, Queenstown	.. 128	,,
Caradoc ..	,, ,,	.. 134	,,

All these vessels sailed about July and were considered crack ships.

In 1898 *Loch Torridon* went out to Adelaide in 79 days. Whilst running her easting down she was swept by a heavy sea, one man being lost overboard, the half-deck burst in like a pack of cards, the donkeyhouse stove, and three of the boats flattened out and left like skeletons in the chocks, whilst their davits were snapped off close to the deck. She came home from Melbourne to London in 90 days.

In 1898-9 she made the splendid run of 72 days 15 hours to Sydney.

She left London 5 a.m., 10th November, 1898—on 11th November she ran 300 miles in the 24 hours—on 12th November she ran 315 miles in the 24 hours—crossed the line in 28° W., 22 days out—ran her easting down in 45° S., best 24 hours 320 miles and was 23 days from the Cape Meridian to Tasmania.

Loch Torridon had between 4000 and 5000 tons of

heavy general cargo in her hold and was very deep. Between 1875-1887 the clippers loaded nothing like such a heavy general cargo outwards, and yet this performance of *Loch Torridon's* is equal to any of that day.

She arrived in Port Jackson on 31st January, 1899. This year for a change she came home from Lyttelton, N.Z., in 86 days.

The next three years she did nothing remarkable.

1899	London to Adelaide	..	..	85 days
	Melbourne to London	..	..	105 ,,
1900	London to Adelaide	..	..	88 ,,
	Melbourne to London	..	..	88 ,,
1901	London to Adelaide	..	..	86 ,,
	Adelaide to London	..	..	112 ,,

In 1902 she went out to Adelaide in 79 days, then loaded coals at Newcastle, N.S.W., for Frisco. Again she made a remarkable run across the Pacific.

She left Newcastle on 27th April—crossed the line on 17th May in 169° 42' W.—arrived at Frisco on 11th June, 45 days out.

At San Francisco Captain Pattman loaded wheat for Liverpool. But when he was ready to sail he found himself 10 men short, so applied to the usual sources. And here is a good instance of the methods of Frisco boarding-house masters at that date. He was informed that each man would cost him $30 blood money, $25 advance, $5 shipping fee, $1 boat hire—total $61 per man. This was more than a resolute man like Captain Pattman could put up with, especially with wheat freights to U.K. at 11s. 3d. Though the boarding-house masters were a law unto themselves in San Francisco and boasted of their power, he determined to brave them and after some trouble managed to get men at $31 inclusive per man. His success broke the ring for a time, and they were soon offering men at $21 a head, less

M

$2.50 commission of the captains. No doubt many a present day officer will remember the episode, which caused quite a stir in windjammer circles at Frisco, and even produced a long poem in one of the leading papers. This poem was entitled "The Lay of the *Loch Torridon*," and the patriotic Frisco newspaper man takes care that the British captain is bested in his efforts. The *Loch Torridon* sailed on 8th November, in company with the four-mast barque *Crocodile*. *Loch Torridon* arrived Liverpool on 14th March, 1904, and the *Crocodile* on 31st March, over two weeks behind.

From 1904 to 1909, when Captain Pattman resigned his command, *Loch Torridon* was kept on the Australian run, her passages being:—

1904	Glasgow to Sydney	..	.. 77 days.
	Sydney to London	..	.. 97 ,.
1905	London to Adelaide	..	.. 85 ,,
	Melbourne to London	..	.. 106 ,,
1906	London to Adelaide	..	.. 83 ,.
	Melbourne to London	..	.. 117 ,,
1907	London to Adelaide	..	.. 83 ,,
	Melbourne to London	..	.. 86 ,,
1908	London to Adelaide	..	.. 94 ,,
	Melbourne to London	..	.. 87 ,,

On her arrival home in 1908, Captain Pattman reluctantly decided to give up his command and go into steam, his reason that vexed one, the lack of real sailormen to man her. Besides which, owing to the unwillingness of good men to remain in sail, he had to put up with an aged " has been " as mate and an apprentice just out of his time for second mate.

In 1912 *Loch Torridon* was sold to the Russians. About the same time Captain Pattman had his leg broken by a sea whilst on the bridge of his new command. He was landed at Falmouth and died there in hospital.

The old *Loch Torridon* survived until 1915, when she

"PORT JACKSON," in the Thames.

[To face page 228.

"PORT JACKSON."

Photo by Captain Schütze, Sydney.

foundered near the entrance to the Channel in the last days of January, and it is possible that a German submarine caused her end. Her Russian crew were rescued by the British steamer *Orduna*, and the Liverpool Shipwreck and Humane Society awarded medals and certificates of thanks to Captain Taylor of the *Orduna* and her chief and second officers.

"Port Jackson."

Port Jackson has always been considered one of the most beautiful iron ships ever built. She was designed by Mr. Alexander Duthie, and built by Hall under the supervision of the Duthie brothers; cost £29,000 to build or at the rate of £13 a ton; was unusually strong and in every way made as perfect as possible. She was one of the most sightly four-mast barques ever launched. Captain Crombie was her first commander, and under him she did some very fine performances, notably a run of 89 days from Sydney to San Francisco, when she was only three days behind the time of the mail steamer. Her best run in the 24 hours was 845 miles. Unfortunately, when Captain Crombie left her, for some years no one attempted to bring out *Port Jackson's* sailing qualities, and for two years before she was bought by Devitt & Moore for their cadet training scheme she lay idle in the Thames. After long years of cadet carrying *Port Jackson* fell a victim to the war, being torpedoed by a German submarine in the Channel in 1916.

PASSAGES TO SYDNEY UNDER 80 DAYS IN 1882.

Ship			From	Left	To	Arrived	Days Out
Thomas Stephens -		-	Channel	Nov. 9	Sydney	Jan. 22, '83	74
Port Jackson	•	-	,,	Oct. 28	,,	Jan. 18, '83	77

PASSAGES TO MELBOURNE UNDER 80 DAYS IN 1882.

Ship	Departure		Crossed Equator		Crossed Cape Meridian		Passed Cape Otway		Arrived		Days Out
Rodney - -	Plymouth	Oct. 15	Nov.	7	Nov.	29	Dec.	22	Dec.	23	69
Ben Voirlich -	Lizard	May 3	May	28	June	18	July	11	July	12	70
Salamis - -	Lizard	Mar. 7	Mar.	31	April	24			May	17	71
Miltiades - -	Lizard	April 19	May	15	June	6			July	1	73
Aristides - -	Start	July 14	Aug.	13	Sept.	4	Sept.	25	Sept.	25	73
Simla - -	Penzance	Sept. 3							Nov.	16	74
Marpesia - -	Tuskar	July 9	Aug.	11	Aug.	30			Sept.	25	78
Thessalus - -	Channel	May 10							July	28	79

Notes on Passages to Australia in 1882.

Port Jackson holds the record of being the first four-poster to go out to Sydney in under 80 days. Her best run was 345 miles in the 24 hours. The *Rodney's* best run was 312 miles, made the day before she sighted the Otway.

Ben Voirlich averaged 300 miles a day from Gough Island to Kerguelen.

Salamis crossed the Cape meridian the same day as the steamship *Aberdeen*, and the steamer only managed to get inside the Heads on 14th May, a bare 70 hours ahead of the gallant little green clipper.

The *Simla* was a fine Liverpool ship with a good reputation for speed. She registered 1260 tons and was built by Royden in 1874. For a change there were no Lochs out to the Colonies in under 80 days this year, and Messrs. Aitken & Lilburn had sent their new four-masters to Calcutta.

Notes on Passages to Australia in 1883.

The *Maulesden*, which figured in these tables in 1877, was a 1500-ton ship, built by Stephen, of Dundee, for David Bruce. She and her sister ship, the *Duntrune*, were very well known clippers with some very fine records to their credit. But this passage of *Maulesden's* to Maryborough, Queensland, made a record which has never been approached. It will be noticed that she crossed the line 17 days out, doubled the Cape 39 days out, and passed Tasmania 61 days out, a truly phenomenal passage. Running the easting down, she made 24-hour runs of 302, 303, 304, 311, 317, 322 and 335 miles, whilst her best weeks were 1698, 1798, 1908 and 1929 miles. From Maryborough she went across to Frisco, and from there to U.K., calling at Queenstown; and the whole voyage, including detention in port, was only 9 months 13 days. I have a photograph of her, and she is a typical iron clipper very like the *Ben Voirlich.*

PASSAGES TO AUSTRALIA UNDER 80 DAYS IN 1883.

Ship	Departure	Crossed Equator	Crossed Cape Meridian	Passed Otway or S.W.Cape	Destination	Date Arrived	Days Out
Maulesden -	Greenock Mar. 2	Mar. 19	April 10	May 2	Maryboro.	May 10	69
Samuel Plimsoll	Plymouth Apl. 6	April 27	May 19	June 10	Sydney	June 17	72
Patriarch -	Start May 16	June 6	June 27	July 24	,,	July 28	73
Salamis -	Dartm'th Feb.24	Mar. 23	April 23	May 6	,,	May 9	74
Loch Torridon	Tuskar Mar. 8		April 29		Melbourne	May 21	74
Dharwar -	Plym'th July 15	Aug. 7	Sept. 1	Sept. 26	Sydney	Sept. 30	77
Cutty Sark -	Channel July 24				N'c'tleN.S.W.	Oct. 10	78
Pericles -	Channel Sept. 27				Sydney	Dec. 14	78
Candida -	Ushant June 15	July 10	Aug. 3	Aug. 27	,,	Sept. 1	78
Miltiades -	Start May 8	June 24	June 27		Melbourne	July 25	78
Mermerus -	Lizard April 29	May 22	June 22	July 16	,,	July 17	79
Aristides -	Start May 28	June 30	July 26	Aug. 14	,,	Aug. 15	79

I have put all the passages together this year; of the ships bound to Sydney, only the *Candida* rounded Tasmania, the skippers generally preferring the shorter route through Bass Straits.

A notable return this year to the Australian trade is the wonderful little *Cutty Sark*, commanded by Captain Moore, this was her first passage to Newcastle, and

I believe she was one of the first ships to load wool at Newcastle. In future we shall see her somewhere near the top of every table.

The *Samuel Plimsoll* did well to the south'ard again, averaging 278 miles for 13 consecutive days, her best day's work being 337 miles.

The little *Salamis* made her second appearance in Port Jackson. She arrived on the same day as her composite sister, *Thermopylae*. *Thermopylae*, however, had a terrible passage, the worst of her career, being actually 107 days from the Start. Held up by continual gales, she did not cross the equator until her 45th day out, 8th March, the day *Salamis* passed the Cape Verd. She crossed the Cape meridian on 7th April, six days before *Salamis*, and passed the Otway on 5th May, only one day ahead of *Salamis*, so *Salamis* had been closing steadily on her the whole passage.

Dharwar arrived with 414 emigrants, and had measles and fever on board so had to go into quarantine.

The *Candida* hailed from Liverpool, a 1200-ton iron clipper. She brought out 35 passengers and a general cargo from London.

Mermerus had now made 12 consecutive passages to Melbourne, averaging 78 days. Her best runs this passage were 311 and 314 miles.

Ben Cruachan and *Ben Voirlich* made passages of 85 and 87 days respectively. *Ben Cruachan* certainly must have been severely handicaped by a foul bottom, as I find this was the third voyage since she had been docked !

The "Derwent."

The *Derwent* was a very up-to-date ship, with numerous innovations. She was built to the specication of Captain Andrew, her first commander, and

"DERWENT," off Gravesend.

"MOUNT STEWART."

Photo by Captain Schnze, Sydney.

[*To face page* 327.

he overlooked her construction with an eagle eye. *Derwent* was one of the first ships to cross steel topgallant yards, substitute rigging screws for deadeyes, to have a donkey with winch barrels, etc.

She sailed on her first voyage on Xmas Eve, 1884, her crew consisting of captain, 8 certificated officers, 8 midshipmen, 12 apprentices, bosun, sailmaker, carpenter, donkeyman and 12 hands in the fo'cs'le. The start was not very propitious. She sailed from Glasgow, dragged her anchors off the Tail of the Bank, and then her crew refused duty. The weather was so bad that she sought shelter at Queenstown, 11 days out from Greenock. Here advantage was taken to prosecute her insubordinate crew, who received sentences of from one to three months' imprisonment.

The *Derwent* was never considered a fast ship, but a good sea boat and excellent cargo carrier; nevertheless she made some very good runs, notably :—

Sydney to Lizard .. .. .. 77 days.
Sydney to Penzance .. .. 74 „

In 1904 Devitt & Moore sold her to the Norwegians, and she was still afloat when the war broke out, being owned in Larvik.

PASSAGES TO AUSTRALIA UNDER 80 DAYS IN 1884.

Ship	Departure	Crossed Equator	Crossed Meridian Cape	Passed Otway	Destination	Date Arrived	Days Out
Miltiades -	Ushant June 3	June 28	July 18		Melbourne	Aug. 13	71
Sobraon -	Plym'th Sept. 29				„	Dec. 13	75
Loch Long -	Clyde June 1				„	Aug. 15	75
Thessalus -	Downs Apl. 11				Sydney	June 27	77
Windsor Castle (D, Rose & Co.)	Dartm'th Mar.26				„	June 12	78
Star of Italy -	Gr'v's'nd Nov.27				Melbourne	Feb.13,85	78
Cutty Sark -	Channel June 18				Newcastle	Sept. 5	79
Cimba - -	Channel May 30	June 23	July 18		Sydney	Aug. 17	79

Notes on Passages to Australia in 1884.

A good many ships this year were just into the 80 days; for instance *Dharwar*, 80 days to Sydney; *Samuel Plimsoll*, 80 to Sydney; *Trafalgar*, 81 to Sydney; *Loch Vennachar*, 80 to Melbourne; *Romanoff*, 80 to Melbourne; *Salamis*, 82 to Melbourne; *Patriarch*, 82 to Sydney.

Miltiades, *Cimba* and *Loch Long* had a good race out. The *Star of Italy* was Corrie's crack jute clipper; this was her tenth voyage, and her first trip to Melbourne. She was nearly lost when about to sail through a fire in her sail-room.

Cutty Sark had a fine weather passage to the Cape, but she scared her crew running the easting down. On one occasion she was pooped by a big sea which jammed the helmsmen in the wheel, and she came up in the wind and swept her decks clean, taking the boats off the after skids, breaking in one side of the monkey poop and gutting the cabin. At the change of the watch at midnight that night, the apprentice keeping the time, in order to call his mates, had to go up the mizen rigging and come down the stay to get to the apprentices' house her decks were so full of water; for three or four days after this she ran like a scared hare before a mountainous sea, which rose up so high astern that it took the wind out of her topsails when she was in the trough.

Captains Bully Martin and Douglas of the two Bens changed ships this year, and Douglas in the *Ben Cruachan* arrived Melbourne on 5th June, 90 days out, whilst Martin in the *Ben Voirlich* arrived Melbourne on 10th August, 88 days out.

" Torridon " and " Yallaroi."

The last of Nicol's clippers were the *Torridon* and *Yallaroi*. They were skysail-yarders, and lying in

"TORRIDON."

Photo by Captain Schütze, Sydney.

[To face page 328.

dock alongside the modern four-poster, looked the real thing, a pair of dainty little thoroughbreds.

Compared to most ships of their size, they had narrow sail plans, and with greater carrying power, they were not as fast as *Cimba* or *Romanoff*. For some reason Nicol gave up the green and gold colours of Aberdeen and gave them the eonventional painted ports. No doubt the days were passed when crowds of landsmen thronged Circular Quay of a Sunday and gaped in awe, reverence and admiration at the tall green clippers.

Captain Shepherd left *Romanoff* to take the *Torridon*, but he could only manage to get her out to Sydney in 90 days from Deal on her maiden trip, and *Yallaroi* took 99 from Grangemouth. However, both ships held on in the Sydney trade until 1906, when they were sold to the Italians, *Torridon* for £4250 and *Yallaroi* for £4400.

Torridon was sunk by a German submarine on 27th August, 1916, but *Yallaroi* disguised as *Santa Catarina* is still sailing the seas.

"Loch Carron" and "Loch Broom."

The last ships to be built for the famous Loch Line were the two fine four-mast barques *Loch Carron* and *Loch Broom*.

The *Loch Carron* was taken from the stocks by Captain Stainton Clarke, one of the best known skippers in the Australian trade and the bosom friend of Captain Pattman, the pair being known in the ports they frequented as the "Corsican Brothers." Captain Clarke was brought up in those beautiful little tea clippers, Skinner's "Castles." At the age of 28 he became master of the *Douglas Castle*, which he used to say was "one of the prettiest models that ever sailed." When she was sold he was given the *Lennox Castle*, and he left her to take the *Loch Carron*.

Loch Carron, though a very fast ship, was also a ticklish ship to handle, being rather tender, and Captain Clarke always sent down royal yards when in port.

The following are some of her best performances :—

Melbourne to London	..	.. 73 days.	
Adelaide to Glasgow	..	.. 75 ,,	
Glasgow to Adelaide	..	.. 78 ,,	
London to Adelaide	..	.. 75 ,,	(twice)
The Semaphore, Adelaide, to			
Cape Otway	..	.. 48 ,,	
Cape Town to Clyde in ballast	..	40 ,,	
Melbourne to the Horn	..	.. 27 ,,	
Cape meridian to the Leeuwin	..	19 ,,	(twice)
Cape Horn to the line	..	.. 20 ,,	

On one occasion when abreast of the Crozets, running her easting down in 45° S., she made three consecutive 24-hour runs of 310, 320 and 332 miles. On her maiden trip she went to Sydney, and then for two or three years left the Australian for the Calcutta trade. In 1887 she took case oil from New York to Calcutta in 112 days.

In 1889 *Loch Carron* had a very nasty experience when rounding the Cape homeward bound from India. It is thus told by Captain Clarke :—

We were bound for London from Calcutta with a cargo of jute and about 500 tons of rice for stiffening purposes. It was new rice and had not been properly dried. When the jute was loaded on top of it, the rice began to get heated and we had to take it out and stow it in the main hatch by itself, boring holes in order to allow the air to enter. This arrangement of the cargo caused the ship to be top-heavy, but it was unavoidable. When we got to the Cape of Good Hope we encountered violent gales, and the vessel could not stand up to them. She was carried right over on her side, although there was very little canvas on her. Her lee side was 5 or 6 feet under water and the crew became so frightened that many of them climbed up the rigging. I let the sails go and sacrificed them in order to save her. She righted herself and we ran before the wind all night, going miles out of our course. Next day we jury-rigged her and I tried hard to make way on the other tack. We tacked for eight days and then the gale again seized her and she turned over once more.   We quickly stripped her of sails, but she was so top-heavy and crank that I decided to send the topgallant masts down.   This was ticklish work, and I shall never forget the scene, as the men struggled against the seas with the topgallants.   The fight against the gales lasted for 30 days and then we got round the Cape, but I had five men down with broken limbs and other injuries.   The voyage from Calcutta to London occupied no fewer than 156 days, and was the most exciting in my experience.   The *Bolan, Glen Padarn* and *Trevelyan,* also bound from Calcutta and Rangoon to London, foundered during the storms and we were lucky to get through with the ship so crank.

In 1904 *Loch Carron* had a great race home from Frisco round the Horn with the French ship *Jules Gommes.* *Loch Carron* hove up her anchor in Frisco Bay on the morning of Christmas Eve, the *Jules Gommes* leaving in the afternoon.   After being six days in company the two ships lost sight of each other.   They met again on the equator in the Atlantic; finally the *Loch Carron* arrived at Queenstown one morning 112 days out, the Frenchman arriving eight hours later at the same port.

On her next passage the *Loch Carron* had the most disastrous event in her career, in her collision with the *Inverkip*.   The two ships were both outward bound, the *Loch Carron* from Glasgow to Sydney with general cargo.   At 11.20 on 13th August, 1904, the *Loch Carron* was about 60 miles to the S. and E. of the Fastnet light, going 6 or 7 knots close-hauled on the port tack, with a moderate gale blowing from the S.W., when the red light of the *Inverkip* was suddenly seen ahead.   But it was too late to avoid a collision, and the *Loch Carron* struck the *Inverkip* abreast of the foremast, stem on. The latter ship went down in a few minutes, only two men, the carpenter and the steward, being saved out of her ship's company.   These two managed to jump aboard the *Loch Carron*. Captain Jones of the *Inverkip* had his wife aboard, and as the ship went down she was seen praying on her knees aft.   They were both great personal friends of Captain Clarke, and he was so distressed by the sad accident that his health broke down and he gave up his command for a voyage. The *Loch Carron*, with a large hole in her bows, her fore topgallant mast and all head gear carried away, besides other damages, managed to make Queenstown.

Her repairs came to £1500, and as she was on the port tack and the *Inverkip* on the starboard, the Loch Line had to pay over £30,000 damages.

When *Loch Carron* was again ready for sea, Captain Henderson, of *Thermopylae* and *Samuel Plimsoll* fame, took her out, Captain Clarke returning to his command on her return home. As late as 1908 *Loch Carron* made the run from Melbourne to London in 80 days.

Loch' Broom was commanded for the greater part of her career by the well-known veteran, Bully Martin.

Though they were absolute sister ships according to the tape-measure, *Loch Broom* was always a stiffer ship than the *Loch Carron*, and her sailing records were not quite as numerous, nevertheless she was a very fast ship.

In 1904 Captain Martin brought her home from Melbourne in 82 days. He left Port Phillip on 12th January, and was only 24 days to the Horn, most of the run being made under six topsails and foresail.

On her following passage out *Loch Broom* took case oil from New York to Melbourne in 96 days. It was a nasty trip for her officers, as the hands before the mast were all hobos, Bowery toughs and hard cases, and had to be driven to their work in the old-fashioned belaying pin style.

In 1907 Captain Bully Martin gave up his command and retired from the sea, being succeeded by Captain Kelynack, who had been mate under him for some years.

I have the abstract log of *Loch Broom's* last voyage under the British flag :—

On 4th September at 7 a.m. she took her departure from the Lizard, had light breezes and calms to the 19th when she took the N.E. trades, crossed the line on 6th October, crossed the meridian of Greenwich on 26th October, ran down her easting on the 40th parallel, her best 24-hour run being 272 miles on 12th November before a moderate gale from W.S.W. in 40° 37′ S., 60° 00′ E., and she anchored off Port Adelaide at 2 p.m. on 4th December, 91 days from the Lizard.

She left Melbourne homeward bound on 23rd February 1912. On 15th March in 50° 58′ S., 135° 26′ W., she ran 278 miles with a fresh S.W. gale, passed Cape Horn on 27th March. On 29th March Captain Kelynack remarks. " Fresh W.S.W. wind, thick misty rain, four-masted barque in company on lee quarter but falling astern﹐ (nothing passes the *Loch Broom* but birds.)"

And on 2nd April I find the following testimony to her qualities :—" Lat. 46° 50′ S., long. 40° 04′ W., distance 213, course N. 51° E. Fresh N.W. gale veering to W.N.W., high sea running, ship going 12 knots, dry as a bone."

The line was crossed on 29th April. On 24th May in 46° N., 20° 55′ W., *Loch Broom* ran 301 miles in the 24 hours before a fresh southerly wind and moderate sea; and on the following day 282 miles. " Fresh S.S.E. wind. Barque in company at 6 a.m. on starboard bow, out of sight astern at noon." On 31st May at 7 p.m. *Loch Broom* anchored off Gravesend, 98 days out.

The *Loch Carron and Loch Broom* were both sold to the foreigners in 1912 for about £5000 a piece, and now, I believe, belong to Christianssand, Norway, being disguised under the names of *Seileren* and *Songdal*.

PASSAGES TO AUSTRALIA UNDER 80 DAYS IN 1885.

Ship	Departure		Passed Equator		Crossed Cape Meridian		Passed Otway		Destination	Date Arrived		Days Out
Salamis -	Start	Mar. 20	April	6	May	9	June	2	Melbourne	June	3	75
Patriarch -	Start	Mar. 9	Mar.	25			May	21	Sydney	May	23	75
Cutty Sark -	Start	April 3	April	23	May	19	June	15	,,	June	19	77
							(SW Cape)					
Siren - -	Start	Mar. 23	April	12	May.	11	June	6	,,	June	8	77
Samuel Plimsoll	Start	April 4	April	28	May	21	June	18	,,	June	21	78
Argonaut -	Start	June 14	July	10	Aug.	1	Aug.	27	,,	Aug.	31	78
Bay of Cadiz -	Start	Mar. 6	Mar.	28	April	20	May	19	,,	May	23	78
Thermopylae -	Start	Jan. 20	Feb.	17	Mar.	9	April	7	Melbourne	April	8	78
Harbinger -	Lizard	June 4	June	30	July	27	Aug.	21	,,	Aug.	21	78
Sir Walter Raleigh	Start	April 4	April	28	May	22	June	20	Sydney	June	22	79
Milton Park -	Tuskar	June 21	July	18	Aug.	12	Sept.	5	,,	Sept.	8	79

Notes on Passages to Australia in 1885.

The race of the year was that between *Cutty Sark*, *Samuel Plimsoll*, *Sir Walter Raleigh* and still a fourth ship, the *City of York*, which was off the Start on 2nd April—crossed the line 23rd April—crossed Cape meridian 26th May—passed the Otway on 18th June—and arrived Sydney on 21st June, 80 days out.

It was Captain Woodget's first voyage in *Cutty Sark*. He went as high as 48° S. in search of good winds, but had a lot of thick misty weather with light northerly winds, and no steady westerlies. He only had two chances. In 70 hours from 21st to 23rd May, the *Cutty* ran 931 miles, braced sharp up against a strong N.E. to E.N.E. wind; and on 4th June, with the wind fresh from N.E. to N.N.E. she ran 330 miles in 47° S., 99° E. None of the other ships made any specially big runs.

Miltiades this year was taken over by Captain Harry Ayling, and arrived in Hobson's Bay on 29th October, 85 days out from Torbay.

Mermerus arrived Melbourne on 24th July, 88 days

"MOUNT STEWART."

Photo by Captain Schutze, Sydney.

"CROMDALE."

[*To face page* 335.

from the Lizard, and *Thomas Stephens* was 87 days from Antwerp to Sydney, arriving on 20th October.

The *Milton Park* was an iron ship of 1500 tons, built by McMillan, of Dumbarton in 1882, a typical Clyde-built ship. The *Bay of Cadiz* was one of the Cardiff "Bays." *Siren* was one of Carmichael's, a 1482-ton ship, built in 1881. She had a number of fine passages to her credit, and came to a curious end, being rammed and sunk by H.M.S. *Landrail* off Portland in July, 1896.

We have now had 12 years of outward tables, and space and, no doubt, the patience of the reader are both growing exhausted.

However, as these beautiful ships kept up their wonderful averages until well into the nineties, fighting all they knew against the ever-growing competition of steam, I give here a table of times from the Channel to port from the year 1886 to 1894 for the seven most regular ships in the trade.

PASSAGES TO AUSTRALIA 1886-1894.

Ship	Distination	1886	1887	1888	1889	1890	1891	1892	1893	1894
Cutty Sark	Newcastle (1887 and 1892) Brisbane 1894 Rest to Sydney	To Shang-hai	88 Dis-masted	76	77	75	79	88	81	79
Salamis - -	Melbourne	78	86	70	84	86	70	77	87	80
Patriarch -	Sydney	97	79	79	77	87	82	80	99	77
Mermerus -	Melbourne	84	96	82	88	89	85	86	85	
Miltiades	Melbourne	83	78	83	82	90	91	86	92	
Cimba - -	Sydney	97	84	88	85	89	93	83	93	88
Samuel Plimsoll	Sydney 1886 & 1887 Rest to Melbourne		93	76	81	84	78	87	79	79

"Mount Stewart" and "Cromdale," the last of the Wool Clippers.

The last two ships to be built specially for the Australian wool trade were the magnificent steel skysail-yard ships *Mount Stewart* and *Cromdale*. The former was launched in May, 1891, and the latter in June, both from Barclay, Curle's yard. They were identical sister ships, and were the very latest development of the full-rig ship. They were of course good carriers, with the modern short poop and long sweep of main deck. Yet, in spite of their carrying powers, they both made some excellent passages out and home.

The *Cromdale* was specially lucky in having Captain E. H. Andrew as her first master, a very experienced and up-to-date sailing ship captain, who had been mate under his father in the *Derwent*.

The *Cromdale* came to grief in 1913 when commanded by Captain Arthur. She was 126 days out, bound home from Taltal with nitrate and was heading for Falmouth. There had been a dense fog for some days, when, most unfortunately, a steamer was passed which advised Captain Arthur to alter his course. Not long after a light was suddenly seen through the fog ahead, but before the ship could be put about she struck on the rocks right at the foot of a cliff. This proved to be Bass Point, close to the Lizard light. The ship was so badly holed that the captain ordered the boats out at once. Luckily it was calm weather, and some rockets brought the Cadgwith and Lizard lifeboats upon the scene, but the *Cromdale* settled down so quickly that there was only just time to save the ship's papers and the crew's personal belongings. Lying on the rocks in such an exposed position, it was of course hopeless to think of salving the ship, and the *Cromdale* became a total loss.

The *Mount Stewart* is, I believe, still afloat, and still has Aberdeen on her stern.

Perforated Sails.

At first glance a sail with a hole in it would hardly be considered superior to a sail without one, yet sails with holes in them, or perforated sails, as they were called, became quite popular with the most experienced of our sailing ship skippers in the early nineties·

Perforated sails were said to be the idea of an Italian shipmaster in the eighties. This Italian captain's theory was that a cushion of air or dead wind, as he called it, was collected in the belly of every sail, and acted as a buffer, thus preventing the sail from receiving the whole strength of the wind. He advocated making a hole in the centre of the belly in order to allow this cushion of air to escape, and allow the true wind to blow against the surface of the sail. An important point was the proper placing of these holes; in fore and aft sails they were cut about the centre of the belly made by the clew; the holes in square sails were also cut near the clews, but they were also cut higher up in the sail on a line from the clews to the bunt: topsails and courses generally had the four holes and topgallant sails and royals only two, one in the lower part of the sail towards the clew on each side. These holes were from $5\frac{1}{2}$ to 6 inches in diameter and roped with grammets.

It is easy to understand that this system was more advantageous when one was close-hauled than when running free. But even when running free many shipmasters claimed that it had its merits and held that, though wind certainly did escape through the holes, it was mostly dead wind and even then was caught up again—the mizen by the main, and the main by the fore, so that in the end there was very little real wind that did not do its work in sending the ship along.

A further advantage of perforated sails was their

aid in spilling the wind out of a sail when the sail had to come in in heavy weather. The advocates of the holes claimed that they prevented a sail from ballooning up over the yard, and made it very much easier to muzzle and put the gaskets on.

The perforated sails were also considered very useful in light airs and calms, because on the calmest day there always seemed to be a draught through the holes, and this kept the sails " asleep " and stopped that irritating flogging of canvas against the masts which is so trying to a skipper's temper and also constantly necessitates the hauling up of courses in the doldrums.

Captain Holmes, who always used them in the *Cimba* and *Inverurie*, wrote to me that he considered them specially valuable in light winds, and he did not adopt perforated sails without testing their efficiency in every way he could.

He even had sand bags made to fit the holes, and thus was able to test his sailing when in company with another ship, first by seeing how he did with holes, and then filling up the holes with sandbags, by seeing how he altered his bearing when without holes.

By this means he proved the benefit of the holes very clearly once when going down Channel.

The *Cimba* was in company with another outward bound ship of nearly the same speed; and it was found that as soon as the sand bags were put in the holes the *Cimba* began to drop astern, whereas, with the holes open, she went ahead. Captain Holmes also tied a rag on the end of a stick, and held it up to the holes, and even in very light airs the rag was sucked through the perforations. In this way with a handkerchief on the end of a long rod, he tried to find out the result of the holes on the crossjack, by walking it all over the after part of the sail. And he told me that the handkerchief flopped stupidly about in the dead wind until it was abreast of the holes, when it at once blew out straight.

Captain Pattman, of *Loch Torridon*, adopted perforated holes in 1892: Captain Poppy used them on the *Aristides*, and Captain Cutler, when he took over *Port Jackson*, had her sails cut for holes, and his successor continued to keep them in the sails.

All these four captains were noted passage-makers, and unless the perforated sails had had very certain advantages, it is hardly likely that they would have adopted them.

Hine's Clipper Barques.

Before turning to the New Zealand trade I must not forget to mention the fine little fleet of barques belonging to Hine Brothers, of Maryport, which brought home wool from Adelaide, Brisbane and the two Tasmanian ports.

The following will still be remembered by the older inhabitants of these ports.

Aline,	wood barque	474	tons, built by	Hardy, Sunderland	1867
Abbey Holme	iron ,,	516 ,,	,,	Blumer, Sunderland	1869
Hazel Holme	wood ,,	405 ,,	,,	at Barnstaple	1890
Aikshaw	iron ,,	573 ,,	,,	Doxford, Sunderland	1875
Eden Holme	,, ,,	794 ,,	,,	Bartram	,, ,,
Myrtle Holme	,, ,,	902 ,,	,,	,,	,, ,,
Castle Holme	,, ,,	996 ,,	,,	,,	,, ,,
Brier Holme	,, ,,	894 ,,	,,	Thompson	,, 1876

They were rarely much over 80 days going out, and generally under 90 days coming home.

The *Myrtle Holme*, under Captain Cobb, and the *Eden Holme*, under Captain Wyrill (late of *Berean*) had perhaps the best records, and maintained their fine average right into the twentieth century.

For instance, in 1899 Captain Wyrill brought the *Eden Holme* from Launceston to the London River in 88 days after experiencing 17 days of calms and variables to the north of the line. This was her fourth passage out of six, in which she had come home in less than 90 days from Tasmania.

In 1895, the *Myrtle Holme* went from Beachy Head to Adelaide in 77 days, and in 1901 went from Dover to Adelaide in 81 days; whilst in 1902 the *Eden Holme* went from the Start to Launceston in 83 days.

The *Eden Holme*, *Brier Holme* and *Castle Holme* were all transferred to the Tasmanian trade from that of Adelaide on the death of Mr. Walker and the dispersal of his fleet.

The *Eden Holme* was wrecked on Hebe Reef in 1907. The *Myrtle Holme* was sold to Arendal, Norway, and renamed *Glimt*, a few years before the war. She was torpedoed in the North Sea in 1915.

The *Brier Holme* came to a tragic end in 1904. She sailed from London for Hobart in September of that year, commanded by Captain Rich, an experienced and skilful seaman who was making his last voyage. She was three months overdue and much anxiety was being felt, when some fishermen landed on a bleak and unfrequented part of the West Coast of Tasmania. They found some jetsom on the shore in the shape of packages of cargo, marked and numbered so that they could be identified. Footprints and the remains of a rude hut also pointed to a wreck on the coast; a close search was made but no signs of the wreck or of life could be found. The fishermen then took the packages back to Hobart and they proved to be part of the cargo of the *Brier Holme*. Thereupon the Government sent out a steamer with a search party. The

" BRIERHOLME."

Photo by De Maus, Port Chalmers.

[To face page 340.

remains of the wreck were found under water, but though the bush was scoured, fires lighted and guns fired to attract attention, no survivor was discovered, and the search party returned to Hobart. Some weeks later the fishermen who had found the packages landed again on the coast and found a man, who proved to be the sole survivor out of the *Brier Holme's* crew. He had been wandering about in the bush trying to find his way to the nearest habitation, first loading himself with provisions washed up from the wreck, he had tried to construct a raft across a river but without success, and he was continually compelled to return to the shore and replenish his stores. He reported that the *Brier Holme* arrived off the S.W. Cape of Tasmania at night during thick stormy weather and was hove to to wait for daylight. But being to the north of the Fairway having overrun her distance, she crashed on to the rocks and soon went to pieces.

The *Castle Holme* is now owned in Frederickstadt, Norway, and sails under the name of *Estar*.

Iron Barques of Walker and Trinder, Anderson.

Hine Bros. were not the only owners of iron clipper barques in the Australian trade. Mr. T. B. Walker had four very well-known ships—the barques *Westbury*, *Decapolis* and *Lanoma* and the ship *Barossa*; whilst Trinder, Anderson & Co. had the *Barunga*, *Oriana*, *Mineru*, *Morialta* and *Kooringa*.

Of the above, Walker's *Lanoma* was probably the fastest. She has been credited with a run from Tasmania to the Horn in 21 days, another of 21 days from the Horn to the line, and again a third of 21 days from the line to soundings, which if they had all been on the same passage would have given her the record from

Tasmania home. The *Westbury* and *Decapolis* were both good for an outward passage round about 80 days.

A year or two ago a correspondent in the " Nautical " claimed that the *Decapolis* went out to Launceston in 56 days on her maiden trip, at the same time he claimed a 57-day trip to Melbourne for my old ship the *Commonwealth*. He had, of course, got his dates wrong somewhere, as the *Decapolis* ran regularly to Brisbane until that trade was captured by steamers, she was then diverted to Launceston.

After the death of Mr. Walker, *Decapolis* was sold to the Italians and renamed *Nostra Madre*. Her name is on the Sailing Ship Roll of Honour, as she was torpedoed in the Mediterranean during the war.

Barossa, a fine little full-rigged ship, ran for many years as a passenger ship to Adelaide. She eventually turned turtle in dock and was sold to be broken up.

The Loss of "Lanoma."

Lanoma was lost in March, 1888, on what promised to be her best passage home. She was coming up Channel, only 76 days out, in thick, blowing south-westerly weather, under a very experienced commander, Captain G. Whittingham.

Berean was also coming up Channel, it was the time when she had the narrow squeak of piling up on the Wight owing to the wrong notice about St. Catherine's light.

In the case of *Lanoma*, Captain Whittingham had had no observations for several days, and so an extra smart look-out was being kept. Just before midnight it must have cleared a bit for the land suddenly loomed up close to on the starboard bow. The helm was at once put down and the ship brought to the wind, and

Captain Whittingham tried to stay her. Unfortunately she missed stays and fell off again, there was no time to wear her, and she stranded broadside on to Chesil Beach, inside the Bill of Portland.

Like many another catastrophe of the same sort, the ship and her crew were hurtled from fancied security to destruction in a few minutes of time. And even so, the crew would probably have all been saved, if she had not fallen over to seaward, so that she at once began to break up in the heavy surf. The rocket apparatus was manned from the shore, but it was only in time to save a few, and Captain Whittingham and 11 of his crew were drowned.

Trinder, Anderson's ships were all well known in the London River at one time, specially the little *Mineru*, a 478-ton barque, built by Stephen, of Glasgow, in 1866. Fremantle, the Ashburton River and Sharks Bay were her wool ports.

Morialta was an iron ship of 1267 tons, built in 1866 by Royden, of Liverpool, for Beazley, her first name being *British Consul*. *Barunga* was the old *Apelles* built in 1868, whilst *Kooringa*, a 1175-ton barque, built at South Shields in 1874, had been the *Ravenstondale*.

Messrs. Trinder, Anderson bought several other well-known ships in their time, notably the *Kingdom of Saxony*, a 588-ton wooden barque, ex-*Deerhound*. Anderson's *Darra*, and Thompson's *Ascalon* also ended their days under the Red Ensign with Trinder, Anderson.

It is a curious coincidence, but in looking through the list of their ships I cannot find two by the same builder, though I find the following all represented : Dudgeon, of London; Moore, of Sunderland; Denton & Gray, of Hartlepool; Scott, of Greenock; Hall, of Aberdeen; Stephen, of Glasgow; Royden, of Liverpool; Hood, of

Aberdeen; Softley, of South Shields; and R. Thompson, Jun., of Sunderland.

At the beginning of the twentieth century, just before going into steam, Trinder, Anderson & Co. bought the fine ships *Wasdale* and *Hornby Castle*, but the century was not ten years old before steamers only were flying the blue with yellow cross and black swan, as the house-flag of the combined firm of Trinder, Anderson and Bethell, Gwyn.

Occasional Visitors in Australian Waters.

Though this part has run to greater length than I had at first intended, nevertheless I fear that many of my readers will complain because old favourites have not been mentioned.

I have tried not to leave out any regular Colonial trader, and space only admits of the bare mention of many beautiful and fast ships which occasionally visited Sydney, Melbourne or Adelaide in the course of their general round.

Of these perhaps the finest were:—Carmichael's *Golden Fleece*, one of the handsomest ships ever launched, with a run from London to Sydney of 72 days to her credit.

Williamson & Milligan's *Cedric the Saxon*, whose 72-day run from Liverpool to Calcutta is the iron ship record. This magnificent clipper once went from Calcutta to the Adelaide Semaphore in 28 days during the S.W. monsoon.

D. Bruce's Dundee clippers *Maulesden* and *Duntrune*; the first famous for her wonderful passage of 69 days from Glasgow to Maryborough, Queensland, in 1882.

The beautiful Belfast ship *Star of Italy*, one of Corry's

Irish " Stars," which in 1884-5 went out to Sydney in 78 days and came home in 79.

Beazley's *British Merchant*, which in 1881 arrived in Melbourne, 78 days out.

The *Sierra Blanca*, one of those yacht-like white " Sierras," which in 1883-4 went out to Sydney in 77 days.

Carmichael's *Argus* and *Argo*, the former with a 76-day run to Melbourne and the latter with a 78-day run to Sydney.

Cuthbert's *Ballochmyle*, Skinner's *Brodick Castle*, Beazley's *John o' Gaunt*, Patton's *Hesperides*, Alexander's *Glengarry*, Bowring's *Othello* and *Desdemona*, and my old ship the *Commonwealth*.

Then coming to the later days of the four-poster, there were McMillan's *Swanhilda*, which in 1894 made the wonderful run of 66 days from Wallaroo to Queenstown ; Mahon's *Oweenee*, which as late as 1913 made the run from Dublin to Newcastle, N.S.W., in 73 days ; Troop's *Howard D. Troop*, which in 1906 brought 3500 tons of wheat from Sydney to Falmouth in 82 days ; that extraordinary four-mast ship, the *Lancing*, which in 1908 ran from Christiania to Melbourne in 75 days; Mackay's *Wendur*, the rival of *Loch Torridon*; the beautiful skysail yarder *Queen Margaret*; Carmichael's *Glaucus*; and the *Lord Brassey*, which went missing on her first voyage, after having made a fine outward passage of 77 days to Melbourne in 1892.

PART IV.—THE NEW ZEALAND TRADE.

THE age of dear tradition has gone by
And steam has killed romance upon the sea,
The newer age requires the newer men,
And dying hard in corners of the world,
The old hands pass forgotten to their graves.
The old Colonial clipper is no more,
Denied the wool freights homeward, she must seek
For nitre on the South Pacific slope,
She need not go to China ports for tea,
She need not haunt the Hooghly for the jute,
Nor beat the Gulf of Martaban for rice,
Her time has come and she must pass away;
Yet still she holds the passage of the Horn,
And when the waterway of Panama
Makes islands of the two Americas,
She'll hold the bleak old headland for her own,
And round its pitch she'll fade away and die.—

JOHN ANDERSON, in *Nautical Magazine*.

The "Mayflowers" of New Zealand.

THE *Mayflower* is a name which every school-child in the United States is taught to reverence. In this part of *Colonial Clippers* I shall deal with the *Mayflowers* of New Zealand—the beautiful sailing ships which brought the settlers from the Old Country to the wonderful New Country.

The memory of these ships and their swift passages round the Cape and through the roaring forties is still green in the hearts of many a man and woman who travelled out to an unknown land with a stout heart and nothing much else, and is now a prosperous and happy member of a great nation. Only lately there

346

was a reunion of all those who had travelled out in one of these ships, that the anniversary of their great adventure might be suitably kept. The name of this ship has already been mentioned in these pages, *The Chariot of Fame*; a name of comfort and good omen it must have been to those who heard the whistle and scream of the mighty westerlies in her rigging on many a dark and sobbing night when the heart of the exile is low and the spirit of the brave pioneer begins to quiver.

Truly running down the easting in a little 1000-ton clipper with a hard driving skipper and big fisted, stony-hearted mates was a fine bracer for the emigrant, who had perhaps never seen salt water up to the date of sailing and who was bound to a country which could only be wooed and won by a clear brain, stout heart and strong arm.

At first the ships in the New Zealand trade were not even 1000 tons in burthen, being mainly little 400 and 500-ton ships and barques, which mostly flew the flag of Shaw, Savill & Co.

The "Edwin Fox."

Of such was the *Edwin Fox*, a country-built Indiaman from Calcutta, built as far back as 1853, with teak decks, quarter galleries, coir running gear and all the quaint characteristics of the East. The hull of this " old timer " is still to be seen, being now used as a landing stage for the freezing works at Picton.

"Wild Duck."

Another favourite passenger ship in the early days was the *Wild Duck*, commanded by Captain

Bishop. She was a main skysail yarder with Cunningham's patent reef single topsails. Though rather short for her beam she had fine ends and made very regular passages.

Shaw, Savill & Co.

The well-known firm of Shaw, Savill & Co. started sending ships to New Zealand about 65 years ago, making 15 sailings a year. At first the outward passage took four or five months, and it was not until the sixties that there was any marked improvement in the time between England and New Zealand, but by the end of the sixties Shaw, Savill had several fast little iron ships, the best known of which were the *Crusader*, *Helen Denny* and *Margaret Galbraith*.

The following is a rather incomplete list of their earlier ships:—

1853	*Edwin Fox*	.. wood barque ..	836 tons.
1856	*Chile* ..	.. iron barque ..	768 ,,
1858	*Dover Castle*	.. wood barque ..	1003 ,,
1858	*Adamant* ..	.. iron barque ..	815 ,,
1859	*Bebington* ..	.. iron barque ..	924 ,,
1862	*Bulwark* ..	.. wood ship ..	1332 ,,
1863	*Chaudiere* ..	.. wood barque ..	470 ,,
,,	*Euterpe* ..	.. iron ship ..	1197 ,,
,,	*Himalaya* ..	.. iron barque ..	1008 ,
,,	*Trevelyan* ..	.. iron ship ..	1042 ,,
1864	*Golden Sea*	.. wood ship ..	1418 ,,
,,	*Soukar* ..	.. iron ship ..	1304 ,,
,,	*Saint Leonards*	.. iron ship ..	1054 ,,
,,	*Glenlora* ..	.. iron barque ..	764 ,,
1865	*Anazi* ..	.. composite barque	468 ,,
,,	*Crusader* ..	.. iron ship ..	1059 ,,
1866	*Helen Denny*	.. iron barque ..	728 ,,
1867	*Forfarshire*	.. composite ship	1238 ,,
1868	*Margaret Galbraith*	iron ship ..	841 ,,
1869	*Elizabeth Graham*	composite barque	598 ,,
,,	*Hudson* ..	.. iron barque ..	705 ,,
,,	*Langstone* ..	.. iron ship ..	746 ,,

1869	*Pleiades* ..	.. iron ship	..	997	,,
,,	*Schiehallion*	.. iron barque	..	602	,,
,,	*Zealandia* ..	.. iron ship	..	1116	,,
,,	*Halcione* ..	.. iron ship	..	843	,,
1870	*Merope* ..	.. iron ship	..	1054	,,

Space forbids more than a few odd notes on the best known of these ships.

The "Crusader."

The *Crusader* was a very handsome little ship, as is well shown in her photograph, and she was considered by many to be the fastest ship in Shaw, Savill's fleet. She was built by Connell, of Glasgow, and launched in March, 1865, her registered measurements being:— Net tonnage 1058 ; gross tonnage 1058 ; length 210.7 ft. ; breadth 35.1 ft., depth 21.4 ft.

In 1877, when commanded by Captain Renaut, she ran from Lyttelton, N.Z., to the Lizard in 69 days, and on her next outward passage in 1878 she went from London to Port Chalmers in 65 days, a performance which has never been beaten. She was eventually sold to the Norwegians for £2950 and was still washing about the seas, rigged as a barque, at the outbreak of the Great War.

"Helen Denny" and "Margaret Galbraith."

The little *Helen Denny* was the last of the fleet to remain under the British flag. She once ran from the longitude of the Cape to New Zealand in 23 days, a really remarkable feat for a small iron barque. She was built by the great Robert Duncan, of Port Glasgow, and was eventually sold by Shaw, Savill, to Christie, of Lyttelton, N.Z., who resold her to Captain F. Holm, of Wellington, N.Z.; she ran regularly in the inter-colonial trade until the end of 1913, being latterly commanded and owned by Captain S. Holm, a son of

Captain F. Holm. She was finally converted into a coal hulk.

Margaret Galbraith was another little Duncan beauty, and for many years a regular passenger ship to Otago. It is surprising to think of these little ships carrying passengers right up to the eighties. Their measurements were :—

Helen Denny, 728 tons; 187.5 feet length; 31.2 feet beam; 19.1 feet depth.

Margaret Galbraith, 841 tons; 198.5 feet length; 32.2 feet beam; 19.9 feet depth.

The *Margaret Galbraith* was sold to the Manica Trading Co., of London. She left Colonia on 26th March, 1905, for Buenos Ayres with a cargo of grain and crew of 13 all told; and whilst in charge of a pilot grounded on Farollon reef, and as she was badly holed her captain abandoned her.

End of Some of Shaw, Savill's Earlier Ships.

Zealandia was a Connell built ship. After being sold to the Swedes, she was resold to the Russians, and her name changed to *Kaleva*. She was stranded in March, 1911, but refloated and again sold to Charles Brister & Son, of Halifax, Nova Scotia.

Pleiades was built by McMillan, of Dumbarton. As late as 1893 she made a good run from New Zealand to the Lizard. She was wrecked at Akiteo, when bound round in ballast from Napier to Dunedin to load wool home.

The *Halcione* was specially built for the New Zealand trade with ⅞ iron plates backed with 3 feet of cement, her saloon was insulated with charcoal, and she had 200 tons of cement stiffening. She was built by Steele, of Greenock, and was lost in 1895 in Fitzroy Bay near Pincarrow Heads, outside Wellington.

The *Euterpe* was sold to the Chileans, and for some years was to be seen in the South Pacific rigged as a barque. Then the Alaska Packers bought her and renamed her *Star of India*. I believe she is still afloat.

The *Himalaya* was also sold to the Alaska Packers Co., and renamed *Star of Peru*.

The *Soukar* was sold to the Spaniards and registered at Barcelona under the name of *Humberto*. She has been broken up.

The *Glenlora* went to the Scandinavians and was still afloat at the outbreak of the Great War. The *Hudson* is also a Scandinavian barque at the present time.

The *Merope* was burnt whilst homeward bound, being off the Plate at the time. Another well-known early Shaw, Savill emigrant ship to be burnt at sea was the *Caribou*, of 1160 tons; she was a wood ship and her cargo of coal caught fire in the year 1869. The Shaw, Savill ships were rather unlucky with fires and collisions, their worst disaster being, of course, the loss of the *Cospatrick*, Dunbar's old frigate-built ship, which they bought in 1873 for £10,000. The tragedy happened on her second voyage under Shaw, Savill's house-flag.

The Loss of the "Cospatrick."

The *Cospatrick* sailed from London for Auckland on the 11th September, 1874, with general cargo, 429 passengers and a crew of 44 men under Captain Elmslie.

Tuesday, 17th November, found the ship to the south'ard of the Cape, the wind being very light from the nor'west. And here is the tragedy as it was given by Henry Macdonald, the second mate, one of the three survivors. He stated that after keeping the first watch, he had not been long below when he was aroused by the cry of " Fire !" Without stopping to dress, he rushed on deck and found that dense clouds of smoke were pouring up from the fore peak, a fire having broken out in the bosun's locker, which was full of oakum, rope, varnish and paint.

The first thing to do was to get the ship's head before the wind, at the same time the fire engine was rigged, and soon the fore part of the ship was being deluged with water. But somehow or other the ship was allowed to come head to wind, which drove the smoke aft in suffocating clouds. From this moment all discipline seems to have been lost; flames began to burst forth in the 'tween decks and out through every scuttle and air vent, and they were soon roaring up the tarred shrouds, so that within an hour and a half of the discovery of the fire the flames had got such a hold that the ship was doomed.

The emigrants now took panic, and, shouting and screaming, made a rush for the boats. The starboard quarter boat was lowered down, but immediately she touched the water such a crowd of demented emigrants swarmed down the ship's side into her that she was capsized. Whilst the longboat was being swung out of her chocks, her bow caught fire, and in the end only the port and starboard lifeboats got safely away from the ship's side, the one with 42 and the other with 39 people.

The two boats stayed by the ship until the afternoon of the 19th, when she sank beneath the waves, a blackened, charred and smoking hull. One can scarcely imagine the horror of the scene during this weary waiting for the end of the ship. The people in the boats watched the main and mizen mast fall, and heard shrieks from the crowded after part of the ship, as many

"CRUSADER."

"COSPATRICK."

Photo by De Maus.

luckless wretches were crushed in their fall.   Then the stern with its old Blackwall quarter galleries was blown out by the flames and smoke.   Lastly the captain was seen to throw his wife overboard and spring after her himself.

But the tragedy was far from finished with the sinking of the ship.   Owing to the panic and confusion the 81 survivors in the boats had only their night clothes and were without food or water, mast or sail, and the starboard lifeboat of which the second mate took command had only one oar.   The rest of the horrible story is best told in Henry Macdonald's own words, and the following is his statement, given at the inquiry afterwards :—

The two boats kept company the 20th and 21st, when it commenced to blow, and we got separated during the night.   I whistled and shouted, but when daylight came we could see nothing of the other boat.   Thirst began to tell severely on all of us.   A man named Bentley fell overboard while steering the boat and was drowned.   Three men became mad that day and died.   We then threw the bodies overboard.   On the 23rd, the wind was blowing hard and a high sea running.   We were continually bailing the water out.   We rigged a sea anchor and rode to it; but it was only made fast to the end of the boat's painter, and we lost it.   Four men died, and we were so hungry and thirsty that we drank the blood and ate the livers of two of them.   We lost our only oar then.   On the 24th, there was a strong gale, and we rigged another sea anchor, making it fast with anything we could get.   There were six more deaths that day.   She shipped water till she was nearly full.   On the 25th there was a light breeze and it was awful hot.   We were reduced that day to eight, and three of them out of their minds. We all felt very bad that day.   Early on the morning of the 26th, not being daylight, a boat passed close to us running.   We hailed but got no answer.   She was not more than 50 yards off.   She was a foreigner.   I think she must have heard us.   One more died that day.   We kept on sucking the blood of those who died.   The 27th was squally all round, but we never caught a drop of water. although we tried to do it.   Two more died that day.   We threw one overboard, but were too weak to lift the other.

There were then five left—two able seamen, one ordinary, myself and one passenger.   The passenger was out of his mind.   All had drunk sea water.   We were all dozing, when the madman bit my foot, and I

N

woke up.   We then saw a ship bearing down upon us.   She proved to be the *British Sceptre,* from Calcutta to Dundee.   We were taken on board and treated very kindly.   I got very bad on board of her.   I was very nigh at death's door.   We were not recovered when we got to St. Helena.

So ends the second mate's statement.   The passenger and ordinary seaman both died a day or two after they were rescued, thus, out of 473 souls on the *Cospatrick,* only three men were saved, the second mate and the two able seamen.

The Loss of the "Avalanche."

The *Avalanche* was another Shaw, Savill ship which took down all but three of its company.   She was outward bound to Wellington with 60 passengers, under Captain Williams, in September, 1877.   At 8.45 p.m. when off Portland, she was on the port tack, the wind blowing strong from the S.W., when a red light was sighted on the starboard bow.   The officer of the watch gave the order "hard up" and "brail in the spanker," but the other ship, which was evidently running up Channel, came straight on, and as the *Avalanche* fell off struck her right amidships on the port side.   Three of the crew of the *Avalanche* managed to clamber aboard the other ship, which was the *Forest of Windsor,* Nova Scotia, and these three, the third mate named Sherrington and two A.B.'s, were the only ones saved.   The *Forest* also sank, but managed to launch four boats in safety.   These were picked up by fishermen the following morning and landed at Portland.

Patrick Henderson's Albion Shipping Company.

The chief rival of the Shaw, Savill before the advent of the New Zealand Shipping Company was Patrick Henderson, who owned the Albion Shipping

" WILD DEER."

" WILD DEER."

[To face page 355.

Company. But in the early days he was also in the China and Rangoon trades. His first ships in the New Zealand emigrant trade were fine, comfortable wooden vessels without any special turn of speed, such as the *Agnes Muir*, *Pladda*, *Lady Douglass*, *Jane Henderson*, *Vicksburgh* and *Helenslee*. But he had some very fast wood and composite clippers, which during the sixties were mostly in the Shanghai trade, and later took their turn at carrying emigrants to New Zealand.

The "Wild Deer."

The fastest of these China ships was the *Wild Deer*. She was launched from Connell's yard in December, 1863, being his thirteenth ship; and was composite built with iron topsides, teak planking to turn of bilge and elm bottom. She had a beautiful figure-head of the goddess "Diana," and was altogether a fine example of an out and out tea clipper.

Her measurements taken from Lloyd's Register were as follows:—

Tonnage net	..	.. 1016 tons
Tonnage under deck	..	955 ,,
Length	..	.. 211 feet.
Breadth	..	.. 33.2 ,,
Depth	..	.. 20.7 ,,

Her poop was 42 feet long, and her foc's'le-head 31 feet. She came out in 1863 with Cunningham's patent single topsails, but owing to her dismasting was one of the earliest ships to send aloft double topsail yards.

The following are the original spar measurements of her mainmast:—

Mainmast—deck to truck	130.6 feet	Royal mast	..	17 feet
Lower mast —deck to cap	64 ,,	Mainyard ..	..	75 ,,
Doubling	13.6 ,,	Topsail yard	..	61 ,,
Topmast	46 ,,	Topgallant yard	..	46 ,,
Doubling	8 ,,	Royal yard	..	34 ,,
Topgallant mast	..	25 ,,		

Wild Deer was taken from the stocks by Captain George Cobb, a well-known racing skipper in the China tea trade who had previously commanded the *Robin Hood*. Her complement consisted of 3 mates, 3 apprentices, carpenter, sailmaker and bosun, 16 A.B.'s and 3 ordinary seamen, it being intended to ship 4 more A.B.'s in China in the event of her getting into the race home with the cracks.

On her maiden passage she lost her foremast in the North Atlantic, owing to the want of angle irons, as *Titania* did a few years later, and this lost *Wild Deer* her chance of loading the first teas of the season. She had to put into Lisbon to refit, and came out of the Tagus with a very mixed sail plan; on the foremast she had an old-fashioned single topsail with three rows of reef points, on the main double topsails and on the mizen her original Cunningham's patent single topsail.

Her first two tea passages from Shanghai were good average runs, but nothing remarkable, her best work being 72 days from Anjer in 1865.

In 1866 she left London on 16th April and arrived at Shanghai on 29th July, 104 days out. Again she did not succeed in getting away with the first ships, but leaving Shanghai on 10th September she made Portland on Christmas Day. A fine S.S.W. breeze was blowing and *Wild Deer* was romping along under all plain sail and starboard fore topmast stunsail, when the American schooner yacht, *Henrietta*, the winner of the first ocean yacht race, hauled out from the land and, closing on the clipper, hoisted her colours and asked her name. The late Gordon Bennett, her owner, was on board the yacht, and evidently wished to try her paces against the tea ship, as the *Henrietta* held on in company with *Wild Deer* for an hour or two, then bore away for the Needles.

On this passage whilst crossing the Indian Ocean in the S.E. trades, *Wild Deer* made three consecutive 24-hour runs of 312, 312 and 327 miles.

On the outward passage in 1867, Captain Cobb had to be landed ill at Anjer and died shortly afterwards. His place was taken by a Hollander skipper. The Dutchman took *Wild Deer* on to Shanghai and loaded tea, then leaving Shanghai in August he took the Eastern Passage, but when he had cleared Dampier Straits took it into his head to alter his course for Anjer. This absolutely spoilt *Wild Deer's* chance of a quick passage, as she had to thread her way up the Java Sea through a succession of light airs and calms, and actually took 84 days to Anjer.

This was a great pity for she made a splendid run home from the Straits of Sunda, arriving in the Thames in January, only 68 days from Anjer, but 152 from Shanghai.

In 1868 her wings were cut, 3 feet being taken off her lower masts.

She was then handed over to a Captain Smith; unfortunately Smith was a regular old woman, but she was fortunate in getting Duncan as mate. This man had served in *Ariel* and *Titania* as chief officer, and was one of the best mates in the China trade, being specially noted for his skilful handling of sails in bad weather.

Wild Deer got away from London at the end of March, and left Shanghai with a tea cargo towards the end of July, a week behind one of Skinner's beautiful little ships, the *Douglas Castle*. In spite of Duncan's remonstrances, Captain Smith, who was frightened of the Gaspar Straits, determined to go east about; but the *Wild Deer* had so good a start south through the Formosa Channel that old Smith plucked up his courage and held on for Gaspar.

The very first day after he had changed his mind, *Wild Deer* ran into the S.W. monsoon and had to be braced sharp up. The following morning about day-break a ship crossed her bows on the other tack. This proved to be the *Douglas Castle*, and the two ships were in company all the way to Gaspar, except whilst passing Tamberlan Islands, which *Wild Deer* went east of, and the *Douglas* west.

The ships were evidently very well matched in light winds, but the *Wild Deer* was handicapped by the want of courage in her skipper. The night before the Straits were made it was clear moonlight, the sea dead smooth and there was a nice little breeze blowing; both ships were close-hauled on the port tack, with *Wild Deer* about a quarter of a mile to windward, neither ship gaining an inch.

Then at the change of the watch at midnight, old Smith backed his mainyard, clewed up his light sails and waited for morning, but young Captain McRitchie of the *Douglas Castle*, a far smarter man and the real sort of skipper for a tea clipper, held on, with the result that when the *Wild Deer* filled away again at daylight the *Douglas Castle* had a lead of several miles. Soon after sun up another ship was observed getting under weigh close to Billiton, where she had evidently anchored for the night; this proved to be the *Peter Denny* from Foochow—another of Patrick Henderson's ships. All three ships now had a fine trial of strength in the beat through Gaspar Straits. In this windward work the *Peter Denny* showed up best, being by far the quickest ship at going about, but she was commanded by a very smart sailorman, Captain George Adams, who had everything arranged for quick working, whilst old Smith was specially slow at getting the *Wild Deer* round—he was generally late with his commands and always hauled his mainsail up, though Captain Cobb always used to work his mainsail in tacking.

At 10 a.m. the *Douglas Castle* kept away for the Macclesfield Channel, and about noon *Wild Deer* made for Clements Channel, whilst the *Peter Denny* held on for the Stolze; this would save her tacking again once she was clear of the Straits, as the S.E. monsoon was blowing steadily in the Java Sea. Thus the ships were parted for a time. That night was another clear moonlight night with a nice little breeze. During the first watch the Brothers were sighted on the *Wild Deer*, and Duncan reported them to Captain Smith, who was lying asleep on the skylight. Smith, however, had none of the alertness of a crack China trader and went off into a heavy sleep again, then during the middle watch he woke up like a bear with a sore head and asked the big Highland second mate if he had seen the Brothers yet. Of course the second mate said he had not seen them, as they had been passed whilst his watch was below. At this old Smith got in a panic; the mainyard was backed, the courses hauled up and the royal yards lowered down. On coming on deck at 4 a.m. Duncan found to his amazement that the ship was hove to, and to his disgust that one of the others had passed her during the night whilst she lay with her head under her wing. On finding out the reason from the second mate, he roused out the " Old Man " and reminded him that he had reported the Brothers during the first watch. And you may be sure that it was " jump and go " for the crew until the *Wild Deer* was off again.

The wind fell light as the ship approached Sunda Straits, and as *Wild Deer* crawled towards Anjer the other two ships were sighted ahead, almost becalmed.

Wild Deer managed to avoid the calm patch by going
to the norrard of Thwarttheway Island and Krakatoa,
and thus stole a march on her rivals; however, they
finally came out of the Straits, neck and neck. Just
before dark the S.E. trade came away. *Wild Deer*
was still leading, but the *Douglas Castle* was so close
astern that each crew could hear the other singing out
as they trimmed sail for the run across the trades.

The next morning found *Wild Deer* still in the lead
with the other two ships one on each quarter, and the
following day the three ships separated until they were
off the Cape. Then, on a day of baffling and squally
winds the *Wild Deer* and *Douglas Castle* passed each
other on opposite tacks, the *Douglas* signalling that she
had spoken the *Denny* that morning.

The *Wild Deer* found a head wind in the mouth of the
Channel, but eventually after two days' beating a fine
slashing breeze came out of the south-west. At Dungeness the pilot had no news of the other two ships; but
just as the *Wild Deer* was making fast to her buoy at
Gravesend the *Douglas Castle* came up, and, as she
passed, hailed to say that the *Peter Denny* was close
astern.

Unfortunately for *Wild Deer* she remained under the
command of Captain Smith for several more voyages,
during which she was not allowed to show her paces and
usually arrived home in such a condition that Captain
Sellers, the ship's-husband (a good old name for the
present day shore superintendent) used to declare that
she was a disgrace to the Albion fleet.

However, on Captain Smith's death Captain Cowan
had her for two voyages, carrying emigrants to New
Zealand; on Cowan leaving her to take the *Wellington*
from the stocks, Captain Kilgour, who had been mate

in her, was given command, and in 1881-2 she came home from Otago in 82 days, arriving on 30th January.

Then Captain Kerr had her; this man had been carpenter of the *Peter Denny* years before, and mate of the *Christian McCausland*, one of Henderson's first iron ships. He was a very steady man, but no sailor.

On 12th January, 1883, when outward bound with emigrants, he piled the poor old *Wild Deer* up on North Rock, Cloghy, County Down, and she became a total loss.

Duncan's Method of Taking in Sail.

It may be of interest, perhaps, to describe the method used by Duncan, the crack racing mate of *Ariel*, *Titania*, and *Wild Deer*, when taking in sail. For a topgallant sail he sent as many men as were available to the lee buntline and leachline; one hand, generally an apprentice, stood by the clewline, and another attended to the weather brace. Duncan himself would ease away a few feet of the halliards, then sing out:— " Let go your lee sheet ! " Away would fly the sheet, followed by Duncan letting go the halliards; the hands on the buntline and leachline hauling away for all they were worth, the yard would run down and round itself in so that the boy on the weather brace only had to take in the slack. With smart hands on bunt and leachlines, the lee side of the sail would be spilt and up on the yard before it was well down and the apprentice on the clewline had only to get in the slack and make it fast. The lee side of the sail being well up, there was no trouble with the weather side. A hand in the top was almost unnecessary as the lee sheet needed no lighting up—it did that itself quick enough. The success of this method, of course, depended on the smartness of the hands on the bunt and leachline, but there were not many indifferent sailormen in a tea clipper's foc's'le.

In taking in a course Duncan used to man the lee bunt and leachlines well, with two hands only on the clew garnet; on the sheet being eased away bunt and leachlines were hauled smartly in, the sail was at once spilt and hauled up to the yard without a flap, the slack of the clew garnet being rounded up; then there was no trouble with the weather side.

This is also the method advocated by Captain Basil Hall in his *Fragments of Voyages*. Everything depended, of course, on having the necessary beef on the bunt and leachlines.

"Peter Denny."

The *Peter Denny* was built by Duthie, of Aberdeen, of teak and greenheart with iron knees in the 'tween decks, and measured 998 tons.

She was not a very fast ship, her best run in the westerlies being 285 miles, but she was a very handy-easy working ship and, still better, a very comfortable happy ship. She was also well run and beautifully kept under Captain Adams.

The Albion Shipping Company, 1869 Ships.

In 1869 Duncan, of Glasgow, built the two fine little composite ships, *James Nicol Fleming* (afterwards renamed the *Napier*) and the *Otago*, for Patrick Henderson. They were sister ships of 993 tons register. Their top strake and bulwarks were of iron, but their bottoms were of wood with pure copper sheathing.

The *Otago*, by the way, must not be confused with a little iron barque of 346 tons, which was owned in Adelaide and at one time commanded by Joseph Conrad.

Patrick Henderson's *Otago* was eventually sold to the Portuguese and renamed *Ermilla*. She was torpedoed and sunk by the Germans early in the war.

It was in 1869 that Patrick Henderson made his first venture in iron ships, Scott, of Greenock, building him the two sister ships *Jessie Readman* and *Christian McCausland*, of 962 tons register. These were fine handy little ships, good for 11 knots on a taut bowline, and equally good off the wind. They made very good outward passages with their 'tween decks full of emigrants, and loaded wool home. In those early days all the New Zealand wool was pressed on board before being stowed; this was generally done by a temporary crew of beachcombers, as it was the regular thing for a crew to run on arrival in the Colonies, however comfortable the ship was. The crew picked up for the run home was usually a fine one, of real sailormen, who had tired of the land after a short spell of working ashore.

The "Christian McCausland" Loses her Wheel.

In 1878, on the run to the Horn, when homeward bound loaded deep with wool and tallow (it was just before the days of Plimsoll) the *Christian McCausland* had her wheel washed away, and the incident, as showing what a beautiful steering ship she was, is worth recording.

Being very deep, she was making a wet passage of it running before the high westerly seas, and taking a good deal of heavy water aboard, especially in the waist. About eight days after leaving port she was running before a fresh gale on the starboard quarter, under reefed foresail, reefed upper topsails, and fore topmast staysail, the only sail set on the mizen being the lower topsail.

Soon after the change of the watch at 4 a.m., two heavy seas broke over the poop in quick succession, and washed away the wheel, which with the helmsman clinging to it was only brought up by the rail at the break of the poop.

The mate, whose watch it was, ran forward, singing out for all hands, and as he went, let go the topsail halliards. The ship, however, made no attempt to broach to, and ran along as steadily as if someone was at the helm.

As soon as possible the relieving tackles were rigged, and it was found that with five men on each tackle the ship could be steered without any difficulty. So the topsails were hoisted again and away she went.

The gear connecting the wheel to the rudder head was the usual right and left handed screws, which were luckily undamaged. These no doubt acted as a brake on the spindle and had a good deal to do with stopping the ship from coming up in the wind when the wheel went. The wheel and helmsman were found at the break of the poop, the man unhurt, but the wheel with every spoke broken through close to the nave as if cut by a saw.

During the morning watch the weather moderated and the carpenter was able to unship the nave of the wheel, and it was found that one of the main winch handles fitted the spindle as if made for it. This was put on the spindle, and the ship was actually steered by turning the winch handle, the helmsman facing the ship's side and looking over his shoulder at the compass. Later on, the captain improved this curious method of steering, by lashing a small handspike to the vertical arm of the winch handle. which gave the helmsman much more command and also allowed him to stand upright. And in three days the carpenter fitted the

"CHRISTIAN McCAUSLAND."

Photo by De Maus. Port Chalmers.

"PIAKO."

[*To face page* 364.

rim of the wheel and nave with a new set of stout elm spokes, and made such a good job of it that it was not found necessary to replace them on arrival in London. The rest of the passage was uneventful, the Horn was rounded in fine weather, and the *Christian McCausland* finally brought up at Gravesend close astern of the Russian royal yacht, which had just brought over the Czar Alexander on a visit to England.

After having four ships on the stocks in 1869, Patrick Henderson remained content with his fleet until 1874. His ships were always painted black with gold stripe and gingerbread work, whilst Shaw, Savill's were painted green. When the two firms amalgamated in 1882, all their ships came out with painted ports and lead colour under the ports.

The Origin of the Albion House-flag.

The Albion house-flag, a French flag with a small Union Jack in the centre, is supposed to have originated during the Crimean War. It is said that one of their early vessels carried both French and British troops at the same time, and for this reason flew a Union Jack and a French tricolour side by side on separate flagstaffs on the stern—this being later improved upon by the well-known Henderson house-flag.

The New Zealand Shipping Company.

During the early years of the Colony Shaw, Savill and P. Henderson had practically all the carrying trade in their hands. Occasionally an outsider took a load of emigrants out to New Zealand, such as the White Star liner *Chariot of Fame*, but the big Liverpool emigrant ships were really too big for the small volume of trade at that time. However, as both emigration to and trade with New Zealand increased, it was felt that the service of ships could well be improved, and at last in 1873, with this object in view, a number of merchants and run holders in the Colony decided to go in for shipowning and managing, and formed themselves into a company under the style of the New Zealand Shipping Company.

Full of enthusiasm, push and go, the promoters of the N.Z.S. Co. were determined from the first to have a line worthy to class with the Blackwall frigates of Green & Wigram. They had, of course, a great deal to learn, and mistakes were made but never repeated; and so great was their energy that in the first three years of their existence they chartered and despatched no less than 150 ships, carrying 28,675 passengers to the Colony. And before the company was ten years old it owned 16 up-to-date iron clippers, most of which had been built specially for them.

From the start the N.Z.S.Co. proceeded on generous lines, their ships being always well found, well manned and most liberally kept up. Their officers, also, considered themselves the aristocrats of the trade and rather looked down on the more economical Shaw, Savill and Albion clippers, whom they nicknamed the " Starvation Stars," in allusion to the stars in their house-flag, which by the way is the proper New Zealand flag which Queen Victoria presented to the Maoris.

The ships built for the N.Z.S.Co. were none of them specially fast; they aimed chiefly at safety and comfort for their passengers.

All these ships were built of iron, the finest and fastest of the fleet being the beautiful little *Turakina*, which originally belonged to George Smith of the well-known City Line, being then called the *City of Perth.* I shall deal with her in more detail presently.

LIST OF THE NEW ZEALAND SHIPPING COMPANY'S
SAILING FLEET.

Date Built	Ship	Tons	Length Feet	Breadth Feet	Depth Feet	Builders
1855	Pareora (ex-White Eagle)	879	203·3	32·8	20·9	At Glasgow
1863	Waitara	833	182·4	31·4	20·9	Reid, Glasgow
,,	Rangitiki (ex-Cimitar) ..	1188	210·0	35·0	22·7	Samuelson. Hull
1868	Turakina (ex-City of Perth)	1189	232·5	35·4	22·2	Connell, Glasgow
,,	Waimea (ex-Dorette) ..	848	194·3	31·7	19·0	Goddefrog, Hamburg
,,	Mataura (ex-Dunfillan)	853	199·4	33·3	20·3	Aitken, Glasgow
1873	Rakaia	1022	210·2	34·0	19·2	Blumer, Sunderland
1874	Waikato	1021	210·5	34·1	19·2	,, ,,
,,	Waimate (ex-Hindostan)	1124	219·7	35·1	20·7	,, ,,
,,	Waitangi	1128	222·0	35·1	20·8	,, ,,
1875	Hurunui	1012	204·1	34·2	20·0	Palmers Co., Newcastle
.,	Orari	1011	204·1	34·2	20·0	,, ,,
,,	Otaki	1014	204·1	34·2	20·0	,, ,,
,,	Waipa	1017	204·1	34·2	20·0	,, ,,
,,	Wairoa	1015	204·1	32·2	20·0	,, ,,
1876	Opawa	1076	215·2	34·0	20·4	Stephen, Glasgow
,,	Piako	1075	215·3	34·0	20·5	,, ,,
1877	Wanganui	1077	215·3	34·0	20·4	,, ,,

The *Pareora* was broken up in 1889.

The *Waitara* came to her end by colliding with the *Hurunui* in the English Channel on 22nd June, 1883.

The *Rangitiki* was sold to the Norwegians and renamed *Dalston*. She was resold in 1909 for £1500 and went to New Caledonia as a hulk.

The *Waimea* was sold to the Norwegians and wrecked on the South African Coast in 1902.

The *Mataura* brought the first cargo of frozen meat from New Zealand, arriving on 26th September, 1882, being fitted with Haslam's patent dry air refrigerator. She was then rigged as a barque. She was eventually sold to the Norwegians and renamed *Alida*. On 24th August, 1900, she was dismasted in the Pacific and abandoned.

The *Raikaia* also went to the Norwegians and was

renamed *Marie*. She was again sold, to Boston ship-owners, for 4850 dollars, and is once more sailing the seas under her old name.

The *Waikato* was sold to the Germans and her name changed to *J. C. Pfluger*. They sold her in 1900 to Californian owners, who sailed her out of Frisco rigged as a barquentine. She is now a hulk disguised under the name of *Coronado*.

The *Waimate*, from noon on 26th November to noon 27th November, in 1881, covered 354 miles in the 28½-hour day running the easting down in lat. 47° S. In the p.m. the sea was smooth and the wind gradually freshening, Captain Mosey who was making his first voyage in the ship, hung on to his main royal until the first watch, the wind being on the port quarter. By daybreak the wind was dead aft with bright sunshine and a clear sky, but with a very big sea running.

Her best week's run was from the 27th November to 3rd December, being 1807 miles.

Waimate was a skysail yarder, and with the wind abaft the beam could be made to travel, but she was nothing extraordinary with the yards on the backstays.

She was once in company with Shaw, Savill's *Marlborough* off the Snares. With the wind free she had the best of it, but as soon as they hauled up to stand along the New Zealand Coast the *Marlborough* passed her without any trouble.

Two years later *Waimate*, with Captain Mosey still in command, ran from Lyttelton to the Scillies in 71 days. She was sold by the N.Z.S.Co. to the Russians and renamed *Valkyrian*. She went missing in 1899.

Waitangi is still afloat flying Norwegian colours under the name of *Agda*.

Hurunui is also, I believe, still afloat under the Russian flag, her name being *Hermes*.

Orari was sold to the Italians in 1906 and converted into a hulk in 1909.

"Otaki's" Record Passage Home.

Otaki is famous for her wonderful run home in 1877. She left Port Chalmers with Captain J. F. Millman in command at 4 p.m. on 11th March; was becalmed for four days off the New Zealand Coast; was then 22 days to the Horn; reached the Lizard 63 days out from her departure, and docked in London 69 days out. During this passage she only had eight hours of head winds. *Otaki* was nothing special in the way of sailing and never made more than 10 knots, so her passage must really be put down to amazing good luck. She was bought by the Germans and renamed *Dr. Siegert*, being wrecked in 1896.

Waipa went to the Norwegians in her old age, and I believe she is still afloat under the name of *Munter*.

Wairoa was bought by the Russians and renamed *Winnipeg*. She went missing in 1907 whilst bound from Pensacola to Buenos Ayres.

Opawa and *Piako* were two beautiful little ships. In 1877 *Opawa* went from the London Docks to New Zealand and home again with wool in 6 months 9 days. And in 1893 she made the passage New Zealand to Liverpool in 83 days. She was still afloat in quite recent years under the name of *Aquila* and Norwegian colours. The sister ship *Piako* went missing in 1900 on a passage from Melbourne to the Cape, being then German owned.

The *Wanganui*, last ship built for the firm, was still afloat when the war started as the Norwegian barque *Blenheim*.

"Turakina" ex-"City of Perth."

I have left the *Turakina* to the last, as she deserves a longer notice, being one of the most beautiful little iron ships that ever left the ways. She was built of extra thick plates and launched in May, 1868, for Smith's famous City Line to Calcutta.

The following interesting account of her in her early days appeared in the *Nautical Magazine* in 1917 :—

I sailed in this vessel when she was three years old, under Captain Beckett, a native of Saltcoats, Firth of Clyde. Captain Beckett would have no foreigners or negroes sail with him, either as officers or sailors, and he was one of the most upright and good-living men I ever sailed under, and I went to sea first in 1858. His policy was the same for the men as for the cabin, with plenty of good food, no allowance, sufficient without waste, and plenty of work to keep the scurvy out of the bones, as the sailors said.

We left the Clyde at latter end of September, 1871, with a general cargo for Calcutta. We soon got out of the St. George's Channel, and got all the studding sail gear rigged ready for the first favourable wind, and that occurred in lat. 43° N., long. 14° 15′ W. We then set top-gallant, royal, topmast, and square lower stunsails, watersails, ringtail and ringtail watersail, Jamie Green and save-alls every place where a sail could be set; wind N.W. but gradually increasing to a gale.

However we kept everything on her. On the second day after everything had been set, about 11 a.m., we sighted a ship ahead of us; by 2 p.m. we were up alongside of her. She was a New York full-rigged ship from the Tyne for California.

The American captain asked us where we were bound from and where bound to. The whole of his crew came and looked at us, and her master cried to our captain that we were the prettiest sight he had ever seen. Our ship was going fully 17 knots when we passed her, and in three hours we had left her completely out of sight.

I have been in many ships in my time, but never one to equal her for speed. She was built by Connell, on the Clyde, and she was certainly that firm's masterpiece. She was iron, and one of the most beautiful models you could look at in the water. The *Thermopylae* was the largest of the China clippers. She was 948 tons, but the *City* was 1189 tons. She was a far more powerful ship. I have been in many cracks, but I never saw anything that could look at her in a strong breeze, and as for running in a heavy gale she would run before the heaviest gale that ever blew.

"TURAKINA" *ex* "CITY OF PERTH."

Photo by De Maus, Port Chalmers.

"OTAKI" becalmed.

Lent by F. G. Layton.

[*To face page* 370.

And he goes on to give the following week's work from the N.E. trades to Sandy Hook.

Left Calcutta, 16th January, 1872, for New York.   Arrived at New York on 5th April, 1872.   Below are the position and runs in nautical miles.

29th March, 1872, position at noon, lat 28° 01′ N., long. 30° 00′ W.

30th March, 1872, position at noon, lat 30° 40′ N., long. 35° 56′ W. distance 298.

31st March, 1872, position at noon lat. 32° 14′ N., long. 41° 44′ W. distance 300.

1st April,   1872, position at noon, lat. 33° 55′ N., long. 48° 35′ W. distance 363.

2nd April,   1872, position at noon, lat. 35° 30′ N., long. 55° 39′ W. distance 350.

3rd April,   1872, position at noon, lat. 36° 51′ N., long. 62° 36′ W. distance 350.

4th April,   1872, position at noon, lat. 38° 40′ N., long. 69° 10′ W. distance 345.

5th April,   1872, position at noon. lat. 40° 29′ N., long. 73° 58′ W. distance 342.

Time 170 hours.   Nautical miles 2348.

I do not agree with all his distances, but anyhow it is a wonderful week's work and probably the quickest run into New York from 28° N., 30° W., ever made by a sailing ship.

During the seventies Messrs. George Smith & Sons generally sent one or two of their fastest ships out to Australia for a wool cargo home; and in 1873, 1874 and 1875 *City of Perth* went out to Melbourne and loaded wool home.   Her outward passages ran to over 80 days, but in 1874 Captain Beckett made the fine run of 81 days to the Thames.

Owing to the exporters of wool insisting that her bottom was foul, she was docked, with her cargo on board, in the Alfred Graving Dock the day before she sailed.   Her bottom was found to be clean, but Captain Beckett took the opportunity to give her a coat of tallow, and leaving on the following day, 15th November, he caught the February wool sales without any difficulty and eased the minds of the anxious wool exporters. It was his last passage in her, however, for in 1875 Captain Warden took her out to Melbourne in 88 days from the Lizard, but he ran his easting down in 38° S. and did not give her a chance. Again she loaded wool and this time was given a coating of Peacock & Buchan's patent before sailing.

After this she went back to the Calcutta trade until 1881, when she left London under Captain McDonald for Canterbury, N.Z., and went on to Timaru and loaded wheat. She completed her loading, and on 13th May, 1882, was lying at anchor in the inner anchorage close to the *Ben Venue*, when it came on to blow with a big sea making.

8.30 a.m. on the 14th found the *Ben Venue* with two anchors and the *City of Perth* with three, riding out a furious gale. But the outlook was very bad especially for the little *Ben Venue* which had a heavy list to starboard, being almost on her beam ends. Four hours later one of *Ben Venue's* cables parted and she began to drag, and about 1 o'clock stranded in Caroline Bay.

About the same time *City of Perth* was also seen to be dragging her anchors and soon afterwards drifted ashore to the north of *Ben Venue*, but further seaward.

Captain McDonald tried to send a boat ashore, but she capsized and the ship's second mate and carpenter were both drowned and the mate had his leg broken. Meanwhile great rescue efforts were made from the shore, the lifeboat was launched, but she also capsized and six of her crew were drowned, including the harbour-master of Timaru. The gale had moderated sufficiently by the 19th to attempt towing the *City of Perth* off, but without success. Her partner in misfortune, the beautiful little *Ben Venue*, had by this time become a total wreck, and the only gear salved, including some of her spars, was sold for £150.

After the failure to get the *City of Perth* afloat her cargo was got out of her, and with an empty hold she was at last towed off successfully. She was then surveyed and sold, her hull and gear only fetching £900. She was next towed round to Port Chalmers and docked there on 1st July, when it was found that the rudder was carried away, with about 20 feet of the keelson and keel, besides five bottom plates very much damaged. It speaks well for the ship, considering the pounding she must have undergone, that the damage was not worse. Again she was sold privately for £500, I am not certain whether the N.Z.S.Co. bought her on this occasion or after her arrival in London after being patched up. If they did, they got a wonderful bargain, though they might have had a still better, for whilst she was lying stranded she was offered for sale by auction and only a few pounds bid for her.

After being repaired and refitted, she was sent to Invercargill to load for London; and she left Invercargill on 13th April, 1883, in charge of Captain McFarlane, arriving safely in the Thames on 8th July after a good passage of 86 days.

Here she had a thorough refit, and finally left London on 24th October, 1883, under a new captain, with the name of *Turakina* on her stern and flying the N.Z.S.Co. house-flag. She arrived at Auckland on 19th January, 1884, 86 days out.

During the next few years we find her in charge of a Captain Power, who was evidently not a sail carrier, for she did nothing remarkable whilst he had her.

In 1885, on her passage home from Otago, she survived another bad dusting. She left Port Chalmers on 9th March, had strong S.W. gales and heavy weather to the Horn, which was rounded at 6 a.m. on the 5th April, 27 days out.   On 11th April, when in 44° 46′ S., 40° W., she ran into a perfect hurricane, the squalls being at their worst between noon and 5 p.m.   At 2 p.m. the lower main topsail blew away, at 2.30 the foresail was whipped out of her and at 3 the lee quarter boat was washed away.   All this time the ship was swept fore and aft by the terrific sea running, and at 5 p.m. the weight of water on her main deck burst the lee topgallant bulwarks.   Luckily the wind then began to veer to the S.W. and the squalls began to take off and come up at longer intervals.

The equator was crossed on 3rd May, 28 days from the Horn.   She had light trades followed by moderate southerly winds to the Western Isles, then light southerly and easterly winds, with thick fog to the Wight, where she picked up her tug, arriving in the Thames on 11th June, 94 days out.

Like most of the New Zealand clippers *Turakina* was fitted with refrigerating machinery in the late eighties, and it was as a frozen meat ship under Captain Hamon that she made her name as a passage maker in the New Zealand trade.

In 1892 she left Gisborne and arrived home on 31st May, 78 days out.

In 1893 she left Timaru for Liverpool on 2nd February, but carried away her mainyard on the first night out and had to put back to Lyttelton to repair damages. This spoilt her passage.

In 1894 she signalled off the Lizard on 27th May, only 69 days out from Wellington, and docked in the London River, 71 days out.

In 1895 she made the Wight on 1st July, 73 days out from Port Chalmers.

On her previous outward passage she had distinguished herself by sailing past the company's steamer *Ruapehu.* The following account of this incident was given me by one of the officers of the steamship :—

On the 14th February, 1895, in lat. 46° 15′ S., long. 68° 16′ E., the N.Z.S. Co.'s mail steamer *Ruapehu* was running her easting down under whole topsails and courses, the weather dirty and a strong wind from the norrard, force 7 Beaufort scale.   At 9 a.m. a sailing ship was reported astern, topgallant sails up.   Shortly after she sheeted home her royals.   Orders were given on the *Ruapehu* to the engineer to drive the ship and topgallant sails were set, the patent log showing a good 14.

At noon exactly the N.Z.S. Co.'s sailing ship *Turakina* passed along our lee side.   She was then carrying all square sail except mizen royal and topgallant sail (probably griping a good deal).   She was right alongside and you could distinguish the features of the officers, and see the seas breaking over her—I have a very good photo.   She then hauled her wind and crossed our bow, at the same time shortening sail to topsails, reef in mainsail and furled crossjack; even then she held her own with us during a long summer evening light, till 9.30 there she was just ahead on the port bow.

Next day at noon we had run 315 miles.   At midnight the wind came aft and she was therefore not in sight from masthead at daylight. It was a wonderful performance and made a man feel glad to be alive to see it.

And the *Turakina* held her own for 14 days.   She covered the 5000 miles between the meridians of the Cape and the Leeuwin, in 16 days, her best runs being 328, 316 and 308.

I am glad to say that the gallant little ship is still afloat under the name of *Elida,* owned in Tordesstrand.

In 1912 she was in Rio at the same time as the Portuguese *Ferreira* ex-*Cutty Sark.*   I wonder how many of the shipping people there realized that two of the fastest and most beautiful sailing ships ever built were lying at anchor in their wonderful harbour.

Before leaving the *Turakina*, I must not omit to give her official measurements from Lloyd's Register :—

Tonnage (net)	.. .. ..	1189 tons
Tonnage (gross)	.. .. ..	1247 „
Tonnage (under deck)	.. ..	1160 „
Length	.. ..	232.5 feet
Breadth	.. ..	35.4 „
Depth	.. ..	22.2 „
Depth moulded	.. .. ..	23.5 „
Freeboard amidships (summer)		4.5½ „
Raised quarterdeck	.. ..	32 „

Robert Duncan's Six Beautiful Sister Ships.

In 1874 Patrick Henderson launched out by ordering six iron passenger clippers from Robert Duncan and two from Scott, of Greenock, and of the big fleet of splendid iron ships built in the seventies there were few more perfect specimens of the shipbuilders' art than these eight ships. The following are the measurements of the Duncan ships:—

Ship	Date Launched	Tonnage	Length	Beam	Depth	Length of Poop	Length of Foc's'le
Dunedin ..	March 1874	1250	241	36.1	20.9	70	35
Canterbury ..	May 1874	1245	239.7	36	20.8	70	35
Invercargill ..	June 1874	1246	239.7	36	20.7	70	35
Auckland ..	July 1874	1245	239.8	36	20.7	70	35
Nelson ..	Aug. 1874	1247	239.3	36	20.7	70	35
Wellington ..	Sept. 1874	1247	239.8	36	20.7	70	35

All these ships, with the exception of *Dunedin*, which went missing when homeward bound with frozen meat in 1889, were sailing the seas in the twentieth century, and until Shaw, Savill sold them in 1904-5 were still making good passages. Even after they had ceased to carry emigrants, their outward passages were constantly under 80 days; and the frozen mutton did not affect their homeward runs as much as one would expect, for

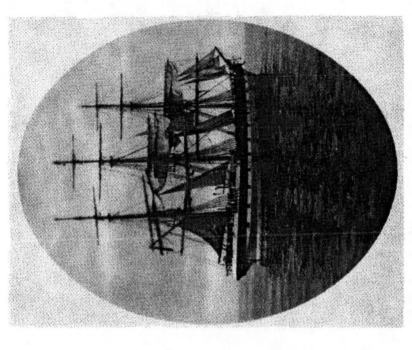

"INVERCARGILL," off Tairoa Heads.

Lent by F. G. Layton

[To face page 377.

"AKAROA."

I find the *Nelson* running from Wellington to the Lizard in 1889-90 in 88 days; the *Auckland* from Wellington to the Lizard in 1899 in 84 days; *Invercargill* from Timaru to the Wight in 1895, in 85 days, and *Wellington* from Timaru to the Lizard in 1900 in 79 days.

The *Canterbury* was credited with a run out of 64 days. She was at her best off the wind in a strong breeze. She was still afloat at the outbreak of the war, owned in Tordesstrand, Norway.

Invercargill, under Captain Bowling, had many excellent passages to her credit. Captain Bowling was a native of Kingstown, in Ireland, and started his sea life in the China trade. He commanded the *Invercargill* for 13 years, at the end of which time he had been 50 years at sea and 30 years in command of sailing ships. He was one of Shaw, Savill's most trusted commanders and was noted for the way in which he handled his beautiful ship.

Not many years ago a writer to the " Nautical " described one of Captain Bowling's skilful bits of seamanship. He wrote as follows:—

The *Invercargill*, fully laden from London, arrived off Wellington Heads one afternoon. A fine southerly breeze was blowing. Very impatient to get anchored, Captain Bowling decided to sail right in without the assistance of a tug. But just as he got well up the entrance, the wind suddenly veered right round to the northward and blew hard, and as his ship was well up inside Barrett's Reef by this time, things began to look rather serious. Notwithstanding his many difficulties— for the slightest error or hesitation in timing the order of the different manœuvres meant disaster—old Bowling managed everything like clockwork, and the *Invercargill* dropped her anchor off Kaiwarra, just as darkness fell.

The *Invercargill's* last passage under the British flag in 1904 was her worst; in it she weathered out the biggest gale of Captain Bowling's experience. She sailed from Sydney, N.S.W., on the 27th August, 1904, loaded with wheat, being bound to Queenstown for orders. On the 30th September she was caught in a Cape Horn snorter, her cargo shifted to port, her port bulwarks were carried away and for some time she lay on her beam ends. At last by hard work the cargo was man-handled to the windward side, she righted and continued her passage. But once again she ran into heavy weather, this time in the Atlantic in 45° N., 20° W., and the morning of the 8th December found her battling with a heavy gale from N.W., the weather being clear. The entry in the log at 4 p.m. said :—

Hard squalls and high confused sea vessel labouring heavily and shipping great quantities of water fore and aft.

At 7 p.m. both wind and sea increased, and a huge mountain of water broke over the port quarter and swept the decks, the whole length of her. The cabin skylight was burst in and the water flooded below, breaking into the saloon and cabins, the sail locker, the lazarette and even into the 'tween decks; the companion hatch on the poop was carried away, and along with it went both compasses, stands and binnacles, side lights and screens, the patent log from the taffrail; in fact, pretty near everything on the decks except the wheel. Mr. Le Sueur, the mate, lost no time in getting a sail over the gaping skylight and all hands were turned to bailing out the water from below, which was up to one's waist in the cabin. 8 p.m. found the gale still blowing with undiminished force, and the ship was rolling heavily as she ran before it. By midnight the seas were mountainous and the squalls became fiercer and more frequent. About 4 a.m. a big sea washed out the carpenter's quarters, and " Chips," under the impression that the ship was sinking by the head, made the best of his way aft. But Captain Bowling and his officers were all below clearing up the wrecked cabin, etc. The carpenter, thereupon, informed the man at the wheel of his fears, with the result that the latter had an attack of nerves, thought he was running the ship under, and allowed her to come to. As the ship broached to, the cargo shifted for the second time and the *Invercargill* went over on her beam ends. The foresail, fore upper topsail, jib, fore topmast staysail and main royal all blew adrift out of the gaskets and were soon in tatters. The lifeboat to leeward was lifted out of her davits and swept away. Then, whilst the ship lay down with her lee foreyard arm dipped 6 feet into the broken water to leeward, the seas worked havoc on the flooded main deck.

Daylight disclosed the extent of the damage; the galley was gutted, the carpenter's shop was bare, all his tools gone and the doors smashed in; the contents of the bosun's locker, paint locker, and the mate's and second mate's cabins were washed clean out of them, and gone overboard. The topgallant bulwarks to leeward were all gone, and the running gear being dragged backwards and forwards through the swinging ports was cut to pieces, two of these ports had been torn off their hinges; the foc's'le-head and poop ladders were gone and all the poop stanchions; whilst the racks for handspikes and capstan bars were empty.

All that day and the next night the *Invercargill* lay like a log with her lee rail buried deep and her main deck full of water. At last, early on 10th December, the wind dropped very light and went into the S.W. with thick weather.

Cargo was jettisoned to bring the ship on an even keel, and at last she was got away on her course. The next difficulty was making a landfall without a reliable compass, as only an old compass which had not been adjusted was available, both the steering and standard compasses having gone overboard.

In spite of a large allowance made for his defective compass, Captain Bowling found himself nearly ashore amongst the Scilly Isles. Again his fine seamanship saved the vessel, and on the 18th December he brought her safely into Queenstown, 113 days out from Sydney.

Orders were received here to proceed to Glasgow, but the crew came aft and refused to proceed in the crippled ship; upon which she was towed round to the Clyde and was docked in Princes Dock, Govan, on Christmas Eve.

After she had been repaired and refitted at a cost of £1000, Shaw, Savill sold the splendid old ship to the Norwegians, who renamed her the *Varg*. She sailed for Christiania in 1905, with coal ballast, and was never seen again after clearing the Tail of the Bank.

The *Auckland*, after a long and successful career with many fine passages to her credit, was sold to S. O. Stray, of Norway, in 1904, but soon disappeared from the Register.

The *Nelson's* finest sailing feat was in 1875, when she ran from Otago Heads to the Horn in 19 days. She was still afloat in 1914 at the outbreak of the war, sailing as a barque under the Chilean flag, and must often have had a chance of trying her sailing powers against the old tea clipper, *Lothair*, which was also still afloat on the West Coast of South America.

"Wellington" and Captain Cowan.

I cannot pronounce an opinion as to which was the fastest of these six beautiful Duncan sisters, but the *Wellington* probably has the best average. She was taken from the stocks by Captain D. Cowan, of Peter-head, and under his able guidance was a most consistent passage-maker.   Captain Cowan, like Captain Bowling, of *Invercargill*, was a magnificent seaman of the old sailing ship type, the survivors of which grow fewer, alas, every day.   He served his time in the Peterhead whale fishery.   Then about 1862 he joined Patrick Henderson's as third officer of the *Pladda*, a slow but com-fortable old wooden packet, which carried 400 emigrants to Port Chalmers.   His next vessel was the *Vicksburgh*. Again after one New Zealand voyage he was transferred, this time with promotion to mate, to the *Jane Henderson*, in which he made three voyages to Rangoon, on the last of which, about 1867, he went in command.   His second voyage as a skipper was in the *Helenslee* with passengers to Port Chalmers.   This ship was sold in New Zealand, and Captain Cowan travelled home as a passenger.   He next had *Margaret Galbraith* for two voyages, then the composite clipper *Wild Deer*, which he left in order to take over the *Wellington*.

Captain Cowan had the *Wellington* for 18 years.   He told me that the *Wellington* was such a fast ship with the wind abaft the beam that he never remembers her being passed under such conditions, but that she was nothing out of the way when braced sharp up.   This indeed may be said to have been the general case with Duncan's ships.   From 1877 to 1884 *Wellington* ran from Glasgow to Otago with first class passengers and emigrants.   Under these favourable conditions her average outward passage was about 80 days, her four best being 73, 75, 76 and 78 days.

Soon after the amalgamation with Shaw, Savill, *Wellington* had freezing machinery put on board, and henceforth came home with 18,000 carcases a trip.   The

Wellington had her freezing machinery on board for four voyages, after which the mutton was sent on board frozen.

"Wellington" Collides with an Iceberg.

Early in the nineties she nearly finished her career by colliding with an iceberg to the eastward of the Falkland Islands. Her bows were stove in, two men being killed in the foc's'le by the deck being driven down on top of them, broken down by a mass of ice falling aboard. The bowsprit and jibboom were, of course, carried away, and also the fore topmast; only the collision bulkhead saved the ship from sinking. Captain Cowan shored up his bulkhead and squared away for Rio de Janeiro. He was a month getting there and repairs were hardly under weigh before the Civil War broke out, and all work was stopped for six months.

Meanwhile in order to keep the mutton frozen, the engine had to be kept going at full speed night and day; owing to the heat not even a rest for an hour to overhaul it could be thought of, and it says a good deal for Captain Cowan and his engineer that they managed to keep the engine running without a breakdown for so many months.

Orders came out from home that the mutton was to be sold; whereupon Captain Cowan rashly sold some of it to the rebels—the Government at once issued a warrant for his arrest—and he had to be smuggled aboard the New Zealand Shipping Co.'s steamer *Norangi*, the mate being left in charge. After this very trying experience Captain Cowan, feeling that he needed a rest, retired from the sea.

In 1904 the *Wellington* was sold to S. O. Stray, of

"TIMARU."

Photo by De Maus, Port Chalmers.

"WELLINGTON."

At Picton, Queen Charlotte Sound.

Lent by F. G. Layton.

[*To face page* 382.

Norway, for £3150.   In December, 1906, she was abandoned on her beam ends and foundered when bound from a Gulf port to Rosario.

"Oamaru" and "Timaru."

Not content with Duncan's six beautiful ships, Patrick Henderson ordered two from Scott, of Greenock, in 1874.   These were the *Oamaru* and *Timaru*, which measured 1306 tons, 239.1 feet length, 36.1 feet beam, 21 feet depth.

The *Oamaru* was launched in October and the *Timaru* in December.   These fine little ships were well worthy of ranking with Duncan's beauties.

The *Timaru* especially, under Captain Taylor, made some fine passages, when she was carrying emigrants.

In March, 1879, she reported off the Scillies, only 68 days out from New Zealand.   On the following outward passage, she went out to Port Chalmers in 78 days.   Whilst running her easting down she averaged 270 miles a day for 17 days.   She had 499 souls on board this passage.

Captain Taylor was rather fond of sending bottles adrift, a common practice in the old days, and he was lucky enough to have two picked up in five years. One which he threw over in 12° N. in the Atlantic was picked up in the Gulf of Guinea, and the other, thrown over just east of the Cape meridian, was washed up on the beach in Western Australia.

These little New Zealand emigrant clippers, like the larger and earlier Australian clippers, constantly carried very rich cargoes of bullion.   On one occasion the *Timaru* had £57,000 in bar gold on board.

Oamaru was finally sold to Norway and renamed *Fox*.   She was broken up in 1912.

Timaru was sold in South Africa as a cold storage ship during the Boer War, and is now, I believe, a freezing hulk at Durban.

"Marlborough," "Hermione" and "Pleione."

In 1876 three very fine little ships were built for Shaw, Savill; these were:—

Marlborough, 1124 tons, 228 feet length, 35 feet beam, 21 feet depth, launched in June from Duncan's yard.

Pelione, 1092 tons, 209.7 feet, length, 34.6 feet beam, 20.3 feet depth, launched in September by Stephen, of Glasgow.

Hermione, 1120 tons, 219.4 feet length, 35 feet beam, 21 feet depth, launched in October by Hall, of Aberdeen.

The longest of the three was also the fastest, as is the general rule where beam and depth are about the same.

Marlborough was certainly a very fast ship and in 1880, under Captain Anderson, ran from Lyttelton to the Lizard in 71 days.

In 1889 she sailed from New Zealand homeward bound with frozen mutton about six weeks behind the *Dunedin*, and a great stir was raised in New Zealand when neither ship reached her destination. No trace of them was ever found, though the *Wellington* which sailed in between the two arrived safely.

Pleione, like so many ships in the New Zealand trade was eventually sold to the Scandinavians, whilst *Hermione* was bought by the Italians and renamed *Mantova*. She was broken up at Genoa in 1918.

"Taranaki," "Lyttelton," and "Westland."

These three were the last sailing ships built for the Shaw, Savill & Albion Companies. *Taranaki* was James Galbraith's last ship and *Westland* Patrick Henderson's.

All three were built by Duncan and were very fast

"WESTLAND."

"TARANAKI."

Lent by Captain T. S. Angus.

To face page 384.

ships, and continued making fine passages right into the twentieth century. They were over 100 tons smaller than Duncan's 1874 ships, their measurements being:—

Taranaki, 1126 tons, 228.2 feet length, 35.2 feet beam, 20.9 feet depth.
Lyttelton, 1111 tons, 223.8 feet length, 35.0 feet beam, 21.0 feet depth.
Westland, 1116 tons, 222.8 feet length, 35.1 feet beam, 21 feet depth.

Of the three, *Westland* was the fastest; in fact, many people considered her to be the fastest of the Shaw, Savill & Albion fleet. One of her best performances was a run of 72 days from Bluff Harbour to the Lizard, where she reported on 81st March, 1895.

Taranaki was sold to the Italians, when Shaw, Savill parted with their sailers, and, owned in Genoa, was still afloat when the Great War burst on Europe. The *Lyttelton* struck on an uncharted rock outside Timaru, when leaving homeward bound. *Westland* went to the Norwegians, she put into Moss, leaking, and was condemned there.

"Lutterworth" and "Lady Jocelyn."

Besides the ships specially built for them, Shaw, Savill occasionally bought a ship; of these probably the best known were the *Lutterworth* and *Lady Jocelyn*.

The *Lutterworth* was a fast little iron barque of 883 tons, built by Denton, of Hartlepool, in 1868. Shaw, Savill & Co. sold her eventually to Turnbull & Co., of Lyttelton, N.Z. Whilst on a passage from Timaru to Kaipara in ballast, she was dismasted and abandoned in Cook Straits. She was, however, picked up as a derelict and towed into Wellington, where she was converted into a coal hulk.

The *Lady Jocelyn* was one of those early auxiliary steamers, which always seem to have had long and adventurous careers. She was originally the *Brazil*,

o

owned by the General Screw Steamship Company, and was built as far back as 1852 by Mare, of London, her measurements being—2138 tons; 254 feet length, 39 feet beam, 24.9 feet depth. Of iron construction, she had a spar deck above her two decks, and no expense was spared in her construction.

As an auxiliary steamer, like most of her kind, she proved to be a money-eater, and when after a few years the company went into liquidation she was bought by Shaw, Savill and put into their emigrant trade as a sailing ship. Then as passengers began to desert the clipper for steam, freezing machinery was put aboard her. Finally Shaw, Savill laid her up in the West India Docks, and used her as a frozen meat store ship, for which owing to her size and the freezing machinery aboard she was well adapted.

Years passed and still she remained the most familiar object in the West India Dock, right up to the present date, during which time she has served a variety of purposes, such as store ship for the Shipping Federation and a home for strike breakers.

Outsiders in the New Zealand Trade.

Though the New Zealand trade was held pretty tightly in the hands of Shaw, Savill, the Albion Shipping Company and the New Zealand Shipping Company, many a distinguished ship paid an occasional visit to Maoriland, notably the beautiful tea clipper *Sir Lancelot* in 1879; the majestic Blackwall frigate *The Tweed* in 1874, when she went out to Otago in 78 days; *The Tweed's* great rival *Thomas Stephens*, which took passengers to Otago in 1879; *Miltiades*, which in 1889-90 came home from Lyttelton in 78 days and the following season came home from Wellington in

"BEN VENUE."

"LADY JOCELYN."

[To face page 386.

82 days; and *Thessalus*, which in 1900 ran from Lyttelton to the Lizards in 87 days, beating the famous coolie ship *Sheila* by a week. *Loch Awe's* record passage to Auckland I have already mentioned in these pages, also *Sam Mendel's* 68 days to Port Chalmers. Some years later, in an attempt to beat this performance and incidentally a fast little City liner, *Sam Mendel* was dismasted and came into port without her foremast, bowsprit and jibbooms, which had all gone by the board.

The Pretty Little "Ben Venue."

A regular trader to New Zealand in the seventies was Watson's pretty little *Ben Venue*, an iron main skysail-yarder of 999 tons, launched by Barclay, Curle in 1867. Under Captain McGowan, she made the very fine average of 77 days for her outward passages, her best homeward being 72 days to the Lizards from Lyttelton in 1879. I have already described her loss in May, 1882.

"Hinemoa."

The distinction of being the only sailing ship specially built for the New Zealand frozen meat trade belongs to the splendid steel four-mast barque, *Hinemoa*, built by Russell, of Greenock, in 1890. She measured 2283 tons, 278.1 feet length, 41.9 feet breadth, 24.2 feet depth. Like many of Russell's carriers she possessed a very fair turn of speed, especially off the wind, and has the following fine passages to her credit.

1894	Downs to Melbourne	.. .. ..	77 days
1901	Newcastle, N.S.W., to Frisco	.. ..	60 ,,
1902	Frisco to Old Head of Kinsale	.. ..	101 ,,

Hinemoa was built at a time when "sail" was making a final effort to hold its markets against the steam tramp. That effort was a truly gallant one, and but for the fact that the windjammer possesses a charm and fascination totally lacking in steam, and has ever been enthroned in the hearts of all lovers of the sea, masts and yards would not have lasted longer in the Mercantile Marine than they did in the Royal Navy.

That there were still sailing ships used commercially in 1914 goes to prove that the most stony-hearted, matter-of-fact business man was ready to sacrifice his pocket for a sentiment, a sentiment indeed which many may find hard to define, yet which has forged the links in the chain of nations which represent the present British Empire.

To sail and the sail-trained seaman more than to any other cause do we owe our nation's greatness. By sail were our homesteads kept safe from the enemy; by sail were our new coasts charted; sail took the adventurous pioneers to the new land, and sail brought home the products of these new lands to the Old Country and made her the Market of the World.

This book is an attempt to preserve in written form what the fading memory is fast forgetting—the Glorious History of the Sailing Ship.

> As o'er the moon, fast fly the amber veils,
> 　For one dear hour let's fling the knots behind,
> And hear again, thro' cordage and thro' sails,
> 　The vigour of the voices of the wind.
>
> They're gone, the Clyde-built darlings, like a dream,
> 　Regrets are vain, and sighs shall not avail,
> Yet, mid the clatter and the rush of steam,
> 　How strangely memory veers again to sail !

APPENDIX

APPENDIX A.

Extracts from " Lightning Gazette," 1855-1857.

SECOND VOYAGE.—LIVERPOOL TO MELBOURNE.

Saturday, 6th January, 1855.—At 8 a.m. the anchor was weighed and the *Lightning* with two steamers ahead proceeded down the Mersey. The morning was cold with a small drizzling rain, the wind being contrary. The steam tender, on leaving with passengers for the shore, came in contact with our main brace and carried away her funnel. The start was anything but a cheerful one; nevertheless, with the aid of two powerful tugs, we progressed at the rate of 7 to 8 knots and at 6 p.m. passed the Skerries Lighthouse.

Sunday, 7th January.—During the night we were nearly run into by a large American clipper, the *Dreadnought,* of New York; she being on the port tack, it was her duty to give way, but true to her name or with the independence of her nation, she held her course disdaining to turn aside; our captain with praiseworthy prudence put his ship about and thus avoided a collision.

Monday, 8th January.—Lat. 52° 14′ N., long. 6° 12′ W. Wind S.W. The night being very dark, we came in contact with a ship on the opposite tack. We saw and hailed, but the stranger evidently did not keep a good look-out and came straight upon us, striking our ship on the starboard bow. All was hubbub and confusion in a moment. The ships were speedily parted and fortunately without doing any damage to us worth mentioning. The stranger did not escape so well, having her jibboom carried away and her bowsprit sprung, as appeared to us in the dark.

12th January.—Lat. 46° 55′ N., long. 10° 41′ W. Wind S.E. Distance 269 miles. About 8 p.m. an alarm of fire was given and great excitement prevailed throughout the ship. This danger was caused by a drunken woman in the second cabin, who set fire to her bonnet; it was soon extinguished and the woman put in irons and confined in the " black hole " for the night as a warning.

13th January.—Lat. 42° 58′ N., long. 14° 24′ W. Wind S.E. Distance 286 miles. It is a week to-day since we left Liverpool and considering that we had two days of contrary winds, two days of calms we have made a very favourable run from the land.

15th January.—Lat. 39° 42′ N., long. 19° 25′ W. Wind S.S.E. Distance 202 miles. Ship going 13 knots close-hauled; in the morning we passed a ship outward bound with topgallant sails in, while we were carrying three royals and main skysail.

20th January.—Lat. 30° 37′ N., long. 19° 24′ W. Wind variable. Distance 130 miles. At 10 a.m. we sighted a steamer on weather bow, homeward bound. In a moment the tables were covered with writing desks. At 11 o'clock we neared her and found she was the General Screw Co.'s Steamship *Calcutta* from Australia bound to Southampton, 69 days out from Melbourne. We sent a boat to her with a bag of letters.

21st January.—Lat. 29° 51′ N., long. 19° 56′ W. Wind S.S.W. At 5 p.m. passed a large ship of war with two tiers of guns supposed to be H.M.S. *Monarch*, bound for the Pacific with Admiral Bruce, to replace the unfortunate Admiral Price, who shot himself before the attack on Petropaulovski.

24th January.—Lat. 24° 24′ N., long. 19° 37′ W. Took the N.E. trades, very light.

26th January.—Lat. 22° 07′ N., long. 20° 45′ W. Wind N.E., ship running 7 knots with smooth sea. A swing was put up on the poop to-day for the amusement of the ladies.

31st January.—Lat. 8° 48′ N., long 22° 7′ W. Wind N.N.E. Distance 130 miles. At 8 p.m. the ship was thrown into instant confusion by the cry of " man overboard." The ship was quickly rounded to, the two quarter boats lowered away and after 10 minutes of intense anxiety a hearty cheer announced that they had found him. The man, who was a second intermediate passenger, could not swim but was kept up by a life-buoy.

1st February.—Lat. 5° 45′ N., long. 21° 50′ W. Wind N.E. Distance 180 miles. Ship running 12 knots before a fresh gale with light sails in. At noon the ship was again thrown into a state of alarm by the cry of " man overboard." A sailor named John Benson, a Swede, had fallen from the jibboom. Lifebuoys were thrown to him and the two boats quickly lowered, but the wind blew strong, the sea ran high with rain and mist so that it was impossible to see any distance and after pulling for nearly an hour they returned with the sad report that they could see nothing of him.

3rd February.—Crossed the equator at 10 p.m. in 23° 9′ W., 28 days out from Liverpool and 23 from Land's End. Took the S.E. trade and lost the favourable north wind this morning.

9th February.—Lat. 18° 15′ S., long. 34° 46′ W. Wind S.E. Distance 308 miles. This is the best day's work since we left; indeed it is the only chance our noble ship has had of displaying her sailing qualities.

14 knots upon a bowline with the yards braced sharp up is certainly
wonderful work and scarcely to be believed if it were not satisfactorily
proved by the observation of the sun at noon, from which it appears
we have sailed 308 miles in last 24 hours with a current against us, which
is always supposed on this coast to run about a knot an hour with the
wind, making an average of 13 knots an hour, and while going at this
extraordinary rate she is as dry as possible, seldom shipping a spoonful
of water. During the greater part of yesterday the carpenter was
employed on a stage below the fore chains, where he worked as easily
as if it had been calm.

14th February.—Lat. 31° 47′ S., long. 34° 54′ W. Wind N.E.
Distance 93 miles. Began to run down our easting on a composite circle.

19th February.—Lat. 41° 41′ S., long. 18° 45′ W. Wind N.W.
Distance 310 miles. Ship running 13 and occasionally 15 knots.

20th February.—Lat. 41° 5′ S., long. 16° 34′ W. Distance 155 miles.
At midnight the wind suddenly flew round from N.E. to S.W. and blew
a heavy gale. The change was so sudden that we were obliged to run
before the wind for six hours to get the sails in, which was not done
without some danger. After taking a reef in the fore and mizen
topsails we hauled up again to E.S.E. The ship went very easy under
the reduced sail and as dry as possible, though there was a heavy cross
sea running. 10 a.m., more moderate, set mainsail and topgallant sails.
Noon going 15 knots with royals set, yards slightly checked, going by
the wind.

21st February.—Lat. 42° 34′ S., long. 9° 10′ W. Wind South.
Distance 342 miles. Ship going 15 and occasionally 16 knots with main
skysail and fore topmast studding sail set, the yards slightly checked.

27th February.—Lat. 46° 22′ S., long. 26° 15′ E. Wind west.
Distance 390 miles. All night it blew a fresh gale with heavy squalls
and occasional showers of hail and snow, the sea running high, ship
running 16 and occasionally 18 knots. During six hours in the morning
the ship logged 18 knots with royals, main skysail and topgallant
studding sails set, the wind blowing a fresh gale from the westward.

28th February.—Lat. 47° 24′ S., long. 33° 32′ E. Wind N.E. Distance 308 miles. At 2 o'clock it blew a hard gale with heavy showers
of rain and hail. Obliged to keep the ship before the wind while shortening sail. By 7 p.m. sail was taken in and ship laid to under trysail
and topmast staysail, to prevent her running too far south for fear of
coming in contact with ice.

7th March.—Lat. 50° S., long. 68° 44′ E. Wind S.W. Distance
280 miles. 10 a.m., sighted Kerguelen or Desolation Island, passing
between Fortune Island and Round Island, small rocks about 20 miles
off the mainland. 2 o'clock, abreast Cape St. George.

8th March.—Lat. 49° 51′ S., long. 76° 24′ E. Wind N.W. Distance 296 miles. Ship running with stunsails both sides, high sea.

9th March.—Lat. 49° 50′ S., long. 83° 47′ E. Wind N.W. Distance 284 miles.

10th March.—Lat. 49° 28′ S., long. 89° 29′ E. Wind N.W. Distance 221 miles.

11th March.—Lat. 49° 11′ S., long. 94° 44′ E. Wind N.N.E. Distance 325 miles. Midnight, fresh gale. Ship going 17 knots with single reefed topsails, foresail, trysail and fore topmast staysail, wind abeam.

12th March.—Lat. 49° 11′ S., long. 106° 38′ E. Wind north. Distance 366 miles. Thick weather and small rain.

13th March.—Lat. 48° 27′ S., long. 114° 16′ E. Wind N.E. Distance 318 miles.

19th March.—Lat. 40° 25′ S., long. 143° 23′ E. Wind E.S.E. Distance 308 miles. 4 p.m., rounded King's Island. 8 p.m., sighted Cape Otway light bearing W. 18 miles. Stood off the land till midnight.

20th March.—During the night strong gale from East. 1 p.m., pilot came aboard. 1.30 p.m., entered Port Phillip Heads.

Passage of 73 days—Liverpool to Melbourne.

Passage of 67 days—Land to land.

The *Lightning* beat the *Red Jacket, Ralph Waller, Eagle,* and *George Waller*, which sailed either previous to her or on the same date.

SECOND VOYAGE—MELBOURNE TO LIVERPOOL, 1855.

11th April.—Early this morning the anchor was weighed and we were taken in tow by two steam tugs. Two guns were fired as a signal of departure, weather delightful but wind light and right ahead. When near the Heads spoke *Frederick*, of Liverpool, 95 days out. In passing she saluted us with two guns, her passengers and crew cheering, a courtesy which we returned. Calm for two days, ship only 11 miles off Port Phillip Heads.

13th April.—Passed through Bass Straits, *Gipsy Bride* and other vessels in company.

17th April.—Lat. 46° 12′ S., long. 156° 28′ E. *Lightning* sweeping along at 17 and sometimes 18 knots.

18th April.—Lat. 49° 5′ S., long. 162° 50′ E. Wind S.W. Distance 314 miles. Sailing 16 knots an hour, wind steady with heavy cross sea. All starboard stunsails set.

21st April.—Lat. 54° 21′ S., long. 175° 45′ W. Wind S.S.W. Distance 327 miles.

24th April.—Lat. 58° S., long. 158° 35′ W. Wind N.N.E. Distance

285 miles. Sailing 14 knots close-hauled. P.M., heavy head gale, royals, skysails, jib and spanker in, ship pitching heavily.

26th April.—Lat. 58° 7' S., long. 150° 49' W. Calm. Distance 79 miles. During night heavy snow squalls.

1st May.—Lat. 58° 53' S., long. 112° 25' W. Wind E.N.E. Sailing 8 knots an hour by the wind. Sighted an iceberg 100 ft. high, 8 miles distant.

5th May.—Lat. 54° 48' S., long. 100° 44' W. Wind E.N.E. to E.S.E., strong gale. Took in foresail and single reefed the topsails. (This was the only occasion during the passage on which the topsails were reefed.)

8th May.—Lat. 55° 56' S., long. 85° 48' W. Wind north. Distance 294 miles. Skysails and staysails in and slab-reefed courses.

10th May.—Lat. 58° 12' S., long. 69° 49' W. Wind N.N.W. Distance 316 miles. 10 p.m., Cape Horn north 100 miles.

17th May.—Lat. 44° 37' S., long. 64° 31' W. Going at the rate of 12 to 14 knots and wind right aft which caused the ship to roll very much. About 3 p.m. a heavy shower of snow was hailed with delight by the passengers. Our captain transferred his command from the Black Ball to the White Ball Line and first commenced snow-balling. Fierce and fast grew the conflict, the ship helping many a valiant snow-baller to a seat on her slippery decks. At 4 we saw an American clipper standing eastward under close-reefed topsails.

1st June.—Crossed the equator at midnight in 30° W. Visit of Neptune in the evening. Neptune made his appearance accompanied by his wife Amphitrite. Their Majesties were received with the usual honours, all the company standing up and the band playing " Rule Britannia." Neptune was dressed in the uniform of a Line regiment, sea-green turned up with cerulean blue. His wife's hair plaited in the most tasteful manner nearly touched her feet, swabbing the decks as she walked along. Neptune put the usual questions to our gallant commander and having received satisfactory replies, his Majesty, leaning upon his three-pronged toaster, made a circuit of the deck, while the fair Amphitrite in passing made a most condescending bow to the Queen of Beauty, who was supported on the arm of Aesculapius, and at this piece of condescension dropped her large blue eyes and looked confused. The salt of the briny element seemed to have excited the thirst of Amphitrite and her attendants, which the Chief Justice en deavoured to quench by draughts from the cup that cheers but inebriates. Neptune having taken the pledge when he visited certain other parts of his dominions would not put the hideous beverage to his lips. The Gods and Goddesses then delighted the company by their vocal melodies and finally descended to their chariot, which went off with fire and smoke.

4th June.—Lat. 6° 30′ N., long. 30° 11′ W. Took the N.E. trades.

28th June.—Four passengers and a number of letters landed off Kinsale.

29th June.—11 a.m., taken in tow by steam tug *Dreadnought*. Anchored in Liverpool at 11 p.m. 79 days out. Since passing the Horn it had been a light weather passage, the moonsail only being lowered on two occasions and the lower deck ports only shut once.

THIRD VOYAGE.

The *Lightning's* third voyage was an unfortunate one. On her arrival home in June, 1855, Messrs. James Baines & Co., whether at Captain Enright's suggestion or not, I do not know, had her hollow bow filled in with deadwood, an action which caused her designer to refer to them as the " wood-butchers of Liverpool," though in the light of modern knowledge in ship designing they were undoubtedly right, as hollow lines for sailing ships have long been proved a mistake.

Unfortunately, however, the blocking in of the bows was not strongly enough done, and one day when she was close-hauled on the starboard tack in the South Atlantic, this false bow, as it was called, was washed away, leaving its frame and ribs bare. This, though in no way affecting the seaworthiness of the *Lightning*, spoilt her sailing, and what promised to be an excellent passage ran to 81 days.

In Australia the bow was repaired, but the accident frightened would-be passengers, as the Government surveyors in Melbourne refused to give her a certificate and she also lost a lot of freight.

LIVERPOOL TO MELBOURNE, 1855.

Wednesday, 5th September.—About 3 o'clock this afternoon, amid the booming of cannon, the sad and solemn strains of the band and the cheers of the passengers, our gallant ship was taken in tow by the tug *Rattler*. The commencement of our voyage is marked with a fair wind, so that the captain is determined to proceed without the aid of a tug. Accordingly at 7.30 the pilot left us and we bade him a cheering farewell. In the evening several songs were sung for " Each sail was set, and each heart was gay."

Thursday, 6th September.—At 2 a.m. we passed Holyhead, going from 7 to 7½ knots, and Bardsey at 9. At 3 p.m. we were abreast of Tuskar. The ship is gliding along under an astonishing cloud of canvas, with stunsails alow and aloft. In the evening the band played several tunes; many of the passengers ventured on a polka and other dances with spirit.

Friday, 7th September.—The light breeze of past two days died away at 4 this morning, leaving us becalmed. Happily the weather is delightful with clear sky and brilliant sun. The sea has the appearance of an immense sheet of glass. All parties are on deck so that the promenades are inconveniently crowded.

Tuesday, 11th September.—About 11 a.m. we passed on the port side close to a Neapolitan brig, which put us in mind of Noah's Ark. She was going ahead about one knot and drifting two, with a fine breeze that would have enabled a ship of any other nation to carry all sail, while these sea-lubbers rolled along under double-reefed topsails and furled mainsail. Lat. 44° 9′ N., long. 12° 5′ W. Distance run 205 miles.

Thursday, 13th September.—About 7 this morning we exchanged colours with a ship steering our course. At 12 she was but a white speck on the horizon and at 3 she was lost to sight.

Thursday, 20th September.—About 8 a.m. we sighted a vessel right ahead about 10 miles distant and at 2 p.m. we were almost within speaking distance. She proved to be the barque *Araquita*, from England bound to Rio Janeiro. At 6, such was our speed, she was lost to sight. At 3.30 entered Tropic of Cancer.

Monday, 24th September.—Lat. 14° 10′ N., long. 28° 14′ W. Distance 78 miles. Early this afternoon we sighted the schooner *Gleam*, from Accra, on the Guinea Coast, bound to London. At 5 p.m. a boat was lowered and in command of Mr. Bartlett, the chief officer, accompanied by a few of the saloon passengers, proceeded to the *Gleam*, conveying a large number of letters and *Lightning Gazettes* for home. A small present of fresh meat and potatoes was also put on board and gratefully received. On the return of the boat we learned she was 47 days out and crossed the line 19 days ago.

Tuesday, 25th September.—Lat. 12° 14′ N., long. 28° 1′ W. Distance 117 miles. In the forenoon we exchanged colours with the brig *Favorite*, from Buenos Ayres to Liverpool. Shortly afterwards we passed a Danish brigantine and a Hamburg vessel.

Friday, 28th September.—Lat. 9° 53′ N., long. 28° 5′ W. Distance 33 miles. At 6 a.m. a boat visited us from the *Evening Star*, of Portland, from the Chincha Islands bound to Cork for orders.

Friday, 5th October.—Crossed the equator.

Monday, 15th October.—Lat. 24° 7′ S., long. 29° 59′ W. Distance 255 miles. Ship sweeping along at the rate of 14½ knots.

Tuesday, 16th October.—Lat. 24° 5′ S., long. 25° 50′ W. Distance 225 miles. About 9 a.m. a considerable portion of the false bow on the larboard side was suddenly carried away.

Sunday, 21st October.—Lat. 36° 4′ S., long. 24° 52′ W. Distance 238 miles. At 5 p.m. sighted a large ship on our weather quarter, sailing under double-reefed topsails, and we apprehend they must have taken us for the *Flying Dutchman* seen occasionally in these latitudes, for notwithstanding the strong breeze we would be observed carrying our skysails with studding sails 'low and aloft.

Monday, 22nd October.—Lat. 38° 24' S., long. 19° 21' W.   Distance 300 miles.

Tuesday, 23rd October.—Lat. 39° 22' S., long. 12° 32' W.   Distance 325 miles.   At 9 a.m. during a sudden squall, carried away our starboard fore topmast stunsail boom—a splendid Oregon spar, which was carried right over the larboard bow.

Saturday, 17th November.—Lat. 48° 00' S., long. 121° 15' E.   Distance 324 miles.   The wind changed during the night to W.N.W., still blowing a fresh breeze with every sail set.

Sunday, 25th November.—Sail was shortened at midnight and Bowman Head Lighthouse sighted at 3 a.m.   Shortly afterwards hove to for a pilot and as his boat came near, at 4.30, every glass in her was levelled in astonishment at the bare ribs of our false bow.   After getting inside the Heads, we again hove to and landed the Geelong mail.   At 10 a.m. met the *James Baines* homeward bound and hove to to communicate with her.   Captain McDonald came on board and we had the pleasure of sending letters and papers home.   At 1 p.m. we were at anchor with sails furled and the Melbourne mail landed.   We had the misfortune to come into port with a broken bow which impeded our progress not less on the average than 3 knots an hour for upwards of 9000 miles.   On the last voyage we were going 17 knots, on the present with the same wind only 14—owing to the accident.

THIRD VOYAGE—MELBOURNE TO LIVERPOOL.

Friday, 28th December.—At 8 a.m. we got outside the bar at Port Phillip Heads, when the agents and a few friends left in the pilot boat. From the captain of the latter we learned the sad intelligence of the loss of the *Schomberg*, off Cape Otway.   The clipper ship *Blackwall* was sighted right ahead of us at the same moment, and at 10.30 we had the satisfaction of overhauling her.   At 7 p.m. she was barely visible on the horizon.   (The *Blackwall* was one of Green's frigate-built Indiamen.)

Friday, 4th January, 1856.—Lat. 56° 34' S., long. 177° 14' W. Distance 334 miles.   Wind S.W.   Run for the week 1908 miles.

Wednesday, 9th January.—Lat. 58° 32' S., long. 136° 06' W.   Distance 311 miles.   Wind S.W.   During the middle watch 7 icebergs were seen, some very large.   During morning several more sighted. Snow fell during the day.

Monday, 14th January.—Lat. 57° 48' S., long. 93° 08' W.   Distance 330 miles.   Wind S.S.E., cold, with showers of snow and hail.   Sighted two large icebergs on starboard bow.

(28th December-15th January *Lightning* ran 5244 knots in 18 days, an average of 12 knots on a direct course from Melbourne to Cape Horn.)

Sunday, 20th January.—At 6 a.m. Cape Horn in sight, 25 miles distant.

Tuesday, 29th January.—Lat. 35° 00′ S., long. 33° 15′ W.   Distance 300 miles.   Wind east.   Heavy cross sea and rattling breeze all night. Ship pitching very heavily and going at rate of 15 or 16 knots.   At 1 p.m. spoke Aberdeen clipper ship *Centurion*, from Sydney bound to London, 46 days out.   She passed during the night the White Star ship *Emma*, of Liverpool, with Melbourne mail of 10th December.   We have beaten the *Centurion* 16 days and the *Emma* 18.

Friday, 1st February.—Spoke the mail ship *Emma*.

Sunday, 17th February.—Crossed the equator at 8.30 a.m.

Tuesday, 26th February.—In the forenoon carpenter fell from the stage on which he was working on the starboard side and immediately the appalling cry of " man overboard " ! echoed through the ship. On rising to the surface of the water, he passed his hatchet over the fore sheet and held on until assistance was tendered.

Wednesday, 5th March.—Lat. 42° 30′ N., long. 25° 33′ W.   Distance 181 miles.   In forenoon sighted large vessel on lee bow under reefed topsails, whilst we carried royals with ease.

Friday, 14th March.—Lat. 50° 43′ N., long. 14° 36′ W.   Distance 174 miles.   Wind S.S.E.   At 6 a.m. sighted two vessels on starboard, another on port bow.   Ship put about at 8 a.m.   Shortly after a schooner to windward of us.   At 10.30 a.m. passed close to ship *Henry Fulton*, of New York, under close-reefed topsails and on opposite tack. During the day the wind blew with great violence from S.S.E.   Towards evening it increased to a perfect gale.   Every stitch of canvas that could be carried with safety was kept on until Captain Enright thought it full time to stow the topgallant sails and single reef the topsails and mainsail, which was done at 8 p.m.   At midnight the foresail was also single-reefed.

Saturday, 15th March.—Lat. 51° 52′ N., long. 12° 23′ W.   Distance 107 miles.   Gale continued from S.S.E. during the night, splitting the fore topsail in two.   At 9 a.m. hove to under a double-reefed fore sail and close-reefed main topsail.

Sunday, 16th March.—Passed a longboat keel up.

Tuesday, 18th March.—Wind S.S.E.   Course full and by.   Made the Skellig Rocks.

Wednesday, 19th March.—Becalmed; nine vessels surrounding us.   A couple of schooners close to and our starboard boat was lowered under

Mr. Bartlett. On its return we learned one was the *Fashion*, 35 days from Antigua, the other the *Breeze*, of Wexford, from Athens, 73 days out and short of provisions, her crew subsisting on wheat which they ground. Kinsale Head light plainly discernible all night.

Thursday, 20th March.—Still becalmed, a large number of vessels in all directions. Visited by Cork pilot boat which landed a number of passengers and portion of the mail at Castlehaven. Learnt that 60 or 80 sail started from Crookhaven on previous day, all of which had been detained by same head winds.

Saturday, 22nd March.—10.30 p.m., tug made fast.

Sunday, 23rd March.—Arrived after a passage of 86 days against head winds and calms.

THE RUN.

From Melbourne to Cape Horn	..	22 days.
„ Cape Horn to Equator	..	29 „
„ Equator to Fayal -	..	14 „
„ Western Isles to Liverpool	..	21 „

A TABLE OF WINDS.

Fair Winds	Light Winds	Calms	Head Winds.
26 days	19 days	17 days	24 days.

FOURTH VOYAGE—LIVERPOOL TO MELBOURNE, 1856.

Tuesday, 6th May.—At noon the signal gun was fired, our anchor weighed and we proceeded in tow of our old friend, the *Rattler*. At 3 p.m pilot left. At 4.30 cast off steamer and set all sail. At 5.20 p.m. passed Point Lynas, the Skerries at 8, Holyhead at 9, and Bardsey at midnight.

Thursday, 8th May.—Lat. 47° 08′ N., long. 10° 44′ W. Distance 274 miles. At noon passed ship *Dauntless*, sailing similar course to our own.

Wednesday, 14th May.—Lat. 33° 39′ N., long. 20° 30′ W. Distance 310 miles.

Monday, 26th May.—Crossed the line in long. 31° 40′ W.

Saturday, 21st June.—Lat. 38° 53′ S., long. 5° 7′ E. Distance 253 miles.

Sunday, 22nd June.—Lat. 40° 07′ S., long 13° 1′ E. Distance 346 miles.

Saturday, 28th June.—Lat. 44° 25′ S., long 42° 58′ E. Distance 232 miles. Wind increasing; whilst taking in lighter canvas, mizen royal and mizen topmast staysail were torn to pieces. P.M., reefs were taken in topsails. Ship running under foresail and reefed topsails.

Sunday, 29th June.—Lat. 43° 36′ S., long. 50° 07′ E. Distance 312 miles.

Monday, 30th June.—Lat. 44° 02′ S., long. 56° 35′ E. Distance 281 miles.

Tuesday, 1st July.—Lat. 44° 39′ S., long. 63° 27′ E. Distance 298 miles.

Wednesday, 2nd July.—Lat. 45° 07′ S., long. 70° 55′ E. Distance 319 miles.

Thursday, 3rd July.—Lat. 45° 07′ S., long. 79° 55′ E. Distance 382 miles. Her run to-day has been only once surpassed since she floated.

Friday, 4th July.—Lat. 45° 07′ S., long. 88° 30′ E. Distance 364 miles. Our week's work of 2188 miles has been the best the *Lightning* has ever accomplished.

Friday, 11th July.—Lat. 45° 47′ S., long. 128° 25′ E. Distance 326 miles. During the night our speed averaged 16 knots an hour. At 4 p.m., split our mainsail and carried away two jibs.

Monday, 14th July.—This morning at 7 a.m. our ears were saluted with the welcome sounds of " Land Ho!" At 8 a.m. we had a fine view of Cape Otway Lighthouse. As the depth of water on the bar was not sufficient to enable us to proceed up the Bay, we came to anchor under the lee of the land. We found the *Champion of the Seas* anchored at some little distance from us, waiting for a favourable wind to proceed to sea. Sailing time from port to port, 68 days 10 hours.

MELBOURNE TO LIVERPOOL.

Wednesday, 27th August.—By 10 a.m. we were fairly underweigh. On approaching the mouth of the Bay a farewell salute of six guns was fired. The wind dropped and we were obliged to anchor inside Port Phillip Heads at 6 p.m.

Thursday, 28th August.—Cleared the Heads at 10.30 a.m. and at 11 a.m. the pilot left us. We passed Lake Liptrap about 9 p.m. and shortly afterwards carried away our port fore topmast studding sail boom, by which accident two men stationed at the look-out had a narrow escape of losing their lives.

Sunday, 31st August.—Lat. 46° 30′ S., long. 158° 46′ E. Distance 313 miles. Wind strong from N.W. We have been going 15 and 16 knots, astonishing all on board, particularly those passengers who have hitherto sailed in London clippers.

Monday, 1st September.—Lat. 49° 39′ S., long. 166° 35′ E. Distance 366 miles. Thick weather and drizzling rain, sun obscured. At 5 p.m. breakers on the lee (starboard) bow were unexpectedly observed, which by some at first were supposed to be icebergs; they soon, however, appeared to be rocks and high land loomed darkly in the background.

The ship was immediately hauled to the wind, when a bold bluff appeared through the fog on the weather bow. The helm was then put down and, contrary to the expectations of all on board, our ship came round; when all sails were trimmed she headed to clear the rocks. But the wind having fallen light and a heavy sea rolling towards the shore. a fearful period of suspense ensued. Thanks to the wonderful powers of our noble ship, she gathered headway and gradually passed the weathermost rocks. The prompt and cool conduct of our worthy captain, his officers and men cannot be too highly praised, as the smallest error or delay in the issue and execution of the order would have involved the certain destruction of the ship. On getting clear of the danger, the captain informed us that the rocks were the Bristows, off Enderby's Island, near the Aucklands.

(Captain Enright allowed 40 miles for the usual southerly set, but, as the occasion proved, this was not enough.)

Tuesday, 9th September.—Lat 55° 08′ S., long. 148° 56′ W. Distance 208 miles. Wind increasing, ship scudding at 16 and 17 knots with all studding sails alow and aloft set.

Wednesday, 10th September.—Lat. 55° 33′ S., long. 138° 33′ W. Distance 355 miles. During the night our fore and main topgallant stunsails were split and also the main skysail, which was immediately unbent and replaced by a new one. Wind veering from W. to W.S.W., very cold with sleet showers. At 9 a.m. an iceberg was sighted right ahead. It was measured by Mr. Bartlett and found to be 420 feet high.

Wednesday, 17th September.—Lat. 57° 18′ S., long. 83° 28′ W. Distance 328 miles. The ship rolled much as she scudded under her topsails and courses with, at times only, the fore and main topgallant sails. We all know it must blow hard before our main royal and mizen topgallant sail are furled.

Thursday, 18th September.—Lat. 57° 35′ S., long. 74° 48′ W. Distance 377 miles.

Friday, 19th September.—At 11.15 a.m. on the meridian of Cape Horn. Distant 69 miles. Saw three ships beating to windward. Exchanged signals with the *Patriot King*.

Wednesday, 24th September.—Lat. 47° 21′ S., long. 47° 05′ W. Distance 227 miles. Squally with rain, but all sail carried bravely—even little " bull-dog " up on the main skysail mast. Ship going 14 knots and sometimes 15 in the squalls.

Thursday, 25th September.—Lat. 44° 40′ S., long. 41° 43′ W. Distance 278 miles. All sail set including topmast, topgallant and royal studding sails, in all 29 sails. Afternoon, the moonsail was sent up and set as the 30th.

Thursday, 9th October.—Crossed the line in 28° 20′ W.

(*Lightning's* average 238 miles daily.)

Tuesday, 14th October.—Lat. 8° 12′ N., long. 28° 00′ W. Distance 52 miles. At daylight two vessels in sight on the other tack, one a large ship with three skysails set, the other a brig. At 7 a.m. tacked ship to N.E. Signalised the ship, which proved to be an American, the *Tornado*; the brig was thought to be a Spaniard. About 11, the clouds and mist enveloped our neighbours, who presently emerged with a fair southerly wind, although only distant about 5 miles, while we retained our northerly wind. For a time all was uncertainty and doubt which wind would gain the day, but when the vessels came close up to us, bringing with them heavy rain and puffs of wind, we trimmed yards and soon were rushing through the water at the rate of 10 knots: anon all was calm and the sails flapped. Again we saw our American companion staggering under a heavy squall, which split his fore topgallant sail and main topmast staysail, and caused his masts to buckle like fishing rods: we had plenty more rain but did not catch the strength of the squall. There was great shortening sail and making sail, for the Yankee was going by us, distant about 2 miles on our starboard side; meanwhile the little brig, with a more steady and strong breeze of his own, came close up on our port quarter. Then again all was lulled. The interval presented an opportunity of further signalling, and the following questions and answers were made.

Lightning—" Where are you from and bound to ? "

Tornado—" Callao and Cape Hatteras."

Lightning—" We are from Melbourne."

Tornado—" How many days are you out ? "

Lightning—" Forty-seven."

At which answer *Tornado* seemed surprised and although we had previously shown our number, again asked:—" What ship is that ? " .

We answered:—

Lightning—" How many days are you out ? "

Tornado—" Fifty-six."

We then exchanged the courtesy of hoisting and dipping ensigns.

It was then about 4 o'clock, and for nearly an hour there was nothing but " box-hauling " the yards, when suddenly Jonathan caught a breeze and crept up alongside, and seemed very much inclined to pass us. All possible sail was set and trimmed most carefully but still *Tornado* gained, and all was anxiety and excitement. At last the strength of the breeze came to us, and for a few minutes there was a most exciting race, some even feared that we were going to be beaten; but the *Lightning* showed her wonted superiority, our antagonist dropped astern, and a hearty cheer from us announced our victory. The wind then fell light again, and twice freshened and caused the same capital match; but the *Tornado*, though evidently a first-rate sailer—being one of the early Californian clippers—could not manage us; and, as the night closed in, and the breeze became more steady, we gradually bid him good-bye.

Wednesday, 15th October.—Lat. 9° 27′ N., long. 27° 45′ W. Distance 77 miles. Our American friend kept in sight until sunset.

16th-19th October.—N.E. trades.

20th-28th October.—Doldrums. The *Lightning* only averaged 55 miles a day for nine days.

Wednesday, 29th October.—Lat. 28° 31′ N., long. 35° 39′ W. Distance 108 miles. At 4 a.m. a light breeze sprang up from the norrard. 5.30 a.m., spoke a large American ship, the *Clarendon*, from Malta to New Orleans. 8 a.m., going 7 knots, almost a " dead on end " wind, but any wind at all is a change. Passed a brig to leeward and are overhauling three ships, which are ahead standing on the same tack. About 3 p.m., passed the *Cid*, of Hambro, a very pretty little clipper barque.

Thursday, 30th October.—7 a.m., tacked ship to N.N.W. A large ship in sight went about at the same time, ahead of us. During forenoon Captain Enright expressed himself confident that she was the *James Baines*. Great excitement and numerous conjectures, bets, etc. One thing certain that she sailed almost as fast as ourselves, and her rigging and sails were similar to those of the *Baines*. By sunset we had both weathered and gained on our companion.

(The ship was the *James Baines* and I have already described the encounter between the two Black Ballers.)

Wednesday, 5th November.—Lat. 36° 30′ N., long. 35° 11′ W. Distance 165 miles. (Distance made since 9th October 2219 miles or 76¾ miles daily.) During the night the wind suddenly shifted, catching the ship all aback; in the first puff the fore topmast stunsail boom was carried away. Passed a three-masted schooner steering to the westward, she showed an English Ensign, but from her rig appeared more like an American. She had no foresail or mainsail, but large main and mizen staysails, and a host of other staysails, square-rigged forward; was about 300 tons.

Friday, 7th November.—The islands of Pico, Fayal, etc., in sight.

Tuesday, 18th November.—Lat. 51° 04′ N., long. 6° 43′ W. Distance 202 miles.

Wednesday, 19th November.—1.30 a.m., Smalls Rocks light bore E.N.E.

Thursday, 20th November.—At 4.30 p.m., Mr. W. Harris, pilot, came on board and took charge off Cape Lynas.

Melbourne to Cape Horn	..	24 days 16 hours
Cape Horn to Equator	..	19 ,, 8 ,,
Equator to Pico, Azores	..	29 ,, 0 ,,
Western Isles to Liverpool	..	11 ,, 0 ,,

WINDS.

Fair Winds	Light Winds	Calms	Head Winds
32 days	23 days	4 days	24 days

FIFTH VOYAGE—LIVERPOOL TO MELBOURNE, 1857.

Thursday, 5th February.—After a little delay the tender brought all off safely to the *Lightning*, and the passengers were mustered and answered to their names to the Government inspector. A minister from the shore gave a parting address and about 4 p.m. the *Lightning* began her voyage to Australia in tow of the steam tug *Rattler*, for unfortunately the wind was dead ahead.

Saturday, 14th February.—Lat. 38° 38′ N., long. 15° 59′ W. Distance 127 miles. Fresh stores were being brought up from the mainhold when a barrel of vinegar fell from a considerable height upon Abraham Le Seur and injured him severely on the back. He was second mate to Captain Enright 18 years ago.

Tuesday, 24th February.—Lat. 12° 01′ N., long. 23° 27′ W. Distance 268 miles In the evening our friend Mr. Taylor paid a visit to the mizen royal yard—much to the consternation of the ladies. He relieved, what we suppose he felt was the monotony of the descent, by descending by the preventer brace. If Mr. Taylor will allow us to advise, we would say " Very well done, but don't do it again for it is a thing which the ladies cannot abide."

Tuesday, 3rd March.—Lat. 0° 30′ N., long. 26° 39′ W. Distance 53 miles. In the evening received a visit from Neptune. He evidently keeps himself well acquainted with what goes on on Terra Firma, for his fifer played him the well-known tunes of " Villikens and his Dinah " and " Jim along Josey," as a triumphal march. It struck us his marine chargers were a little out of condition and one of them had put on the outward resemblance of a donkey. After being regaled with our poor creature comforts, the old fellow very shabbily took himself off without our letters.

Saturday, 7th March.—Last night we passed within 25 miles of Pernambuco.

Wednesday, 11th March.—Lat. 24° 03′ S., long. 35° 40′ W. Distance 213 miles. In a squall this evening we made 14 or 15 knots, and that on a wind.

Sunday, 15th March.—Lat. 38° 47′ S., long. 30° 58′ W. Distance 311 miles. We have been making 16 knots often during the night.

Monday, 16th March.—Lat. 41° 08′ S., long. 24° 23′ W. Distance 334 miles. Wind fell light in the afternoon.

Wednesday, 18th March.—Lat. 42° 34′ S., long. 17° 04′ W. Distance 200 miles. The wind increases towards evening and we make from 15 to 17 knots an hour, yet the ship is so steady that we danced on the poop with the greatest ease.

Thursday, 19th March.—Lat. 43° 0′ S., long. 7° 17′ W. Distance 430 miles. It is very wet and there is a heavy sea on. In the middle of the day the wind lulled a bit, then turned over to the starboard quarter and set to work snoring again as hard as ever.

Friday, 20th March.—Lat. 43° 0′ S., long. 0° 55′ E. Distance 360 miles. This weather is most inspiriting, we have made during the last 47 hours the greatest run that perhaps ship ever made; yet all the time we have carried our main skysail and all sorts and conditions of stunsails.

Saturday, 21st March.—Lat. 43° 03′ S., long. 7° 57′ E. Distance 308 miles. The sea to-day has been really magnificent, the waves were grand and swept along in majestic lines. In the afternoon our weekly concert took place in the after saloon.

Sunday, 22nd March.—Lat. 43° 51′ S., long. 15° 51′ E. Distance 348 miles. (1446 miles in four days, an average of 361¼ miles per day.)

Friday, 27th March.—Lat. 44° 38′ S., long. 35° 36′ E. Distance 152 miles. About 2 p.m. a sail was just visible on the port bow. We very soon overhauled her, made her out to be a fine American clipper barque, passed her as if she was at anchor, although she was going 10 knots at least and by 4 o'clock she was almost out of sight astern.

Thursday, 2nd April.—Lat. 46° 11′ S., long. 70° 40′ E. Distance 328 miles. To-night the wind freshened considerably and the sea got up with it. Our main royal sheet and sundry stunsail tacks parted.

Friday, 3rd April.—Lat. 47° 14′ S., long. 79° 22′ E. Distance 364 miles. Wind blew strongly from the north, sea high; during the night main topsail, main topgallant stunsail and main royal sheets carried away.

Sunday, 5th April.—Lat. 45° 54′ S., long. 93° 31′ E. Distance 326 miles. Yesterday afternoon the fore topmast stunsail boom snapped like a carrot, the sail shook itself to pieces, then its yard dashed through the main topgallant sail, tore it, then tore a large hole in the main topsail.

Monday, 6th April.—Lat. 45° 34′ S., long. 99° 40′ E. Distance 260 miles. A fine day with the wind still dead aft. The sea is not so high as was yesterday, but the rolling of the ship brings it often very near our ports. The *Lightning* is, however, a very dry ship, and it is extraordinary how few seas we have shipped.   She rolled tremendously last night, her feelings appeared to be hurt, for she creaked piteously.

Thursday, 9th April.—Lat. 45° 34′ S., long. 118° 03′ E.   Distance 302 miles.   The spanker boom broke adrift and tore a large piece out of the starboard rail to the eminent peril of every person on deck, but also of the printing office of the *Lightning Gazette*.

Wednesday, 15th April.—7 a.m., Cape Otway bore N. 4¾° E., 30 miles. About 10 we signalised the *William Miles* on the other tack.   We have run from the line to Cape Otway in 35 days 15 hours—9449 miles.

Thursday, 16th April.—Entered Port Phillip Heads at 8 a.m., having completed the passage in 69 days 6 hours.

MELBOURNE TO LIVERPOOL, 1857.

Saturday, 9th May.—We came on board the good ship *Lightning* and find her busily preparing for her journey, with steamers and lighters alongside, discharging their contents on to her decks.   Passengers, their friends and luggage all pouring on board, amidst the noises of the sailors, the cackling and crowing of poultry innumerable, the squeaking of pigs and the occasional altercations of watermen; while, at the after end of the vessel, may be observed sundry small sealed boxes, many of them seemingly of ponderous weight, being lowered into their place of safety and containing the precious metal that has made Australia so famous.

Sunday, 10th May.—Got underweigh at 7 o'clock with the assistance of two steam tugs and slowly moved from Hobson's Bay.   Wind light and calm.   At dusk we anchored off the Lightship.

Monday, 11th May.—Got away from our anchorage at daybreak and proceeded for the Heads, saluting with a gun the *Morning Glory* in quarantine, as we passed her.   Got clear of Port Phillip Heads at 8 o'clock, with wind barely sufficient to move the ship.   Several barracoutas were caught in the evening.

Tuesday, 12th May.—Head winds and very light.   Cape Otway visible on our starboard bow.   In the evening quite becalmed with the Otway light on starboard quarter.

Thursday, 14th May.—Lat. 44° 9′ S., long. 145° 57′ E.   Distance 270 miles.   Dashing along at 14 to 16 knots with a fine fair wind.   S.W. coast of Tasmania visible through the gloom on our port beam.

Friday, 15th May.—Lat. 46° 55′ S., long. 154° 10′ E.   Distance 384 miles.   Strong breezes and heavy seas with rain squalls and occasional glimpses of sunshine.   During one of the squalls our fore topsail was split and for some time after dark the crew were busy bending a new one.

Saturday, 30th May.—Lat. 51° 56′ S., long. 126° 34′ W.   Distance

250 miles. We are now 18 days from Port Phillip Heads, and have experienced two days calm, two days westerly winds and for 14 days the winds have been from E.S.E. and S. The last 10 days we have sailed close to the wind. She makes no more water in a storm than she does in a calm.

Thursday, 11th June.—Lat. 56° 40′ S., long. 67° 12′ W. Distance 170 miles. About midday we were about 50 miles to south of Cape Horn. In the evening the wind changed round to N.E. and blew with great fury, and we had to lay to under single-reefed fore and main topsail. I believe it may with truth be said that few vessels have had · a more trying passage to the Horn than our good ship *Lightning*. On our clearing Port Phillip Heads, the winds were light and baffling from the east, compelling us to take the western passage round Van Dieman's Land. Shortly after we encountered a heavy gale from the south, during which we were at one time reduced to close-reefed main topsail and main trysail, the ship behaving nobly. After this the wind headed us and continued to blow from S. by E. to S.E. by E. for space of 23 days, during which time we ran 4237 miles from long. 160° E. to 84° W., rendering it quite impossible to get further to the south than 54°, keeping us between the parallels of 51° and 54°, blowing very heavy—reducing our canvas at times to close-reefed topsails and courses. During all this, our noble ship behaved admirably, making, as our parallel of sailing will prove, very little leeway. This is the fifth trip the writer. has made round the Horn in less than four years, in various ships, and it is not saying too much when he states that he does not believe any one of them would have made the distance in the same time, having the same difficulties to contend with. It has been done in the short space of 31 days, in the face of unprecedented difficulties as the following short summary will show.

Calms and Light Winds, 3 days; Variable, 3 days; From S.W. to N.W., 2 days; From S. by E. to S.E. by E., 23 days. Total 31 days.

On the 2nd May, 1855, the writer sailed from Port Phillip in the *Red Jacket* and reached Cape Horn in 34 days, but without one day's check from head winds.

Sunday, 14th June.—Staten Island in sight to eastward. A sail visible on lee bow, steering same course as ourselves. At 11 o'clock came up to her and spoke the American ship *Aspasia*, of Mystic, from California for New York.

Wednesday, 1st July.—Lat. 12° 44′ S., long. 37° 30′ W. Distance 192 miles. At 9 a.m. we were opposite Bahia and later in the day the land was just visible.

Monday, 6th July.—Lat. 0° 45′ N., long. 32° 23′ W. Distance 258 miles. At 7 a.m. crossed the line.

Wednesday, 15th July.—Lat. 24° 59′ N., long. 45° 22′ W.   Distance 300 miles.   The wind keeps steady and strong.

Tuesday, 21st July.—Lat. 40° 57′ N., long. 38° 25′ W.   Distance 254 miles.   Wind S.W., a strong breeze, running before it with stunsails set on both sides at rate of 10 to 12 knots.   The 'tween deck passengers presented the baker (Mr. W. Grainger) with an address to-day, thanking him for his attention to their comfort.

Friday, 31st July.—At 9.30 a.m., Land Ho! Ould Ireland is in sight.   At 5 p.m. passed the Tuskar.   Wind right aft.

THE RUN.

From Melbourne to Cape Horn	..	31 days
„ Cape Horn to Equator	..	25 „
„ Equator to Azores ..	..	15 „
„ Azores to Liverpool	..	11 „
		82 days.

75 days on the starboard tack.

Longest run in 24 hours ..   .. 384 miles
Shortest run in 24 hours ..   .. 25 „
Best week's run, 11th to 17th July   1723 „

APPENDIX B.—Later American-built Passenger Ships to Australia.

Name of Ship	Original Name if Name changed	Reg. Tonnage	Builders	Where Built	Date Built	Last Owners
Southern Empire	Jacob A. Westervelt	1418	Williams	New York	1849	Black Ball Line
Tornado		1801A		Williamsburg,N.Y.	1851	,,
Flying Cloud		1793A	Don. Mackay	Boston	,,	,,
Invincible		1767A	W. H. Webb	New York	,,	White Star Line
Queen of the Colonies	Wizard	1346	Hall	Boston	1852	Black Ball Line
Chariot of Fame		1640	Don. Mackay	Boston	1853	White Star Line
Empress of the Seas, No. 1		1647	,,	,,	,,	,,
Neptune's Car		1616		Portsmouth, Va.	,,	,,
Young Australia		1020		,,	,,	Black Ball Line
Landsborough		1066		United States	,,	,,
Golden Age		1241		St. John's	,,	Tyson & Co.
Whirlwind		1003		Medford, Mass.	,,	Black Ball Line
Saldanha		1257	J. O. Curtis	Quebec	,,	,,
Fiery Star	Comet	1361	Webb	New York	1851	,,
Morning Star		1534		St. John	1854	Fernie Bros.
Light Brigade	Ocean Telegraph	1495		Medford, U.S.	,,	Black Ball Line
Royal Dane	Sierra Nevada	1616		Portsmouth, U.S.	,,	,,
Florence Nightingale		1362	Don. Mackay	New Brunswick	1855	Brocklebank
Elizabeth Ann Bright		1920	McLachlan	St. John	1856	Black Ball Line
Sovereign of the Seas, No. 2	Tam o' Shanter	1226		Boston		White Star Line
Blue Jacket, No. 2		986		St. John	1858	,,
Prince of the Seas		1316				
Dawn of Hope		1215	Nevins	New Brunswick	1859	Wright & Co.
Mistress of the Seas		1740	Gass		1861	,,
Empress of the Seas, No. 2		1243	Hilyard	,,	1863	Black Ball Line
Legion of Honour, No. 2		1219	McDonald	,,	1863	White Star Line
Southern Empire, No. 2		1142	Baldwin	Quebec		Cannon & S.
Palm Tree		1473	Smith	New Brunswick	1865	J. Smith
Sunda		1556	Desmond	Miramichi	,,	Black Ball Line

APPENDIX C.—*Iron Wool Clippers.*

Date Built	Name of Ship	Best known Commander	Ton.	L'th	Bre'th	Depth	Builders	Owners
1852	*Darling Downs*	Wakeham	1634	258.6	40	29.9	Built on the Thames	Taylor, Bethell & Roberts
1860	*City of Agra*	T. Young	1074	213.6	34.7	20.6	Pile, W. Hartlepool	Blyth & Co.
1861	*Sam Mendel*	Steele	1034	215.6	35	20.6	"	Coupland Bros.
1864	*Dharwar*	T. Frebody	1300	226.2	37.2	23.3	Harland & Wolf	J. Willis
1866	*Marpessa*	T. Storey	1443	234.2	38.4	23.9	Reid, Glasgow	J. Heap & Sons
"	*Antiope*	Black	1443	242.3	38.4	23.7	"	"
1868	*Theophane*	Follett	1525	248.4	38.9	23.7	"	Williamson, Milligan
"	*Ivanhoe*	Burgess	1383	235.2	37.4	23.7	"	Glasgow Shipping Co.
"	*Loch Rannoch*	Ross	1185	217.8	35.5	21	Thomson, Glasgow	Watson Bros.
"	*Ben Nevis*	Mackie	1061	218	34.6	21	Barclay, Curle, Gl'gow	G. Thompson & Co.
1869	*Patriarch*	Pile	1339	222.1	38.1	22.3	Hood, Aberdeen	J. & R. Wilson
"	*Loch Awe*	Weir	1053	217.7	34.5	21	Barclay, Curle, Gl'gow	Ismay, Imrie
"	*Hoghton Tower*	Trimble	1598	247	40.1	23.7	Clover, Birkenhead	T. Stephens & Sons
"	*Thomas Stephens*	Richards	1507	263	38.2	23.1	Potter, Liverpool	Glasgow Shipping Co.
"	*Loch Katrine*	J. Burton	1200	226	35.8	21.5	Lowrie, Glasgow	"
"	*Loch Ness*	Foreshaw	1190	225.5	35.6	21.6	Barclay, Curle, Gl'gow	"
"	*Loch Tay*	Bennett	1191	225.4	35.5	21.6	"	
1870	*Loch Lomond*	J. Strachan	1200	226.3	35.8	21.5	Lowrie, Glasgow	
"	*Loch Leven*	Branscombe	1200	226.3	35.8	21.5	"	
1871	*Miltiades*	Perrett	1452	240.5	39.3	23.3	Hood, Aberdeen	G. Thompson & Co.
1872	*Mermerus*	Fife	1671	264.2	39.8	23.7	Barclay, Curle, Gl'gow	Carmichael
"	*Collingwood*	Forbes	1011	211.1	34.8	21	Hood, Aberdeen	Devitt & Moore
1873	*Hesperus*	Legoe	1777	262.2	39.7	23.5	Steele, Glasgow	Anderson, Anderson
"	*Ben Cruachan*	W. Martin	1468	255.5	37	21.7	Barclay, Curle, Gl'gow	Watson Bros.
"	*Ben Voirlich*	W. Ovenstone	1474	255.6	37.1	21.8	"	"
"	*Samuel Plimsoll*	R. Boaden	1444	241.3	39	23.1	Hood, Aberdeen	G. Thompson & Co.

APPENDIX C.—*Iron Wool Clippers*—Continued.

Date Built	Name of Ship	Best known Commander	Ton.	L'th	Bre'th	Depth	Builders	Owners
1873	Loch Maree	A. Scott	1581	255.8	38.6	22.9	Barclay, Curle, Gl'gow	Glasgow Shipping Co.
	Loch Ard	G. Gibbs	1624	262.7	38.3	23	Connell, Glasgow	,,
	Gladstone	J. Jackson	1159	248.2	34.2	20.9	McMillan, Dumbarton	F. H. Dangar
1874	Rodney	A. Loutitt	1447	235.6	38.4	22.6	Pile, Sunderland	Devitt & Moore
	Romanoff	W. Shepherd	1226	222.1	36.3	22.2	Hood, Aberdeen	A. Nicol
	Cairnbulg	Birnie	1567	261.3	39	23	Duthie, Aberdeen	Wm. Duthie, Jun.
	Thessalus	E. C. Bennett	1782	269	41.1	23.6	Barclay, Curle, Gl'gow	Carmichael
	Carpathian	Pennecuik	1444	240.1	36.6	22.6	Humphreys, Hull	McDiarmid, Green-shields
1875	Old Kensington	Underwood	1777	262	42.1	23.8	Potter, Liverpool	Smith, Bilbrough & Co.
	Loch Garry	Horne	1493	250.5	38.4	22.6	Thomson, Glasgow	Glasgow Shipping Co.
	Loch Vennachar	Ozanne	1485	250.1	38.3	22.4	,,	,,
	Salamis	Phillip, Sen.	1079	221.6	36	21.7	Hood, Aberdeen	G. Thompson & Co.
	Trafalgar	Muir	1429	242	38.4	22	E. I. Scott, Greenock	D. Rose & Co.
	Woollahra	Barneson	942	202.4	33.6	20.4	Osburne, Sunderland	Cowlislaw Bros.
	Cassiope	Withers	1559	253	40	23.6	Whitehaven S. Co.	J. Heap & Sons
	Parthenope	Goody	1563	250.6	39.9	23.6	Evans, Liverpool	
1876	Sir Walter Raleigh	Purvis	1492	243.4	38.9	21.9	Thomson, Glasgow	D. Rose & Co.
	Anglo-Norman	Davidson	822	192.4	32.2	18.9	Russell, Glasgow	Frost, Cook & Co.
	Loch Fyne	Martin	1213	228.5	36	21.3	Thomson, Glasgow	General Shipping Co. (Aitken, Lilburn & Co.)
	Loch Long	McCallum	1203	228.5	35.8	21.3	Hood, Aberdeen	G. Thompson & Co.
	Aristides	Kemball	1661	260	39.5	24.5	,,	,,
	Smyrna	Spalding	1305	232.3	38.5	22.2		
	Harbinger	Bolt	1506	253.5	37.6	22.4	Steele, Greenock	Anderson, Anderson
	Argonaut	Hunter	1488	254.4	38.6	23.2	Barclay, Curle, Gl'gow	Carmichael
1877	Brilliant	Davidson	1613	254.8	39.7	24.2	Duthie, Aberdeen	J. Duthie, Sons & Co.

APPENDIX C.—*Iron Wool Clippers*—Continued.

Date Built	Name of Ship	Best known Commander	Ton.	L'th	Bre'th	Depth	Builders	Owners
1877	Pericles	Largie	1598	259.6	39.4	23.6	Hood, Aberdeen	Thompson & Co.
	Loch Ryan	Black	1207	228.5	35.8	21.3	Thomson, Glasgow	General Shipping Co.
	Loch Etive	Stuart	1235	226.5	35.9	21.6	Inglis, Glasgow	"
	Loch Sloy	Horne	1225	225.3	35.6	21.2	Henderson, Glasgow	"
	Loch Shiel	Erskine	1218	225.3	35.6	21.1	"	"
1878	Nebo	Coleman	1383	246.9	37.1	21.1	Dobie, Glasgow	J. Smith
	Cimba	J. W. Holmes	1174	223	34.6	21.7	Hood, Aberdeen	A. Nicol & Co.
1879	Loch Sunart	G. Weir	1231	223.4	34.7	21.7	Inglis, Glasgow	Glasgow Shipping Co
	Sophocles	Smith	1138	223.4	34.7	21.7	Hood, Aberdeen	G. Thomson & Sons
1881	Illawarra	Corvasso	1887	269.1	40.6	24	Dobie, Glasgow	Devitt & Moore
	Orontes	Bain	1383	234.8	36.1	22.5	Hood, Aberdeen	G Thompson & Co.
	Loch Moidart		2000	287.4	42.6	24	Barclay, Curle, Gl'gow	General Shipping Co. (Aitken, Lilburn & Co.)
1882	Loch Torridon	R. Pattman	2000	287.4	42.6	24	"	General Shipping Co.
	Port Jackson	A. S. Cutler	2132	286.2	41.1	25.2	Hall, Aberdeen	Devitt & Moore
1884	Derwent	Andrew	1890	275	40.2	23.7	McMillan, Dumbarton	
1885	Torridon	Shepherd	1564	246	38.1	22	Hall, Aberdeen	A. Nicol & Co.
	Yallaroi	J. Brown	1565	245.8	38.1	22		"
	Loch Carron	S. Clarke	2075	287.7	42.5	24.1	Barclay, Curle, Gl'gow	General Shipping Co.
	Loch Broom	W. Martin	2075	287.7	42.5	24.1	"	"
	Strathdon	J. Paterson	2093	282.8	40.5	23.6	Harland & Wolf	G. Thompson & Co.
1891	Mount Stewart	Green	1903	271.6	40.1	23.4	Barclay, Curle, Gl'gow	D. Rose & Co.
	Cromdale	Andrew	1903	271.6	40.1	23.4	"	"

APPENDIX D.

Log of Ship " Theophane," 1868—Maiden Passage.

		Lat.	Long.	Miles.	Winds.
Oct.	19	Left. Liverpool in tow.			
,,	20	Tug left ship off Tusk. 6 p.m.			
,,	21	49° 20′ N.	8° 30′ W.	215	N.W.
,,	22	45° 54′	10° 46′	224	W.N.W.
,,	23	42° 42′	10° 53′	199	W.N.W.
,,	24	39° 32′	11° 11′	202	N.
,,	25	37° 35′	13° 11′	160	N.N.E.
,,	26	35° 15′	15° 31′	182	E.N.E.
,,	27	33° 00′	17° 12′	162	Variable.
,,	28	30° 38′	19° 50′	200	N.E.
,,	29	26° 44′	21° 20′	243	E.
,,	30	23° 29′	23° 55′	254	E.N.E.
,,	31	20° 7′	25° 52′	230	E.N.E.
Nov.	1	16° 17′	26° 30′	234	E.S.E.
,,	2	13° 47′	25° 45′	158	S.E.
,,	3	11° 4′	25° 6′	172	E.
,,	4	9° 26′	24° 20′	110	E.
,,	5	8° 47′	25° 10′	40	Variable
,,	6	8° 10′	25° 29′	44	Variable
,,	7	7° 6′	24° 19′	91	S.S.E.
,,	8	5° 50′	24° 6′	79	S.S.E.
,,	9	4° 55′	23° 43′	63	S.
,,	10	4° 13′	23° 19′	50	S.
,,	11	2° 37′	24° 50′	133	Variable
,,	12	00° 19′	26° 30′	180	S.S.E.
,,	13	2° 60′ S.	28° 50′	203	S.S.E.
,,	14	5° 29′	30° 39′	235	S.E.
,,	15	9° 15′	31° 49′	242	S.E.
,,	16	12° 51′	31° 48′	220	S.E.
,,	17	16° 27′	31° 58′	269	E.S.E.
,,	18	18° 15′	31° 34′	113	E.S.E.
,,	19	19° 44′	31° 38′	108	E.S.E.
,,	20	21° 50′	29° 2′	150	S.E.
,,	21	24° 2′	27° 4′	176	N.E.
,,	22	26° 24′	24° 34′	185	N.E.
,,	23	28° 24′	22° 42′	174	N.E.
,,	24	30° 6′	21° 28′	125	N.W.

Log of Ship " Theophane," 1868—Cont.

		Lat.	Long.	Miles.	Winds.
Nov.	25	32° 10′	19° 50′	160	W.
„	26	34° 24′	15° 48′	240	N.N.W.
„	27	37° 6′	12° 11′	246	N.N.W.
„	28	39° 14′	8° 5′	241	N.N.W.
„	29	39° 88′	2° 6′	306	W.
„	30	42° 00′	2° 18′ E.	252	W.
Dec.	1	43° 36′	8° 26′	254	N.
„	2	44° 22′	15° 20′	296	N.
„	3	44° 40′	21° 6′	286	N.W.
„	4	44° 4′	27° 9′	270	N.W.
„	5	44° 32′	33° 24′	276	W.N.W.
„	6	44° 53′	40° 3′	280	W.
„	7	44° 41′	45° 00′	214	W.
„	8	44° 30′	51° 40′	218	W.
„	9	45° 00′	38° 00′	277	N.
„	10	45° 9′	65° 37′	294	N.
„	11	44° 57′	71° 39′	295	N.
„	12	44° 59′	79° 10′	320	N.N.E.
„	13	45° 28′	86° 00′ E.	304	N.N.E.
„	14	45° 29′	93° 40′	328	N.
„	15	46° 19′	100° 10′	260	N.N.E.
„	16	46° 45′	105° 53′	250	N.N.E.
„	17	47° 25′	110° 40′	212	E.N.E.
„	18	47° 50′	115° 40′	230	E.N.E.
„	19	48° 50′	122° 26′	210	E.N.E.
„	20	47° 28′	127° 11′	208	N.E.
„	21	44° 53′	134° 11′	316	N.N.E.
„	22	41° 45′	138° 11′	276	N.N.E.
„	23	39° 57′	140° 13′	115	N.E. by N.
„	24	Passed Cape Otway		100	N.E.

Liverpool to Melbourne 66 days

APPENDIX E.

List of Clipper Ships still Afloat and Trading at the Outbreak of War, August, 1914.

Date Built	Original Name	Present Name if changed	Present Nationality of Owners	Yrs Old
1864	*Glenlora*		Norwegian	50
1866	*Antiope*		Australian	48
1868	*Turakina*	*Elida*	Norwegian	46
1868	*Decapolis*	*Nostra Madre*	Italian	46
1868	*Ivanhoe*		Chilean	46
1869	*Cutty Sark*	*Ferreira*	Portuguese	45
1869	*Thomas Stephens*	*Pero d'Alemguer*	Portuguese	45
1869	*Otago*	*Emilia*	Portuguese	45
1869	*Loch Awe*	*Madura*	Norwegian	45
1869	*Hudson*		Norwegian	45
1870	*Lothair*		Peruvian	44
1870	*Aviemore*		Norwegian	44
1872	*Collingwood*		Norwegian	42
1873	*Hesperus*	*Grand Duchess Marie Niholaevna*	Russian	41
1873	*Rakaia*		Barbadian	41
1874	*Nelson*		Chilean	40
1874	*Waikato*	*Coronada*	American	40
1874	*Canterbury*		Norwegian	40
1874	*Romanoff*		Norwegian	40
1874	*Charlotte Padbury*		Norwegian	40
1875	*Trafalgar*		Norwegian	39
1875	*Maulesden*	*Ostend*	Italian	39
1875	*Hurunui*	*Hermes*	Finnish	39
1875	*Myrtle Holme*	*Glimt*	Norwegian	39
1875	*Castle Holme*	*Ester*	Norwegian	39
1876	*Argonaut*	*Argo*	Portuguese	38
1876	*Pleione*		Norwegian	38
1876	*Opawa*	*Aquila*	Norwegian	38
1877	*Taranaki*		Italian	37
1877	*Pericles*		Norwegian	37
1877	*Wanganui*	*Blenheim*	Norwegian	37
1877	*Loch Ryan*	*John Murray*	Australian	37
1878	*Cimba*		Norwegian	36
1879	*Sophocles*		Italian	35
1881	*Loch Torridon*		Finnish	33
1882	*Port Jackson*		British	32
1884	*Derwent*		Norwegian	30
1885	*Torridon*		Italian	29
1885	*Loch Broom*	*Songdal*	Norwegian	27
1885	*Loch Carron*	*Seileren*	Norwegian	27
1885	*Strathdon*	*Gers*	French	27
1890	*Hinemoa*		British	24
1891	*Mount Stewart*		British	23

APPENDIX F.

The Wool Fleet, 1874-1890.

Four Best Wool Passages, 1874-1890—Port to Port.

Ship	Best Four Passages	Total Number of Days	Average Number of Days	Total Number of Passages
Cutty Sark ..	72, 73, 72, 76	293	73¼	7
Thermopylae ..	75, 79, 79, 79	312	78	10
Mermerus ..	78, 80, 81, 84	323	80¼	15
Salamis	77, 83, 84, 85	329	82¼	13

Cutty Sark's passages are far superior to those of any other ship; in fact, if we take the average of all her wool passages between 1874 and 1890, it only comes to 77 days from port to port.

The Wool Fleet, 1873-4.

Ship	From	Left	To	Arrived	D'ys Out
Patriarch	Sydney	Oct. 25	London	Jan. 27	94
Miltiades	Melbourne	Nov. 12	,,	Feb. 16	96
Mermerus ..	,,	,, 15	,,	,, 16	93
Jerusalem ..	,,	,, 18	,.	,, 12	86
Sam Mendel ..	,,	Dec. 17	,,	Mar. 12	85
Collingwood ..	,,	,, 24	,,	,, 23	89
Loch Tay ..	,,	,, 30	,,	,, 23	83
The Tweed ..	,,	Feb. 3	,,	Apl. 27	83
Star of Peace ..	,,	,, 10	,,	May 29	108
Ben Cruachan ..	,,	Mar. 5	,,	June 13	100
Samuel Plimsoll	Sydney	April 14	,,	July 5	82
Loch Maree ..	Melbourne	June 14	,,	Sept. 7	85
Ben Voirlich ..	,,	,, 14	Lizard	,, 30	108

P

The Wool Fleet, 1874-5.

Ship	From	Left	To	Arrived	D'ys Out
Loch Tay	Melbourne	Oct. 23	London	Jan. 31'75	100
Ethiopian ..	Sydney	,, 24	,,	,, 23	91
Macduff	Melbourne	,, 30	,,	,, 26	88
Collingwood ..		Nov. 1	,,	Feb. 4	95
Miltiades		,, 4	,,	Jan. 20	77
Loch Ard		,, 10	,,	Feb. 11	93
Patriarch	Sydney	,, 14	,,	,, 6	84
Oberon	Melbourne	,, 15	,,	Jan. 31	77
Holmsdale ..		,, 15	,,	Feb. 6	83
City of Perth ..		,, 15	,,	,, 4	81
Sam Mendel ..		,, 18	,,	Mar. 1	103
Ben Nevis ..		,, 18	.,	Feb. 3	77
Moravian ..		,, 25	,,	Mar. 4	99
John o' Gaunt ..		,, 25	,,	,, 27	122
City of Agra ..		,, 30	,,	,, 29	119
The Tweed ..	Sydney	Jan. 11'75	Lizard	April 7	86
Ben Cruachan ..	Melbourne	,, 19	London	,, 27	98
Samuel Plimsoll ..	Sydney	Mar. 3	,,	June 14	103
Romanoff ..	Melbourne	,, 11	,,	,, 15	96
Ben Voirlich ..		,, 16	,,	,, 17	93
Loch Maree ..		,, 21	Wight	,, 17	88
Thomas Stephens		April 30	Lizard	Aug. 4	96
Loch Lomond ..		May 1	London	,, 2	93
Cairnbulg ..	Sydney	,, 6	,,	,, 27	113

The Wool Fleet, 1875-6.

Ship	From	Left		To	Arrived		D'ys Out
Queen of Nations	Sydney	Oct.	16	London	Feb. 18 '76		125
Hawkesbury ..	,,	,,	25	,,	,,	15	113
Salamis	Melbourne	,,	23	,,	Jan.	25	94
Thessalus ..	,,	,,	30	,,	,,	31	93
Oberon	,,	Nov.	5	Deal	Feb.	17	104
Lincolnshire ..	,,	,,	7	London	,,	17	102
City of Agra ..	,,	,,	10	,,	,,	17	99
La Hogue ..	Sydney	,,	11	,,	,,	17	98
Ben Cruachan ..	Melbourne	,,	11	Dover	,,	16	97
Miltiades	,,	,,	14	London	,,	17	95
Ben Ledi	,,	,,	16	Dungen's	,,	16	92
Loch Ard	,,	,,	17	,,	,,	16	91
Moravian ..	,,	,,	20	,,	,,	18	90
Abergeldie ..	Sydney	,,	21	,,	,,	20	91
Holmsdale ..	Melbourne	,,	21	,,	,,	19	90
Patriarch	Sydney	,,	26	..	,,	18	84
The Tweed ..	,,	Dec.	10	,,	,,	17	69
Romanoff ..	Melbourne	,,	10	,,	Mar.	14	94
Centurion ..	Sydney	,,	21	,,	April	11	111
Loch Maree ..	Melbourne	,,	29	,,	Mar.	29	90
John Duthie ..	Sydney	Jan.	1 '76	,,	April	12	101
Rodney	Melbourne	,,	6	Deal	,,	13	97
ThomasinaMcLellan	,,	,,	10	London	,,	20	100
Samuel Plimsoll ..	Sydney	,,	2	,,	,,	5	83
Loch Vennachar ..	Melbourne	,,	13	,,	,,	11	88
Mermerus ..	,,	,,	17	,,	,,	20	93
Parramatta ..	Sydney	Feb.	1	,,	,,	21	79
Nineveh	,,	,,	5	,,	May	26	110
Loch Ness ..	Melbourne	,,	22	,,	,,	24	91
Loch Garry ..	,,	,,	22	,,			
Thomas Stephens	Sydney	Mar.	8	,,	June	8	92
Cairnbulg ..	,,	,,	9	,,	,,	7	90
Darling Downs ..	,,	,,	9	,,	,,	24	107

The Wool Fleet, 1876-7.

Ship	From	Left		To	Arrived		D'ys Out
Sir Walter Raleigh	Melbourne	Oct.	6	London	Jan.	10	97
Macduff	Geelong	,,	25	,,	,,	15	82
George Thompson	,,	,,	25	,,	Feb.	5	103
Miltiades	Melbourne	,,	27	,,	Jan.	24	89
City of Agra ..	Geelong	Nov.	3	,,	Feb.	9	98
Loch Katrine ..	Melbourne	,,	6	,,	,,	8	94
Ben Lomond ..	,,	,,	6	,,	,,	9	95
Loch Vennachar ..	,,	,,	8	,,	,,	9	93
Centurion ..	,,	,,	9	,,	,,	7	90
Romanoff ..	,,	,,	11	,,	,,	6	87
Ben Cruachan ..	Sydney	,,	12	,,	,,	8	88
Samuel Plimsoll	,,	,,	19	,,	,,	19	92
Loch Maree ..	Melbourne	,,	27	,,	Mar.	6	99
Collingwood ..	,,	,,	27	,,	,,	6	99
Aristides	,,	,,	28	,,	Feb.	17	81
Patriarch	Sydney	Dec	4	,,	Mar.	6	92
Sam Mendel ..	Melbourne	,,	11	,	,,	26	105
Ben Voirlich ..	,,	,,	18	,,	,,	26	98
Loch Garry ..	,,	Jan.	25	Deal	May	10	105
Darling Downs ..	Sydney	Feb.	1	London	,,	22	110
Cairnbulg ..	,,	,,	5	,,	,,	10	94
Loch Lomond ..	,,	,,	17	,,	,,	10	82
Parramatta ..	,,	,,	17	,,	,,	10	82

The Wool Fleet, 1877-8.

Ship	From	Left		To	Arrived		D'ys Out
Ben Cruachan	Melbourne	Oct.	24	London	Jan. 22 '78		90
Romanoff ..	,,	,,	27	,,	Feb. 12 '78		108
John Duthie ..	Sydney	Nov.	1	,,	,,	15	107
Ben Voirlich ..	Melbourne	,,	6	,,	,,	15	101
Samuel Plimsoll ..	Sydney	,,	8	,,	,,	12	96
George Thompson	Melbourne	,,	9	,,	,,	12	95
Loch Maree ..	,,	,,	11	,,	,,	13	94
Macduff	,,	,,	12	,,	,,	15	95
Miltiades ..	,,	,,	16	,,	,,	21	97
Patriarch	Sydney	,,	21	,,	,,	28	99
Sir Walter Raleigh	Melbourne	,,	23	,,	Mar.	1	98
Salamis	,,	,,	24	,,	Feb.	19	87
Mermerus ..	,,	,,	24	,,	,,	12	80
Cairnbulg ..	Sydney	Dec.	3	,,	Mar.	2	89
City of Agra ..	Melbourne	,,	4	,,	,,	7	93
Old Kensington ..	,,	,,	7	,,	,,	7	90
Aristides	Adelaide	,,	14	,,	,,	21	97
Loch Garry ..	Melbourne	,,	20	,,	April	4	105
True Briton ..	,,	,,	21	,,	,,	4	104
Thyatira	,,	Jan.	12	,,	,,	16	94
La Hogue ..	Sydney	,,	16	,,	,,	16	90
Thomas Stephens	Melbourne	,,	17	,,	,,	18	91

The Wool Fleet, 1878-9.

Ship	From	Left	To	Arrived	D'ys Out
Loch Katrine	Melbourne	Sept. 23	London	Jan. 15'79	114
Ascalon	Sydney	Oct. 14	,,	,, 16	94
Romanoff ..	Melbourne	,, 26	,,	,, 27	93
Nineveh	Sydney	,, 29	,,	Feb. 7	101
Ann Duthie	,,	Nov. 2	,,	,, 3	93
Slieve More ..	Melbourne	,, 4	,,	,, 8	96
Ben Cruachan ..	Geelong	,, 5	,,	,, 8	95
Loch Maree ..	Melbourne	,, 8	,,	Jan. 30	83
Miltiades	,,	,, 11	,,	Feb. 8	89
Mermerus ..	,,	,, 13	,,	,, 5	84
Merope	,,	,, 16	,,	,, 20	96
Cimba	Sydney	,, 16	,,	,, 17	93
Jerusalem ..	Geelong	,, 16	,,	,, 8	84
Ben Voirlich ..	Melbourne	,, 17	,,	Mar. 6	109
Melbourne ..	,,	,, 18	PrawleP	Feb. 16	90
Samuel Plimsoll ..	Sydney	,, 19	London	,, 7	80
Aristides	Melbourne	,, 23	,,	,, 18	87
Cynisca	Sydney	,, 26	,,	Mar. 14	108
Macduff	Geelong	Dec. 1	,,	,, 4	93
Loch Lomond ..	Melbourne	,, 3	,,	,, 6	93
Hawkesbury ..	Sydney	,, 5	,,	,, 6	91
Old Kensington ..	Melbourne	,, 7	,,	,, 7	90
Thomas Stephens ..	Sydney	,, 7	,,	,, 6	89
Loch Garry ..	Geelong	,, 13	,,	,, 13	90
Thyatira	Melbourne	,, 14	,,	,, 6	82
Patriarch	Sydney	,, 16	Lizard	,, 15	89
Cairnbulg ..	,,	,, 20	,,	April 8	109
Superb	Melbourne	,, 21	Dover	,, 1	101
La Hogue	Sydney	Jan. 18'79	Lizard	,, 18	90
Parramatta ..	,,	Feb. 5	Plym'th	,, 26	80
Windsor Castle (D. Rose & Co.)	,,	Mar. 11	PrawleP	June 13	94

The Wool Fleet, 1879-80.

Ship	From	Left		To	Arrived		D'ys Out
Sam Mendel ..	Melbourne	Nov.	3	London	Feb.	6	95
Cimba	Sydney	,,	6	Channel	Mar.	4	119
Ben Cruachan ..	Geelong	,,	9	London	Feb.	6	89
Romanoff ..	Geelong	,,	16	,,	Mar.	10	114
Thermopylae ..	Sydney	,,	18	,,	Feb.	7	81
Salamis	Melbourne	,,	19	,,	Mar.	8	109
Samuel Plimsoll ..	Sydney	,,	22	,,	,,	9	107
Macduff	Melbourne	,,	23	,,	,,	9	106
Thyatira	,,	,,	26	,,	,,	8	102
Old Kensington ..	,,	,,	29	,,	,,	9	100
Sir Walter Raleigh	,,	,,	29	,,	,,	9	100
Mermerus ..	,,	Dec.	4	,,	,,	4	90
Cynisca	Sydney	,,	5	,,	April	6	122
Dunbar Castle ..	,,	,,	11	,,	,,	3	113
Superb	Melbourne	,,	13	,,	,,	3	111
Nineveh	Sydney	,,	18	,,	,,	2	105
Darling Downs ..	,,	,,	30	,,	,,	2	94
Ben Voirlich ..	,,	Jan.	1	,,	,,	17	106
Aristides	Melbourne	,,	1	,,	,,	3	92
Loch Tay ..	,,	,,	3	,,	,,	19	106
Loch Vennachar ..	Geelong	,,	16	,,	,,	19	93
Patriarch	Sydney	,,	17	,,	,,	19	92
Loch Garry ..	Melbourne	,,	22	,,	,,	19	87

The Wool Fleet, 1880-1.

Ship	From	Left		To	Arrived		D'ys Out
Woollahra ..	Sydney	Sept.	3	London	Dec.	1	88
Hawkesbury ..	,,	,,	30	,,	,,	27	88
The Tweed ..	,,	Oct.	1	,,	,,	28	88
Samuel Plimsoll ..	,,	,,	12	,,	Feb.	2	113
Thermopylae ..	,,	,,	14	,,	Jan.	12	90
Miltiades	Melbourne	,,	20	Motherb'nk	Feb.	3	106
Cimba	Sydney	,,	23	London	,,	2	102
Sir Walter Raleigh	Melbourne	,,	26	,,	,,	13	110
Loch Vennachar ..	,,	,,	27	,,	Jan.	31	96
Loch Maree ..	,,	,,	28	,,	Feb.	3	98
Melbourne ..	,,	,,	29	,,	Jan.	31	94
Romanoff ..	,,	,,	29	,,	Feb.	2	96
Patriarch	Sydney	,,	29	,,	,,	3	97
Ben Voirlich ..	Melbourne	Nov.	5	,,	,,	7	94
Mermerus ..	,,	,,	5	,,	,,	4	91
Salamis ..	Geelong	,,	9	,,	,,	5	88
Sam Mendel ..	Melbourne	,,	10	,,	Mar.	8	118
Windsor Castle .. (Green's)	,,	,,	11	,,	Feb.	5	86
Windsor Castle .. (D. Rose)	Sydney	,,	13	,,	Jan.	31	79
Aristides	Melbourne	,,	17	,,	Feb.	4	79
Thyatira	Geelong	,,	20	,,	Mar.	5	105
Loch Garry ..	Melbourne	,,	29	,,	Feb.	24	87
Darling Downs ..	Sydney	Dec.	5	,,	April	13	129
Collingwood ..	Melbourne	,,	5	,,	Mar.	20	105
Thessalus ..	,,	Jan.	14	,,	April	28	104
Parramatta ..	Sydney	,,	24	,,	,,	30	96
Brilliant	,,	Feb.	2	,,	May	1	88
Loch Tay ..	Melbourne	,,	25	Falm'th	June	8	103
Argonaut	,,	April	7	London	,,	30	84

The Wool Fleet, 1881-2.

Ship	From	Left		To	Arrived		D'ys Out
Windsor Castle .. (D. Rose) ..	Sydney	Oct.	15	London	Jan.	30	107
Salamis	Geelong	,,	29	,,	Feb.	7	101
Romanoff ..	Melbourne	Nov.	7	,,	,,	18	103
Holmsdale ••	,,	,,	10	,,	,,	17	99
Loch Garry ..	..	..	11	Wight	,,	16	97
Ben Cruachan ..	..	..	12	London	,,	18	98
Sir Walter Raleigh	..	,,	12	,,	Mar.	6	114
Parthenope ..	,,	,,	13	..	Feb.	15	94
Theophane ..	Geelong	,,	14	Dover	,,	16	94
Miltiades	Melbourne	.,	14	Downs	,,	16	94
Patriarch	Sydney	,.	15	London	Mar.	6	111
City of Agra ..	Melbourne	,,	17	,,	Feb.	20	95
Mermerus ..	,,	,,	17	Lizard	,,	14	89
Samuel Plimsoll ..	Sydney	,,	17	Downs	,,	16	91
Ben Voirlich ..	Geelong	,,	18	London	Mar.	22	124
Loch Rannoch ..	,,	,,	29	,,	,,	29	120
Thyatira	Melbourne	Dec.	3	,,	,,	18	105
Loch Vennachar ..	,,	,,	9	,,	,,	3	84
Thessalus ..	Sydney	,,	19	,,	,,	28	99
Aristides	Melbourne	Feb.	6'82	,,	May	11	94

P*

The Wool Fleet, 1882-3.

Ship	From	Left		To	Arrived		D'ys Out
Windsor Castle (D. Rose & Co.)	Sydney	Oct.	13	Falm'th	Jan.	20	99
Thermopylae ..	,,	,,	14	London	Dec.	28	75
Salamis	Melbourne	,,	17	,,	Jan.	19	94
Loch Garry ..	,,	Nov.	3	,,	Feb.	14	103
Samuel Plimsoll ..	Sydney	,,	4	,,	,,	4	92
Orontes	,,	,,	6	,,	,,	15	101
Loch Vennachar ..	Melbourne	,,	8	,,	,,	15	99
Macduff	,,	,,	8	,,	,,	11	95
Ben Voirlich ..	,,	,,	9	,,	,,	9	92
Holmsdale ..	,,	,,	9	,,	,,	15	98
Ben Cruachan ..	,,	,,	13	,,	,,	12	91
Hallowe'en ..	Sydney	,,	14	,,	,,	13	91
Miltiades	Melbourne	,,	14	,,	,,	14	92
Romanoff ..	,,	,,	16	,,	,,	14	90
Loch Sloy ..	,,	,,	23	,,	,,	23	92
Mermerus ..	,,	,,	25	,,	,,	14	81
John Duthie ..	Sydney	,,	29	,,	Mar.	25	116
Collingwood ..	Melbourne	,,	6	,,	Mar.	26	110
Melbourne ..	,,	,,	14	,,	,,	27	103
Patriarch	Sydney	,,	26	,,	April	10	105
Woollahra ..	,,	Jan.	6	,,	,,	7	91
Cimba	,,	,,	7	Channel	,,	22	105
Smyrna	,,	,,	7	London	,,	30	113
Anglo-Norman ..	,,	,,	10	,,	,,	23	103
Christiana Thompson	,,	,,	19	,,	May	12	113
Darling Downs ..	,,	,,	23	,,	April	30	97
Loch Etive ..	,,	,,	24	,,	May	16	112
La Hogue ..	Sydney	Jan.	25	,,	April	30	95
Dharwar	,,	Feb.	8	,,	June	4	116
Hawkesbury ..	,,	,,	8	,,	May	12	93
Trafalgar ..	,,	,,	8	,,	,,	12	93
Gladstone	,,	,,	26	,,	,,	13	76
Rodney	Melbourne	Mar.	4	Prawle	June	11	99
Parramatta ..	Sydney	,,	6	London	July	7	123
Abergeldie ..	,,	April	15	,,	Aug.	1	108
Brilliant	,,	,,	19	,,	,,	4	107
William Duthie ..	,,	,,	20	,,	,,	15	117
Port Jackson ..	,,	,,	28	,,	July	30	93

The Wool Fleet, 1883-4.

Ship	From	Left		To	Arrived		D'ys Out
John Duthie ..	Sydney	Oct.	12	London	Jan.	10	90
Salamis	Melbourne	,,	19	,,	,,	27	100
Sir Walter Raleigh	Sydney	,,	20	,,	,,	19	91
Woollahra ..	,,	,,	26	,,	Feb.	6	103
Thermopylae ..	,,	,,	31	,,	Jan.	26	87
Loch Vennachar ..	Melbourne	Nov.	3	,,	Feb.	25	114
Ben Cruachan ..	,,	,,	3	,,	Jan.	27	85
Holmsdale ..	,,	,,	3	,,	Feb.	10	99
Loch Garry ..	Geelong	,,	3	,,	,,	2	91
Patriarch	Sydney	,,	3	,,	,,	2	91
Windsor Castle (D. Rose)	,,	,,	3	,,	,,	6	94
Anglo-Norman ..	,,	,,	4	,,	,,	1	89
Samuel Plimsoll ..	,,	,,	5	,.	Jan.	28	84
Ethiopian ..	Geelong	,,	7	,.	Feb.	12	97
Ben Voirlich ..	,,	,,	11	,.	,,	10	91
South Australian	Melbourne	,,	14	,,	,,	20	98
Romanoff ..	,,	,,	17	,,	,,	12	87
Mermerus ..	,,	,,	21	,,	,,	24	93
Loch Tay ..	,,	,,	24	,,	Mar.	3	99
Thyatira	,,	,,	28	,,	,,	10	102
Hawkesbury ..	Sydney	Dec.	7	,,	,,	10	93
Loch Long ..	Melbourne	,,	8	,,	,,	14	96
Melbourne ..	,,	,,	12	,,	,,	18	96
Cutty Sark ..	Newcastle	,,	28	,,	,,	20	82
Dharwar	Sydney	,,	29	,,	April	21	113
Cimba	,,	,,	29	,,	,,	22	114
ChristianaThompson	,,	,.	29	,,	,,	21	113
Miltiades	Geelong	Jan.	4	,,	,,	22	108
Smyrna	Sydney	,,	14	,,	,,	30	106
Rodney	Melbourne	,,	19	,,	,,	28	99
Jerusalem ..	Sydney	Feb.	6	,,	May	3	87

The Wool Fleet, 1884-5.

Ship	From	Left		To	Arrived		D'ys Out
Loch Long ..	Melbourne	Oct.	5	London	Jan.	9	96
Thermopylae ..	,,	,,	6	,,	Dec.	24	79
Patriarch ..	Sydney	,,	12	Channel	Jan.	10	90
Sir Walter Raleigh	,,	,,	14	London	,,	27	105
Samuel Plimsoll ..	,,	,,	15	Plym'th	,,	22	99
Salamis	Melbourne	,,	19	London	,,	11	84
Thyatira ..	,,	,,	31	,,	Feb.	14	106
The Tweed ..	Sydney	Nov.	4	..	,,	14	102
Hawkesbury ..	,,	,,	26	,,	,,	28	94
Ben Cruachan ..	Melbourne	,,	28	,,	,,	27	91
Gladstone	Newcastle	Dec.	2	,,	Mar.	20	108
Mermerus ..	Melbourne	,,	5	,,	Feb.	27	84
Loch Garry ..	Geelong	,,	5	,,	Mar.	30	115
Orontes	Sydney	,,	5	,,	,,	31	116
ChristianaThompson	,,	,,	6	,,	,,	27	111
Woollahra ..	,,	,,	7	,,	,,	27	110
Cutty Sark ..	Newcastle	,,	9	,,	Feb.	27	80
Cimba	Sydney	,,	12	,,	Mar.	27	105
Dharwar	,,	,,	12	,,	,,	27	105
Harbinger ..	Melbourne	,,	24	,,	April	2	99
Loch Vennachar ..	,,	,,	27	,,	Mar.	29	92
Miltiades	,,	,,	28	,,	,,	30	92
Trafalgar ..	Sydney	Jan.	19	,,	April	29	100
Cairnbulg ..	,,	,,	20	,,	,,	23	93
Rodney	Melbourne	Feb.	2	,,	,,	26	83
Port Jackson ..	Sydney	,,	12	,,	May	17	94
Centurion ..	,,	Mar.	21	,,	June	20	91

The Wool Fleet, 1885-6.

Ship	From	Left		To	Arrived		D'ys Out
Patriarch	Newcastle	Oct	5	London	Jan.	7	94
Sir Walter Raleigh	Sydney	,,	12	,,	,,	5	85
Loch Vennachar ..	Melbourne	,,	14	,,	,,	7	85
Cutty Sark ..	Sydney	,,	16	,,	Dec.	27	72
Salamis	Melbourne	,,	17	,,	Jan.	2	77
Woollahra ..	Sydney	,,	17	,,	,,	7	82
Thermopylae ..	,,	,,	18	,,	,,	5	79
Samuel Plimsoll ..	,,	,,	24	,,	,,	23	91
Cimba ..	,,	,,	24	,,	,,	28	97
Harbinger ..	Melbourne	Nov.	7	,,	Feb.	5	90
Ben Cruachan ..	,,	,,	13	,,	,,	2	81
Mermerus.. ..	,,	,,	30	Lizard	Mar.	19	109
Illawarra	Sydney	Dec.	7	London	,,	21	104
The Tweed ..	,,	,,	7	,,	,,	25	108
Thomas Stephens	,,	,,	11	,,	,,	21	100
Ben Voirlich ..	Melbourne	,,	22	,,	,,	21	89
Rodney	,,	,,	22	,,	,,	19	87
Loch Ness ..	,,	Jan.	4	,,	May	3	119
Loch Ryan ..	,,	,,	8	,,	,,	8	120
Mount Stewart ..	,,	,,	10	,,	,,	3	113
Darling Downs ..	,,	,,	16	,,	,,	11	115
Dharwar	,,	,,	19	,,	,,	11	112
Trafalgar ..	Sydney	,,	23	,,	,,	10	107
Loch Sloy ..	Melbourne	,,	30	,,	,,	27	117
Brilliant	Sydney	Feb.	3	,,	,,	7	93
Port Jackson ..	,,	,,	8	,,	,,	27	108
Miltiades	Melbourne	Mar.	22	,,	June	24	94

The Wool Fleet, 1886-7.

Ship	From	Left		To	Arrived		D'ys Out
Loch Vennachar ..	Melbourne	Oct.	21	London	Jan.	20	91
Salamis	,,	,,	24	,,	,,	17	85
Patriarch	Sydney	,,	24	,,	,,	21	89
Thermopylae ..	,,	,,	24	,,	,,	19	87
Blackadder ..	Newcastle	,,	27	,,	Feb.	23	119
Derwent	Sydney	Nov.	6	,,	,,	22	108
Cimba	,,	,,	27	,,	,,	24	90
Woollahra	,,	,,	30	,,	,,	26	88
Aristides	Melbourne	Dec	7	,,	Mar.	10	93
Mermerus	,,	,,	10	,,	Feb.	26	78
Sir Walter Raleigh	,,	,,	11	,,	Mar.	1	80
Harbinger ..	,,	,,	13	,,	,,	25	102
Samuel Plimsoll ..	Sydney	,,	14	,,	,,	25	101
Rodney	Melbourne	,,	17	,,	April	17	121
Loch Garry ..	Geelong	,,	18	,,	,,	13	116
City of Agra ..	Melbourne	Jan.	1	,,	,,	23	112
South Australian	,,	,,	1	,,	,,	23	112
Cairnbulg ..	Sydney	,,	8	,,	,,	22	104
Illawarra	,,	,,	13	,,	,,	22	97
Port Jackson ..	,,	,,	15	,,	,,	24	99
Orontes	,,	,,	16	,,	,,	23	97
Smyrna	,,	,,	18	,,	,,	24	96
Trafalgar	,,	Feb.	15	,,	May	21	95
Dharwar	,,	,,	15	,,	,,	21	95
Cutty Sark ..	,,	Mar.	26	,,	June	6	72

The Wool Fleet, 1887-8.

Ship	From	Left		To	Arrived		D'ys Out
Sir Walter Raleigh	Sydney	Sept.	14	London	Jan.	2	110
Thermopylae ..	,,	Oct.	16	,,	,,	3	79
Patriarch	,,	,,	16	,,	,,	20	96
Loch Vennachar ..	Melbourne	,,	17	,,	,,	5	80
Woollahra ..	Sydney	,,	23	,,	,,	23	92
Cimba ..	,,	,,	24	,,	,,	22	90
Samuel Plimsoll ..	,,	,,	25	,,	,,	27	94
Salamis	Melbourne	,,	26	,,	,,	17	83
Romanoff ..	,,	Nov.	2	,,	Mar	11	130
Smyrna	Sydney	,,	12	,,	,,	13	122
Derwent	,,	,,	17	,,	Feb	20	95
Thyatira	Newcastle	,,	21	Dungen's	Mar.	8	108
Dharwar	Melbourne	,,	23	London	,,	5	103
Loch Ryan ..	Geelong	,,	23	,,	,,	12	110
Harbinger .	Melbourne	,,	28	,,	,,	10	103
Mermerus ..	,,	,,	29	,,	,,	9	101
Orontes	Sydney	Dec.	1	,,	,,	13	103
Illawarra	,,	,,	5	,,	,,	8	94
Aristides ..	Melbourne	,,	5	,,	,,	5	91
Yallaroi	Sydney	,,	10	,,	,,	10	91
Trafalgar ..	,,	,,	12	,,	,,	11	90
Collingwood ..	Melbourne	,,	12	,,	,,	11	90
City of Agra ..	,,	,,	17	,,	,,	10	83
Loch Garry ..	,,	,,	21	,,	,,	15	85
Cutty Sark ..	Newcastle	,,	28	Dungen's	,,	8	71
Gladstone	Sydney	Jan.	7	London	April	5	89
Miltiades	Melbourne	,,	11	,,	,,	11	91
Brilliant	Sydney	,,	26	,,	,,	18	83
Thomas Stephens	,,	Feb.	4	,,	May	17	103

The Wool Fleet, 1888-9.

Ship	From	Left		To	Arrived		D'ys Out
Derwent	Sydney	Oct.	10	London	Jan.	17	99
Cimba	,,	,,	18	,,	,,	15	89
Orontes	,,	,,	20	,,	,,	22	94
Star of Italy ..	,,	,,	20	,,	,,	14	86
Woollahra ..	,,	,,	24	,,	,,	18	86
Salamis	Melbourne	,,	24	,,	,,	17	85
Cutty Sark	Sydney	,,	26	Start	,,	18	84
Loch Vennachar ..	Melbourne	,,	27	London	,,	19	84
Gladstone	Sydney	,,	30	,,	Feb.	15	108
Centurion ..	,,	,,	31	,,	,,	21	113
Mermerus ..	Melbourne	Nov.	3	,,	Jan.	31	89
Blackadder ..	Newcastle	,,	17	,,	Feb.	15	90
Loch Ryan ..	Geelong	,,	23	,,	Mar.	9	106
Harbinger ..	Melbourne	,,	26	,,	,,	8	102
Nebo	Sydney	,,	28	,,	Feb.	16	82
Thomas Stephens	,,	,,	29	,,	Mar.	20	111
Dharwar	Melbourne	Dec.	1	,,	,,	7	96
Trafalgar ..	Sydney	,,	6	,,	Mar.	18	102
Yallaroi	,,	,,	10	,,	,,	20	100
Collingwood ..	Melbourne	,,	15	,,	,,	20	95
Loch Garry ..	,,	,,	21	,,	,,	20	89
Sophocles ..	Sydney	,,	22	,,	April	15	114
Samuel Plimsoll	Melbourne	,,	23	,,	,,	2	100
Rodney	Sydney	,,	24	,,	Mar.	27	93
Romanoff ..	Geelong	,,	31	,	April	23	113
Torridon	Sydney	Jan.	12	,,	,,	29	107
Thermopylae ..	,,	Mar.	26	,,	June	29	95

The Wool Fleet, 1889-90.

Ship	From	Left		To	Arrived		D'ys Out
Derwent	Sydney	Oct.	14	London	Jan.	2	80
Cairnbulg ..	,,	,,	15	,,	,,	24	101
Orontes	,,	,,	17	,,	,,	24	99
Loch Vennachar ..	Melbourne	,,	21	,,	,,	15	86
Salamis	,,	,,	22	,,	,,	15	85
Cimba	Sydney	,,	22	,,	,,	5	75
Woollahra ..	,,	,,	22	,,	,,	15	85
Rodney	,,	,,	31	Lizard	,,	16	77
Cutty Sark ..	,,	Nov.	3	Start	,,	16	74
Loch Ryan ..	Melbourne	,,	3	London	Mar.	11	128
Mermerus ..	,,	Dec.	7	,,	,,	10	93
Thomas Stephens	,,	,,	10	,,	,,	28	108
Loch Tay ..	Geelong	,,	12	,,	,,	15	96
Samuel Plimsoll ..	Melbourne	,,	14	,,	,,	26	102
Yallaroi	Sydney	,,	20	,,	April	8	109
Trafalgar ..	,,	,,	21	,,	,,	8	108
Harbinger ..	Melbourne	,,	22	,,	,,	10	109
Collingwood ..	,,	,,	23	,,	Mar.	28	95
Loch Rannoch ..	,,	,,	23	,,	April	10	108
Illawarra ..	Sydney	,,	23	,,	,,	5	103
Romanoff ..	Melbourne	Jan.	1	,,	,,	6	95
Thermopylae ..	Sydney	,,	9	Deal	,,	8	89
Loch Long ..	Geelong	,,	18	London	,,	27	99
Loch Sloy ..	Melbourne	,,	18	,,	,,	28	100
Brilliant	Sydney	,,	25	,,	,,	22	87
Torridon	,,	,,	25	,,	,,	26	91
Patriarch	,,	,,	27	,,	,,	26	89
Hesperus	Melbourne	,,	31	,,	May	14	103
Port Jackson ..	Sydney	Feb.	8	,,	,,	8	89

LaVergne, TN USA
03 December 2010

207197LV00003B/9/P